FATHER GABRIEL OF ST. MARY MAGDALEN, O.C.D.

DIVINE INTIMACY

Volume III

Ninth Sunday through
Twenty-first Week of Ordinary Time

From the Library of:

Jehane Jones

IGNATIUS PRESS   SAN FRANCISCO

This enlarged and revised edition was
previously published by Dimension Books, Inc.
Translated from the Sixteenth Italian Edition
Carmelite Monastery of Pittsford, N.Y.

206. NINTH SUNDAY OF ORDINARY TIME

YEAR A

Be my rock of refuge, a strong fortress to save me   *(Ps 31:2)*

"I set before you this day a blessing and a curse: the blessing if you obey the commandments of the Lord your God; . . . the curse if you do not obey" (Dt 11:26-28). Israel's whole perfection was contained in the law and was expressed in its observance. God blessed and cursed man according to whether he obeyed or disobeyed the law. The New Testament established a new order: God blesses and therefore saves man, not for keeping the old law, which is now no longer in force, but through faith in Christ the Savior. St. Paul strongly supports this: "But now the righteousness of God has been manifested apart from the law . . . the righteousness of God through faith in Jesus Christ for all who believe" (Rom 3:21-22). This is a great change: Jews who faithfully observe the Mosaic law have no greater right to salvation than those who are ignorant of this law; for both the one and the other, salvation is a free gift offered by God's infinite goodness to all those who believe in Jesus Christ. Likewise we read in John's Gospel " . . . that whoever believes in him may have eternal life" (3:15). And St. Paul states specifically: "For we hold that a man is justified by faith apart from works of the law" (Rom 3:28). It must be understood, however, that the works which are excluded are only those of the Mosaic law, not the good works which are the fruit of faith in Christ. For, indeed, the same Apostle explains elsewhere that for salvation, all that counts is "faith working through love" (Gal 5:6), that is, faith which is not just an adherence of the intellect to Christ, but an adherence of the whole person: intellect and will, thought and works.

This is exactly what Jesus was teaching when he declared "Not everyone who says to me, 'Lord, Lord' shall enter the kingdom of heaven, but he who does the will of my Father who is in heaven" (Mt 7:21). Faith must encompass the whole of life, and lead, not to a simple abstract recognition of God's existence, but to a practical acknowledgement which brings with it the submission of our own will to God's, and behavior that is regulated by his commandments. Therefore those who reduce their profession of faith to prayer, to the apostolate, or even to the simple practice of the ministry—"did we not prophesy in your name and cast out demons . . . " (ib. 22)—but who do not extend it to every sector of personal life through accomplishing God's will, will one day hear him say: "I never knew you" (ib. 23). Only faith which is made concrete in full adherence to the will of God enables us to build "our house upon rock," without fear that it will be knocked down by winds or storm. This house is Christian life, which, founded on faith in Christ and on carrying out his words, can defy any hurricane and even time and death as they change at last into eternal life.

> *The soul of the just yields to no temptation, because it rests upon "rock," that is upon the firmness and stability of your teaching, O Lord Jesus. Indeed your precepts are more solid than rock. Any one who practices them is raised above all the unexpected disasters of this world. What happier situation in life can there be than this? Neither wealth, nor physical strength, nor glory, nor power, nor any other privilege can secure for us an interior steadiness like this. Only the possession of virtue can make all this possible...*
>
> *O Lord, you spur me on to virtue, not only by the promise of future realities by making me remember the kingdom of heaven, with all the inexpressible rewards and consolations and other endless blessings to be enjoyed there, but also by showing me the unshakeable steadiness and stability which virtue confers upon me in this life.*
> St. John Chrysostom, *Commentary upon Gospel of St. Matthew*
> 24:2-3

> *O Jesus, with a strong faith I get as near you as I can, in order to know God in you and through you, and to know him in a manner that is worthy of God, that is in a way that makes me love and obey him, according to what your beloved disciple says: "He who says 'I know him,' but disobeys his commandments is a liar;" and you yourself said: "If you love me, keep my commandments."*
>
> *So my whole reason for wanting to know you is to love you; and I want to know and love you in order to force myself to do your will, for I am convinced that I will not be able to know you well except by being united to you by a love that is pure and chaste... May the light of faith enlighten and guide me so that I may succeed in loving you, since it is really through faith, according to St. Paul, that we "work and act out of love."*
> cf J.B. Bossuet, *Elevations*

YEAR B

Let us sing aloud to God our strength; shout for joy to our God
(Ps 81:2)

Keeping holy the Lord's day holds a special place in Sacred Scripture. We read in Deuteronomy: "Observe the sabbath day to keep it holy as the Lord your God commanded you. Six days you shall labor and do all your work; but the seventh day is the sabbath to the Lord, your God" (5:12-14). "To keep holy" the sabbath means to separate it, distinguish it from the other days to devote it to God. Further on (ib. 15), the sacred text suggests how this is to be done: by remembering God's great favors to his people, among which the "passover" holds first place, for it was their liberation from slavery in Egypt. Remembering this should lead them to thanksgiving and to a renewal of their promise of loyalty to God.

In the New Testament, the old passover is replaced by the new: Christ's paschal mystery; the old sabbath, Saturday, yields place to Sunday, the blessed day of the resurrection. For the Christian the Lord's day is meant to be a "memorial" of the pasch of Jesus, the mystery of love and salvation, the center and supreme act of worship. Abstaining from daily labor does not suffice to fulfill the precept of keeping this day holy; that is simply a preliminary step to free us from the bustle of everyday life so that we can engage more easily in dialogue with God, recall his love and favors, rekindle our desire and hope for eternal blessings, strengthen our soul by meditation on the divine word, and catch our breath again on the road to our heavenly homeland. When Sunday loses this religious meaning it is no longer the Lord's day, but frequently becomes the day on which men give free rein to pleasure; or the feastday rest may be reduced to a petty formalism as had happened with the Jewish sabbath.

In thus renewing the old law, Jesus affirmed his authority in regard to the sabbath. When the disciples had gathered and husked corn on the sabbath to satisfy their hunger, Jesus defended them, saying: "The sabbath was made for man, not man for the sabbath" (Mk 2:27). Its purpose is especially man's spiritual benefit, attained through a more intense relationship with God in acts of worship which are not only individual but communitarian; and also his material welfare by its procuring him justified repose and giving him time for works of charity on behalf of his neighbor. By declaring himself "Lord of the sabbath" (ib. 28), Jesus freed the sabbath from the narrow interpretations of the Pharisees; at the same time he admonished his disciples to use it with suitable freedom, but always in conformity with his teaching and example. In fact he did not hesitate on the sabbath itself to cure the man "who had a withered hand" (Mk 3:1). He did it in spite of the malevolent attitude of the Pharisees in order to demonstrate that not only is it lawful to do a good deed on the sabbath (ib. 4), but that good deeds for the relief of our suffering brethren should complete the sanctification of the Lord's day.

We call upon you, Lord God ... You desire to save all men and to make them know the truth. All together, we now offer you praise and hymns of thanksgiving to glorify you with all our hearts and voices. You deigned to call us, to teach and invite us, to grant us wisdom and understanding of truth, for eternal life. You have redeemed us with the precious and immaculate blood of your only Son, from all corruption and slavery . . . We were dead and you have given us new life, body and soul, in the Spirit. We were dirty and you made us clean.

Therefore we beg you, Father of mercy, and God of every consolation: strengthen us in our vocation, in adoration and fidelity. We consecrate ourselves to your divine words and to your holy law. We desire to come closer to you today. Enlighten our souls so that we may know and serve you. We pray you to give us strength to achieve our holy purposes, and do not remember the sins which we have committed and continue to commit . . . Remember, Lord, that we fall so easily: your creatures are weak by nature and in their resources: our ills are hidden . . .

Help us to consider, to seek, and to contemplate the good things of heaven and not those of this world. In this way, through the strength of your grace, glory will be given to your almighty power, so holy and worthy of all praise, in Christ Jesus, your beloved Son, with the Holy Spirit, world without end! Amen.

Sabbath Prayer from *Early Christian Prayers*, 94

YEAR C

Praise the Lord, all you nations; extol him, all you peoples (Ps 117:1)

After Solomon had built the temple in Jerusalem, he offered this prayer to God: "Likewise when a foreigner, who is not of your people Israel, but comes from a far country for your name's sake . . . when he comes and prays toward this house, hear (him) in heaven your dwelling-place . . . that all the peoples of the earth may know your name" (1 Kings 8:41-43). It was a beautiful prayer, characterized by the prophetic spirit which saw in Yahweh not only the God of Israel, but the Lord of all peoples, to whom every man could turn to obtain grace.

There is an episode in the Gospel which could be considered a verification of this prayer. At Capharnaum a Roman centurion had heard people talking about the miracles performed by Jesus and would have liked to ask for the recovery of a very dear servant of his, but because he was a pagan he did not dare approach Jesus and so sent a message through some of his Jewish friends. These remarked to the Lord: "He is worthy to have you do this for him, for he loves our nation, and he built us our synagogue" (Lk 7:4-5). Although a foreigner, the centurion was a friend of the Jews, and admired their religion—perhaps even practiced it—so much so that he had had a synagogue built at his expense; still he did not feel that this gave him the right to deal directly with the Master; rather, when Jesus was on the way to his house, the centurion sent

Ninth Sunday of Ordinary Time

him word: "Lord, do not trouble yourself, for I am not worthy to have you come under my roof . . . But say the word, and let my servant be healed" (ib. 6-7). His humility was great, but his faith greater still, so that "when Jesus heard this he marvelled at him . . . and said: 'I tell you, not even in Israel have I found such faith'" (ib. 9). He answered this faith with a miracle performed from afar; and thus was heard the prayer of a foreigner who turned to the God of Israel made present in the person of Christ. The centurion's goodness of heart, his anxiety over his sick servant, his humility, and his faith, prepared him for receiving the grace of the Savior more than many who belonged to the chosen people. Jesus is the universal Savior: his salvation is for every one, he makes no distinction between Jew or pagan; where he finds humility and faith he gives of himself, even from afar, even when he is still not well known, just as he had done with the centurion.

Moreover, for all mankind there is but one Savior, but one faith, and one gospel, and it is impossible to find salvation elsewhere. For this reason St. Paul warned against those who "want to pervert the gospel of Christ" and he did not hesitate to say: "Even if we, or an angel from heaven, should preach to you a gospel contrary to that which we preached to you, let him be accursed" (Gal 1:7,9). The apostle was not afraid that his intransigence in defense of the gospel might bring him enemies, but declared with courage: "If I were still pleasing men, I should not be a servant of Christ!" (ib. 10).

Eternal Savior, King of heaven, you alone are all-powerful and Lord, God of all creation, all-holy God of our holy fathers who lived before us, O God of Abraham, Isaac, and Jacob, full of pity and compassion, of goodness and forbearance. Every heart is laid bare before you, and the most secret of thoughts does not escape you. The souls of the just call upon you and put their trust in you. Father of the just, you hear those who pray to you with uprightness, you also hear silent appeals; your providence penetrates even to our deepest depths, your knowledge searches the will of each of us. From every corner of the earth the incense of prayer and petition rises up to you.
Early Christian Prayers, 174

O my Savior, after being called to your faith and to being your son through grace, do not permit me to lose this gift through my own fault, and be disinherited from your kingdom and thrown into the darkness outside your light and your friendship . . . Oh grant that many may come to your faith . . . so that your kingdom may be peopled by a multitude of just souls! But Lord, do not permit the faithful who are already in your church to become estranged and be cast out from the kingdom to which you have called them.
L. De Ponte, Meditations III 30:3

207. PRAYER IN GENERAL

To you, O Lord, I lift up my soul ... For you I wait all the day long
(Ps 25:1,5)

1. A Christian is by vocation one called to communion, to dialogue with God: a communion and a dialogue which are an exchange of life and of love, an outpouring of man's heart into that of God; an intimate, silent prayer, yet a voice raised to heaven; a desire and a search for the Lord; a supplication, a sigh, a groan, a song of praise and thanksgiving, an entreaty for forgiveness. There can be nothing more personal, free, and spontaneous than prayer, which becomes progressively the habitual breath of Christian life, thus fulfilling the great admonition: we "ought always to pray and not lose heart" (Lk 18:1). Already in the paslms of the Old Testament we have some beautiful examples of this continual raising of the heart toward God: "O God, you are my God, whom I seek ... I think of you upon my bed, and meditate on you in the watches of the night" (Ps 63:1,6). "But I call upon God ... Evening, and morning, and at noon, I utter my complaint and moan, and he will hear my voice" (Ps 55:17). "To you, O Lord, I lift up my soul, my God, in you I trust" (Ps 25:1-2). Jesus himself was accustomed to pray in phrases taken from the psalms which he habitually recited according to the Jewish custom; he did so even on the cross, adding his own personal stamp by his tender appeal to the Father: "Father, into your hands I commit my spirit" (Lk 23:46). Jesus repeatedly inculcated the necessity of continual prayer: "Take heed to yourselves lest your hearts be weighed down ... with the cares of life; ... watch at all times and pray" (Lk 21:34,36). "Will not God vindicate his elect who cry to him day and night?" (Lk 18:7). St. Paul had deeply absorbed this teaching, and in his turn handed it down: "Pray at all times in the Spirit, with all prayer and supplication ... Keep alert with all perseverance" (Eph 6:18). "Rejoice always, pray constantly, give thanks in all circumstances, for this is the will of God in Christ Jesus for you" (1 Thes 5:16).

We must not be content to pray just in our own name; it must also be in the name of all creation. Since man "was appointed (by God) as master of all earthly creatures that he might subdue them ... to God's glory" (GS 12), we have the duty to take them into our prayer, so that the entire universe may become one hymn of praise to the Lord. "Bless the Lord, all you works of the Lord ... You heavens, sun and moon, rain and dew, fire and heat, frost and chill, nights and days, light and darkness, ice and snow, lightnings and clouds ... bless the Lord" (Dan 3:35-51).

Instead of looking upon creatures with an eye greedy for possession and an unrestrained desire of enjoying them selfishly, a Christian should "receive them from God, and respect and reverence them as flowing constantly from the hand of God" (GS 37). Then all creation becomes a precious help to prayer, both because it continually speaks to us of God and because it urges us to thank and bless and love the Giver of so many blessings. St. John of the Cross comments: "This reflection on creatures, this observing that they are things made by the very hand of God, her Beloved, strongly awakens the soul to love him" (Sp 4:3). A Christian respects creatures and uses them in the measure willed by God, and they reciprocate by revealing God's presence and infinite goodness. It is the full realization of what St. Paul affirms: "His invisible nature, namely his eternal power and deity, has been clearly perceived in the things that have been made" (Rom 1:20). The more we approach creatures with a pure heart and an eye enlightened by faith, the more we shall be able to understand their mute language, and transform it into prayer, becoming thereby the voice of every creature. Thus we perform our priestly function in respect to creation, directing every earthly reality toward the worship and praise of God, in a kind of universal liturgy through which creation begins to share "in the glorious liberty of the children of God" (Rom 8:21).

> *Grant, O Lord, that my heart may rise up to you and think constantly of my faults with sorrow and determination to correct myself...*
>
> *Lord, give me a heart so watchful that no vain thought can distract it from you, a noble heart that no unworthy passion can seduce, an upright heart that no evil intention may contaminate, a sturdy heart that is not crushed by tribulation, a free heart that does not let itself be overcome by troubled passion.*
>
> *Grant me, O Lord my God, an understanding that knows you, a love that seeks you, a wisdom that finds you, conversation that pleases you, perseverance that waits for you with confidence, and hope that will finally embrace you.*
>
> St. Thomas Aquinas, *Prayers*

> *Father in heaven, it is right to give you thanks and glory. You alone are God, living and true. Through all eternity you live in unapproachable light.*
>
> *Source of life and goodness, you have created all things to fill your creatures with every blessing and to lead all men to the joyful vision of your light.*
>
> *Countless hosts of angels stand before you to do your will, looking upon the glory of your face and singing your praises day and night. United with them, and become the voice of every creature, we too, exultingly sing: Holy, holy, holy Lord, God of power and might. Heaven and earth are full of your glory. Hosanna in the highest heaven.*
>
> Roman Missal, *Preface Eucharistic Prayer IV*

208. LITURGICAL PRAYER

O Lord, let my prayer be counted as incense before you   (Ps 141:2)

1. Prayer, even most personal prayer, is always a communion with Christ and with his Church, for a Christian is always a member of Christ and of his Church; in this we are treating of prayer as an interior and intimate communion which takes place only between God and the soul. There is another kind of prayer in which this communion has also a dimension that is external, visible, and communitarian: this is liturgical prayer, through which the Church, united to Christ, her Head and her Bridegroom, offers God complete worship.

Man is not only spirit, but an incarnate spirit; therefore, for him prayer must involve not only his spiritual faculties: intellect and will, but also his affective powers: his heart and sensitive faculties, and even the imagination, the senses, and also external behavior. The whole man must pray. This is exactly what is accomplished in liturgical prayer, which is not only an interior worship, but also an exterior one, expressed in common prayer, in singing, gestures, and ceremonies. Although interior worship is essential, for without it external worship would be formality and phariseeism, we must, nonetheless, be careful not to downgrade the external, whose purpose is to manifest our interior devotion in a public and tangible way. This not only corresponds to our nature but also to that of the Church; since the Church is a visible society, it cannot be without an external social worship. The sacred liturgy expresses precisely "the real nature of the true Church. It is of the essence of the Church that she be both human and divine, visible and yet invisibly endowed with truth, eager to act, and yet devoted to contemplation" (SC 2).

Liturgical prayer is thus at the summit of the other forms of prayer, because it epitomizes them all and involves all our faculties, and also because it expresses not just the prayer of a single believer, but that of the whole community of the faithful, that is, of the whole Church in which Christ is present as Head and leader in prayer.

2. From the very beginning of the Church, the faithful began to gather "in fellowship to the breaking of bread and prayers . . . praising God" (Acts 2:42,47). These were the first ecclesial meetings, of which Christ, present in the Eucharist, was the center. In fact, the sacred Liturgy, wholly founded upon the eucharistic Sacrifice and on the sacraments, is the perfect worship that Christ himself offers to the heavenly Father for his glory and for the salvation of men. "Christ indeed always associates the Church with himself in the truly great work of giving perfect praise to God and making men holy. The Church is his dearly beloved bride who calls to her Lord, and through him offers wor-

ship to the eternal Father" (SC 7). By participating in the sacred Liturgy, we officially participate in the worship rendered to God by the whole Christ, that is, by Christ united to his Church and hence to her members. Hence liturgical prayer has an intrinsic and objective value which is derived from the infinite value of Christ's sacrifice and prayer; liturgical prayer is thus the main support of private prayer, by supplying for its deficiencies and nourishing it with the grace which comes from the presence and life-giving action of Christ. When we suffer from the poverty of our own personal prayer, it is a great comfort to take refuge in liturgical prayer, the great prayer of Christ and the Church. On the other hand, liturgical prayer itself, from the fact that the faithful participate in it, needs to be accompanied by their personal prayer. Though it is true that liturgical prayer has an intrinsic value, through which it always continues to be the prayer of Christ and of the Church, even if the individual participant is distracted, it is likewise true that its benefit to the individual is in direct proportion to his faith, his devotion, and his personal attention. Therefore, liturgical prayer and personal prayer are never opposed nor separated from one another, but are always joined in such a way that one compenetrates the other, each animating and completing the other.

My God, how discouraged I should be because of my weakness and nothingness, if I did not have Jesus Christ, my only Good, to praise, reverence and glorify you, as he does so perfectly. I entrust my weaknesses to him and I rejoice that he is all and I am nothing ...

O Jesus, I possess everything in you. You are my Head, and I am really one of your members. You pray, adore, humble yourself, and give thanks, in me and for me, and I do the same in you, for the member is entirely one with the head. Your holy, magnanimous life absorbs mine, which is so vile and mean.

You are super-eminently my gratitude. I will take the chalice of salvation and offer with you a host of praise, a sacrifice that is pleasing and worthy of God and superabundant.

Bl. M. Theresa de Soubiran

O Jesus, I adore you as center of the Liturgy; it is you who give unity to this Liturgy, which I may define as the public and official worship of the Church ...

Everything in the Mosaic worship prepares for the Christian Liturgy of which you, O Jesus, are the center and the life. You alone are the perfect hymn, since you are the true glory of the Father; no one can glorify the Father worthily but through you. "By him, with him, and in him, all honor and glory are given to you, O God the Father."

O Christ, you are the link between the liturgy of earth and the liturgy of heaven in which you more directly associate your elect.

Your incarnation has come to unite in a living, substantial manner, humanity and all creation in a divine liturgy. A God gives praise to God: a praise, full and perfect, which reaches its highest pitch in the sacrifice of Calvary.

G.B. Chautard, *Soul of the Apostolate* V:3

209. THE SACRED LITURGY

O God, may I offer you spiritual sacrifices, acceptable to you through Jesus Christ (1 Pet 2:5)

1. The Liturgy is not limited to being the perfect worship rendered to God, in union with Christ her Head. It embraces, expresses, and prolongs the whole mystery of Christ the Redeemer in its fundamental aspects of glorification of the Father and of the salvation of men. Jesus, the "one mediator between God and men" (1 Tim 2:5), the one eternal Priest, accomplished his work "in redeeming mankind and giving perfect glory to God . . . principally through the paschal mystery of his blessed passion, resurrection from the dead and glorious ascension" (SC 5). This took place once for all at a definite moment of history, but in order to prolong his work throughout the centuries for the benefit of all men, Christ continues his priestly office without interruption both in the glory of heaven where "he always lives to make intercession for them" (Heb 7:25), and here on earth where he exercises it through his bride, the Church, whom he has made the depository of his Sacrifice and of his sacraments. The Sacrifice and sacraments constitute the essential contents of sacred Liturgy, through which the Church, intimately united to Christ and through him, both continues to offer God perfect worship, and to bring about man's salvation. Just as a Christian must associate himself with the liturgical actions and prayers if he wants to share in this perfect worship, so, in order to nourish the life of grace in himself, he must have recourse to the Liturgy which opens up the source of grace to him through the sacraments. Even when the sacraments are administered most privately, as is the case with penance, they are always liturgical acts which link the faithful to the mystery of Christ, and apply to them the fruits of his redeeming work. Moreover, this insertion into the mystery of Christ always takes place within the Church and by means of the Church. Hence living the liturgical life means living the mystery of Christ as he desired to extend and express it in his Church.

2. Christ is always present in the various liturgical acts by his action within his Church and by her means. "He is present in the Sacrifice of the Mass . . . especially under the eucharistic species. By his power he is present in the sacraments . . . He is present with his word since it is he himself who speaks when holy Scrip-

ture is read in the Church. He is present finally when the Church prays and sings, for he promised 'where two or three are gathered in my name, there am I in the midst of them' (Mt 18:20)" (SC 7). Thus it clearly appears that the Liturgy simply expresses in a tangible way and effectively carries out the two great and inseparable dimensions of Christ's priesthood: the glory of the Father and the redemption of the world. In fact, in the eucharistic Sacrifice he renews his own self-sacrifice for that purpose. Then, through the sacraments Christ sanctifies believers by inserting them into his paschal mystery in such a way that in baptism we die, are buried, and rise again with him (Rom 6:4); in penance we are absolved and purified by virtue of his passion, and in the Eucharist we are nourished by his Body and Blood, given for our salvation. And while the sacraments regenerate and sanctify us in Christ, by that very fact they make us capable of participating in the perfect worship that he offers to his Father. "Rightly then"—says the Council—"the liturgy is considered as an exercise of the priestly office of Jesus Christ. In the liturgy the sanctification of man is manifested . . . and effected . . . by signs perceptible to the senses; full public worship is performed by the Mystical Body of Jesus Christ, that is, by the Head and his members" (SC 7). By participating in liturgical acts we are associated with the double function of Christ's priesthood: glorification of the Father and the sanctification of men. "It follows that every liturgical celebration, because it is an action of Christ the priest and of his Body the Church, is a sacred action surpassing all others. No other action of the Church can match its claim to efficacy" (ib.).

Before leaving the earth O divine Savior, you instituted the Sacrifice of the new law to renew your immolation; this is the source from which everything comes. You also instituted the sacraments to communicate the fruits of your Sacrifice to the faithful. But you left to your Church the care of surrounding this Sacrifice and these sacraments with symbols, ceremonies, exhortations, prayers, so that thus she gives more honor to the mystery of the Redemption, makes it easier for the faithful to understand it, and helps them to profit more from it . . .

With the love of the spouse, which the Church has for you, with the mother's solicitude that your heart has put in her for us, she has performed this double task . . . This praise and prayer of the Church, by being united with that of the God-man, becomes divine, and the liturgy of the earth mingles with that of the heavenly choirs in the Heart of Jesus, to make an echo to that eternal praise which flows from the furnace of infinite love, which is the Holy Trinity . . .

To be united with the Church to your Sacrifice, O Jesus, even imperfectly, by thought and intention—to mingle my prayer with the unceasing prayer of your Church—how great a boon is this already! The heart thus wings its way more surely to God, borne along by your praise, adoration, thanksgiving, reparation and petition.

But help me, O Lord, never to lose sight of the fact that all the resources offered by the Liturgy are only means... to put to death the old man, so that you, O Jesus, may live and reign in his place. May the Mass and the prayers and official rites of the Church help me to share more fully in your interior life and in your virtues, so that I may mirror them the more to the faithful!

G.B. Chautard, *Soul of the Apostolate* V 3

210. I SHALL GO UP TO THE ALTAR OF GOD

Your word, O Lord, is a lamp to my feet, and a light to my path
(Ps 119:105)

1. The Sacred Liturgy reaches its climax in the eucharistic Sacrifice, the supreme act of worship in which is renewed "the one sacrifice of the New Testament, namely the sacrifice of Christ, offering himself once and for all ... as a spotless victim" (LG 28). Rightly then is the Church careful to surround the Mass with prayers, ceremonies, and doctrinal instruction that will make the participation of the faithful truly "conscious and active" (SC 14). The first part is dominated by the Liturgy of the Word whose purpose is to instruct the people in the truths of faith, in the mysteries of the life of Christ, and especially in the paschal mystery which the holy Sacrifice will make living and present amid the faithful. "In the celebration of Mass'—the Council teaches—"the proclamation of the death and resurrection of the Lord is inseparably joined to the response of the people who hear and to the very offering ... [of] Christ" (PO 4). Through the reading of scriptural passages and especially those of the Gospel, inserted in the Mass, Christ is present through his word which is the light of Christian life and the nourishment of faith; the devout and attentive listening of the faithful is almost immediately followed by the common recitation of the Creed as their response and adherence to the word of God. Then, in this climate of renewed faith, the eucharistic mystery is accomplished, through which Christ himself becomes substantially present under the species of bread and wine. In this way, at one same altar, the faithful are nourished by the word of God and the Body of Christ. "The liturgy of the word and the eucharistic ligurgy are so closely connected with each other that they form but one single act of worship" (SC 56). The first makes Christ present in his word, the second in the Eucharist. Both the one and the other are directed toward the worship of God who is glorified by the people's profession of faith and by the oblation of his divine Son. When Mass is over, the light which has been received from the word of God will be the guide of our daily life, just as our reception of the Body of Christ will be our sustenance and our strength.

2. From the very beginning of Mass the faithful are invited to share in the "sacred mysteries" and in order to become less unworthy they are urged to acknowledge their faults. The priest finishes by saying: "May Almighty God have mercy on us, forgive us our sins, and bring us to everlasting life." This is both the most suitable preparation for the eucharistic celebration that is about to begin, and at the same time its anticipated gift, "for when we proclaim the death of the Lord, you continue the work of our redemption" (RM II Sun. in the year). At every Mass the fruits of Christ's offering are applied to the faithful: the remission of sins and the gift of eternal life which begins here on earth with the life of grace. But above all the eucharistic Sacrifice is "a giving of thanks," and therefore the celebrant hastens to intone a joyful hymn of praise and thanksgiving taken up by all the faithful: "Glory to God in the highest." It is significant that the first reason for this praise is not the wonderful gifts with which God overwhelms us; it is the greatness, the very glory of God in which the Church finds her joy: "We worship you, we give you thanks, we praise you for your glory." The glorification of God is the primary purpose of the Mass and will be carried out in the most perfect way possible when, after the Consecration, the faithful are able to offer the Eucharist to the Father: the Christ-Victim for his glory.

After listening to the word of God in the readings of the Mass and in the living voice of the priest, there follow the offering of gifts and the presentation of the materials for the sacrifice. These are precious moments of recollection for readying ourselves for sharing most intimately in the sacred act in which we are all called to exercise our holy priesthood "to offer spiritual sacrifices acceptable to God through Jesus Christ" (1 Pet 2:5). This involves our accompanying the offering of bread and wine with the offering of our own lives, our works, prayers, sufferings, weariness, sacrifices and resolutions, so that Christ may take them into his own offering and offer them to the Father, "as a living sacrifice, holy and acceptable to God" (Rom 12:1).

O divine Spirit, divest my soul of all worldly affections, cleanse it of every stain, and set it aflame with holy fervor, so that it may be worthy to take part in the adorable Sacrifice which is being prepared upon the altar. To obtain this grace I repeat with that most devout king, David: O God, create a clean heart in me; O Lord, and a steadfast spirit sustain in me. Take not your holy Spirit from me.

O Lord, pour out the Holy Spirit upon me, that he may make me ready and worthy of being perfectly united with the adorable Victim who comes down from heaven . . .

In this eucharistic Sacrifice, O Jesus, you immolate yourself as our Head and you immolate us as your members; I abandon myself wholly into your hands in order to have the happy fortune of being one same victim with you . . . But I need to be filled by your Spirit

*for the sacrifice of myself, which I intend to offer you, to be accept-
able to the eternal Father.*

Bl. Elena Guerra, *Il fuoco che Gesu porto sulla terra*

*O Jesus, grant that your sacrifice, the holy Sacrifice of the altar,
may be the source and model of my sacrifice, for my life must also be
a holy sacrifice. It certainly is a sacrifice, for life is all interwoven
with mortification, detachment and suffering . . . But that my
sacrifice be "holy," like yours on Calvary and in the Mass, it must
be vivified, offered and consumed by love. O Jesus, give me a great
love which will give value to my sacrifice and make it fruitful for the
glory of the Father, the triumph of the Church, and the good of
souls.*

*O Jesus, divine Priest, what shall I offer you as matter in the
sacrifice, as a victim of love who shares in your Sacrifice? I offer you
my heart, my will, my very love, to be entirely transformed into
yours. In fact, in your holy Sacrifice you give me an example of this
perfect docility, this conformity to the divine will, and this abandonment. This is the offering which I, too, make: a generous, total
acceptance of every decree of divine Providence, of every divine
wish.*

Sr. Carmela of the Holy Spirit, OCD

211. EUCHARISTIC PRAYER

*Holy Father, in union with the sacrifice of your divine Son, accept
this offering of my whole self, as a living sacrifice, holy and acceptable to you* (Rom 12:1)

1. In the eucharistic prayer of the canon of the Mass there
stand out the two great purposes of the holy Sacrifice, which are
identical with those of Christ's eternal priesthood: God's glory
and the redemption of men. In the preface, immediately before the
canon, the faithful are once again invited to offer to God a solemn
act of thanksgiving. The motive, the means and the object of this
thanksgiving are one: Christ, the perfect praise of the Father,
Christ our mediator, Christ, himself the object of our praise:
"Father, we do well to give you thanks . . . through Jesus Christ
our Lord . . . Blessed is he who comes in the name of the Lord"
(RM). Christ is the center of the Mass: he is the Priest who offers
the Father a "sacrifice of praise," a sacrifice of which he is at the
same time priest and victim. But while Jesus offered his sacrifice
on Calvary alone, here all the faithful offer it together with him:
"We offer you this sacrifice of praise" (Euch. Pr. I). We are invited
not only to offer Christ's oblation to the Father, but to unite our
own to it, so that "receiving the offering of the spiritual victim, he
fashion us for himself as an eternal gift" (SC 12). Immediately
after the consecration the offering is renewed: "Father, we, your

people and your ministers . . . from the many gifts you have given us, offer to you, God of glory and majesty, this holy and perfect sacrifice" (Euch Pr I). It is no longer a matter of offering bread and wine, but of the Body and Blood of Christ, now present upon the altar: a memorial of the Lord's death through the separation of the species, and of his resurrection through his living and lifegiving presence. Christ is God's supreme gift to men—"God so loved the world that he gave his only Son" (Jn 3:16)—and in the Mass mankind offers him to the Father as the supreme act of worship, for the Father is pleased only in his Son. "Through him, with him, in him, in the unity of the Holy Spirit, all glory and honor is yours, almighty Father, for ever and ever."

2. The eucharistic Sacrifice rises to God as a sacrifice of praise and descends again upon earth as a gift for the redemption of mankind. This second aspect also is repeatedly in evidence in the prayers of the canon. Before the consecration the priest prays: "Accept this offering from your whole family . . . save us from final damnation, and count us among those you have chosen." As upon the cross, so also upon the altar, Christ's Sacrifice is presented to the Father for our salvation. Later, calling down upon the bread and wine the "power of . . . the divine blessing" which is to accomplish the eucharistic miracle, the celebrant says: "Accept this offering for our good . . . that it may become for us the Body and Blood of your beloved Son . . . " For "our good" and "for us," the bread and wine will be changed into the Body and Blood of Christ: we need this as the expiatory sacrifice for our sins and as the sacrament which nourishes our supernatural life. Without the Eucharist we cannot live: it is "the fount and apex of the whole Christian life" by which "the Church constantly lives and grows" (LG 11,26). This concept culminates in the consecration with the words of the Lord: "Take this, all of you, and eat it: this is my body . . . Take this, all of you, and drink . . . this is the cup of my blood, the blood . . . [that] will be shed for you and for all men, so that sins may be forgiven." Christ himself makes known the redemptive intention of his sacrifice and invites the faithful to participate through eucharistic communion. This is a communion so intimately joined to the sacrifice, that it is, for our part, its supreme consummation. When we receive the Body and Blood of the Lord, we complete the memorial of his death as well as that of his resurrection, because the Eucharist grants us a share in the glorious life of Christ our Head. This wonderful communion with the paschal mystery of Christ should not end with Mass, but should be spiritually prolonged in our daily life by the offering of our sufferings as a participation in our Lord's death, and by an intense life of grace on our part as a participation in his resurrection.

Father, it is . . . our duty and our salvation always and everywhere to give you thanks through your beloved Son, Jesus Christ. He is the Word through whom you made the universe, the Savior you sent to redeem us.

... We offer you in thanksgiving this holy and living sacrifice. Look with favor on your Church's offering and see the Victim whose death has reconciled us to yourself. Grant that we who are nourished by his body and blood may be filled with his Holy Spirit, and may become one body, one spirit in Christ.

May he make us an everlasting gift to you and enable us to share in the inheritance of your saints ... Father, may this sacrifice which has made our peace with you, advance the peace and salvation of all the world.

Roman Missal, *Eucharistic Prayer* II and III

"What shall I render unto the Lord for all that he has rendered unto me? I will take the chalice of salvation." Yes, O my God, if I take this chalice, crimsoned with the blood of my Master, and in utterly joyous thanksgiving, mingle my blood with that of the sacred Victim, he will impart to it something of his own infinity, and it will give you, O Father, wonderful praise. Then my suffering will become a message that will proclaim your glory.

O Jesus, grant that I may become so identified with you that I may ceaselessly express you in the sight of your Father. What were your first words on entering the world? "Behold I come to do your will, O God!" May this prayer be like the beating of my heart. You made a complete offering of yourself to accomplish the will of the Father; grant that that will may be my food, and, at the same time, the sword which immolates me. Thus, peaceful and joyous, I shall go to meet all sacrifices with you, my adored Master, rejoicing to be known by the Father, since he crucifies me with his Son.

cf Elizabeth of the Trinity, *Second Retreat* 7, 14

212. EVERLASTING PRAISE

Praise the Lord, O my soul! I will praise you, O Lord, as long as I live; I will sing praise to you while I have being   (Ps 146:1-2)

1. The Mass, the supreme act of worship, is not an isolated act; from the very beginning the Church has been mindful of the gospel precept "that they ought always to pray and not lose heart" (Lk 18:1), and has wished to surround the Mass with the recitation of hymns and psalms in order to prolong its prayer of praise and thanksgiving and intercession throughout the hours of the day and the night. St. Paul was already writing to the Ephesians of this time: "Addressing one another in psalms and hymns and spiritual songs; singing and making melody to the Lord with all your heart" (Eph 5:19). Thus in the course of time there came to be established that form of prayer which is called the Divine Office, because it truly performs in the name of the entire Church, the office of perennial praise to the Most High. Even more than this, Catholic tradition and with it Vatican Council II look upon

this prayer as the extension of the hymn of praise that Christ himself began on earth with his incarnation, to which he has desired to join all mankind. "Christ Jesus . . . " says the Council—"by taking human nature introduced into this earthly exile that hymn which is sung throughout all ages in the halls of heaven. He joins the entire community of mankind to himself, associating it with his own singing of this canticle of divine praise. For he continues his priestly work through the agency of his Church, which is ceaselessly engaged in praising the Lord and interceding for the salvation of the whole world. She does this, not only by celebrating the Eucharist, but also . . . by praying the Divine Office" (SC 83). This explains the special dignity of this prayer in which "the voice is truly the voice of the Bride [the Church] addressing her Bridegroom; it is also the very prayer which Christ himself, together with his Body, addresses to the Father" (SC 84).

When priests, religious, or groups of the faithful recite the Divine Office, they have every right to believe that their weak voices are lifted up to God, sustained by the all powerful voice of Christ; "Jesus prays for us as our priest"—says St. Augustine—"he prays within us as our head . . . Consequently we recognize our voice in him and his voice in us" (In Ps 85:1).

2. The Divine Office, or the *Liturgy of the Hours,* is composed, for the greatest part, of texts drawn from holy Scripture and hence inspired by the Holy Spirit. Through these texts, and particularly the psalms, "the Spirit himself intercedes for us with sighs too deep for words" (Rom 8:26), while in the biblical readings he instructs us with the word of God. Therefore, the Divine Office, as the Council says, "is a source of piety and nourishment for personal prayer" (SC 90); but in order to be this effectively, it is necessary that those "who take part" should "attune their minds to their voices when praying it" (ibid). In the thought of the Church, the Divine Office is to be authentic praise of God, not only because of its intrinsic value, but also through the zeal of the one who recites it, so that his prayer personifies and represents the fervor, love and devotion with which the Church herself wants to praise her Lord. In fact, by reciting the Divine Office, we "are fulfilling a duty of the Church" (SC 85), which really expresses her prayer by means of the hearts and lips of her children. The celebration of the Liturgy of the Hours must be animated and sustained by this ecclesial sense which instills fervor into the spirit and urges us on, beyond narrow personal horizons, to embrace in our own prayer the intentions and needs of the entire Church, indeed of all mankind, praising, giving thanks, and entreating help for all men. Only in this way does the Divine Office attain its purpose of "making the whole course of the day and night holy by the praises of God" (SC 84), and so become a true Liturgy of the Hours, at one and the same time as an effective means of sanctification, and hence of spiritual progress and union with God, for the person who

celebrates it. The word of God with which it is interwoven will become the soul of personal prayer—and this not just for the time of its recitation; often in fact, a verse of the paslms or some other phrase of holy Scripture, garnered during devout celebration, will serve as the point of departure for lifting up the heart to God during the day, and sometimes even for nourishing our interior life for long periods of time.

> *O Lord, your ears are not turned toward our lips, but toward our hearts; they are not open to the speech, but to the life of him who praises you (In Ps 146:3).*
>
> *I sing with my voice to awaken piety within me; I sing with my heart to please you . . . Let not my voice be alone in praising you, but may my works also praise you. (In Ps 147:5; 149:8).*
>
> *Grant that I may not cease to live a good life, so that I may praise you without interruption . . . If my tongue must be silent sometimes, let my life speak to you; your ears will not be attracted by my voice, but may you attend to my heart . . .*
>
> *I shall not confine my praise to my voice, but I wish my praise to come from my whole being! Let my voice sing, let my life sing, let all my works sing. And if I must sigh, suffer and be tempted here on earth, I hope that it will all pass away and the day will come when my praises will not fail (In Ps 148:2).*
>
> *It is better for me to use my strength in praising you, than to take breath to praise myself. It is impossible to faint in praising you. To give you praise is like taking food. The more I praise you, the stronger I become, because you are always giving me your sweetness, you, the object of my praise (In Ps 145:4; 99:17).*
>
> *Help me, then, to praise you, by my voice as well as by my mind and by my good works, so that, as you exhort me in the scriptures, I may sing to you a new canticle . . . To the old man, the old canticle; to the new man, the new canticle . . . If I love the things of the world, my song is old; I must love the things of eternity. Your love is ever new and eternal, it is always new because it never grows old . . . Sin is what has made me grow old; rejuvenate me by your grace (In Ps 149:1).*

St. Augustine

213. TENTH SUNDAY OF ORDINARY TIME

YEAR A

To him who orders his way aright you will show salvation, O Lord
(Ps 50:23)

Israel was always wavering between Yahweh and idol worship, and when shaken by God's just punishments sought forgiveness. But God who knew the fickleness of his people, and saw that their acts of worship were not accompanied by conversion, caused the prophet to say: "For I desire steadfast love and not sacrifice" (Hos. 6:6). God does not disdain the ceremonies of worship, but they do not please him unless they express the interior piety through which man turns to God with sincere love, and turns to his neighbor with a good heart, ready to lend aid in any kind of physical or spiritual distress.

In both word and conduct, Jesus gives us a beautiful commentary on Hosea's words. One day, as he was passing by the customs desk where Matthew was seated, he said to him: " 'Follow me.' And he rose and followed him" (Mt 9:9). The terse swiftness of the narrative vividly expresses the unexpectedness of the call and the immediateness of the response. This is so much the more significant because Matthew belonged to the class of tax-collectors—those who collected the public taxes—who were considered sinners on account of their often unjust profits, and were, therefore, hated and avoided by the people. Yet Jesus chose one of his Apostles from among them, and Matthew's promptness in following him showed that these despised people really understood the Savior and could teach respectable folk how resolutely they ought to separate themselves from their "old life" in order to follow Christ. In response to our Lord's action, Matthew "made a great feast for Jesus in his house, and there was a large company of tax collectors and others sitting at the table with them" (Lk 5:29). Jesus and his disciples sat among them at table; for this they were bitterly criticized by the Pharisees: "Why does your Teacher eat with tax collectors and sinners?" The question was directed to the disciples, but Jesus intervened directly: "Go and learn what this means: 'I desire mercy and not sacrifice' " (Mt 9:13). The Pharisees, who considered themselves experts in Scripture, were sent back to study the sacred text again in order to understand the meaning of Hosea's words. To start them off toward the right interpretation, Jesus added: "I came not to call the righteous, but sinners" (ibid). God does not change: what he had said to Israel through the prophets, he repeats now in the words of his Son who came to manifest his infinite mercy and to teach us that piety toward God is sincere only when it is accompanied by mercy and goodness toward our neighbor. In choosing an Apostle from among the excise collectors Jesus was demonstrating that God can call whomever he wishes, and that his call can in a moment transform any one who is open to his grace. By sitting at the table with sinners, he teaches that no one should despair of salvation, that all can confidently trust in him who came not to seek out the healthy but the sick, not the just but sinners—for the simple reason that he is doctor and savior.

O Christ, instead of restoring the old man, you make him into a new man. And this latter, being a new creature, offers you a banquet that you may be pleased with him and that he may be worthy to have his portion of happiness with you. He follows you at once, full of joy and enthusiasm, and says to you: I am no longer the publican . . . I have taken off Levi, to reclothe myself with you.

Like him, I too want to escape my old life and to follow only you, Lord Jesus, for you heal my wounds. Who will be able to separate me from the love of God that is in you? . . . I am bound to the faith as though nailed to it, I am bound by the holy chains of love. All your commandments will be like a cauterizer which I will always keep close to my body . . . the medicine stings, but it draws out the infection from the wound. So cut away the rottenness of my sins, Lord Jesus, while you keep me united to you with the bonds of love; cut away everything that is infected. Come quickly to lance my hidden, secret and multiform passions; lance the wound lest the unhealthy infection spread throughout my body . . .

I have found a doctor who lives in heaven but dispenses his remedies on earth. Only he can heal my wounds, since he has none himself; he can take away the heart's sorrow and the soul's fear, for he knows our inmost secrets.

St. Ambrose, *Commentary on the Gospel of St. Luke* V, 27

YEAR B

For with you, Lord, is steadfast love; with you is plenteous redemption   *(Ps 130:7)*

Today the Liturgy opens the first page of the history of salvation. Man and woman, guilty of transgressing the divine commandment, are being questioned by God. Adam blames Eve and she blames the serpent. The chain of sin is thus lengthened, and through these ancestors of ours it will entangle the whole human race in its snares. But God has pity on his creatures, and while he condemns the serpent in absolute terms, he gives man a glimpse of future salvation: "I will put enmity between you and the woman, and between your seed and her seed; he shall bruise your head" (Gen 3:15). From that moment Satan becomes man's eternal enemy, and will do his utmost to make him perish in sin. "The Lord himself"—the Council teaches—"came to free and strengthen man, renewing him inwardly and casting out that prince of this world (Jn 12:31), who held him in the bondage of sin" (GS 13). Jesus, born of woman, the Son of Mary, came to put an end to Satan's power.

"He went throughout all Galilee"—says the Gospel—"preaching in their synagogues, and casting out demons" (Mk 1:39). This event aroused such enthusiasm among the people that the scribes—incredulous and malevolent—unable to deny the evidence, and not willing to recognize Jesus as the Messiah, attributed his power to the influence of Beelzebub. The

Master responded: "If Satan has risen up against himself and is divided he cannot stand" (Mk 3:26). Satan is in fact giving way, but for quite another reason: one stronger than he has come, the Son of God, who has the power to "bind him" by virtue of the Holy Spirit acting within him. The debate concludes with the fearful words: "All sins will be forgiven the sons of men . . . but whoever blasphemes against the Holy Spirit never has forgiveness, but is guilty of an eternal sin" (ib. 28-29). The sin against the Holy Spirit is to attribute to Satan that which is the work of the Spirit of God, and because—as with the scribes—this sin originates in pride, which denies and rejects God, the person who commits it excludes himself from salvation of his own accord. God does not save any one who does not want to be saved.

This episode, painted in such strong colors, is followed in St. Mark's Gospel by another which brings hope to the heart. His mother and other relatives have come looking for him, and Jesus answered: "Whoever does the will of God is my brother and sister and mother" (ib. 35). All who, following his example, embrace the will of the Father and fulfill it perfectly, are united to him by bonds so intimate that they may be compared to the closest of family ties. And from this union with Christ in the sole will of the Father, they draw the strength to conquer Satan. Just as Christ, by his obedience even to death on the cross, repaired Adam's disobedience and conquered Satan, so will the Christian defeat him by associating himself with the obedience of the Savior, yet not without traveling the way of the cross like Jesus. He is not frightened in the stress of the battle, because he relies on the victorious Christ and knows that through Christ's merits "this slight momentary affliction is preparing for us an eternal weight of glory beyond all comparison" (2 Cor 4:17).

Savior and Lord of all men, author of all deliverance and ransom, and hope of those who have found themselves under your strong protection! You have abolished sin; through your only Son you have destroyed the works of Satan; you have frustrated his stratagems, you have freed those he had bound.

Every diabolical undertaking, Lord, every power of Satan, every snare of the adversary, every wound, every torment, every anguish, blow, shock or evil shadow—let these all fear your name which we are invoking, and the name of your only Son; keep them far removed from the souls and bodies of your servants, so that there may be made holy the name of him who was crucified and raised from the dead for us, who took upon himself our ills and our infirmities, Jesus Christ, who will come to judge the living and the dead.

Early Christian Prayers, 181; 207

You are blessed, Lord; teach me your commandments. Lord, you have been our refuge from age to age. I have said, O Lord, have mercy on me, heal my soul for I have sinned. Teach me to do your will,

for you are my God, for in you is the source of life: in your light we
shall see light. In your mercy preserve those who acknowledge you.
Early Christian Prayers, 225

YEAR C

O Lord, my God, I cried to you for help and you have healed me
(Ps 30:2)

We find in Jesus all the messianic signs contained in the prophecies: "Then the eyes of the blind shall be opened, and the ears
of the deaf unstopped. Then shall the lame man leap like a hart,
and the tongue of the dumb sing for joy" (Is 35:5-6). Jesus himself,
as proof that he was the Messiah, sent word to the Baptist: "The
blind receive their sight, the lame walk, lepers are cleansed, and
the deaf hear, the dead are raised up" (Lk 7:22). It is what took
place as he passed along, even death could not resist him.

Near Naim the Savior came upon a funeral procession; a poor
widow was mourning the death of her only son, "and when he saw
her, he had compassion on her, and said to her: 'Do not weep!' "
(ib. 13). Perhaps the weeping woman made him think of another
mother, his own, who would one day see him dying on the cross,
and, later, contemplate him risen. He wanted to restore her son to
this widow of Naim also. He did not wait to be asked, he demand-
ed no act of faith—as he almost always did before a miracle—but,
moved solely by his compassion, he said: "Young man, I say to
you, arise" (ib. 14). Just as he had told the mother not to weep, he
now ordered the dead son to get up. Only one who was master of
life and death could speak in this manner, with words which effected what they expressed. "The dead man sat up and began to
speak. And Jesus gave him to his mother" (ib. 15).

The Old Testament also records the raising to life of a
child—the son of the widow of Sarepta, through the work of Elijah. But what a difference! The prophet had turned to God in supplication, then three times stretched himself over the boy's
corpse, saying: "O Lord, my God, let this child's soul come into
him again" (1 Kgs 17:21). Jesus, on the contrary, had no need to
interpose actions or supplications, but, with the authority of one
who was acting from his own power, gave a simple command: get
up!

In commenting upon this fact, St. Augustine says: "In the
Gospel we find three dead persons visibly brought back to life by
the Lord, but he raised up a thousand of invisibly dead" (Ser 98:3).
The Saint himself was one of these, raised from the awful death of
sin by the grace of Christ, and there were innumerable others. Today's second reading treats of Paul's great conversion. Of this he
personally wrote to the Galatians with utmost candor: "You have
heard of my former life in Judaism . . . how I persecuted the

Church of God violently, and tried to destroy it" (1:13). But when grace threw him to the ground on his way to Damascus, "at once, without conferring with flesh and blood" he changed his course and consecrated himself entirely to the gospel of Christ. These are the miracles which the Lord never ceases to perform, raising up to new life so many souls ravaged by sin. But to attain that resurrection someone has to weep and suffer. "May Mother Church weep for you"—says St. Ambrose, turning to a sinner—"for she intervenes for each of her children as the widowed mother intervened for her only son . . . And may a multitude of people [the people of the faithful] share in the grief of the good mother" (Comm Gosp St. Luke, V,9).

> *I will extol you, O Lord, for you have drawn me up and have not let my foes rejoice over me. O Lord, my God, I cried to you for help and you have healed me. Lord, you brought up my soul from the nether world; restored me to life from among those gone down to the pit . . .*
>
> *To you, O Lord, I cry; and to the Lord I make supplication. What point is there in my death, if I go down to the pit? Will dust praise you? Will it tell of your faithfulness? . . .*
>
> *You have turned for me my mourning into dancing; you have loosened my sackcloth and girded me with gladness, that my soul may praise you and not be silent. O Lord, my God, I will give thanks to you for ever.*
>
> *Psalm* 30:1-3; 9-13

> *From what great sadness have you often delivered me, O good Jesus, by coming to me! How often, after anxious tears, inexpressible moaning and sobbing, you have healed my wounded conscience with the balm of your mercy, and washed it with the oil of gladness! How often when I began prayer in an almost hopeless state, did I finish it exultant and boldly certain of forgiveness! Those who are similarly afflicted know well how truly the Lord Jesus is the physician who heals the contrite of heart . . . Let those who have not experienced it believe the one who said: The Spirit of the Lord has anointed me and has sent me to bring good tidings to the poor and to heal the contrite of heart. If they still doubt, let them draw near with assurance, and find out by experience; and learn for themselves the meaning of: I desire mercy and not sacrifice.*
>
> St. Bernard, *On the Canticle of Canticles* 32:3

214. THE REAL PRESENCE

I adore you devoutly, O God, hidden beneath the eucharistic veil (Adoro te devote)

1. "The Word was made flesh" (Jn 1:14). The incarnation of the Word, the ineffable mystery of the merciful love of God, who so loved man that he became flesh for his salvation, is prolonged and extended through the ages, and will be until the end of time, by the Eucharist. God was not content with giving us his only Son once for all, willing him to take flesh in the womb of a Virgin—flesh like ours, so that he might suffer and die for us on the cross—but he wished him to remain with us for ever, perpetuating his real presence and his sacrifice in the Eucharist.

In reality there are various ways in which Christ is present in the Church. Vatican II teaches that Christ is present "especially in her liturgical functions; he is present in the sacrifice of the Mass" . . . in the administering of "the sacraments," in preaching, and finally "when the Church prays" (SC 7). We are always dealing with a spiritual presence, yet one that is real, substantial, and operative. The eucharistic presence is above all others because Christ is really present in the Eucharist, not only in a spiritual manner, but also corporeally. "In fact, in this Sacrament, in a unique way, Christ is present wholly and entirely, God and man, substantially and uninterruptedly. This presence of Christ under these species is called real, not by way of exclusion, as if other ways were not real, but rather as a particularized title" (Euch Myst 9). In the Eucharist we find the same Jesus whom Mary brought into the world; whom the shepherds found lying in a manger; whom Mary and Joseph watched over as he grew before their eyes; the Jesus who captivated and tamed those who were mad, who performed miracles; who said he was the "light" and the "life" of the world, who to save mankind died on the cross; the same Jesus who rose again and appeared to the Apostles and in whose wound Thomas put his finger; who ascended into heaven and is now seated in glory at the right hand of his Father, and who, in union with the Father, sends us the Holy Spirit. O Jesus, you are always with us, always the same "yesterday, today and for ever!" (Heb 13:8). Always the same in eternity by the immutability of your divine Person; always the same in time by the Sacrament of the Eucharist.

2. Jesus is present in the Eucharist with all his divinity and all his humanity. Although his humanity is present in substance and not in corporeal extension, it is whole and entire in the consecrated Host—body and soul, and this latter with its faculties of intellect and will. Therefore our Eucharistic Lord knows and loves us as God and as man. He is not a passive object for our adoration but is *living;* he sees us, listens to us, answers our prayers with his graces. Thus we may have with the gentle Master of the gospel living, concrete relations which, although imperceptible to our senses, are similar to those which his contemporaries had with him. It is true that in the Eucharist not only his divinity but even his humanity is hidden; however, faith supplies for the senses, it substitutes for what we do not see or touch; "to convince a sincere

heart"—St. Thomas sings—"faith alone is sufficient" (Pange lingua). As Jesus, disguised as a traveler, once taught the disciples of Emmaus and inflamed their hearts, so too, Jesus hidden under the eucharistic veil illumines our souls, inflames them with his love and inclines them ever more effectively toward the good.

The Son of God who became incarnate for us, makes himself present in the Eucharist to be our companion on our earthly pilgrimage, to be the viaticum of our journey. God, as pure Spirit, is present everywhere, it is true; and in his Unity and Trinity, he even deigns to dwell within our souls, vivified by grace. Nevertheless, we always have need of contact with Jesus, the Word made Flesh, God made Man, the only Mediator who can take us to the Trinity. This is the reason the Church urges us to seek out and venerate in the Eucharist "the presence of the Son of God, our Savior, offered for us on the sacrificial altar [. . . and] to respond with grateful hearts to the gift of him who through his humanity constantly pours divine life into the members of his Body" (PO 5).

> O Jesus, since you are always with us in the Holy Eucharist, grant that we may always be with you, always keep you company at the foot of the tabernacle, and not lose through our fault a single moment that we can spend before you . . . Our Beloved, our all, you are there, you invite us to keep you company; then should we not run to you? Or should we spend elsewhere a single one of the moments you permit us to spend at your feet? . . .
>
> O my beloved Jesus, you are whole and entire, completely alive in the Holy Eucharist, as fully as you were in the house of the holy Family of Nazareth, or in the house of Magdalen at Bethany, as you were in the midst of your Apostles . . . You are here in the same way, O my Beloved, my all! Oh, let us never be distracted from your presence in the holy Eucharist for a single moment of the time you let us be with you.
>
> C. de Foucauld, Ecrits spirituels

> O my Lord, if you did not hide your grandeur, who would approach so often a union of something so dirty and miserable with such great majesty! May the angels and all creatures praise you, for you so measure things in accordance with our weakness that when we rejoice in your sovereign favors your great power does not so frighten us that, as weak and wretched people, we would not dare enjoy them.
>
> O Wealth of the poor, how admirably you know how to sustain souls! And without their seeing such great wealth, you show it to them little by little. When I behold majesty as extraordinary as this concealed in something as small as the host, it happens afterward that I marvel at wisdom so wonderful, and I fail to know how the Lord gives me courage or strength to approach him. If he who has granted, and still does grant me so many favors, did not give this

*strength, it would be impossible to conceal the fact or resist
shouting aloud about marvels so great.*
St. Teresa of Jesus, Life 38:19, 21

215. MYSTERY OF FAITH

Lord . . . you have the words of eternal life; we have believed
(Jn 6:68-69)

1. In the canon of the Mass, the Eucharist is called *the
Mystery of faith;* indeed only faith can make us see God present
under the appearances of bread. Here, the senses do not help at
all—sight, touch, and taste are deceived, finding only a little
bread. But we have the word of the Son of God, the word of Christ,
who declared: "This is my Body . . . This is my Blood" and we
firmly believe in his word. I believe everything the Son of God has
said; nothing can be truer than this word of Truth (Adoro te
devote). "Therefore"—Paul VI teaches—"the Savior in his
humanity is present not only at the right hand of the Father
according to the natural manner of existence, but, at the same
time, also in the sacrament of the Eucharist by a mode of existence which we can hardly express in words, but which, with a
mind illuminated by faith, we can conceive and must most firmly
believe to be possible for God" (Myst Fid 45).

Many people believe in the Eucharist and have no doubts
about it, yet often their faith is weak and dull. Habit deadens im-
pressions and thus it comes about that even the holiest things
leave us indifferent if we regard them in a superficial way. Even
frequenting the Church and perhaps living under the same roof as
Jesus in the Sacrament, it is easy to become rather cool and insensitive. We believe in the real presence of Jesus, but pay little attention to the greatness of this inexpressible reality, and we lack
that lively, concrete faith which those saints had who fell down in
adoration before the Sacrament. Judging by the attitude of the
majority of Christians toward the Eucharist, one could say that
they are "men of little faith" (Mt 8:26). Perhaps we all somewhat
deserve this reproach of Jesus. We must ask for a livelier faith,
and repeat very humbly and confidently the Apostles' beautiful
prayer: "Lord, increase our faith" (Lk 17:5).

2. When Jesus announced the Eucharist, "many of his
disciples drew back and no longer went about with him" (Jn 6:66).
But Peter, in the name of the Apostles, gave this beautiful
testimony of faith: "Lord, you have the words of eternal life, and
we have believed and have come to know that you are the holy one
of God" (ib. 68-69). Faith in the Eucharist is the touchstone of the
true followers of Jesus, and the more intense it is, the more it
reveals an intimate and profound friendship with Christ. Anyone

Tenth Sunday of Ordinary Time

who, like Peter, firmly believes in him, also believes and accepts all his words and all his mysteries: from the Incarnation to the Eucharist. Faith is above all a gift of God. In the same discourse in which he promised the Eucharist, Jesus affirmed this principle, declaring to the incredulous Jews that no one could come to him or believe in him, "unless the Father draws him" (ib. 44). To have a deep and living faith in the Eucharist—as in every other mystery—we must have that interior "attraction" which can come only from God, but toward which everyone can and must dispose himself, by asking for the grace through prayer. "Have you not yet been drawn to it?"—says St. Augustine—"Pray to God that you may be" (In Io 26:2). And while we are asking the Lord to attract us ever more, we do not cease exercising ourselves in faith. In fact, since God infused this virtue into us at baptism and since faith is a voluntary adherence of the intellect to revealed truth, it depends on us to will to believe and to put into this act all the strength of our will.

Faith in the Eucharist must above all lead to zeal for the Mass, the vital center of the Eucharist itself, and therefore to frequent, fervent and active participation in the holy Sacrifice which must also extend to the worship of the "eucharistic Sacrament outside the celebration of the Mass... since"—as Paul VI teaches—"not only while the sacrifice is offered, but also afterwards as long as the Eucharist is kept in our churches ... Christ is truly the Emmanuel, that is, 'God with us.' Day and night he is in our midst, he dwells with us full of grace and truth" (Myst Fid 56;67).

> O Sacrament of love, O Chalice of sublime benignity! O Lord, what gift this is to receive your love itself within me and be transformed in it by grace. I no longer care about seeing you visibly, because the eye of faith, more certain and sure than any of the senses or intellect, gives me consolation enough and as long as I possess you with certainty in my soul, nothing is lacking and nothing else can I desire.
>
> Indeed, I feel urged to praise you in wondering admiration, and to extol the great height of your wisdom and the richness and treasure of your knowledge... O profound Counsel, O Love immense... O food most pure, adorable and ineffable Sacrament! But, O Lord, if you are so great and wonderful and incomprehensible in your gifts and in your outpourings of grace and love, what must you be in yourself?
>
> Bl. Henry Suso, *Dialogue of love 24, Life and works*

> How then, my Creator, can a heart as loving as yours allow that the deeds done by your Son with such ardent love and so as to make us more pleasing to you (for you commanded that he love us) be esteemed so little? Nowadays they have so little regard for the Blessed Sacrament that they take away its dwelling places... Was

something still to be done to please you? But he did everything ... Hasn't he already paid far more than enough for the sin of Adam? Whenever we sin again must this loving Lamb pay? Don't allow this, my sovereign Lord! Let your Majesty be at once appeased! ...

O my God, would that I might have begged you much more ... Lord, perhaps I am the one who has angered you so that my sins have caused these many evils to come about. Well, what is there for me to do, my Creator, but offer this most blessed bread to you, and even though you have given it to us, return it to you and beg you through the merits of your Son to grant me this favor since in so many ways he has merited that you do so? Now, Lord, now; make the sea calm! May this ship, which is the Church, not always have to journey in a tempest like this. Save us, Lord, for we are perishing.

St. Teresa of Jesus, Way 3:8; 35:5

216. MYSTERY OF HOPE

May I hunger for you, O living Bread, who came down from heaven
(Jn 6:51)

1. Jesus said: "I am the living bread which came down from heaven; if anyone eats of this bread, he will live for ever; and the bread which I shall give for the life of the world is my flesh" (Jn 6:51). The Jews disliked this speech; they began to question and dispute the Master's words. But Jesus answered them still more forcefully: "Truly, truly, I say to you, unless you eat the flesh of the Son of man and drink his blood, you have no life in you" (ib. 53). These are peremptory words which leave no room for doubt; if we wish to live, we must eat the Bread of life. We have been grafted into Christ through baptism, and in him and from him have received the life of grace; but this life has to be nourished by a deeper penetration into Christ. "The faithful"—Vatican II teaches—"already marked with the sacred seal of baptism and confirmation, are through the reception of the Eucharist fully joined to the Body of Christ" (PO 5); the Eucharist perfects the work of the other sacraments and nourishes the life of grace in a special way. In very deed, in this sacrament "the extraordinary and unique fact of the presence of the Author of holiness himself" (Euch Myst 4) is made evident; Christ the Lord, made himself food, the bread of man. "There are many mothers today"—says St. John Chrysostom—"who entrust the children they have borne to others to be nursed. Christ does not do that, but feeds us with his own blood, and by every possible means unites us closely to himself." (In Mt 82:5). And while the Eucharist is the sacrament which assimilates us into Christ and makes our union with him always more intimate, it is also the sacrament which unites us

more closely to each other. "Because there is one bread; we who are many are one body, for we all partake of the one bread" (1 Cor 10:17). To aspire to an intimate union with Christ, and to a sincere and cordial fellowship with our brethren, is neither utopian nor a foolish hope. These aspirations correspond to the will of Christ, who gives himself to us as food, precisely to assimilate us to himself, and to make all who share in his body and in his blood, one in him.

2. By nourishing us with Christ's life, the Eucharist nourishes in us a life which has no end; by uniting us to him who is Life, it frees us from death. In fact, Jesus has said: "He who eats my flesh and drinks my blood has eternal life, and I will raise him up at the last day" (Jn 6:54). He *has* eternal life, not *will have,* because the Eucharist not only gives us the right to rise again on the last day, but even now infuses in us the seed of resurrection: "In our frail and weak bodies . . . Christ's immortal body plants the seed of immortality which will one day sprout and blossom" (Leo XIII, Mirae caritatis). The Eucharist, the memorial of the Lord's death, is also the memorial of his resurrection; by it Christ feeds the faithful with his flesh, sacrificed for them, but now risen and forever glorious: "Through his very flesh, made vital and vitalizing by the Holy Spirit, he offers life to men" (PO 5). From this point of view, the Eucharist is truly the sacrament of hope: hope of eternal life, where communion with the risen Christ will have no end. The Eucharist "is the sacred banquet [. . . which] in faith and hope prefigures and anticipates the eschatological banquet in the Father's kingdom" (Euch myst 3a). Eternal communion with Christ begins here on earth, precisely in the eucharistic communion, which is its pledge and its prelude. This is what the Liturgy of the feast of the most blessed Body and Blood of Christ asks for us: "Grant, O Lord, that we may be filled with you in our eternal banquet, of which you give us a foretaste today in the sacrament of your Body nd Blood" (RM). Moreover, because the Eucharist especially prepares us for the eternal banquet, it is a great source of hope and confidence for us in the vicissitudes of daily life. When our road is made rough by temptations, struggles, and troubles, we need to have recourse to the Eucharist, the bread of the strong and the pure. In recommending daily Communion, St. Pius X used to say that "when the faithful are united to God through this sacrament, they receive from it the strength to restrain their passions, to purify themselves of the lesser faults into which they fall daily, and to avoid the serious offenses to which human frailty is exposed" (Scr Trid Synodus). And St. Augustine exclaims: "O great mystery of love! . . . Anyone who wishes to live, has a place in which to live and the means to live: let him draw near, and believe . . . and he will share in life" (In Io 26:13).

O heavenly Father, since you have already given us your Son and, just because you wanted to, sent him into the world, the Son, just because he wants to, desires not to abandon us but to remain here with us, to the greater glory of his friends and the affliction of his enemies . . . It is a fact that you have given us this sacred bread for ever. You gave us, O Father, the manna and nourishment of his humanity that we might find him at will and not die of hunger, save through our own fault.

In no matter how many ways the soul may desire to eat, it will find delight and consolation in the Blessed Sacrament . . . There is no need or trial or persecution that is not easy to suffer if we begin to enjoy the delight and consolation of this sacred bread.

Let whoever wants be concerned with asking for material bread. As for me, O eternal Father, I ask you to let me merit to receive this heavenly bread in such a way that the Lord may reveal himself to the eyes of my soul and make himself thereby known, since my bodily eyes cannot delight in beholding him, because he is so hidden. Such knowledge is another kind of satisfying and delightful sustenance that maintains life.

St. Teresa of Jesus, *Way* 34:2,5

O most loving Father, grant that I may forever contemplate openly your beloved Son, whom I am now, as a pilgrim on earth, about to receive hidden under the eucharistic veils. Lead me, a sinner, to that indescribable banquet of yours, where you, with your Son and with the Holy Spirit, are the true light, full satiety, complete joy, and perfect happiness for your saints.

May your most holy Body and Blood, sweet Jesus, be for my soul sweetness and gentleness, health and strength in every temptation, joy and peace in every tribulation, light and final protection in death.

St. Thomas Aquinas, *Prayers*

217. MYSTERY OF LOVE

O Jesus, that I may eat you, and live because of you   *(Jn 6:57)*

1. All God's activity for man's benefit is summed up in the immense mystery of love which causes him, the sovereign, infinite Good, to raise man to himself, and to make him share in his very life. It was to communicate this divine life to men, to unite men to God, that "the Word became flesh and dwelt among us" (Jn 1:14); in his Person, the divinity was to be united to our humanity in a most complete and perfect way. It was united directly to the most holy humanity of Jesus, and through it, to the whole human race. The way of union with God is thus opened to man: by becoming incarnate and dying on the cross, the Son of God not only removed the obstacles to this union, but also provided all we need to gain it, or rather, he himself became the *Way:* through union with him, man is united to God. And here the love of Jesus, surpassing all

measure, is impelled to find a means of uniting himself to each one of us in the most intimate and personal manner; he found this in the Eucharist. "He whom the angels contemplate trembling..."—says St. John Chrysostom—"is he who made himself our food; we are mingled and fused with him, and thus we are made one body and flesh with Christ" (In Mt 82:5). By assuming our flesh in the Incarnation, the Son of God united himself once and for all with mankind; in the Eucharist the Son of God made man continues to unite himself with each individual person. This is why the Eucharist, "according to the mind of the holy fathers, may really be considered as a continuation and extension of the Incarnation. In fact, through it the substance of the incarnate Word is united to individual men, and the supreme sacrifice of Golgotha is wonderfully renewed" (Leo XIII, Mirae caritatis). The plan of infinite love which desires to unite men with God, and to let them share in the divine nature and life, thus finds its supreme and highest fulfillment in the Eucharist.

2. The eucharistic Mystery is the compendium of all the work of God's infinite love for man's salvation. Indeed, in the Sacrifice of the altar, from which the Eucharist proceeds, there is renewed and perpetuated the sacrifice of the cross by which Christ redeemed the world. "Greater love has no man than this, that a man lay down his life for his friends" (Jn 15:13), are our Lord's own words, and he was not satisfied to give this testimony of love once on Calvary, but willed to renew it continually through the centuries in the eucharistic celebration. In the Mass Christ continues to immolate himself mystically but really for the salvation of men, so that the Church can pray: "Lord ... we offer to you, God of glory and majesty ... this holy and perfect sacrifice, the bread of eternal life and the cup of eternal salvation" (Euch Prayer I); and each of the faithful, adoring Christ present under the sacred species can say: "He loved me and gave himself for me" (Gal 2:20). But Christ's love seems to go beyond even the sacrifice, wishing that it be completed in the banquet in which he offers himself as food for those who love him; even more, the banquet is so intimately linked to the sacrifice that the one cannot exist without the other. "The Lord is ... immolated ... in the Sacrifice of the Mass ... when he begins to be sacramentally present as the spiritual food of the faithful under the appearances of bread and wine" (Myst fidae 34); and the faithful participate more fully in the Sacrifice when they approach the eucharistic table. The Eucharist is so bound to the Sacrifice that the sacred species "are reserved so that the faithful who are unable to participate in the Mass may be united with Christ and to his Sacrifice through sacramental communion received with proper dispositions ... Participation in the Lord's Supper is always truly communion with Christ, who offers himself up for us in the sacrifice to the Father" (Euch Myst 3e, 3b). The Eucharist, the sacrament of love that unites us with Christ immolated and risen, should lead the faithful to live his life of love, and hence his sacrifice for the

Father's glory and the salvation of their brothers, until the day when they will share for ever in his glorious resurrection. "Truly, participation in the Body and Blood of Christ has no other end than to transform us into that which we eat" (St Leo the Great, Ser 63:7).

O eternal Trinity, O Trinity eternal! O fire and abyss of charity! O enamored of your creature! . . . How could our redemption benefit you? It could not, for you, our God, have no need of us. To whom then comes this benefit? Only to man. O inestimable charity! Even as you, true God and true Man, gave yourself entirely to us, so also you left yourself entirely for us, to be our food, so that during our earthly pilgrimage we would not faint with weariness, but would be strengthened by you, our celestial Bread.

O man, what has your God left you? He has left you himself, wholly God and wholly man, concealed under this whiteness of bread. O fire of love! Was it not enough for you to have created us to your image and likeness, and to have re-created us in grace through the Blood of your Son, without giving yourself wholly to us as our food, O God, divine Essence? What impelled you to do this? Your charity alone, in the excess of your love.

St. Catherine of Siena, *Prayers*

Lord of power . . . to you we offer this living sacrifice, this bloodless oblation, to you we offer this bread, figure of the Body of your only Son . . . When we celebrate "the memory of his death," we offer you this bread and pray: Through this sacrifice be propitious to us all, be propitious to us, O God of truth . . . And we offer you this chalice, figure of his Blood . . . God of truth, may your holy word come upon this bread, so that it may become the body of the Word; and upon this chalice, that it may become the blood of truth. And grant that all who communicate may receive the medicine of life, for the healing of every infirmity, for the strengthening of growth in every virtue; let this not be cause for condemnation . . .

Make us worthy of this communion, God of truth, and give chastity to our bodies, and to our souls understanding and knowledge; give us wisdom, God of mercy, through sharing in your Body and Blood. For yours is the glory and the power through your only Son, in the Holy Spirit, now and for ever.

St. Serapion, *Early Christian Prayers*, 191; 192

218. MYSTERY OF UNITY

May all of us who share in the body and blood of Christ be brought together in unity by the Holy Spirit   *(Euch Prayer II)*

1. In his discourse on the bread of life, Jesus himself spoke of

the Eucharist as the Sacrament of our union with him. "He who eats my flesh and drinks my blood abides in me, and I in him" (Jn 6:56). It is a true interpenetration: Christ is in us and we are in Christ. Of course, his life and ours, his Person and ours, remain distinct; and yet, "having received the Body and Blood of Christ, we are in Christ and Christ is in us . . . he himself is in us by his flesh and we are in him, and with him all that we are is in God" (St. Hilary, De Trinit. VIII: 14). We are never so close to Jesus, so penetrated by him, transformed, deified, and plunged into the divinity as at the moment of sacramental Communion: "with him, all that we are is in God."

But Jesus goes further still and adds: "As the living Father sent me, and I live because of the Father, so he who eats me will live because of me" (Jn 6:57). The whole life of Christ comes from the Father; he has no life other than that which he shares with the Father. Similarly, one who is nourished by the flesh of Christ lives by the life Christ communicates to him; it is a life which has already been received through baptism, but which, through the Eucharist, is shared with greater immediacy by Christ who is its source, since he comes in person to infuse it. Jesus lives by the Father, because the Father is the source of his life; and the communicant lives by Jesus, because Jesus, by becoming his food, becomes the source of his life in the most direct, profound and intimate manner. Having received his life from the Father, Jesus lives solely for his glory, dedicating himself completely to the mission entrusted to him; so too the communicant should no longer live a life concerned only with personal cares and interests, should no longer live for himself, but for Jesus, in order to accomplish his will and to seek his glory. "None of us lives to himself"—exclaims St. Paul—" . . . if we live, we live to the Lord" (Rom 14:8).

2. Vatican II affirms that Christ, "before offering himself up as a spotless victim upon the altar of the cross, prayed to his Father for those who believe, saying: 'that all may be one even as you, Father, in me and I in you; that they also may be one in us . . . ' (Jn 17:21). He instituted in his Church the wonderful sacrament of the Eucharist, by which the unity of the Church is both signified and brought about" (UR 2). From the beginning of the Church, the Eucharist has been considered as the symbol of the union of all believers: "Regarding the Eucharist, give thanks"—says an ancient eucharistic prayer—"As this broken bread was scattered over the hills and when gathered became one mass, so may your Church be gathered from the ends of the earth" (Didache 9). And since the sacraments effect the reality that they signify, the Eucharist not only represents, but accomplishes unity among believers; they, by feeding upon the one bread, the immaculate flesh of Christ, become incorporated in him and form one single body, his Mystical Body, which is the Church. The unity of all the faithful in Christ, begun with baptism, is strengthened, perfected and brought to completion by the Eucharist, on account

of which we can truly say that "the Church constantly lives and grows" through the Eucharist, for it "completes the building up of the Body" (LG 26,17). Speaking of the early Church, the Acts of the Apostles assert that the assembly of believers was as a single heart and soul, united and nourished by the Eucharist (Acts 4:32; 2:42); this is the fruit that the eucharistic Bread must continue to produce in the Church: unity of heart and mind among all believers, a precious and logical consequence of the union of each of them with Christ. The deeper the union of each individual with Christ, by virtue of the Eucharist, the more it generates mutual unity among those who are nourished at the same Table, thus accomplishing the prayer of our Lord; "that they may become perfectly one" (Jn 17:23). For this reason, then, the Church prays to the Father during Mass: "Grant that we who are nourished by his Body and Blood may be filled with his Holy Spirit, and become one body, one spirit in Christ" (Euch Prayer III).

> *O Lord, who must be more pure from everything than he who takes part in your Sacrifice? What under the light of the sun must be more pure than the hand that distributes your flesh, or the mouth about to be filled with spiritual fire, or the tongue to be reddened by your blood? ... Lord, make me realize with what an honor I have been honored, in what a banquet I am sharing. You whom the angels contemplate trembling, upon whom they dare not even look without fear because of the splendor that comes forth from you, you have made yourself our food; we ... are fused with you, and are thus become one body and one flesh through you. "Who will tell your great wonders, O Lord, and make known all your praises?" What shepherd feeds his flock with his own flesh? ... There are many mothers who entrust the children they have borne to others to be nursed. You do not do that, you feed us with your own blood, and unite us closely to yourself by every possible means ... You join yourself to each of the faithful through the mysteries; you nourish with yourself those whom you have brought to life without entrusting them to others, and so convince me yet again that you have truly taken my flesh.*
>
> *O Lord, let me not remain indifferent and lazy after receiving such great love and honor! With what desire children cling to their mother's bosom, and how eagerly their lips draw near for nourishment! Let us approach this table and this spiritual chalice in like manner and with the same ardor; or rather, with even greater desire and ardor ... Help us to attract to ourselves the grace of the Spirit, and let our only grief be that of being deprived of this food. What is being offered to us is not the work of human hands, but you who worked this miracle during the Supper, work this same miracle also today.*
>
> St. John Chrysostom, *Commentary on Gospel of St. Matthew* 2:5

> *Just as this bread, once scattered over the hills, was gathered up*

to become one, in like manner, O Lord, gather together into one in your Church people from every race, every country, every city, every town and every home ... and make them all one living, Catholic Church.

St. Serapion, *Early Christian Prayers*, 191

219. EUCHARIST AND LIFE

O Lord, grant that we who partake of one bread, although many, may be one body   *(1 Cor 10:17)*

1. The Eucharist unites us to Christ directly; this physical union is the same for all who partake of his Body and Blood. However it does not produce the same effects in everyone, so much so that St. Paul says: "Whoever therefore eats the bread or drinks the cup of the Lord in an unworthy manner, will be guilty of profaning the body and blood of the Lord" (1 Cor 11:27-29). But even for those who approach the Eucharist in the state of grace, the effects which are derived from it are not the same, but are proportioned to their dispositions.

Since the actual effect of the Eucharist is union with Christ and with our brethren, the best preparation for the eucharistic Banquet is love, without which there can be no union. Union with Christ requires that sincere love which is conformity with his will, his desires, and with what pleases him. "Have this mind among yourselves, which is yours in Christ Jesus" (Phil 2:5), St. Paul would say. Whatever runs counter to Christ's sentiments, to his will, to his precepts, and especially to his commandment to love, is an obstacle to union with him. Then it can happen, as St. Augustine says, that we eat the Body of the Lord materially, without doing so spiritually, thus remaining deprived of the fruit of the sacrament (In Io 26:12). In order that the Eucharist may bring about and strengthen fraternal unity, we must rid ourselves of everything that disturbs a cordial and sincere relationship with our neighbor, and carefully cultivate genuine, universal charity. "Love one another as I have loved you" (Jn 15:12), said the Lord, and more precisely: "If you are offering your gift at the altar, and there remember that your brother has something against you, leave your gift there ... first be reconciled to your brother" (Mt 5:23-24). Before approaching the altar, each of us must examine ourself, for no one should dare receive the Body of the Lord who has broken his commandment, even slightly. "Forgive and you will be forgiven"—says St. Augustine—"then you may approach with assurance: it is bread, not poison. But forgive sincerely; because if you do not forgive sincerely ... you are lying to one whom you cannot deceive" (In Io 26:11).

2. If we must prepare ourselves in an always worthier manner

for the eucharistic Sacrifice and Banquet, we must also strive to live, in our daily conduct, the grace that flows from the Eucharist. "The Liturgy in its turn"—says Vatican II—"inspires the faithful to become one heart in love, when they have tasted to their full of the paschal mysteries; it prays that 'they may grasp by deed what they hold by creed' " (SC 10). It is a matter of harmonizing our own way of life with that holiness and charity which the Eucharist expresses and produces; it is a matter of bringing into the accomplishment of our daily duties that union with Christ and our brothers which is the fruit of eucharistic Communion. Since the Eucharist brings us close to the death and resurrection of our Lord, we must also share in his death by dying to ourselves and to sin, and share in his resurrection by living more and more that divine life which he transmits.

The daily visit to the Blessed Sacrament, which the Church has always recommended, is most useful for preserving the effects of the Eucharist and for becoming better disposed toward it. Christ, present under the sacred species, "restores morality, nourishes virtues, consoles the afflicted, strengthens the weak, and proposes his own example for imitation to all those who come to him . . . Therefore anyone who approaches this august Sacrament with special devotion, and endeavors to return generous and ardent love for Christ's own infinite love, experiences and fully understands, not without great spiritual joy and profit, how precious is life hidden with Christ in God, and how great is the value of converse with Christ; for there is nothing more consoling on earth, and nothing more efficacious for advancing along the road of holiness" (Paul VI Myst Fidei 67).

The Holy Eucharist truly contains all our good, "Christ himself, our Passover and living bread . . . He offers life to men. They are thereby invited and led to offer themselves, their labors, and all created things together with him" (PO 5).

O Jesus, divine food of the soul, this immense multitude turns to you. It wishes to give to its human and Christian vocation a new, vigorous power of interior virtue, and to be ready for sacrifice, of which you were such a wonderful pattern in word and example.

You are our elder Brother; you have trodden our path before us, O Christ Jesus, the path of every one of us; you have forgiven all our sins; you inspire us, each and all, to give a nobler, more convinced and more active example of Christian life.

O Jesus, our "true bread" and only substantial food for our souls, gather all the peoples around your table. Your altar is divine reality on earth, the pledge of heavenly favor, the assurance of a just understanding among peoples, and of peaceful rivalry in the true progress of civilization.

Nourished by you and with you, O Jesus, men will be strong in faith, joyful in hope, and active in the many varied expressions of charity.

Our will will know how to overcome the snares of evil, the temptations of selfishness, the listlessness of sloth. And the eyes of men who love and fear the Lord will behold the vision of the land of the living, of which the wayfaring Church militant is the image, enabling the whole earth to hear the first sweet and mysterious voices of the City of God.

O Jesus, "feed us and guard us, and grant that we may see the good things in the land of the living! Amen."

John XXIII, Prayers and Devotions April 9

Lord, I am unclean; I am not worthy that your blessed body should come sacramentally into my dirty dwelling. Lord, I am altogether unworthy of any honor or of any good or of any of the consolations that virtuous people obtain from you. There is nothing left for me to do but to weep and lament continually, and to walk before you with unshakeable confidence. And although poor and abandoned, I will not stray far from you, but will cry out and implore you without ceasing, until my faith obtains from you the cure of my "servant"—my sensible part. Then I shall praise you and seve you with body and soul, with all my being and all my strength.

Ruysbroeck, Oeuvres, vol. 1

220. ELEVENTH SUNDAY OF ORDINARY TIME

YEAR A

We rejoice in God through our Lord Jesus Christ, through whom we have now received our reconciliation   *(Rom 5:11)*

God put this stipulation at the base of his covenant with Israel: "If you will obey my voice . . . you shall be my own possession among all peoples . . . and you shall be to me a kingdom of priests and a holy nation" (Ex 19:5-6). God was entrusting Israel with a priestly mission, a position of mediation which established that faith and salvation should come to all mankind through Israel. In the New Testament this office is given to the Church, the new People of God. Every Christian shares in this office, for his baptism pledges him not only to live personally the faith and grace he has received, but also to radiate his faith to those about him, so that it may penetrate into the world. "You are a chosen race"—St. Peter writes to the early Christians, repeating God's words to Israel almost to the letter—"a royal priesthood, a holy nation" (1 Pet 2:9). Vatican Council II has restored the value of this doctrine in a special way by recognizing in it the foundation of the common priesthood of the faithful and hence of their apostolic duty.

Beside this priesthood which involves every one who is baptized, Jesus instituted another, the ministerial priesthood, to which is entrusted magisterial and sacramental functions. His first step in reference to this latter one was the choice and sending out of the Twelve. "And he called to him his twelve disciples and gave them authority over unclean spirits, to cast them out, and to heal every disease and every infirmity" (Mt 10:1). Jesus shared his mission with them, and therefore his powers also; like him, they were to preach "that the kingdom of heaven is at hand" (ib. 7), and like him, they were to give proof of the truth of their words by miracles. Like him too, they were to bring the message of salvation "to the lost sheep of the house of Israel" (ib. 6). This did not mean that other nations were excluded, but was rather an expression of God's fidelity to his choices. Since he had chosen Israel as a privileged, priestly people, he offered it the first-fruits of salvation; if Israel would not accept, it would be only through its own fault.

This leads us to reflect that the initiative in any election always comes from God. Neither Israel was chosen, nor the Twelve picked out because of personal merits, but solely because God had so desired. "You did not choose me, but I chose you" (Jn 15:16). However, this free choice creates a special responsibility for those who are chosen. No one can read without trembling the list of the Twelve which ends with the name of Judas Iscariot. If God is so faithful to his choices that Israel always remained the chosen people notwithstanding its transgressions, and Judas was not expelled from the apostolic college in spite of his traitorous designs, it is clear that every divine calling pledges one to extreme fidelity. The chosen ones of today are even more responsible than was ancient Israel, because their priesthood is based now on that of Christ, the only true Priest, who sacrificed himself for the world's salvation. "For, if while we were enemies, we were reconciled to God by the death of his Son, much more, now that we are reconciled, shall we be saved by his life" (Rom 5:10). Christ, who reconciled men with God, is the foundation of all priesthood, he is its strength, and at the same time confers upon it the grace to be faithful.

> *O Lord, protect your work, preserve in me the grace you have granted me. It is through your grace that I am what I am; I am in truth the least and last of your bishops.*
>
> *Since you have permitted me to work for your Church, always bless the fruits of my labor. You called me to the priesthood when I was a lost child; do not let me be lost now that I am a priest.*
>
> *But most of all, give me the grace to know how to have compassion for sinners from the depths of my heart . . . Grant that I be compassionate every time I witness the fall of a sinner; that I may not punish him with arrogance but rather weep and sorrow with him. In weeping for my neighbor, let me weep over myself also.*
>
> St. Ambrose, *Early Christian Prayers*, 283

*O most pure Virgin, Mother of God and of the "whole" Christ,
you who still always have the essential mission of giving Jesus to
the world, form in me the spirit of Christ. Associated like you with
all the sentiments of the incarnate Word, may I be able to express
Christ Jesus before the eyes of the Father with every deed I do. Like
you, O Virgin, I desire to be a victim for the Church, and to love her
even to giving up my life for her, enveloping her with the same love
with which Jesus loved her.*

M.M. Philipon

YEAR B

Open our hearts, Lord, and we will give heed to your word
(Acts 16:14)

God resists the proud and humbles them so that his divine
omnipotence may be the more evident through human
powerlessness. Thus, when Israel grew arrogant because of the
privileges of her election, God humbled her and pruned her severely by reducing her, through exile and slavery, to a "remnant" of a
poor, humble, despised people. It was to this "remnant" that the
prophets addressed themselves in order to keep alive hope in the
divine promises. Hence, Ezekiel speaks of the "shoot" that God
will cut from the strong, sturdy cedar to transplant it "upon a
high hill." "It will spread its branches" to such an extent that
"under it will dwell all kinds of beasts" (Ezek 17:22-23). This messianic prophecy ties in with that of Isaiah: "A shoot will come
forth from the trunk of Jesse, a sapling will sprout from its roots"
(11:1). As God had promised, the Savior will come from Israel, not
from an Israel that is strong and powerful—the great cedar—but
from one that is humble and faithful, like the Virgin Mary; from
her will come forth the "little shoot" from which the new people of
God will spring.
    God continues to work in the world in this manner in order to
establish his kingdom and to save mankind. He leaves the great
and the powerful to one side and makes use of small, humble
creatures and things, just as the seed thrown on the ground is
small, and a mustard seed a negligible thing. Jesus used just these
images to make it understood that God's kingdom is not a reality
which imposes itself through power and visible greatness, but is a
hidden reality, sown in humble hearts, which nevertheless has the
vitality and strength to expand in an incredible degree. Man cannot fathom it, just as the farmer cannot comprehend how the seed
put into the ground sprouts and grows; its growth is certain even
if he "does not know" how it comes about.
    Although the parables in the Gospel about the seed and the
grain of mustard (Mk 4:26-34) are a summons to humility, which is
the only fit ground for the development of God's kingdom, they

are also a call to a healthy optimism which is based on the unfailing efficacy of the divine action. Even though men have become perverted to the point of denying God, of considering him "dead," of acting as if he did not exist, he is always present and operative in human history and continues to scatter the seed of his kingdom. The Church itself which cooperates in this seeding often does not see its fruits, but it is certain that one day these "ears of corn" will ripen. Meanwhile we have to await the hour appointed by God in patience, just as the farmer waits without anxiety for the winter to pass and the seed to germinate. We also must wait in humility, accepting our status as "a grain of mustard" or "a small flock," without any pretense of becoming a strong, powerful people. What is true for the Church is likewise true for the individual, for in man's heart also, the kingdom of God, which is holiness, develops secretly, and we must not be discouraged if after repeated efforts we find ourselves always weak and imperfect. While persevering in our effort, we need to put our trust in God alone, for only he can make our actions efficacious.

O God, strength of those who hope in you, hear the cry of mankind, weighed down by mortal weakness: we can do nothing without your help; come and aid us with your grace, so that by following your precepts, we may be able to please you in our intentions and in our deeds.

Roman Missal, *Collect*

O all powerful God, to show us your omnipotence you choose those things that are weak to confound the great, and use those that are weak to destroy the strong, and work wonderful things with humble tools, so that no one may glory in himself, but may only glory in you, Grant that I may love and embrace with all my heart the little things you have chosen so that I may be worthy to obtain the great things that are enclosed within them. O my Savior, make me a little grain of mustard that is crushed like you by mockery and torment so I may merit to obtain eternal rest.

L. De Ponte, *Meditations* III 46:1

YEAR C

Lord, forgive the guilt of my sin   (Ps 32:5)

King David had sinned; blinded by passion, he had had Uriah killed so that he could possess his wife. The prophet Nathan, sent by God, wanted to make him understand by way of a story, the gravity of his wrong doing. The king became indignant as he listened to the story of the rich man who had many sheep who, in order to prepare a dinner for a guest, had robbed a poor man of his only sheep, and David judged the man worthy of death. But when

Nathan said to him: "You are that man!" (2 Sam 12:7), he understood and wept for his sin. God had had him anointed, had given him riches and every variety of material goods, but all this had not been enough for him, and despising the divine law, he had carried off another man's wife. It was a serious sin, yet God forgave him because David acknowledged his guilt and humbly confessed: "I have sinned against the Lord" (ib. 13). But he still had to pay the penalty for it: "the child that is born to you shall die" (ib. 14). God in his mercy forgives the sinner who acknowledges his guilt, and in that same mercy punishes him so that he may not sin again.

The themes of mercy and forgiveness are taken up again in the Gospel, but in a new light: that of the salvation that is now in progress. God no longer sends prophets to reproach sinners; he has sent his Son to save them, who goes everywhere to seek them, in their homes and in the streets. We see Jesus in the house of Simon the Pharisee who had invited him to dinner more with the intention of criticizing him than through any friendship. While Jesus was at the table, he allowed a sinful woman to kiss and anoint his feet. Simon shuddered at the daring deed: "If this man were a prophet, he would have known who and what sort of woman this is who is touching him" (Lk 7:39). He too—like David, but even more wrongly—is scandalized at another's behavior, and is very far from examining his own. But Jesus, like Nathan, seeks to enlighten the Pharisee through a story: which of two debtors whose debts had been remitted would love their creditor more? "The one to whom he forgave more" (ib. 43), was Simon's answer. Like David, he did not realize that his answer contained his own condemnation. It was true that the woman had committed many sins, but these were forgiven her in view of the great love she had shown by bathing the Lord's feet with her tears, and drying them with her hair, kissing them and anointing them with ointment. Simon had not committed "many sins" (ib. 47), but he had closed his heart to love—"you gave me no kiss—you did not anoint my head with oil" (ib. 45-46)—on the contrary, his heart was open to criticism and ready to take scandal. If Simon had acknowledged his fault—particularly that overriding desire to catch the Lord in error—he would have been pardoned and God's mercy, flowing into his soul, would have filled him with love.

The forgiveness of sins is, at one and the same time, an initiative of God's merciful love and his response to man's penitential love. The more a man repents through a motive of love, the more abundant is God's pardon, and it cancels not only guilt, but also punishment. Jesus did not impose any penance on the sinful woman, not simply because her love was so great, but above all because he himself had taken its burden upon himself by offering his own life for the sins of men.

Lord, I offer you my past, I confide it to your mercy, hoping for forgiveness from your goodness alone. I do not want to try to excuse myself, or to reassure myself about my past by pointing to any good trait of mine, or any good deed or act of reparation or some good resolution; both as to the past and to the future, I leave myself to your mercy...

I stand before you, my holy God, with the painful memory of my sin, of the betrayal of friendship, with the certainty of my weakness and my impotence, yet confiding in your wonderful love, of which I never have enough and yet of which I have never been lacking. Have pity on me! put no confidence in me, keep me close for you know how stubborn and capricious I am as soon as yo relax your vigilance; still do not overwhelm me beyond my strength, Lord, for I am ridiculously weak; take me as I am, as I was made, to remake me in your way and make me capable of following your will.

I do not even dare to tell you that I love you; I would like to be able to prove it to you, but see, I need you here already: I cannot love you without your loving me. O God, create a new heart within me... Make me a true son, worthy of your kingdom and your promise, a son in whom your blood will flow, in whom your life will circulate... I know that I have no strength... be always with me, work with me, fight in me. Lord, I blush while offering you my contrite love.

P. Lyonnet, *Spiritual Writings*

221. UNDERSTANDING THE MYSTERY OF CHRIST

Grant, O Father, that I may understand the love of Christ which surpasses knowledge (Eph 3:19)

1. Together with the apostle John, St. Paul can be considered the first theologian of the mystery hidden in the heart of Christ. In his letter to the Ephesians he does not hesitate to declare that he has received the mission to announce to all men without discrimination "the unsearchable riches of Christ, and to make all men see what is the plan of the mystery hidden for ages in God" (Eph 3:8-9). It is the mystery of the salvation of mankind, realized "in Christ Jesus Our Lord" (ib. 11), which shows "God's grace in kindness toward us" (Eph 2:7). Deeply impressed by the immense greatness of such a mystery, and feeling himself powerless to communicate the understanding of it to others, Paul turns to God with ardent entreaty: "For this reason I bow my knees before the Father ... that you may have power to comprehend with all the saints what is the breadth and length and height and depth, and to know the love of Christ which surpasses knowledge" (Eph 3:14, 18-19). He makes use of every dimension to explain in some manner that which it is impossible to put into human words. The mystery of God's love, from which flows his plan of salvation, the

mystery of that plan realized by the Word made flesh (Jn 1:14), the mystery of the charity of Christ, who loved us and gave his life for us (Gal 2:20), are ineffable realities which surpass the limits of all human understanding. No man, however holy and learned, could give other men an understanding of these things; this can come only from God, and Paul begs for it from God for all who believe. Any one who does not intuitively sense the mystery of God's love, of Christ's love, cannot grasp the intimate essence of Christianity, which springs precisely from this love. This is why the Apostle begs of the Father that the faithful may be "strengthened through his Spirit . . . that Christ may dwell in [their] hearts through faith; that you . . . [may be] rooted and grounded in love" (Eph 3:16-18). Only the Holy Spirit, substantial love, who causes the faithful to be reborn in Christ and pours love into their hearts (Jn 3:5; Rom 5:5), can put them in a position to sense "the love of God which surpasses understanding." It is an intuition which is the fruit of love much more than of understanding.

2. "The Son of God walked the ways of a true incarnation that he might make men sharers in the divine nature . . . He took up . . . our entire human nature such as it is found among us in our misery and poverty, though without our sin" (AG 3). The apostles who knew Christ and lived with him bear witness to the truth of this assertion. John, as though speaking in the name of all, writes: "That which we have seen with our eyes, which we have looked upon and touched with our hands concerning the Word of Life . . . that which we have seen and heard we proclaim also to you (1 Jn 1:1,3). Through the life, the teaching, and the works of Christ, John has grasped the essence of his mystery: love; and this love announces to us all "that we may have fellowship with the Father and with his Son Jesus Christ" (ib.). The Apostle briefly traces the history of God's love: "In this the love of God was made manifest among us, that God sent his only Son into the world, so that we might live through him" (1 Jn 4:9). And he adds in the excited tone of one who has been an eye-witness: "We have seen and testify that the Father has sent his Son as the Savior of the world" (ib. 14). John had lived and dealt intimately with the Son of God become son of man: he had received his confidences, and understood the feelings of his heart, and he summed it all up as: "We know and believe the love God has for us. God is love" (ib. 16). The habitual intimacy of St. John's life with Christ had given him a kind of intuitive perception of the profound nature of God: love. God is love, Christ is love; Christianity is love. "Beloved, if God has loved us, we also ought to love one another . . . God is love, and he who abides in love, abides in God, and God abides in him" (ib. 11,16). Understanding the mystery of God-as-Love cannot remain an abstraction, it must become life. Only in this way are the faithful introduced into the mystery of Christ and with him into the mystery of the Trinity "by which we are filled with all the fullness of God" (Eph 3:19).

My God, I can only fall on my knees beside the great revealer of the mystery of grace, begging you, my Father, to increase my spiritual capacity, my faith and charity, through your Holy Spirit, so that I may have the strength to contemplate the breadth, the length, the height and depth of the charity of Christ, and to realize that it surpasses all understanding and that I must let myself be penetrated by the outflowing of divine life . . .

O Father, let Jesus live in me, and through him I shall share in your love . . . I am not pure, but the blood of your Son purifies me; I am far distant from you, in darkness and falsehood and death, but he is the Way, the Truth, the Life. Teach me to let go of myself, to deny myself, to strip myself and die; and when Christ shall have become my only life, O Father, you will be lovingly pleased with me . . .

O my Lord Jesus, you are in our midst and we do not know you; you are the lamb of God who take away the sins of the world and we do not recognize you.

D. Mercier, La vie interieure 3,4

O Christ, the venerable voices of the prophets who foretold the liberating plan of your blessed coming . . . are but fleeting images and pallid figures . . . compared to the revelation of your good news and of our redemption by your cross.

In fact, you have set up everywhere the tabernacle . . . of the covenant in your Blood which cries out continually . . . the victorious outcome of your struggle, the sweet, immortal life of your graces: baptism, resurrection, renewal, friendship with you, union with your Holy Spirit, atonement, freedom, enlightenment, eternal purity, true blessedness . . . besides that of which we scarcely dare speak: . . . the mystery of being divinized through our election by grace, of our union with you, O Creator, through our communion with your Body, O Lord . . .

O Redeemer, you have come with the wealth of your Father; you have fulfilled and brought to its culmination the long expectation which had remained confidently alive in men's hearts, O you who atone for us all! Glory be to you with your Father, in the praise and blessing of your Holy Spirit, for ever and ever.

St. Gregory of Narek, Le livre des prieres

222. YOU ARE MY FRIENDS

O Jesus, may I abide in your love   (Jn 15:10)

1. In the Word made flesh "human nature as he assumed it was not annulled . . . The Son of God . . . worked with human hands, he thought with a human mind, acted by human choice, and loved with a human heart" (GS 22). The Son of God, burning

away all distances between us with his love, was made one of us and was involved with us, like to us in everything but sin (Phil 2:7-8; Heb 4:15). He wanted to share our life and our lot: he worked, suffered and loved like us. He made his divine love for us known through all the ordinary indications of human love: tenderness, compassion, friendship, even tears. The Gospel shows him wanting to have the little children around him: "And he took them in his arms and blessed them" (Mk 10:16); it presents him, deeply moved by the tears of the widow for her dead son: he said to her: "Do not weep" (Lk 7:13), and a miracle blossomed from his compassion. He was moved to pity by the lepers, the lame and the blind who cry out to him: "Have mercy on us, Son of David" (Mt 20:30); he felt pity for the crowd which had been following him for three days and did not want to send them away hungry. He manifested compassion for sinners with whom he did not disdain to share a meal, for the adulteress whom he sent away absolved of sin, for the sinful woman who prostrated herself at his feet in Simon's house. When men resisted his love, Jesus suffered even to tears; gazing at Jerusalem, he "wept over it, saying: 'Would that even today you knew the things that make for peace!'" (Lk 19:41-42).

The heart of Christ was also acquainted with the most tender feelings of human friendship: when the Jews saw Jesus crying at the death of his friend Lazarus, they said: "See how he loved him!" (Jn 11:36); and when John, his favorite, who had experienced the exquisite wonder of Jesus' friendship, wanted to write about himself, he concealed his identity under the affectionate expression: "the disciple whom Jesus loved" (Jn 13:23). When on the eve of his passion our Lord would say: "Love one another as I have loved you" (Jn 15:12), the disciples would be able to measure themselves against the concrete, authentic and experienced reality of the Master's love.

2. Christ himself revealed the depth of his love for mankind when he said: "I am the good shepherd; I know my own [sheep] and my own know me, as the Father knows me and I know the Father" (Jn 10;14-15). Jesus wanted to establish with his disciples a sharing of his life, his thoughts and his affections like that which existed between his Father and himself. This was no cold, superficial acquaintance, but a profound knowledge that springs from love. Jesus made himself known to his own in the way a friend lays himself open to a friend. He revealed the profound mysteries of his divine life, of his ceaseless communion with the Father and with the Holy Spirit, of the mission the Father had entrusted to him, of the love that impelled him to sacrifice himself for men, and of the relationship he desired to set up with them. In a word, in regard to himself, the Father, and the Trinity, Jesus told them all that the human mind could comprehend; and on the evening of the Last Supper he would conclude: "You are my friends . . . No longer do I call you servants, for the servant does not know what his master

is doing; but I have called you friends, for all that I have heard from my Father I have made known to you" (Jn 14:14-15). This was an explicit declaration of that deep friendship that he had come to establish between God and men at the command of the Father. He wished to give this friendship the assurance of a boundless dimension when he said: "As the Father has loved me, so have I loved you" (ib. 9); here he revealed its greatest height, for what greater love could there be than that uncreated, eternal love which exists in the Trinity between the Father and the Son in the Holy Spirit? Jesus did not think it out of place to refer to it and to add: "Abide in my love . . . just as I . . . abide in my Father's love" (ib. 10). Together with the divine measure of his love, Jesus also gave the human measure which was only possible inasmuch as that he had assumed an earthly life. He had already said this in his discourse on the good shepherd: "I lay down my life for the sheep . . . No one takes it from me, but I lay it down of my own accord" (Jn 10:15,18). This voluntary sacrifice of his life was the utmost proof of love: "Greater love has no man than this, that a man lay down his life for his friends" (Jn 15:13).

> Lord, you are just what I needed, but I would never have dared to hope to have you, wonderful as you are. My thought was of speaking to God in the way I talk to a man.
> And behold, you are God, living as a man . . . O the revelation of God to the world . . . O God, Jesus Christ, I no longer need to torment myself trying to know you; the best thing is for you to be truly a man. Inasmuch as you have assumed my nature, there is nothing human that cannot be part of my religion: that is, a link with you.
> I come to you with my own way of thinking, because now, in order to know God made man, the best thing is to have eyes of flesh and human intelligence. I come to you with my own way of loving, O Sacred Heart, whose heart beats in love's rhythm in unison with mine . . . I come to you as my brother, and in every man—oh! miracle—behold, I revere God. I come to you with my way of suffering, O crucified One, whose blood the earth has tasted and whose groans and repugnance men have heard . . .
> I come to you with my way of praying, because you have lips to answer me, because you had for a mother a woman of flesh as I did . . .
> I bring you my very sins, O Lamb of God, who came to take them, and to cancel them at the very moment in which you took them upon yourself.
> P. Lyonnet, Spiritual Writings

> O my Lord, how good you are! May you be blessed for ever! May all things praise you, my God, for you have so loved us that we can truthfully speak of this communication which you engage in with souls even in our exile! And even in the case of those who are good, this still shows great generosity and magnanimity. In fact it is your

communication and you give it in the manner of who you are. O in-
finite Largess, how magnificent are your works! It frightens one
whose intellect is not occupied with things of the earth that he has
no intellect by which he can understand divine truths. That you
bestow such sovereign favors on souls that have offended you so
much certainly brings my intellect to a halt, and when I begin to
think about this I am unable to continue. Where can the intellect go
that would not be a turning back since it does not know how to give
you thanks for such great favors? Sometimes I find it a remedy to
speak absurdities.

St. Teresa of Jesus, Life 18:3

233. GENTLE OF HEART

O Lord, infuse in me that gentle and quiet spirit that is precious in
your eyes   *(1 Pet 3:4)*

1. To the simple, the poor, the sick and the suffering who crowded around him, Jesus said: "Come to me, all who labor and are heavy laden, and I will give you rest. Take my yoke upon you, and learn from me, for I am gentle and lowly in heart, and you will find rest for your souls" (Mt 11:28-29). In his desire to draw men to himself, he offered them his doctrine, his law, and his very person under the image of that meekness and humility which he had already proclaimed in the beatitudes. The prophet, too, had so depicted him: "Behold, my servant whom I have chosen . . . will not wrangle or cry aloud . . . He will not break a bruised reed or quench a smoldering wick" (Mt 12:18-20). Jesus would gain the hearts of men by the gentleness of his own; he, who "is our Master and Lord, is also meek and humble of heart, and, in attracting and inviting his disciples, he acted patiently" (DH 11). James and John, who wanted fire to rain down from heaven upon the Samaritans, were rebuked because, as Jesus would say later: "This is the will of him who sent me, that I should lose nothing of all that he has given me" (Jn 6:39). To the Pharisees who were scandalized because he sat at table with publicans, he repeated: "Go and learn what this means, 'I desire mercy, and not sacrifice'" (Mt 9:13). He imposed himself upon no one with violence, and condemned no one, but declared: "I did not come to judge the world, but to save the world" (Jn 12:47). Jesus fulfilled his mission as savior especially through meekness and self-sacrifice. "I am the good shepherd. The good shepherd lays down his life for the sheep" (Jn 10:11). This was the meekness he proposed to his disciples as the condition for interior peace. Too often men lose their peace of heart and consequently disturb the peace of their relationships with others because they let anger agitate them. To these Christ repeats: "Learn of me for I am gentle of

heart." But he also proposes gentleness as a condition for doing good and for winning over our brothers to God. Violence convinces no one, rather it turns away and hardens hearts; while meekness bends and saves.

2. Christ, "gentle of heart," does not avoid the fight when the glory of the Father and men's salvation are at stake. He welcomes sinners with infinite kindness, but he openly condemns sin, especially pride, hypocrisy, and hardness of heart. He also uses strong language, like the invectives he hurled against the Pharisees (Lk 11:42-52), and forceful actions like that against those who were profaning the temple. (Jn 2:15). But on the other hand, when the issue is his own person, he lets any offense pass with absolute gentleness. Thus some can take him for a fool, others as possessed by the devil; relatives may have doubts about him, and the people of Nazareth can try to throw him from the brow of the hill without provoking any reaction from him: "But passing through the midst of them he went away" (Lk 4:30). Jesus spoke firmly in discussions with his persecutors, seeking to enlighten their minds; but for calumnies and insults he had but one answer: "I do not seek my own glory; there is one who seeks it and he will be the judge" (Jn 8:50). At the Last Supper, his heart filled with sorrow, he denounced the coming betrayal on the part of one of the Twelve, but did it in such a way that the guilty one was not discovered; he said to him alone: "What you are going to do, do quickly" (Jn 13:27); later in the garden of Olives when Judas kissed him, feigning sentiments of friendship, Jesus did not repulse him, and once again called him "friend" (Mt 26:50). He treated as friends those who betrayed him, denied him, and condemned him to the cross: he died for them, and prayed for them to the Father, excusing them and imploring forgiveness. Only for the dearest of friends can one act in such a way.

Jesus' meekness is the remedy for our wrath and anger, and for our violence and intolerance. Anger darkens our intellect and carries our will away into committing actions which are unconsidered and therefore are less than human; while whoever imitates Jesus' meekness, "whoever follows after Christ, the perfect man, becomes himself more of a man" (GS 41). Meekness knows no enemies, is forgiving and loving, and "overcomes evil with good" (Rom 12:21). Meekness soothes life's sufferings and disposes us to accept the will of God and to abandon ourselves into his hands in times of tribulation.

"Come to me, all you who are weary and tired." O Lord, we are all weary because we are mortal men, fragile, infirm, clothed in earthen vessels which are our common reason for a thousand anxieties. But though our vessels of flesh may keep us in distress, help us to enlarge the horizons of our charity. Otherwise, why do you say: Come to me all you who are weary, except that we should not weary ourselves any more? After all, your promise is immediate: and I will

refresh you, and you add: Take my yoke upon you and learn of me; not how to build the world, not how to create all things visible and invisible, not how to work miracles in this world nor to revive the dead, but to be "gentle and humble of heart."

cf St. Augustine, Sermon 69:1-2

O most Sacred Heart of Jesus, you desire so ardently to shower your favors upon the unfortunate, and to teach those who want to advance in the school of your love; you continually invite me to be meek and humble of heart like you. For this reason you convince me that in order to gain your friendship and to become your true disciple, I can do nothing better than to try henceforth to be truly meek and humble. Grant me, then, that sincere humility which keeps me subject to everyone, which makes me bear little humiliations in silence, which even makes me accept them willingly and with serenity, without excuse or complaint, remembering that I really deserve more and greater ones than I receive.

O Jesus, permit me to enter your Heart as I would a school. In this school teach me the science of the saints, the science of pure love. O good Master, I shall listen attentively to your words: "Learn of me for I am gentle and humble of heart, and you will find rest for your souls."

cf St. Margaret Mary, Life

224. HUMBLE OF HEART

O Jesus, humble of heart, teach me to humble myself "under the mighty hand of God"   *(1 Pet 5:6)*

1. St. Paul wrote the most beautiful of hymns to Christ's humility: "Though he was in the form of God, he did not count equality with God a thing to be grasped, but emptied himself, taking the form of a servant, being born in the likeness of men; and being found in human form, he humbled himself and became obedient unto death" (Phil 2:6-8). Nothing more profound can be said about Jesus, "humble of heart." The Apostle has touched the essence of this mystery: above all of his self-emptying, his stripping himself of the external splendor of his infinite majesty, in order to put himself on man's level, concealing his divinity under the veil of flesh in order to appear a man like other men. Then there is the humbling of himself in his human form: a poor man among the poor, "the carpenter's son" (Mt 13:55), and he himself a humble artisan, who came "not to be served, but to serve" (Mt 20:28); he is to extend his service even to giving his life to ransom mankind, and he will carry his self-emptying even to the ignominious death of the cross. Man's humility is child's play compared to that of the Son of God. Man is so very small in comparison to him: weak, wretched, poor, limited, a sinner, and still so

much inclined to pride, so incapable of true humility. He has an immense need for Jesus to encourage him by his example: "Learn from me, for I am gentle and lowly in heart" (Mt 11:29).

It was not by chance that the Lord preached humility and meekness together, for humility is the immediate basis for the latter. Jesus was meek because he was humble: he did not seek to assert himself, nor to be applauded, neither did he pursue his own glory, but desired only the honor and glory of the kingdom of the Father; his one aim was to accomplish the mission entrusted to him in total dedication to its cause and to the salvation of mankind.

We are not meek, because we are not humble, and even in performing good works, we do not know how to renounce our affirmation of self to its very core.

2. Jesus was essentially humble because he acknowledged and fully lived his dependence on the Father. As the Word, he was equal and co-eternal with the Father in all things; at the same time, he was mysteriously begotten by the Father, he lived the life which the Father communicated to him; everything came to him from the Father, and he rejoiced in it infinitely. As the incarnate Word, he received temporal life from the Father—that human nature which he assumed solely in order to sacrifice it according to the will of the Father. "Consequently when Christ came into the world, he said: 'Sacrifices and offerings you have not desired, but a body you have prepared for me; in burnt offerings and sin offerings you have no pleasure. Then I said: 'Lo, I have come to do your will, O God' " (Heb 10:5-7). This was Christ's unchanging will throughout his life. The first words that the Gospel records of him point this out: "Did you not know that I must be in my Father's house?" (Lk 2:49). His whole life was at the service of the Father; his mission was to make his Father known and loved, and to make his Father's doctrine, law, and will prevail. "I live because of the Father—My doctrine is not mine, but his who sent me—I do nothing on my own authority, but speak thus as the Father taught me. He who believes in me, believes not in me, but in him who sent me" (Jn 6:57; 7:16; 8:28; 12:44). Before working any miracles, he awaited the hour set by his Father, he went to his passion because he had received "this charge . . . from his Father" (Jn 10:18). Christ was truly the "Servant of Yahweh" foretold by Isaiah: "The will of the Lord shall prosper in his hand" (Is 53:10). Christ's essential humility, founded upon his total dependence on the Father, put him entirely at his service and hence at the service of mankind, since that was the Father's will.

We are not humble because we are not fully conscious of our total dependence on God; although we may be convinced of it in theory, we are not so convinced in practice, but are always, to a greater or less extent, escaping from the service of God to serve ourselves, our own pride and self-love. Consequently we do not know how to practice humble service of our brother, but only too often let ourselves be motivated by presumed rights and interests and personal causes to the detriment of others. "Do nothing from selfishness or conceit, but in humility count others better than yourself" (Phil 2:3).

O divine Jesus, you so forgot yourself that you accepted being humiliated and despised by all, and judged and condemned by men and dying ignominiously on the cross; how can I who want to be your disciple and who have promised to follow you conduct myself in such an opposite way from you ... and be concerned only about myself and seeking my own advantage in everything I do? How can I be so easily offended, and so jealous, and find it so difficult to put up with small faults in others, when I have so many myself? O God, make me ashamed of being so far from you and of living in a way so little in harmony with your teaching and example!

O Jesus, through the intercession of the Blessed Virgin, so humble and little in her own eyes, let me not seek myself in anything, but accept everything with humility and charity; let me forget myself and never talk about myself, nor be concerned about self any more, and make no account of what others may think or say about me; help me to put my whole trust in you alone, seeking to please you in everything and not concerning myself about the judgments of men, silencing within me any thoughts that are contrary to Christian charity and humility.

A. Chevrier, *L'esprit et les vertus*

Grant me your grace, most merciful Jesus, that it may be with me, and labor with me, and continue with me unto the end. Grant me always to will and desire that which is most acceptable to you, and which pleases you best. Let your will be mine, and let my will always follow yours, and agree perfectly with it. Let me always will or not will the same with you; and let me not be able to will or not to will otherwise than as you will or will not. Grant that I may die to all things that are in the world, and for your sake love to be despised, and to be unknown in this world. Grant me, above all things to be desired, that I may rest in you and that my heart may be at peace in you.

Imitation of Christ III 15:3-4

225. HE HAS WASHED US WITH HIS BLOOD

O Jesus, you were slain and by your blood did ransom men for God
(Rev 5:9)

1. On the first page of the Apocalypse, the prophetic book that celebrates the triumph of the Word of God, Christ is exalted as the savior who shed his blood for the redemption of the world. "To

him who loves us and has freed us from our sins by his blood . . . to him be glory and dominion for ever and ever" (Rev 1:5). The mystery of Christ's love for men is principally revealed in his passion, whose dreadful aspect is particularly emphasized by the blood he shed to its last drop. The Gospel records its culminating moments. "Then Pilate took Jesus and scourged him. And the soldiers plaited a crown of thorns and put it on his head" (Jn 19:1-2). Scourges and thorns quickly reddened the Savior's head and face and back with blood. He is presented to the crowd in this condition: "Behold the man!" (ib. 5). Then one of the most disconcerting developments of the story took place. Pilate, a pagan, declared: "I am innocent of this man's blood!" (Mt 27:24), and the chosen people, so loved by God and so favored by Jesus, cried out at the instigation of the high priests and the elders: "His blood be on us and on our children!" (ib. 25). The words indicate the full responsibility for Jesus' condemnation to death which the people were taking upon themselves. It is perhaps not rash to say that it unconsciously expressed the cry of all mankind which is so in need of the blood of Christ to wash away the filth of its sins. The whole of Scripture bears witness to this reality. "For it is impossible that the blood of bulls and goats should take away sins"—said St. Paul—"Consequently when Christ came into the world, he said: 'Sacrifices and offerings you have not desired, but a body you have prepared for me' . . . Then he said: 'Lo, I have come to do your will, O God' " (Heb 10:4-7). The body which the Father had prepared for him, the blood which human nature had supplied him, is completely immolated and poured out in sacrifice for the redemption of mankind. St. Peter reminds us: "You know that you were ransomed not with perishable things such as silver and gold, but with the precious blood of Christ, like that of a lamb without blemish or spot" (I Pet 18-19).

2. Alone among the evangelists, Luke has recorded the first blood shed by Christ during his passion, when in the Garden of Olives through the intensity of his interior anguish, "his sweat became like drops of blood flowing upon the ground" (Lk 22:44). It is a particularly precious detail which demonstrates the cruel reality of the passion our Lord suffered in his human flesh, which was like ours, and like ours too in its repugnance to suffering and death. But Jesus came forth victorious from this most sorrowful agony, repeating his "yes" to the will of the Father who offered him this bitter chalice.

On the other hand, John, the only Apostle present at Calvary, tells of the last drops of blood shed from Christ's pierced side: "One of the soldiers pierced his side with a spear, and at once there came out blood and water" (Jn 19:34). The writer had been an eyewitness and still had before his eyes the vision of the bloody lacerated body of the crucified Jesus. Every drop of his blood had been shed for our sins! A really profound meditation on this point should be enough to make us resolve to face any renunciation in an effort to eradicate sin from our lives.

Eleventh Sunday of Ordinary Time

St. Paul, greatly moved by the remembrance of all that Jesus had suffered during his passion, adds: "In your struggle against sin you have not yet resisted to the point of shedding your blood" (Heb 12:4). Which of us can say that we have fought "to the point of shedding blood" to conquer pride or selfishness or whatever passion it is that inclines us toward evil? Jesus, the most innocent Lamb, has punished the sins of men in himself, even to a disgraceful and bloody death; and we do not know how to chastise them in ourselves even by sacrificing our own depraved tendencies. To yield to sin is to despise the blood of Christ; it is to despise the love and the sorrow with which it was shed.

Every day in the eucharistic Sacrifice this precious Blood is offered to the Father as a propitiation for sins, and to the faithful as the drink of salvation. "Take this, all of you, and drink from it: this is the cup of my blood . . . of the new and everlasting covenant. It will be shed for you and for all men, so that sins may be forgiven" (Eucharistic Prayer). Let us approach with faith, and drink with love, because "the cup of blessing which we bless is a participation in the blood of Christ" (I Cor 10:16).

O crucified Christ, we were the ground in which the standard of your cross was set: we were like a vessel for receiving your blood which ran down from the cross . . . The earth itself was not enough to hold the cross erect, it would even have rejected such an injustice, nor were the nails enough to keep you fastened and held down, if your inexpressible love for our salvation had not held you. So it was your burning love for the honor of the Father and for our salvation which kept you [on the cross] . . .

If I acknowledge and espouse this Truth, O Christ, I shall find grace in your blood, the richness and the life of grace; I shall find my nakedness covered and my soul clothed in the wedding garment of the fire of charity, of mixed and mingled blood and fire, that [blood] which you shed and united with the Godhead through love.

O crucified Christ, through your blood may I be nourished with your merciful love; in your blood may the darkness be dispersed and the light shine forth, for in your blood the cloud of sensitive self-love will disappear, together with the slavish fear that gives rise to anguish, and I shall be given a holy fear and the security of divine love—all through your blood. Whoever will not wish to be found among the lovers of this Truth . . . such a one will be in darkness and divested of the garment of grace . . . not through any defect in your blood, but because he has disdained it and, as though blinded by self-love, neither sees nor understands the Truth of the blood.

Then let me be drowned in your blood, O Christ, let me bathe in it and be clothed in it. If I should be unfaithful, baptize me again in blood; if the devil should darken the eye of my understanding, wash my eye with blood; if I fall into ingratitude for gifts I have not appreciated, make me grateful through your blood . . . In the warmth of your blood, dissolve my tepidity; and in the light of your blood

dispel the darkness, so that I may be a bride of the Truth.
                                    St. Catherine of Siena, *Letters* 102 v 2

226. THROUGH CHRIST TO THE FATHER

May our fellowship be with you, Father, and with your Son, Jesus Christ
                                                              (1 Jn 1:3)

1. God's revelation to men began in the earthly paradise when, before there was sin, God himself walked with our first parents (Gen 3:8); then it continued through the patriarchs and prophets, but only reached its fullness in Christ, the Son of God. "In many and various ways God spoke of old to our fathers by the prophets; but in these last days he has spoken to us by a Son" (Heb 1:1-2). The revelation of the most sublime mystery of the intimate life of God, the mystery of the Blessed Trinity, was reserved to the Son of God. Only the Only-Begotten of the Father, who is "God from God, light from light, true God from true God ... one in Being with the Father" (Creed), could reveal to us that mysterious, incessant flow of divine life which is always pouring itself out in the bosom of the Trinity: the flow of infinite light and love and fecundity which circulates in three perfectly equal Persons who are co-eternal and infinite, yet also distinct, in the unity of one identical nature.

Jesus had said in his prayer to the Father: "This is eternal life, that they may know you, the only true God and Jesus Christ whom you have sent" (Jn 17:3); and he had indeed used every possible facet of his divine teaching to make men know the true God, one and three: the Father, the Son, and the Holy Spirit. He had made known the Father, his Father and our Father (Jn 20:17), his goodness, his mercy, his providence, his infinite love, and had said of him: "The Father loves you" (Jn 16:27). In making his Father known he made himself known, and vice versa: "I and the Father are one—He who has seen me has seen the Father ... I am in the Father and the Father is in me" (Jn 10:30; 14:9-10); and he had spoken of the Holy Spirit who was to complete his work: "The Counselor, the Holy Spirit, whom the Father will send in my name, he will teach you all things and bring to your remembrance all that I have said to you" (Jn 14:25-26). The evangelist quite rightfully comments: "No one has ever seen God; the only Son, who is in the bosom of the Father, he has made him known" (Jn 1:18).

2. Christ reveals the Trinity to man and leads him to the Trinity. "I am the way," he repeats, and adds: "No one comes to the Father but by me" (Jn 14:6). The more closely we are united to Christ through faith and love, the more we are united, in him and through him, to the Trinity: "If a man loves me ... my Father will

love him, and we will come to him and make our home with him" (ib. 23). Christ puts us into contact with the Trinity in an entirely special way in the Eucharist. Vatican II teaches that it is especially through the eucharistic Liturgy that "through an outpouring of the Holy Spirit the faithful gain access to God the Father through the Son, the Word made flesh, who suffered and was glorified. And so, 'made partakers of the divine nature,' they enter into communion with the most holy Trinity" (UR 15). In the Eucharist in which he is really present, Jesus continues his mission as Mediator between man and the Trinity. By giving himself to us in the wholeness of his person as the Word made flesh, he puts us in a more direct, intimate, and unifying contact with the three divine Persons. Present in the heart of the faithful by means of the Sacrament, he can repeat the great words: "He who sent me is with me, he has not left me alone—I am in the Father and the Father in me" (Jn 8:29; 14:11); because the three divine Persons cannot be separated, where the Son is, there is the Father and the Holy Spirit also. Sacramental communion with Christ therefore becomes union with the "Three," a union which renders deeper and more intimate the relationship already established in faith and love between the soul and the Trinity dwelling within it. When the Eucharist is viewed in this light, it manifests its profound Trinitarian value; just as the purpose of the incarnation of the Word is to guide us to the Trinity, so the purpose of the Eucharist, which is the prolongation of the incarnation, is to bring us to the Trinity. The Eucharist nourishes not only our life of union with Christ, but also our unceasing union with the three divine Persons.

Moreover, the Eucharist is the gift of the Trinity: "My Father gives you the true bread from heaven" (Jn 6:32), said Jesus; and "it is the Spirit that gives life" (ib. 63). Just as the Word made flesh comes from the Trinity and leads back to the Trinity, so the Eucharist comes from the Trinity and leads us to the Trinity.

> O Christ, make me live by your life, and, since you are God, live of God and in God, through you and in you. Our life is now hidden with you in the mysterious depths of the Father's bosom, but the day will come in which your glory will shine forth, O Christ, life of our souls, and then we too, united with you, will be resplendent in glory . . .
>
> O Christ, if you came into the world and became the way, the truth, and the life for us, it was in order to lead us to the Father. When Philip gave vent to the cry of his heart and asked: "Master, show us the Father and that will be enough," you answered: "Philip, whoever sees me, sees my Father" . . . O my divine Jesus, My King, my Teacher, my high priest, my living head, let me see the Father! And what else do we need but him? Let us see yourself, so that we may see him in you and through you; send us your Spirit to reveal your glory to us and show us him from whom that glory comes to you.

> D. Mercier, *La vie interieure* 3;6

Lord Jesus, Word made flesh, I believe that you are God; true God from true God; Deum verum de Deo vero. I do not see your divinity, but because the Father said to me: "This is my beloved Son," I believe it, and because I believe it I want to submit myself entirely to you, body and soul, judgment, will, heart, sensibilities, imagination, all my powers. I want the word of your psalmist to be realized in me: "That everything be laid in homage at your feet" . . . I want you to be my head, your Gospel my light, your will my guide. I wish to think of nothing but you for you are infallible truth, and never to act but with you, for you are the only way to go to the Father, and to seek no joy outside your will, for you are the very source of life. Make me yours in the most absolute way through the Holy Spirit for the glory of the Father.

C. Marmion, *Consecration to the most Blessed Trinity* 6

227. TWELFTH SUNDAY OF ORDINARY TIME

YEAR A

Praise the Lord, for he has delivered the life of the needy from the hand of evildoers   *(Jer 20:13)*

Perhaps no prophet has suffered as Jeremiah did. Timid and gentle by nature, he had led a tranquil life, and trembled with fear when confronted with the mission of preaching the word of God to an obstinate and rebelious people. His keenly sensitive heart was constantly irritated by this continual interior conflict and by the never ending contests and persecutions he had to endure from his people, while he was trying to save them at any cost. Yet the strength of the divine call prevailed, and Jeremiah had the courage to face a life of peril and endless battle. Faith and trust in God sustained him: "The Lord is with me as a dread warrior . . . to you I have committed my cause" (Jer 20:11-12). The vicissitudes of this prophet, who was so human in expressing his innermost sufferings, can be a great encouragement to the many apostles who even today have to face painful struggles. But these are more fortunate than Jeremiah, for to comfort them they have the example and teaching of Jesus, of whom Jeremiah is a figure.

When Jesus entrusted the Twelve with the mission of preaching the good news, he forewarned them of the dangers they would encounter: "They will deliver you up to councils, and flog you in their synagogues, and you will be dragged before governors and kings for my sake" (Mt 10:17-18). All this is harsh, but it should not be surprising, because a disciple cannot expect to meet a different fate than his master's. "If they persecuted me, they will persecute you" (Jn 15:20). When the Apostles would see Jesus dragged to the tribunal, slapped in the face, crowned with thorns, condemned to death, and crucified, they would understand the meaning of his words, and later on, illuminated by the Holy Spirit, they would understand that though it is necessary to share the Master's lot, it is also an honor. Besides, what is there to fear from men? They can deride, persecute, deprive us of material goods, imprison, and even kill, but this is not the worst evil. In fact the Lord says: "Do not fear those who kill the body, but cannot kill the soul; rather fear him who can destroy both soul and body in hell" (Mt 10:28). There are times when a believer can find himself faced with an extreme alternative: either to renounce his faith out of fear of men, and lose his soul; or, out of fear of being separated from Christ for ever, to face serious harm or even death, with the assurance of eternal life. Martyrdom, the supreme act of love for God, becomes a duty for every Christian when to escape from it involves denial of his faith.

To keep his disciples from feeling abandoned in their struggles and persecution, Jesus encouraged them by speaking of the providence of his heavenly Father, who is present in even the most minute circumstances of his creatures' lives. If he does not disregard even a sparrow, how could he forget his children who are exposed to danger on his account? "Fear not, therefore; you are of more value than many sparrows" (ib. 31). Just as the Father takes an interest in them, so will Christ one day give testimony in their behalf before the Father, as if in return for their witness before men. "So every one who acknowledges me before men, I also will acknowledge before my Father who is in heaven" (ib. 32).

> *God's wheat am I, and by the teeth of wild beasts I am to be ground that I may prove Christ's pure bread...*
> *At last I am well on the way to being a disciple. May nothing seen or unseen fascinate me, so that I may happily make my way to Jesus Christ. Fire, cross, wild beasts, torture... the most cruel tortures inflicted by the devil—let them come upon me, provided only I make my way to Jesus Christ...*
> *Of no use to me will be the farthest reaches of the universe or the kingdoms of this world. I would rather die and come to Jesus Christ than be king over the entire earth. Him I seek who died for us; him I love who rose again for us... Suffer me to receive pure light. Once arrived there, I shall be a man. Permit me to be an imitator of your suffering, O my God!*
> St. Ignatius of Antioch, *Letter to the Romans* 4-6

> *O Lord, you continuously manifest your strength through your weakness; you have permitted your Church to grow in the midst of vicissitudes; when she seems overwhelmed, she rebounds the more vigorously, because trial is an experience of faith. And after she has faithfully persevered during this present life, be pleased to grant her glory.*
> *Early Christian Prayers,* 319

YEAR B

O Lord, you deliver us from our distress, you make the storm be still
(Ps 107:28-29)

Today the Liturgy of the Word centers on the theme of God's omnipotence and his sovereignty over the universe. The Old Testament presents the remarkable vision which Job had in answer to his complaints and tormenting questions about the grave misfortunes that had befallen him. God showed himself as creator and Lord of all the elements, as master of the sea which is contained by him within fixed limits. "Thus far shall you come, and no farther, and here shall your proud waves be stayed" (Job 38:11). By thus showing Job his power and infinite greatness, God wanted to make him understand that man should not dare to argue with God and ask his reasons for acting as he does. Job was a just man and withdrew his protests, submitting himself to God's unfathomable judgment. Job's resigned submission ever remains a shining example for us, who, as Christians, are in a position to add trust and filial abandonment to our heavenly Father's providence, which has been revealed to us by Jesus.

The same theme is taken up again in the Gospel in a divine context, enlightened by the presence of Christ who possessed divine omnipotence. It was night: the Master was with his followers in a boat on the lake and, being tired after the day's labors, he fell asleep. Without warning, "a great storm of wind arose, and the waves beat into the boat, so that the boat was already filling" (Mk 4:37). The frightened disciples awakened him and with a simple command he calmed the storm's fury: "He rebuked the wind, and said to the sea: 'Peace, be still!'. The wind stopped, and there was a great calm" (ib. 39). The disciples had been saved from the storm, but then they were seized by a new fear: they had seen Jesus sleeping in the boat like any other man and then suddenly doing things it was impossible for a man to do. They asked each other: "Who, then, is this that even wind and sea obey him?" (ib. 41). But the Master had already answered them implicitly when he had said: "Why are you afraid? Have you no faith?" (ib. 40). In reproving them for their lack of faith, Jesus was implying that he was God, for only God can demand that we believe in his power to dominate storms and preserve us from death. Panic had shaken their still weak faith and made them forget the miracles they had already seen him perform.

Today also, misfortune, suffering, danger and the stormy turn of events in our own lives and in the life of the Church cause the too weak faith of many believers to waver. Then they grumble like Job, or tremble like the disciples on the lake, forgetting that Christ is always with his faithful ones and with his Church, and never ceases to help them, even though his presence is hidden and silent, as when he, the Master, was asleep in the boat; in fact it is more hidden now, because he does not awake to perform miracles, nor is there any reason for us to expect him to work any. The great miracle is that Christ guides the Church and individuals to salvation through storms and adversity. Whoever believes firmly will not be lost, but will become "a new creation" (2 Cor 5:17), no longer upset by affliction, because anchored in faith in him who died and rose again for us.

> To you, O Lord, I call; my rock, be not deaf to me, lest, if you be silent to me, I become like those who go down to the pit. Hear the voice of my supplication, as I cry to you for help, as I lift up my hands toward your most holy sanctuary.
> The Lord is my strength and my shield; in him my heart trusts; so I am helped, and my heart exults, and with my song I give thanks to him. The Lord is the strength of his people, he is the saving refuge of his anointed. O save your people, and bless your heritage.
>
> Psalm 28:1-2, 7-9

> Lord, we beg that peace may be quickly restored to us, that we may be given immediate help in this darkness, and that the promises you have deigned to make known to us may be fulfilled: that the Church will be restored, eternal salvation assured, that after the rain will come calm, after darkness light, and after the tempests and storms sweet tranquillity.
> We beg too for the kindly help of your fatherly love and the wonders of your divine majesty, through which our persecutors may be confounded, the repentance of those who have fallen made more sincere, and the strong, sturdy faith of those who persevere exalted.
>
> St. Cyprian, Letters 7,8

YEAR C

O Lord, my soul clings to you to follow you   (Ps 63:8)

When the prophet Zechariah spoke about the messianic era, he described it as a time in which God would pour out on Jerusalem "a spirit of compassion and supplication" (12:10). But this joy was to be disturbed by the violent death of a mysterious personage, "him whom they have pierced" (ib.), over whom the whole nation would mourn bitterly. It was a prophecy of the suffering Messiah which repeated in another form the predictions of Isaiah about the Servant of Yahweh, who "was wounded for our transgressions, and was bruised for our iniquities" (Is 53:5). John, who was present at the death of Jesus, would recall Zechariah's words and use them later in his Gospel as proof that the Scriptures had been fulfilled in Christ crucified and pierced by the lance (Jn 19:37). Jesus himself was the first to make this connection when, desiring to give his disciples an accurate conception of his person and of his mission, he had foretold the sufferings which were awaiting him.

At the end of the first year of his ministry, Jesus gathered his disciples around him and after he had prayed together with them—for no one can understand Christ unless the Father enlightens him—he lifted the veil from his mystery. First of all, he questioned them: "Who do the people say that I am? . . . But who do you say that I am?" (Lk 9:18,20). Although the crowds looked upon him as a prophet, the disciples ought to understand something more, for they had lived so intimately with him and witnessed his miracles and been privileged to receive his teaching. In the name of them all Peter answered: you are "the Christ of God" (ib.). The answer was precise, the echo of Isaiah's prophecy of "the Anointed of the Lord" who was sent "to proclaim liberty to the captives" (Is 61:1). But this was not all. Jesus completed the picture by speaking for the first time about his passion: "The Son of man must suffer many things . . . and be killed" (Lk 9:22). Thus he presented himself as the Servant of Yahweh who would be "despised and rejected by men; a man of sorrows, and acquainted with grief" (Is 53:3). This revelation must have been very hard and upsetting for his disciples who, like their countrymen, thought only in terms of a Messiah-king. But Jesus did not back down; in fact he went on to inform them that they too would have to pass by the way of suffering: "If any man would come after me, let him deny himself and take up his cross daily and follow me" (Lk 9:23). He would go before to give the example and would be the first to bear the cross; whoever wished to be his disciple would have to imitate him, not only once, but "every day," by denying himself—his will, his inclinations, his pleasures—in order to become like the suffering and crucified Master. St. Paul says: "For as many of you as were baptized into Christ have put on Christ" (Gal 3:27); that is, clothed in his passion and death. After being baptized in Christ's death, a Christian must live in the image of him who was the "man of sorrows" before being glorified. Just as it was the Lord's passion that opened the way to the joy of his resurrection, so also, the Christian must carry his cross even to the point of losing his own life for Jesus' sake; he will save it by finding it once again in him in eternal glory.

> O Christ, Son of God, as I meditate upon your passion and death, your words sound in my soul; "My love is without deceit." They strike me with mortal grief, for they open the eyes of my soul and make me realize how true they are. I consider the works of your love and all that you have done to show me your love, O Son of God. There rushes upon me all that you have endured during your life and in your death, always on account of your immense love for me. I see in you every sign of steadfast love, and I cannot doubt in any way the truth of your words: that you have not loved me falsely, but with the most perfect and ardent love.
>
> Then I consider how everything is the opposite with me—that I love you so insincerely and so deceptively, and the great grief of my soul makes me cry out: "O Master, all that you say has no place in

you is all too truly present in me. I have never loved you except with deceit and falsehood. I never wanted to come close to you in order to share the sufferings you bore for me. I never served you except in appearance, never sincerely."

I see how truly you have loved me and perceive in you all the signs and works of the truest love, how you gave yourself completely in order to serve me, and came so close to me as to become man and feel my afflictions in yourself. You say to me: "Those who love and imitate my poverty, my grief, and my humility are my real children; those who keep their spirit fixed on my passion and death, wherein is true salvation (and nowhere else), all these are my real children."

cf Bl. Angela of Foligno, *The Book of Divine Consolation* II

228. O BLESSED TRINITY!

"To you be praise, glory and thanksgiving, through eternal ages, O blessed Trinity" (RB Feast of most Holy Trinity)

1. We are absolutely incapable of even glimpsing the mystery of the Trinity by the use of our reason alone, nor have we any right to know it; this mystery transcends us in the most absolute way. That God has made it known to us shows that he wants to admit us into the intimacy of his family as sons and friends. "No longer do I call you servants"—says Jesus—"for the servant does not know what his master is doing; but I have called you friends, for all that I have heard from my Father I have made known to you" (Jn 15:15). This "all" that has been revealed by Christ extends even to the deepest, most personal mystery of God, the mystery of the Trinity. As a friend reserves for his friend his dearest and most intimate secrets, and manifests these to him in an act of friendship, so, in an act of trusting love, the Word made flesh, himself God, perfectly equal to the Father and to the Holy Spirit, has revealed to us the mystery of the most Holy Trinity which only he has contemplated and continually contemplates in the bosom of the Father; only after this revelation has he called us friends.

Christ confided to his disciples "all" that he had heard from the Father, all that they were capable of comprehending in regard to God's inner life; he did so in order that they too might rejoice in it with him: "These things I have spoken to you, that my joy may be in you, and that your joy may be full" (ib. 11). He finds infinite joy in his Father, in being his Son, in being his perfect and substantial image; he rejoices in loving him and in being loved in return in the infinite power of uncreated Love; he exults in the mutual love which proceeds from him and from the Father, and which is in its turn a divine Person, the Holy Spirit. He wants to share this joy with us, that we also may rejoice in the Father, the Son, and the Holy Spirit. But the ultimate reason why Christ reveals this mystery is God's glory, so that God may be glorified by men not only in the unity of his nature, but also in the Trinity of his Persons; that on earth, too, the song of praise may rise: "Glory to the Father, and to the Son and to the Holy Spirit."

2. The Preface of the feast of the Trinity expresses the mystery of the Trinity thus: "Holy Father, almighty and everlasting God, who with your only-begotten Son and Holy Spirit, are one God, one Lord; not in the oneness of a single Person, but in the Trinity of one substance" (MR—Cabrol).

The Father is the fountainhead of the Trinity. From all eternity the Father knows himself perfectly, and, knowing himself, generates the Word, the substantial Idea in which the Father expresses and contemplates himself fully, the only-begotten Son, to whom he communicates his whole essence, divinity, and infinite goodness. Thus the evangelist says: "In the beginning was the Word, and the Word was with God, and the Word was God" (Jn 1:1). The Son is "the brightness of the Father's glory, the figure of his substance" (Heb 1;3 Douai); but he is a substantial splendor and glory, since the Son has in himself the same nature and the same perfections as the Father. From all eternity the Father and the Son contemplate and love each other infinitely by reason of the infinite indivisible perfection which they have in common. Loving each other, they are attracted to each other in a mutual giving of themselves, one to the other, diffusing their whole nature and divine essence into a third Person, the Holy Spirit, who is the terminus, the pledge, and the substantial gift of their mutual love. Thus the same nature and the same divine life circulates from Father to Son, and from the Son and the Father is poured out in the Holy Spirit to flow back again to the Father. The Trinity is the mystery of the intimate life of God which surges from the most perfect operations of knowledge and love by which God knows and loves himself.

The mystery of the Trinity shows us God in three Persons who are equal and distinct, but subsist in a single nature, as the pseudo-Athanasian Creed clearly states: "The Catholic faith is this: that we worship one God in Trinity and Trinity in Unity. Neither confusing the Persons, nor dividing the substance. For there is one Person of the Father, another of the Son, and another of the Holy Spirit. But the Godhead of the Father, of the Son, and of the Holy Spirit is one, the glory equal, the majesty co-eternal." The Liturgy echoes this: "In confessing the true and everlasting Godhead, we shall adore the Trinity of Persons, the unity of nature, the equality in majesty" (Pref. Holy Trinity).

O Lord our God, we believe in you, Father, Son and Holy Spirit... I have directed my efforts to this truth of faith according to the ability you gave me, and have sought you and desired to

Twelfth Sunday of Ordinary Time

understand what I believed and have debated and so labored over. O Lord, my God, my only hope, hear me and never let me grow weary of seeking you, but ever ardently seek your face. So grant me strength, for you have let me find you and have given me the hope of finding you still more and more.

See, my strength and my weakness are before you: preserve the one and heal the other. My knowledge and my ignorance stand before you. Where you have unlocked the door, bid me a welcome entrance; where it is locked, open when I knock. Make me remember you, understand you, love you. Make these desires grow in me until I am completely renewed . . .

When we shall have reached you, then will cease all these words that we multiply without reaching you; you alone will be all in all, and we shall endlessly say only one word, praising you in one single movement, being made one in you.

St. Augustine, *The Trinity*, XV 28, 51

Glory to the Father and to the Son and to the Holy Spirit, O holy, strong, immortal One; have mercy on us and save us. Alleluia! Alleluia! Alleluia!

May the whole of God's wonderful creation be silent neither morning nor evening! Let not even the bright stars be silent, nor the high mountains, not the depths of the sea nor the sources of the swift running rivers, while we sing our hymns to the Father, the Son, and the Holy Spirit. May all the angels in heaven reply: Amen! Amen! Amen!

Power, praise, honor and everlasting glory to our God, the only giver of every grace! Amen! Amen! Amen!

Early Christian Prayers 98

229. THE MYSTERY OF THE LIVING GOD

"My heart and flesh sing for joy to the living God"   *(Ps 84:2)*

1. More than any other mystery the mystery of the Trinity shows us that God is the "living God," whose life is essentially and incessantly fecund, so fecund, that the Father communicates to the Son his whole divine nature and essence, and the Father and the Son communicate these to the Holy Spirit without suffering any loss, all three possessing them with the same infinite perfection. "In this Trinity there is nothing before or after, nothing is greater or less, but the whole three Persons are co-eternal together and co-equal" (Pseud-Athan. Creed).

More than any other mystery, the Trinity reveals God's infinite goodness, that is to say that God is good not only because he is infinite good, but also because he communicates all his good: from the Father to the Son, from the Father and the Son to the

Holy Spirit. The life of the Trinity is a mutual incessant exchange of self-giving in perfect communion. The Father gives himself totally to the Son, and the Son gives himself totally to the Father, and from their mutual giving proceeds the Holy Spirit, the substantial Gift who in turn flows back into the Father and the Son. It follows that "the Father is wholly in the Son and the Holy Spirit, the Son is wholly in the Father and the Holy Spirit, and the Holy Spirit is wholly in the Father and the Son" (Ecumen. Council, Florence). This is the mystery of the living God, "true God, one in Trinity, and Trinity in Unity" (Brev).

By following Revelation and the teaching of the Church, we can know about this sublime mystery, though not comprehend it. We experience more than ever in its regard the infinite disproportion between human intelligence and the divine mysteries, and become more than ever aware of the immense distance that exists between God and his creature; for God is the supreme Being, the Most High, God, one and three. But if human reason always remains blinded by the depth of the mystery, reason illuminated by faith does not go astray: it humbles itself in the acknowledgement of its own insufficiency, it believes and adores. "The more the things of faith go beyond what is natural"—writes Teresa of Jesus—"the stronger the faith—and this thought enkindled great devotion in me. Just believing that you are all powerful was enough for me to receive all the grandeurs that you work" (Life 19:9).

2. Completely happy and perfect in themselves, the three divine Persons do not shut themselves up in their own life and good and happiness, but desire to let creatures share all this in some way. Thus the Trinity is accessible to the world: the Father gives the Son, the Son by the action of the Holy Spirit takes flesh, and through him, made man, men have access to the Trinity, provided that they desire it. St. Paul says that "through Christ we . . . have access in one Spirit to the Father" (Eph 2:18). The Blessed Trinity loves us and is open to us; the three divine Persons give themselves to us in order to draw us to themselves. All the wonders of Christian life have their ultimate origin in the mystery of the Trinity. It is in virtue of the Trinity that the believer is the son of the Father, the brother of the incarnate Son and the temple of the Holy Spirit.

If the Trinity is the essential and absolute gift of God's intimate life, it is likewise a gift—although a free, proportionate, shared, and created one—in reference to men. The Father gives himself to us, and after creating us in his image and likeness, sacrifices his only-begotten Son to redeem us; the Son gives himself, he became man and died on the cross for us, and continues to give himself to us as food; the Holy Spirit gives himself, dwelling within our hearts, and diffusing peace and love in us. In all this the three divine Persons give themselves to creatures for the purpose of raising us to the status of sons, of introducing us into the circle of the divine family of the Trinity, making us participants in the life and love and eternal beatitude of the Trinity. The Gospel shows us the Father enveloping us in his paternal mercy and providence, the Son taking us by the hand and teaching us to live as true children of God, and the Holy Spirit renewing us and sanctifying us by causing us to be born into divine life. The Apostle was thinking of all this when he ended his letter to the Corinthians with his great wish: "The grace of the Lord Jesus Christ and the love of God and the fellowship of the Holy Spirit be with you all" (2 Cor 13:14). We should have all this in mind when we mention the most Blessed Trinity, in order to excite ourselves to love, gratitude, and adoration: "We call upon you, we praise you, we adore you, O Blessed Trinity" (RB).

> *I invoke you, O happy, blessed and glorious Trinity: Father, Son and Holy Spirit; God, Lord, and Paraclete, love, grace and communication.*
>
> *I invoke you, O Begetter, Begotten and Regenerator; true light of true light and true brightness; spring, stream, and flowing channel; all from one, all through one, all in one; from whom, through whom and in whom all things are; living life, life that proceeds from the living One, and lifegiver of the living; one in itself, one from one, and one from both ... Father truth, Son truth, Holy Spirit truth ...*
>
> *God highest and true blessedness, from whom, through whom, and in whom is blessed everything that is blessed. God, true and highest life, from whom, through whom, and in whom everything lives that truly and blessedly lives.*
>
> Pseudo-Augustine, Meditations 31-32

> *O my Hope, my Father, my Creator, and my true Lord and Brother! When I consider how you say that your delights are with the children of men, my soul rejoices greatly. O Lord of heaven and earth, what words these are that no sinner might be wanting in trust! Are you, Lord, perhaps lacking someone with whom to delight that you seek such a foul-smelling little worm like myself? That voice that was heard at the Baptism says you delight in your Son. Well, will we all be equal, Lord?*
>
> *Oh, what extraordinary mercy and what favor so beyond our ability to deserve! And that mortals forget all of this! Be mindful, my God, of so much misery, and behold our weakness, since you are the Knower of everything.*
>
> *O my soul: Consider the great delight and great love the Father has in knowing his Son and the Son in knowing his Father; and the enkindling love with which the Holy Spirit is joined with them; and how no one of them is able to be separate from this love and knowledge, because they are one. These sovereign Persons know each other, love each other, and delight in each other. Well, what need is there for my love? Why do you want it, my God, or what do*

*you gain? Oh, may you be blessed! May you be blessed, my God,
forever! May all things praise you, Lord, without end, since in you
there can be no end.*

St. Teresa of Jesus, Soliloquies VII 1-2

230. WE SHALL DWELL IN HIS HOUSE

*Great source of light, blessed Three in One, infuse your love into our
hearts (RB Solemnity of the most Blessed Trinity)*

1. God already wanted to give himself to our first parents, not
only as Creator but also as the Trinity; but sin cut off this intimate communication of friendship by which God would have
liked to treat man as a son, as a friend for whom he could unveil
the mystery of his intimate life in order to share it with him. All
this would be given back to man through the incarnation of the
Word, through Christ, the God-Man, who was to be Mediator between God and man. By ransoming us from sin, Jesus endowed us
anew with the capacity of receiving the divine gift of sanctifying
grace, and therefore of love, through which we could once again
participate in the divine nature and life. And thus in virtue of the
redemption he had wrought for us, Jesus could make the wonderful promise: "If a man loves me ... my Father will love him, and
we will come to him and make our home with him" (Jn 14:23). The
Holy Trinity takes pleasure in dwelling in those who love, that is
in those who live in grace and love, because, as St. John says:
"God is love and he who abides in love abides in God, and God
abides in him" (1 Jn 4:16). God himself infuses love into us, a
created sharing of his being and of his divine nature; it is infused
by the Father who is its original source, by the Son who merits it,
by the Holy Spirit who communicates it. It is a free gift which
originates entirely from God because "he first loved us" (ib. 19),
but we are expected to open our hearts to the effusion of this gift,
and not put obstacles in its path, nor resist it. The more we are
able to welcome divine love and to live in it, the more the Trinity
will be pleased to abide in us, just as a friend is happy to stay with
a friend, lingering with him in pleasant intimacy. "Behold"—says
the Lord—"I stand at the door and knock; if any one hears my
voice and opens the door, I will come in to him and eat with him,
and he with me" (Rev 3:20). What will our answer be?

2. If we live in love, God not only dwells in us, but since he is
the living God, he lives in us; he lives his intimate life, the life of
the Trinity. The Father is living in us, continually generating his
Son, the Father and the Son are living in us and from them the Holy Spirit unceasingly proceeds. Our soul is the little heaven where
this magnificent divine life is always unfolding. Why do the three
divine Persons live in us, if not to give a share in their life? The

Father begets his Son in us and gives him to us in order to make us also his children. The Father and the Son breathe forth the Holy Spirit within us and give him to us, so that the Spirit, who is the terminus and bond of their love and union, may also be the bond of our love and union with the Trinity.

The divine Persons are within those of us who welcome them and participate in their divine life through faith and charity. By *faith* we believe in them and by *charity* we are united to them. We are united to the Father and are received into his paternal embrace, sustained by his almighty power and drawn with him to contemplate and love his Son, according to the words of Jesus himself: "No one can come to me unless the Father who sent me draws him" (Jn 6:44). When we are united to the Son, he clothes us with his splendor, penetrates us with his infinite light, teaches us to know the Father; he covers us with his merits and draws us with him to praise and love the Father, thus fulfilling his words: "No one comes to the Father but by me" (Jn 14:6). When we are united with the Holy Spirit, he infuses into us the grace of the adoption of the children of God, and pours into our soul an ever-increasing participation in the divine life; thus he draws us with him into an ever more intimate communion with the Father and the Son, so that our union with God may be made perfect.

"O souls created for this greatness and called to it"—cries out St. John of the Cross—"what are you doing? What is holding you back?" (Sp C 39:7). The most Blessed Trinity desires to share divine life with us, and shall we turn our gaze elsewhere?

> *Holy and undivided Trinity, unfailing goodness, hear my petitions: just as you made me share in your sacraments without any merit on my part, but only through your free goodness, so also grant that I may persevere to my last hour in faith, hope and charity...*
>
> *God, three and one, accept the prayers of your humble servant. Give me, O Lord, diligence to seek you, wisdom to find you, a soul to know you, eyes to see you, words to please you, and perseverance to the end, a happy end, the eternal reward.*
>
> *To you, O Lord, I reveal the secrets of my heart, to you I confess all my sins... Dispose of all my actions according to your good pleasure, so that I may advance day by day and go from virtue to virtue. O Lord I pour out my pleading prayer before you, the cry of my heart...*
>
> *O Trinity, blessed light, increase my faith, my hope, my charity; free me, save me, justify me...*
>
> *Come, O merciful Lord, and dwell among us, so that we may experience your presence in our hearts.*
>
> St. Anselm *Prayers* 1

> *O holy Trinity, Father, Son, and Holy Spirit, may your divine omnipotence rule and confirm my faith; let your divine wisdom instruct and enlighten it, and your divine goodness help and perfect it,*

*that, at the hour of my death, I may render up this, my faith, unde-
filed and unaltered before your face, together with all the virtues
which it will have gained for me.*

*God the Father of heaven and King of kings, deign to wed me
within my soul to Christ the King, your Son. Jesus Christ, Son of the
living God, let my love be wedded unto you, for you yourself are my
King and my God. Holy Spirit, the Paraclete, join my heart for ever
unto Jesus by that connecting tie of love wherein you unite the
Father and the Son.*

St. Gertrude, Exercises I, p. 6; III p. 38

231. WE WILL COME TO HIM

*O holy Trinity, grant that, abiding in love, I may abide in you and
you in me*   *(1 Jn 4:16)*

1. At the very moment of baptism, the three Persons of the holy Trinity take up their abode in the Christian; yet, the Church
teaches us in the *Veni, Sancte Spiritus* (Come, Holy Spirit) to ask
continually for the coming of the Holy Spirit, and consequently of
all the Blessed Trinity, because by reason of their indivisible unity, no one of the three Persons comes to us without the others.
But if the three divine Persons are within us already, how can they
come again? A soul needs only to be in the state of grace in order
to have God—who is already present as creator—present also as a
friend, inviting us to live in intimacy with himself. However, this
intimacy has different degrees. It becomes closer and deeper according as the soul, growing in grace and charity, acquires a
greater capacity of entering into a deeper relationship with the
Trinity. It is somewhat like what takes place between two persons
who are friends, and who live in the same house: as their mutual
affection increases, their friendship becomes more intense; thus,
therefore, although they were already present to each other, their
reciprocal presence acquires a new aspect, one that is proper to the
presence of a very dear friend. Likewise the Trinity already in-
habits the souls of the just, but the presence of the three divine
Persons can always be made stronger in the terms of a more intimate affection; that is, they can always enter into deeper relations of friendship with us. This is realized progressively, as the
soul acquires additional degrees of grace by advancing in charity.
Since these new effusions of the Trinity present aspects and produce effects which are always new, we can rightly call them new
comings, new visits of the divine Persons. But, in reality, they are
always present in the soul; their visit does not come from without,
but from within the soul itself where they dwell and give
themselves; and even, to a certain degree, reveal themselves to the
soul, according to the words of Jesus: "He who loves me will be

loved by my Father, and I will love him and manifest myself to him" (Jn 14:21). It is an interior revelation based on love, and reserved for those who love; through love the Trinity is made known to man in a most intimate and personal way, and infuses in him an awareness of the divine presence.

2. The first effusion of the Trinity in our souls took place on the day of our baptism. The Father sent us his Son, the Father and the Son sent us the Holy Spirit, and, because of the indissoluble unity of the Three, the Father himself came without being sent. This visit of the Trinity is renewed every time we grow in grace and charity through receiving a sacrament or advancing in love. Jesus' promise: "We will come to him" (Jn 14:23) is never exhausted; it is always new, always ready to be actualized whenever the conditions for it are renewed, that is, every time we love more intensely. This divine gift which is offered to us so generously ought to spur us on to generosity, and to constant progress in love, for only in this way shall we be able to enjoy it fully. If we put no obstacles in the way of the growth of charity and grace in our soul, the Blessed Trinity will set no limit to the effusion of charity and grace within us.

The Trinity lives in the baptized person, and dwells in him that he may live in union with the three divine Persons. This is the reason Jesus revealed the mystery of the Trinity when he redeemed us, and why he shared with us the glory of his divine Sonship; this is the reason why before going to his Passion he prayed: "As you, Father, are in me and I in you, that they also may be in us" (Jn 17:21). As Christ lives in the Father in the unity of the Holy Spirit, so must we live in the Trinity, dwelling within us. The channel of union with the three divine Persons is always Christ our Lord. He is the door: "I am the door" (Jn 10:9); he is the way: "I am the way" (Jn 14:6) through which we needs must pass. Through Christ, with Christ, and in Christ, we are permitted to live in communion with the "Three" who live in us; it is up to us to accept the invitation and to effect this marvellous divine life through the theological virtues, especially those of faith and charity. Through faith we believe and adore the Trinity present within us, but by love we enter into the circle of divine life, because—it is good to repeat it—"God is love, and he who abides in love abides in God, and God abides in him" (1 Jn 4;16).

"O my God, Trinity whom I adore! Help me to become utterly forgetful of self, that I may bury myself in you as changeless and as calm as though my soul were already in eternity. May nothing disturb my peace or draw me out of you, O my immutable Lord! but may I at every moment penetrate more deeply into the depths of your mystery!

Give peace to my soul; make it your heaven, your cherished dwelling place, your home of rest. Let me never leave you there alone, but keep me there, all absorbed in you, in living faith, adoring you and wholly yielded up to your creative action!

O my Christ, whom I love, crucified by love, fain would I be the bride of your heart; fain would I cover you with glory and love you ... until I die of very love. Yet I realize my weakness and beseech you to clothe me with yourself, to identify my soul with all the movements of your own. Immerse me in yourself; possess me wholly; substitute yourself for me, that my life may be but a radiance of your own. Enter my soul as Adorer, as Restorer, as Savior! O eternal Word, utterance of my God! I long to pass my life in listening to you, to become docile that I may learn all from you. Through all darkness, all privations, all helplessness, I crave to keep you ever with me and to dwell in your great light. O my beloved Star! so hold me that I cannot wander from your light!

O consuming Fire! Spirit of love! descend within me and reproduce in me, as it were, an incarnation of the Word; that I may be in him another humanity wherein he renews his Mystery! And you, O Father, bend down toward your poor little creature and overshadow her, beholding in her none other than your beloved Son, in whom you have set all your pleasure.

O my "Three," my All, my Beatitude, infinite Solitude, Immensity wherein I lose myself! I yield myself to you as your prey. Bury yourself in me that I may be buried in you, until I depart to contemplate in your light the abyss of your greatness!
Elizabeth of the Trinity, *Spiritual Doctrine* by M.M. Philipon, O.P.

232. IN THE NAME OF THE FATHER

May I live in the name of the Father who created me, of the Son who redeemed me, and of the Holy Spirit, who is poured out in me. (RRo)

1. The whole of Christian life proceeds from the Trinity, and returns to the Trinity as its final end. "Go therefore"—said the risen Jesus to his disciples—"make disciples of all nations, baptizing them in the name of the Father and of the son and of the Holy Spirit" (Mt 28:19). Christian life thus begins in the name of the Trinity and is based on the Trinity. Any one who seeks to become a member of the Church is consecrated through baptism as a temple of God's glory, the dwelling place of the Holy Spirit, through Christ our Lord (*Baptism of infants*). In after years, he is absolved of sins, confirmed with holy chrism, ordained priest or united in matrimony "in the name of the Father and of the Son and of the Holy Spirit." When his life reaches its final moments, the Church prays: "Go forth from this world, O Christian soul, in the name of God the almighty Father, who created you; in the name of Jesus Christ the Son of the living God, who suffered for you; in the name of the Holy Spirit, who has been poured forth upon you" (RRo). This impressive formula sums up the whole action of the Trinity

on man's behalf; it shows how all we are and all we have as creatures and as Christians originates in the holy Trinity. The eucharistic Sacrifice likewise begins and ends in the name of the Trinity; the Eucharist itself is the gift of the Trinity: The Father gives us "the true bread from heaven" (Jn 6:32), and this living and life-giving bread is his very Son made man, whose "flesh is food indeed . . . and whose blood is drink indeed" (ib. 55). But none of this takes place without the Holy Spirit, for "it is the Spirit that gives life" (ib. 63); by giving life to Christ's glorious humanity, the Spirit renders it capable of communicating life.

All this great reality is expressed in the sign of the cross: all the sacred rites begin with it, all the sacraments are completed with it, the Church repeatedly blesses the faithful with it, and the faithful themselves make the sign of the cross many times a day. Everything in the life of a Christian is, and should be, done in the name of the most blessed Trinity; everything should be worthy of testifying to faith and love, gratitude and dedication to the Father, the Son, and the Holy Spirit.

2. The life of the Church also is based on the mystery of the Trinity. "The Church"—Vatican II teaches—"shines forth as a people made one with the unity of the Father, the Son, and the Holy Spirit" (LG 4). The object of Jesus' prayer to his Father was the union of all believers in a single Church: "The glory which you have given me I have given to them that they may be one even as we are one; I in them and you in me, that they may become perfectly one, so that the world may know that you have sent me" (Jn 17:22-23). Jesus, the Only-Begotten of the Father, has shared his glory as Son of God with us, that we too might be brought into the mysterious movement of the life of the Trinity, a movement of love and unity. Christ desires that the love and union of believers mirror the love and unity of the Blessed Trinity. He wants each of us to love the other to the point where we shall be "one even as [the three divine Persons] are one." Such a union among men of diverse civilizations, diverse ways of thinking, diverse outlooks and aspirations is not possible except in God; that is, it is not possible unless every believer personally lives united to God in charity. Jesus had already said this: "Even as you, Father, are in me, and I in you, that they also may be in us" (ib. 21). Without this being and living in God, it is impossible for a genuine union to exist, one that is lasting and deep beyond any divergence or discordant interest. Only love which comes from God and unites to God can accomplish this miracle. This is what Christ was asking of his Father when he implored that all believers might "be perfect in unity" and proposed the indissoluble unity of the holy Trinity as their model.

This concept was very dear to Vatican II and frequently found a place in its documents. "The highest exemplar and source of this mystery [the union of the faithful] is the unity, in the Trinity of Persons, of one God, the Father and the Son in the Holy

Spirit" (UR 2). So sublime an ideal is beyond our natural understanding, yet it is the goal toward which we must tend, and it is the witness the Church is called to give to the world, "that the world may know that you have sent me." The example of unity among the faithful should induce the world to recognize the truth of Christianity and to recognize Christ as the true Son of God.

Every morning at Mass ... I shall offer myself to the Father, I shall immolate myself with the Son in order to be transformed and consumed in Communion through the Holy Spirit, and in that Communion I shall strengthen my union with you, O most holy Trinity ..., reveling in the joyful thought that your invisible purposes will be carried out in me in every good work of my day.

Yes, O Father, beget your Word in me, so that recognizing him in me, you may love him and be loved in return, and with him breathe your Love into me; and, since love transforms the lover into the beloved, so transform me into the Holy Spirit.

O fount of life, O beneficent light, O infinite charity, remain in me, and make your permanent abode in me. Establish me in you in the peace and joy of your Spirit, making me calm, free and simple. I desire to cooperate with your sanctifying action. I desire to conceal myself in you and be wholly concentrated on you so that I may embrace all souls in you and love and serve you in my neighbor with most generous fraternal charity, forgetting myself.

Remain in me as in your temple, where I desire to live in company with you, in the light of faith made bright by the gift of wisdom, while waiting to contemplate you without veil, face to face in Paradise in the eternal banquet of love.

St. Carmela of the Holy Spirit, *Unpublished Works*

Receive me, O Father most holy, in your all-clement fatherhood, that at the end of this course I may receive you yourself as my crown and my eternal inheritance.

Receive me, O Jesus most loving, in your bounteous brotherhood, that you may bear with me all the burden of the heat of the day, and that I may have you as my comforter in all my labor and as my tutor, guide, and companion on my journey.

Receive me, O Holy Spirit, Love divine, in your most compassionate mercy and charity, that I may have you as the master and instructor of my whole life, and the dearest Lover of my heart.

St. Gertrude, *Exercises* 4

233. PRAISE OF HIS GLORY

Holy Trinity, may I be a praise of your glory   *(Eph 1:12)*

1. "Blessed be the God and Father of our Lord Jesus Christ, who has blessed us in Christ with every spiritual blessing . . . even as he chose us in him before the foundation of the world that we should be holy and blameless before him. He destined us in love to be his sons through Jesus Christ, according to the purpose of his will to the praise of his glorious grace" (Eph 1:3-6). In these few words St. Paul announces the plan of salvation willed by the Father and carried out by the Son, "sealed with the promise of the Holy Spirit" (ib. 13), for the glory of the Trinity. If "the heavens are telling the glory of God, and the firmament proclaims his handiwork" (Ps 19:1), because they testify to his power, wisdom, and infinite beauty, so much the more do the works which effected our creation and elevation to the supernatural state magnify the glory of the Trinity, since they are the most glorious manifestation of his goodness. What more could the three divine Persons do than to share themselves with man to the point of dwelling within him in order to draw him into the blessed vortex of their divine life? And how could man not live for the glory of the Trinity? This is the Christian's great vocation, as St. Paul states so clearly: "We have been destined to live for the praise of his glory" (Eph 1:12). For this reason the Father has "chosen us . . . to be holy and blameless before him" (ib. 4).

In perfect harmony with the divine plan, Vatican II exhorts all the faithful, especially those who are consecrated, to "persevere and excel increasingly in their vocation . . . for a more vigorous flowering of the Church's holiness and the greater glory of the one and undivided Trinity, which in Christ and through Christ is the fountain and the wellspring of all holiness" (LG 47). The holier each individual is, the holier the Church is; her holiness glorifies the Trinity and at the same time makes the Trinity, in a certain way, visible to men. "It is the function of the Church, led by the Holy Spirit who renews and purifies her ceaselessly, to make God the Father and his incarnate Son present and in a sense visible" (GS 21).

2. God "has generously poured out his divine goodness and does not cease to do so. Thus he who made all things may at last be 'everything to every one' (1 Cor 15:28), procuring at one and the

same time his own glory and our happiness" (AG 2). Such is God's way of acting; since he is the supreme and infinite Good, he cannot direct his actions to any one except himself; but at the same time his goodness is so great that he wishes to make his glory coincide with man's happiness, that is, he wishes to be glorified in the effusion of his goodness, his life, and his love into man. All this comes to pass solely through love, through pure generosity. "But God, who is rich in mercy, out of the great love with which he loved us, even when we were dead through our trespasses, made us alive together with Christ . . . that in the coming ages he might show the immeasurable riches of his grace in kindness toward us in Christ Jesus" (Eph 2:4-7). God is not content with glorifying himself in inanimate works, however great and beautiful—such as the heavens and oceans and space—but he has desired and continues to desire to glorify himself in creatures—like angels and men—who are capable of enjoying his gifts, and whom he has destined to share in his eternal happiness. The most humble and unknown Christian who knows how to receive the divine gifts with love and gratitude and to find reason in them for praising God, glorifies him more than all the beauty that is spread through the entire universe. The Christian who opens himself totally to the gift of the Trinity dwelling within him, who lives in union with the three divine Persons, renders the Trinity the greatest glory that man can offer.

Yet there is a higher glory still, a truly divine glory, that the Christian is called to offer to the Trinity: that which Christ himself offers to his divine Father in the eucharistic Sacrifice. The Eucharist is the infinite thanksgiving that the whole Christ—Christ united to his Church—renders to the Father in the name of all humanity. "Through Christ, with Christ, and in Christ in the unity of the Holy Spirit, all glory and honor is yours, almighty Father, for ever and ever" (RM). Though we suffer from being utterly incapable of ourselves of giving God a glory that is worthy of him, we have the joyous certainty of offering the Trinity a praise that is truly fitting God's infinite majesty.

O silent Trinity, supreme source of light and love and unchangeable peace, everything in heaven, on earth, and even in hell, is ordered to the praise of the glory of your most holy name.

In order to unite myself to the unceasing praise of the Word which rises to you from the depths of Christ's soul, through him, with him, and in him in imitation of the Virgin of the Incarnation and through her immaculate hands, I offer myself as a sacrificial victim of the Trinity.

Beloved Father, the grace of adoption of my baptism has made me your son. Take care of me and let no voluntary fault come to darken even slightly the purity of my soul. Let my life, ever more faithful with each passing day, rise toward you with the boundless filial surrender of an infant who knows he is immersed in the tender love of an all-powerful Father.

O Word, eternal Thought of my God, figure of his substance and splendor of his glory, I no longer desire any light but you. Light up my darkness with the light of life that I may journey on, rooted in faith and ever more docile to the illumination of your wisdom, your understanding and your knowledge, while I await the day when all other light will disappear before the radiant splendor of your divine face.

Holy Spirit, who unite the Father and the Son in one endless beatitude, teach me how to live at every moment and in every circumstance in intimacy with my God, in ever greater union with the Trinity . . .

Grant that after this world which is passing away, when earthly shadows will have disappeared, my life in eternity may flow by before the face of the most holy Trinity in unending praise of the glory of God, the Father, the Son, and the Holy Spirit.

M.M. Philipon

How fitting it is that every mouth should glorify, every voice confess, every creature venerate and celebrate your adorable and glorious name, O most holy Trinity, Father, Son, and Holy Spirit, who have created the world through your grace and its inhabitants through your clemency; who in your mercy saved mankind and have granted immense beatitude to mortal beings.

Thousands upon thousands of heavenly spirits venerate and exalt you . . . With the Cherubim and Seraphim they glorify and adore your greatness, unendingly proclaiming and answering each other: Holy, holy, holy is the Lord of hosts; heaven and earth are filled with his magnificence, with his presence, and with the splendor of his grandeur.

Early Christian Prayers, 167

234. THIRTEENTH SUNDAY OF ORDINARY TIME

YEAR A

May I be dead to sin and alive to God in Christ Jesus (Rom 6:11)

Today the Liturgy of the Word leads us to consider the characteristics of the true disciple of Jesus. They are outlined by the Lord himself in austere words which cannot be lightly dismissed: "He who loves father or mother more than me is not worthy of me; and he who loves son or daughter more than me is not worthy of me; and he who does not take his cross and follow me is not worthy of me" (Mt 10:37-38). The following of Christ demands a radical commitment expressed in a total love which is high above every other love; Jesus must be loved more than father or mother or children or self, more than life itself. This does not mean denying ourselves the love of family or neighbor—that would be absolutely contrary to the law of God—but it does mean never putting love for creatures ahead of our love for Christ. When circumstances bring us to a cross-road in life where it is either creatures or God, as Christians we have to make a resolute choice even if it imposes heavy sacrifices on our hearts. In fact we really become capable of a greater love for our neighbor and for those close to us, precisely when we have consecrated our whole heart to Christ, for only supernatural love can make us surmount all the barriers and reservations of selfishness. Jesus' admonition to take up our cross and follow him is, in great part, particularly directed toward overcoming our selfishness, which not only stands in our way of our loving God, but is also an obstacle to our love for neighbor and even for those very close to us. If sometimes we have to oppose creatures in order to be faithful to Christ, it is not because we do not love them but rather that we love them with a truer love, which by not descending to compromise is capable of raising them up to God.

"He who finds his life will lose it"—says Jesus—"and he who loses his life for my sake will find it" (ib. 39). Just as by handing our heart over entirely to Jesus, we find it again, enriched with a divine power of love, so also, by renouncing self to the extreme limit—even to the loss of life itself—we find our true life again in Christ, that eternal life which no one can take from us. Few are asked to witness to their love by giving up their life for Christ, but every Christian is asked to live so disposed as never to recoil before sacrifice.

With this in mind we meditate upon the second reading in which St. Paul reminds us of our duty as persons baptized "in the death" of Christ. He speaks incisively: "We were buried therefore with him . . . into death" (Rom 6:4). We have not only died with Christ, but are positively "buried" in his death, that death which has destroyed sin. The consequence is clear: one who is baptized must be so dead to sin as to eliminate it from his life. The Apostle considers any other line of behavior abnormal; according to his thought, any one baptized in Christ's death is to rise again for ever with him and like him, "in newness of life" (ib.). The "newness" is precisely our freedom from sin. St. Paul thoroughly understood what was required to follow Christ. So it was necessary to repeat that we need to die to whatever diverts us from generous service of the Lord, and to renounce everything that compromises that absolute preference, that primacy of the love we owe him. Only thus is a Christian a worthy disciple of Christ, intimately associated with him in death and life. "The death he died, he died to sin, once for all, but the life he lives he lives to God. So you also must consider yourselves dead to sin and alive to God in Christ Jesus" (ib. 10-11).

Charity that is well-ordered is a sincere affection for you, O most merciful Lord Jesus, and for our neighbor ... Love is not in order if you are not loved above all things, for you are infinitely above every creature. So love for our neighbor is well-ordered when he is loved through you ... Now if parents and relatives are loved more than you, such love is not in order, nor is one who loves in this way worthy of you ...

O kindest Lord, these are the precepts that should constantly direct our attention, our thought, our memory, and which we should always perform and carry out with all our strength! Now, our love for you, O Lord, can be seen by our charity towards our neighbor and by this it is preserved and grows: in fact, any one who neglects loving you does not know how to love his neighbor either ...

O most loving Lord Jesus Christ, who set charity and love in order, please help me by pardoning me my sins, and by mercifully letting me share in your immense mercy. Bend my stony heart and make it turn to you and love you and my neighbor for your sake through love, so that I may live eternally with you in well ordered charity.

R. Jourdan, *Contemplations*

O Jesus, let nothing upset me, let nothing stop me along the way. You alone are the object of my life, nothing else matters; provided that I love you and am journeying toward you, the rest matters little. Oh, that I might know how to offer up to you with all my heart all the sufferings of my spirit and my heart. The earth is nothing, the world is nothing; you alone, O Jesus, are everything to me who am all yours.

A. Chevrier, *L'esprit et les vertus*

YEAR B

"I will extol you, O Lord, for you have drawn me up ... you have brought up my soul from Sheol"   *(Ps 30:1,3)*

The double phrase "life-death" constitutes the central theme of today's Liturgy. God, essential life, defined himself as: "I am who I am" (Ex 3:14); he can be only the author of life. "God"—says the book of Wisdom—"did not create death and takes no pleasure in the destruction of the living" (1:13). When he created man in his image and likeness he could not destine him for death. Scripture is explicit on this point: "For God created man incorruptible, and to the image of his own likeness he made him" (Wis 2:23). Then where does the sad reality of death, which no one can escape, come from? From the very first pages of the Bible death is depicted as the punishment of sin (Gen 3:19), and today's reading from Scripture renews this concept in precise terms: "By the envy of the devil, death came into the world" (Wis 2:24). By leading man into sin the devil dragged him down to death, understood in a total sense: physical death and spiritual death, which is eternal separation from God. While bodily death, although a consequence of sin, is the passage to eternal life for the just, for the wicked it is the equivalent of eternal damnation. "Justice is immortal" (Wis 1:15), Scripture declares; that is, immortality is assured to those who live according to virtue and according to God; but by their sins the wicked "have called death to them" (ib. 16), eternal death, irreparable separation from God, the source of life.

When Jesus redeemed man from sin, he also redeemed him from death; he fully restored him to his destiny of eternal life. This power of Christ was demonstrated in the miracles of resurrection he performed; today's Gospel (Mk 5:21-43) refers to the raising of the daughter of Jairus. Jesus speaks of her, as he did of Lazarus, as asleep, not dead: "The child is not dead, but sleeping" (ib. 39); as if to indicate that death, like sleep, is subject to awakening; that for him it is no more difficult to bring a dead person back to life than for one of us to awaken someone who is sleeping.

The resurrection miracles performed by Jesus are certainly exceptional deeds, yet they conceal a much greater reality, which will come to pass at the end of time for all of us: the resurrection of the body. Commenting upon the Gospel account, St. John Chrysostom says: "You say Christ did not restore your daughter to life? Well, one day, he will raise her again with absolute certainty, and with a greater glory. After that child was restored to you, she died again; but when your child is raised to life, she will be immortal forever" (In Mt 31:3). This is the faith and sure hope of the Christian for himself and his dear ones. "We look for the resurrection of the dead, and the life of the world to come" (Creed). We need to strengthen such faith and hope in order to be able to look upon our own death and that of others from a Christian viewpoint as our birth into eternal life, our decisive meeting with God.

Charity, too, has its contribution for making us face death serenely. In the second reading (2 Cor 8:7,9,13-15), St. Paul is urging the Corinthians to contribute generously toward relieving the poverty of their brothers in Jerusalem. He reminds them that Jesus "though he was rich, yet for your sake became poor, so that by his poverty you might become rich" (ib. 9), and he invites them to make their present abundance supply for the need of others, so that in their turn "their abundance may supply your want" (ib. 14). In other words, the alms that alleviate the material misery of the destitute heal the moral misery of the affluent and of any who give alms. Charity, good-will and generosity toward the poor obtain from God the forgiveness of our sins and make us rich for eternal life.

Forgive me, Lord, before I go and am no more. Free me from sin before I go, so that I may not go away with my sins. Forgive me that I may be at peace in my conscience, that it may be freed from the burning of the anguish I suffer because of my sin.

Forgive me, so that I may have some comfort before I go and am no more. For if you do not forgive me and relieve me, I shall go away and be no more.

O Lord, you have given me a glimpse of that blessed land, that happy country, that blessed home in which the saints share in eternal life and unchangeable truth; I am afraid to go out where there is no being, for I want to be where you are, O supreme Being . . .

Forgive me that I may know some gladness before I depart and am no more. For if you will not take away my sins, I shall go far from you for all eternity. And to whom shall I go, far away from you for all eternity? From you who said "I am who am," and from you who said: "Tell the children of Israel, he who is sent me to you." Anyone who goes in the opposite direction from him who truly is, goes toward that which is not.

St. Augustine, In Ps 38: 22

YEAR C

Lord, "I will follow you wherever you go"   (Lk 9:57)

The requirements of God's service form the connecting thread of the reflections to which today's readings give rise.

During the mysterious manifestations of God on Mount Horeb, Elijah received a command from God to consecrate Elisha as a prophet. As he came down from the mountain he met Elisha plowing his field; Elijah "passed by him and cast his mantle upon him" (1 Kgs 19:19); it was a symbolic gesture which indicated the prophetic mission with which he was being invested. Elisha's response was immediate; he abandoned his oxen—"twelve yoke," states the sacred text succinctly, for he was rich—and ran after Elijah, asking but one thing: "Let me kiss my father and mother, and then I will follow you" (ib. 20). It is a very human and moving detail which shows that the divine call does not make one insensitive to family affections, although it may demand their sacrifice, when necessary, in order to dedicate ourselves completely to the service of God and neighbor. God has the right to ask us to leave everything—profession, property, home, and family—in order to follow his call.

There is a strong parallel with this episode in the passage of St. Luke's Gospel which is read today (9:51-62). After the theophany on Tabor, Jesus and his disciples set out on the long journey to Jerusalem, where he was to be tried and crucified. On the way he met three men aspiring to be disciples, who represented the innumerable souls who would follow him throughout the centuries; in precise terms he gave them the conditions for following him. "I will follow you wherever you go" (ib. 57), said the first, and our Lord answered in return: "Foxes have holes and birds of the air have nests; but the Son of man has nowhere to lay his head" (ib. 58). Anyone who desires to be a follower of Christ cannot expect security or worldly advantages. To the second Jesus himself addressed a peremptory invitation that was like a command: "Follow me!" (ib. 59), and to him, as also to the third one who was asking a delay in favor of his family, Jesus did not hesitate to declare that there must be no time wasted in following his call. There are cases in which a delay or a return to one's previous ways could jeopardize everything: "No one who puts his hand to the plow and looks back is fit for the kingdom of God" (ib. 62). Once, when Cardinal Roncalli was speaking to clerics, he said: "We give up our country and our family, without losing our love for our country and our family, but this undoubtedly raises this love to a higher and broader significance . . . Woe to us if we should even now be thinking of a comfortable home . . . of a pattern of life which brings us glory or honor or worldly satisfaction!" (Venice, Mar. 3, 1957).

Obviously such requirements belong to special vocations: those of the priesthood, of religious and the like. But we ought not think that they have no meaning for the ordinary faithful: the hour can sound when an heroic dedication, to be paid for at a high price, can become an obligation for anyone—even for those involved in family or professional or social life. Such as these must also have the courage to meditate upon the *strong* words of the gospel in order to react against a concept of a Christianity that is mediocre, easy, lazy, reduced to the measure of our own convenience and interests.

In the second reading (Gal 5:1,13-18), St. Paul reminds us that Christians have been called by Christ to freedom, but that this freedom must not be confused with caprice and our own convenience which sooner or later reduces us to the slavery of sin; instead it must be in the service of charity: "through love be servants of one another" (ib. 13). The generous service of our brothers, undertaken for the love of God, frees us more than ever from selfishness, and not uncommonly demands sacrifices like those Jesus described to the three aspiring disciples whom he met on the way to Jerusalem.

> I say to the Lord: You are my Lord, I have no good apart from you . . . you are my chosen portion and my cup, you hold my lot . . . Yes I have a goodly heritage.
> I bless the Lord who gives me counsel; in the night also my heart instructs me. I keep the Lord always before me; because he is at my right hand, I shall not be moved. Therefore my heart is glad, and my soul rejoices; my body also dwells secure . . .
> Lord, you show me the path of life; in your presence there is

fullness of joy, in your right hand are pleasures forevermore.
Psalm 16:2, 5-11

Lord Jesus, I beg you to set my affections in order; I am so afraid of failing in what I owe you, in the jealousy of your love, and in the intimacies of your tenderness. You see whom and how I love, and that I do not hold anything back; I give you full power, and put myself at your disposal: break me and mortify me, keep me and purify me, sanctify me and make holiness blossom in me. I ask only that there may be nothing in me that is displeasing to your loving regard.

O Lord, you see that all I want is to please you, but you also see how miserable I am, how worldly and attached to every created beauty, how poor in every real virtue, how unstable and irritable and weak I am. Protect me from my weakness, and at any cost make me yours, just as you want me to be. I do not know the measure of your grace, nor the designs of your providence; I feel that I can do nothing but be weak and fall, waste my energies and abandon your ways, and seek myself, even in the good that I do. Oh, have pity on me, Lord.

L. de Grandmaison, *Life* (Lebreton)

235. I AM WITH YOU ALWAYS

"O God, you are my God . . . my soul clings to you; your right hand upholds me"   *(Ps 63:1,8)*

1. God "is not far from each one of us, for in him we live and move and have our being" (Acts 17:27-28). God not only surrounds us everywhere with his presence, which is active in all creatures and in ourselves, but dwells within us through grace: "we are the temple of the living God" (2 Cor 6:16). This is a spiritual presence which escapes the control of the senses, but is nevertheless real. If then God is always with us and in us, why can we not remain in continual contact with him? This is the deep yearning of those who live their faith intensely, and who are convinced that God's presence is more real than any other presence. It is, in fact, the one necessary Presence, without which no creature can exist; the Presence that rules and upholds the universe; the Presence which is the indwelling of the Trinity in the souls of the just, the offer of intimate friendship in a continuous relationship of knowledge and love. Meditating upon this mystery, Sister Elizabeth of the Trinity wrote: "Let this be our motto: God in me, and I in him. What a joy is this presence within us in the intimate sanctuary of our souls; we can always find him there, even when, as far as feeling goes, we no longer perceive his

presence! What do feelings matter? He is there all the same, maybe even closer. There is where I love to seek him! Oh, let us try never to leave him alone, so that our lives may be one continual prayer." (Letters 47)

Anyone who has grasped the greatness of the mystery of God present in his heart will have an ardent desire to live with him, to prolong his contact with him during the whole day, amidst any occupation whatsoever. How can we have God so near and forget him? "In my opinion"—exclaims St. Teresa of Jesus—"if I had understood as I do now that in this little palace of my soul dwelt so great a king, I would not have left him alone so often. I would have remained with him at times and have striven more, so as not to be so unclean" (Way 28:11).

2. "Walk before me and be blameless" (Gen 17:1), says the Lord. The psalmist replies: "I am continually with you; you hold my right hand" (Ps 73:23). Putting ourselves in God's presence and staying with him during the time of prayer is relatively easy, but remaining with him *always* is more difficult. The actual fact is that when we return to our usual occupations, the awareness of God which had been enkindled during prayer gradually dissipates, and we often behave as if God were no longer present, as if he were no longer with and in us. St. Teresa of Avila writes: "We must . . . even in the midst of occupations, withdraw ourselves. Although it may be for only a moment that I remember I have that company within myself, doing so is very beneficial" (Way 29:5). A quick, interior act of the mind, of the will, of the heart, is enough to put us back in God's presence and to renew our contact with him. This is possible not only for those who live in solitude, but also for those who are deeply involved in business and in continual dealings with people and things, although a greater effort may be necessary in such cases. In fact, the Saint is addressing precisely persons in such conditions when she says: "If you speak, strive to remember that the One with whom you are speaking is present within. If you listen, remember that you are going to hear One who is very close to you when he speaks. Bear in mind that you can, if you want, avoid ever withdrawing from such good company . . . If you can, practice this recollection often during the day; if not, do so a few times" (ib. 7). The more often we practice this, the more we shall learn to walk in God's presence and to live with him.

This method can also be used in another way; it can be applied to God's presence in our neighbor. If, unfortunately, God is not always present in everyone through grace, he is nevertheless present in essence, as Creator and preserver of life. This thought helps us to acknowledge and to adore the divine presence in every person, and hence to deal with each individual not only on a professional basis or through some social obligation, but also, and especially, in homage and in relation to God's presence in that person. This requires good will and constant diligence in order not to let ourselves be carried away by our activities; those who can persevere through love will not be long in tasting its rewards, and will be able to declare as the psalmist does: "Lord, I am continually with you" (Ps 73:23).

O God, you are continually present to me, with all your love, your tenderness and your divine power, and I did not know this! I, who am so afraid of being alone, am never alone. Your omnipotence and your love, O my God, protect me, and constantly surround me with gentleness; you love me with a love that wishes to communicate, to lower itself to the object it loves in order to raise it up then to yourself, to protect it from all harm and to shower all your good things upon it.

How improper, and how weak it is of me to doubt this love on account of my own preoccupations, and at the same time, what boldness! O God, strengthen me against my own weakness.

Bl. M. Teresa de Soubiran

My God, you say to all of us what you said to Abraham: "Walk in my presence and be perfect." Being in your presence is the means, the reason; to be perfect is the result, the effect, the end.

"Be perfect as your heavenly Father is perfect"... You tell us to be perfect and at the same time you show us the way to become so, which is to be unceasingly in your presence... When we are under the eyes of one we love, can we do anything but try with all the energy of our being to please that one in every thing?...

At every moment of our lives we are under your eyes, O God, much more closely and much more intimately than we can possibly be with any human being in the most intimate fellowship... You are not only near us, you are around us and in us; you envelop us and you fill us; you not only know our words and our actions, but even our most secret and fleeting thoughts... O my God, let me think without ever ceasing about this blessed truth: if a single moment of the company of the one we love seems so sweet and is worth more than the entire world... what will our infinite happiness be when at every single moment we shall enjoy your presence?

O my God, make me feel this presence, make me rejoice in it, think of it unceasingly, and, thanks to it, be perfect!

C. de Foucauld, *Meditations upon Old Testament*

236. PERSEVERING IN PRAYER

"My soul yearns for you in the night, my spirit within me earnestly seeks you" (Is 26:9)

1. "Prayer is an exercise of love and it would be incorrect to think that if there is no time for solitude, there is no prayer at all" (T.J. Life 7:12). For the very reason that prayer is based especially on love and springs from it, it is possible to prolong it beyond the time devoted exclusively to it. Though it is not possible to be always thinking of God, partly because our mind gets tired, or because our many occupations demand full attention, still it is always possible for the heart to love and to desire God, even while our thoughts are necessarily occupied elsewhere. Charity consists in just this intimate orientation of the will toward God, and this can, and must, exist even in the performance of duties which absorb our intellect; in fact, such an orientation can be intensified by the desire to accomplish every action for the love of God, to please him, and give him glory. "The reason for prayer"—according to St. Thomas—"is a desire moved by charity ... And this desire within us must be continuous, either in act, or at least potentially ... We can say that one prays continuously ... by reason of the continuity of his desire" (2-2,83,14). The more this desire for God is living and constant, capable of inspiring and dominating our entire life, the more continuous is our prayer and the more in harmony with what holy Scripture admonishes: "Whether you eat or drink, or whatever you do, do all to the glory of God" (1 Cor 10:31). For the glory of God and through the love of God who is not far from us but is within us, more intimately than our very selves, God arouses a longing for himself from the depths of our being; and pours out and revivifies charity in us. If we are not closed to God's impulses nor deaf to his invitations, we shall find within ourselves, originating from him, an inexhaustible source of an ever more intense longing and love. "Pray always, with a constant desire rooted in faith, hope and charity"—says St. Augustine—"Even when there is no time for long prayer, we need to pray always through having such a desire" (Ep 130).

2. "But watch at all times, praying ... " (Lk 21:36). "Continue steadfast in prayer, being watchful in it with thanksgiving" (Col 4:2). "Is anyone among you suffering? Let him pray. Is any cheerful? Let him sing praise" (Jas 5:13). Holy Scripture is full of such calls to continual prayer in both the Old and New Testaments. And it is evident that these calls are not directed just to hermits in the desert, to monks, or to the cloistered, but to everyone. For anyone with a living faith, prayer is the breath of the soul; it is the soul's habitual atmosphere without which it cannot live, just as the body cannot live without air. But just as we cannot always be thinking of God, neither can we be continually reciting long prayers. "It is more a matter of sighing than of speaking"—St. Augustine says expressively, and recalls that the monks of Egypt used to offer "very frequent, but very short prayers, like swift shots of an arrow, so that the alert attention, so necessary for prayer, might not vanish through being prolonged

too long" (Ep 130). In other words, it means frequently using short aspirations or ejaculations formulated more by the heart than by the lips; because they are brief and spontaneous, they do not grow tiresome, and through their frequency and intensity they are very helpful in nourishing charity and maintaining our contact with God. It is in this sense that Vatican II says that in order to develop charity, all the faithful "must apply (themselves) constantly to prayer" (LG 42); it recommends to members of institutes of perfection that they "energetically cultivate the spirit of prayer" (PC 6); it makes the same exhortation to clerics and priests, that "by constancy in prayer and burning love," they may do "all for the glory and honor of God" (LG 41). If it is true that potential desire is sufficient to keep us united with God, it is equally true, considering the weaknesses of human nature, that to keep our yearning kindled, and therefore effective, we must express it from time to time in explicit acts, which at one and the same time serve as a summons, a control and a stimulus. "Direct your affections habitually toward God and your spirit will be divinely enkindled" (J.C., Maxims on Love 1).

> O my God, my soul pines with longing to be united to you, to be intimately close to you in the sweet and holy bond of indissoluble love! What do I seek in heaven? What do I want on earth? The God of my heart, the God who will be my heritage for all eternity! Oh, when will the world's clamor finally cease for me? When shall I finally be free from the ties, the preoccupations, and the vicissitudes of time? When will my pilgrimage end, the unhappy imprisonment of this place of exile? When shall I see the shadow of mortality decline, and the dawn of eternal light begin to shine? When, free at last of the weight of this body, shall I enjoy you, and praise you eternally and without hindrance, together with your saints? O my God, my love, my only yearning, my only good!
>
> Louis de Blois, (Blosius) *Works*

> All my desire is before you. Not indeed before men, who cannot see into the heart; but before you . . .
> Set my desire before you, and you, O Father, who see in secret, will repay me. This very desire of mine is my prayer; and if my desire is continual, my prayer is continual too . . . Can we unceasingly bend our knees, bow down our bodies or uplift our hands, that you should tell us: Pray without ceasing? . . . Make me understand, Lord, that there is another way of praying, interior and unbroken, the way of desire . . . Grant that I may never cease desiring so that I may not cease to pray.
> Your unceasing desire is your unceasing prayer. You will lapse into silence if you lose your longing . . . The coldness of charity is the heart's silence; its glowing ardor the heart's outcry. O Lord, make charity always present in me, so I may be ever crying out; if always crying out, I am ever longing . . .

All my desire is before you. What if my desire is before you and the actual groaning is not? Would it be possible, since the groaning is just the expression of the desire? . . . If the desire is always within, so too is the groaning; it does not always come to the ears of men, but it is never absent from the ears of God.

St. Augustine, *In Ps* 37:14

237. TOWARD DIALOGUE WITH THE FATHER

O Lord, I keep you always before me; you show me the path of life
(Ps 16:8,11)

1. "By its very nature, religion is a relationship between God and man. Prayer expresses this relationship through dialogue . . . This dialogue becomes complete and trusting; the child is invited to it, the mystic is consumed in it" (Paul VI, Eccl Suam, 41). Conversation with God is not just an episode in the life of a fervent Christian; it is a loving practice which tends to become continuous. It is not something studied or imposed, like certain conversations that are part of etiquette or propriety, but something entirely spontaneous like a meeting of father and son. Neither is it an exterior event that is confined to formulas, or to spoken words; it is an interior event which bespeaks a profound relationship with God, a lively desire to listen to him and to linger with him.

Although the time of prayer is directly devoted to this dialogue, prayer must not, however, be restricted to such a time. The purpose of prayer is to intensify our conversation with God, to nourish it, and to renew its fervor; but the end of formal prayer should not be the end of our dialogue with him who is always with us; we should not stop listening to him who, even when silent, always has something to communicate to those who love him, if only by his presence which is never lacking, and by grace and charity which he is continually infusing into our souls.

"O that today you would hearken to his voice! Harden not your hearts!" (Ps 95:7-8). God is not obliged to speak with us only at specified times or in specified ways. He has no need of words in order to make himself heard: his inspirations, the movements of his grace and the circumstances permitted by his divine providence are more eloquent than any human language, and can reach us at any moment, in any place. But in order to recognize them, we need interior recollection, we need to have our will constantly directed toward him, and to be desirous of welcoming every least sign of his divine will, of what gives him pleasure. "Behold, as the eyes of servants look to the hand of their master . . . so our eyes look to the Lord our God" (Ps 123:2).

2. The entire life of a Christian should be drawn into dialogue with God; in fact, life itself should become dialogue. "God is faithful"—says St. Paul—"by whom you were called into the fellowship of his Son, Jesus Christ our Lord" (1 Cor 1:9). Because of this faithfulness he never lets the interplay of his dialogue with man cease, so that we may truly live in communion with him. He always takes the initiative, it is he who calls. God is the good shepherd who knows each of his sheep individually and calls each by name (Jn 10:3). Our response consists not so much in words as in deeds, that is, in adhering by our life to what God says, proposes, asks, or offers and gives. The rich young man who did not accept Jesus' invitation and went away to take care of his wealth, put an end to his dialogue with the Master (Mk 10:17-22). On the contrary, Zacchaeus accepted the words of the Lord with enthusiasm and immediately came down from the sycamore tree to welcome him into his house, and thus began his dialogue with the Lord (Lk 19:1-10).

The dialogue that pleases God is not one that consists only of words, but one that expresses sincere friendship. "You are my friends if you do what I command you" (Jn 15:14). In the midst of our worldly duties, it is good to repeat some acts of love and of offering, but our actions must bear witness to what our lips affirm. Moreover, we must not expect to attain perfect charity through telling God that we love him, although this is a way of arousing our love and of keeping us united to him; there is still need for our dialogue to become progressively the authentic expression of our life. Vatican II says this very well when referring to the laity: "While properly fulfilling their secular duties in the ordinary conditions of life, they do not disassociate union with Christ from that life. Rather, by performing their work according to God's will, they can grow in that union" (AA 4). God initiated dialogue with man by revealing his love through his works: creation, redemption, the offer of his friendship; and we must respond in like manner: telling God that we love him not only in word, but much more by our life.

> *"I will hear what the Lord God will speak in me."* Happy is the soul which hears you, Lord, speaking within and receiving from your mouth the word of comfort! Happy ears which are attentive to the breathings of the divine whisper and take no notice of the whisperings of the world! Happy ears which hearken not to the voice sounding without, but to the Truth itself teaching within. Happy eyes which are shut to outward things, but intent on spiritual things! Happy they who penetrate into the interior and endeavor to prepare themselves more and more by daily exercises for receiving heavenly secrets.
>
> *Imitation of Christ* III 1:1

237. Toward Dialogue with the Father

*Let all my life be yours, O Lord: I resolutely offer you my whole
self. May all my spirit, all my heart, all my body, and all my life live
for you, O my Life, because you have freed me wholly in order to
possess me wholly; you made me completely over, so you could completely have me again.*

*So I will love you, O Lord, my strength, I will love you, my inex-
pressible delight, and my whole life will be lived, not for myself, but
for you. I was perishing in my wretchedness, and you raised me up
again in your mercy, O merciful God, who are so prodigal with your
benefits for those who love your name. This was the reason, O Lord
my God, my sanctifier, that you commanded me in your laws to love
you with all my heart, with all my soul, with all my mind and with
all my strength from the very depths of my heart, in each and every
hour and moment in wich I enjoy the gifts of your mercy . . .*

*Since there is not an hour nor an instant in all my life in which I
am not sustained by your generosity, so there should also be no moment in which I should not have you before my eyes in my memory,
nor love you with all my strength. But I am not able for so much
unless you help me, for every good gift is from you, and every best
gift comes down from the Father of lights, with whom there is no
variation, nor shadow of change. In fact, loving you, O Lord, is not
the privilege either of those who want to, or of those who are anxious to do so, but rather of those to whom you show mercy. It is your
gift, Lord, since every good gift comes from you. You command me
to love you: give me what you command, and then command what
you will.*

Pseudo Augustine, Soliloquies 18

238. LISTEN TO THE VOICE OF THE LORD

*Happy is the man who listens to you, Lord, watching daily at your
gates*   *(Prov 8:34)*

1. Dialogue supposes listening. How many times in sacred
Scripture the call rings out: "Hear the word of the Lord"
(Jer 31:10). It was the incessant cry of the prophets who were sum-
moning the people back to their essential calling: that of listening
to God and of following him. "Obey my voice!"—says the Lord
through the mouth of Jeremiah—"and I will be your God and you
shall be my people" (7:23).

But the fullness of the word of God was given to the world
when the Word became flesh, the Logos became man and came
among men to speak with them and among them. Then a voice
from heaven was heard: "This is my beloved Son—listen to him"
(Mt 17:5). The whole gospel is an invitation to listen. Faith comes
from hearing (Rom 10:17); it is by hearing that men receive
Christ's message, that they receive even Christ himself, and in

him become children of God: "To all who received him, he gave power to become children of God" (Jn 1:12). Hearing or not hearing the Lord is a matter of life or death. Those who listen to him, follow him, and embrace his teaching, become part of his flock: his sheep "hear his voice" (Jn 10:2). A superficial listening is not enough, nor an occasional listening; we need to be always listening. One who loves is always attentive to the voice of the loved one.

The world is full of voices. Men are eager to listen: to news, to information, to novelties and to curiosities. All too easily these voices become a hubbub which bewilders us and makes us superficial, incapable of interior life, and incapable too of hearing the one true Voice. We also often stay on the surface when praying: physically we hear the voice of the priest or listen to the sacred book that speaks to us of God, but rarely do we let this voice penetrate to the depths of our soul, like a seed placed in a furrow so that it may sprout in due time. Yet only those who receive the "word of the kingdom" in good soil, that is hear it, practice it, and live it, will bring forth fruit (Mt 13:19-23).

2. Christ, the Word of the Father, is not only the object of our listening, but he himself personifies listening to the Father, and is hence the model for our listening. "I declare to the world"—he said—"what I have heard from him . . . I speak thus as the Father taught me" (Jn 8:26,28). Jesus is the Word of the Father, and he speaks to the world because he contains in himself all the Father's wisdom, for he unceasingly listens to the Father and transmits only what he hears from him. Jesus is the perfect listener to the Father, the only Man who listens to him in an adequate measure. Following in his footsteps, the Christian must be constantly listening in order to be taught by God. Jesus said so: "And they shall be taught by God" (Jn 6:45); this means that all men are intended to receive a training, a divine teaching: the word of God must reach them, enlighten them, guide them and shape them. They must become attentive disciples, docile and ready at hand. Christ lives and talks with men, but he never ceases to listen to his Father, and he teaches us that our listening must also be unceasing.

Likewise, in the midst of everyday affairs and the service of our brothers, we need that vigilant attention of the spirit which knows how to understand God's word. The world is filled with his voice. When men or circumstances or daily duties demand service and dedication and sacrifice, it is God who is asking it by means of them; when people or events put our virtue to a hard test, it is always God who is desirous of testing it. When the Church, the Pope, the hierarchy, and superiors speak, it is God who is speaking. When we listen to them, we are listening to God (Lk 10:16). When we are inwardly urged toward good, to forgiveness, to forget ourselves, or to greater recollection and intimacy with God, again it is God speaking. How often God's word falls on heedless ears! "When I spoke to you . . . you did not listen, and when I called you, you did not answer" (Jer 7:13). God's omnipotent voice is never wasted: it always accomplishes what he wishes; but those who do not heed him are going to be lost; and those who do not welcome him wholeheartedly will remain in mediocrity. "Happy is the man who listens to me"—says the Lord—"watching daily at my gates . . . For he who finds me, finds life" (Prov 8;34-35).

Speak, Lord, for your servant hears. I am your servant: give me understanding that I may know your precepts. Incline my heart to the words of your mouth, let your speech distill as the dew.

Of old the children of Israel said to Moses: speak to us, and we will listen; let not the Lord speak to us or we will die. My God, it is not thus that I pray, but rather with the prophet Samuel, I earnestly entreat: "Speak, Lord, for your servant hears you. Let not Moses, or any of the prophets speak to me, but rather do you speak to me, Lord God, who inspire and enlighten all the prophets, for you alone without them can perfectly teach me, but they without you, can do me no good.

Prophets may sound forth words, but they do not give the spirit; they say beautiful things, but if you are silent, they do not inflame the heart; they proclaim your mysteries, but you open our understanding to what has been hidden from us. They make your commandments known, but you enable us to put them into practice; they show the way, but you give us the strength to walk in it; they see to the external, while you instead instruct and enlighten the heart; they water outwardly, but you give the increase; they say words, but you give understanding to the hearing . . .

Then speak, Lord: your servant listens, for you have the words of eternal life.

Imitation of Christ III 2:1-3

In you, O Jesus, and in your Father, there is but one spirit, one way of thinking and acting, one same spirit which always works in union with the Father and the Son; so when I listen to you, I listen to the Father . . . When I see you act, I see the very actions of the Father, since the Son does nothing of himself and the Father accomplishes the works. What beautiful harmony and concord between the Father and the Son and the Holy Spirit in you, O Jesus!

What then must I do but study you closely, listen to your word, and examine your actions, that I may conform myself to you, and thus be filled with the Holy Spirit? . . . The Spirit of God is diffused in your whole life . . . Every word of yours, every example, is like a ray of light which comes from heaven to enlighten me and to communicate life to me. Help me study you closely every day that I may be filled with the Spirit of God.

A. Chevrier, *Il vero discepolo di Cristo*

Thirteenth Sunday of Ordinary Time

239. LORD, WHO IS LIKE YOU?

Great is the Lord, and greatly to be praised, and his greatness is unsearchable ... On your wondrous works I will meditate (Ps 145:3-5)

1. "You must be perfect as your heavenly Father is perfect" (Mt 5:48); with these words Jesus turns our attention to God's infinite perfection. The only possible way for us to grasp even some pale reflection of his perfection is by considering the limited perfections we find in creatures, but we cannot understand it in itself for no human mind is capable of embracing and comprehending the infinite. Our ideas tell us something about God and his infinite perfections, but they cannot show him to us as he is. "God"—St. Paul informs us—"dwells in unapproachable light" (1 Tim 6:16), a light which infinitely exceeds the capacity of the human intellect, and is too bright for the eye of our mind to gaze at directly. It is a little like the sun in the full power of its brilliance that no human eye can look at fixedly.

Yet on several occasions when Jesus spoke about the divine perfections, he invited us to raise our eyes to these heights. He taught us that although we can understand very little about them, this little is precious. In fact the more a soul advances in the knowledge of God, the more it understands that what it does know about him is nothing compared to what he is in reality, and the more it senses that far beyond its ideas—however lofty and beautiful—there is an infinite ocean of splendor, beauty, goodness, and love which no human intellect can ever fathom. This awareness of God's immensity, which infinitely surpasses the capacity of our mind, is a great grace. "One of the outstanding favors"—St. John of the Cross states—"that God grants briefly in this life is an understanding and experience of himself, so lucid and lofty as to make one know clearly that he cannot be completely understood or experienced" (Sp Cant 7:9). This is a very precious grace, because it infuses into the soul an ever deeper realization of God's immensity and infinite transcendence; and, by contrast, it also gives it a greater understanding of its own nothingness and the extreme limitation of any human perfection.

2. Only in heaven shall we be permitted to see God "face to face" without the intermediary of ideas. "Now we see in a mirror dimly, but then face to face. Now I know in part; then I shall understand fully, even as I have been fully understood" (1 Cor 13:12). This partial knowledge of God—all that is possible on this earth—reaches us through the "mirror" of creatures. They give us a reflection of his infinite perfections: his goodness, wisdom, justice and beauty, but a reflection which is very imperfect and limited. For example, there is no man so wise that he knows everything that exists; no man so good that he does not sometimes fail in goodness because of his frailty, or so just that he

is not sometimes unjust through too great severity. Only by stripping created perfections of their defects and limitations shall we be able to form a vague idea of the divine perfections. God is good, he is always good, infinitely good. "One there is who is good" (Mt 19:17), said Jesus, meaning that God alone possesses goodness preeminently; rather, he is goodness itself, unlimited goodness which never diminishes or fails.

Therefore it is a serious error to become attached to any creature, however beautiful, good, or wise it may be; its beauty, goodness and wisdom are nothing in comparison with God's perfections. Indeed, St. John of the Cross goes further and says: "All the beauty of creatures compared with the being of God, is supreme ugliness . . . All the goodness of creatures in the world, compared with the infinite goodness of the Creator, can be called evil . . . Since evil does not comprehend goodness, a man who sets his heart on the good things of the world . . . will be incapable of union with God, who is supreme goodness . . . " (Asc. I 4:4). This does not mean that we should despise or belittle creatures, but that we should recognize the absolute preeminence of the Creator and make use of created perfections to rise again to the source of every perfection. We can never go too far in our praise of the Lord: "How can we glorify him worthily? Truly, he is superior to all his works . . . When you glorify the Lord, exalt him as much as you can, because we can never glorify him enough" (Sir 43:28,30).

> Truly you dwell in inaccessible light, O Lord. In fact nothing can penetrate this light in order to discover you there. The reason I do not see it is because it infinitely transcends me. Still, whatever I do see, I see through your light: just as our weak eyes see what they see through the light of the sun, even though they are incapable of gazing at the light of the sun itself.
>
> My intellect is powerless in the presence of your excessively brilliant light; it cannot contain it nor can the eye of my soul bear to fix upon it for long. It is struck by its brilliance, conquered by its extent, overpowered by its immensity, and staggered by its infinity.
>
> O Supreme, inaccessible light! O full and happy truth, how far you are from me, who am yet so near to you! How far from my view you are, although I am so present to yours! You are fully present everywhere, and I do not see you. In you I move, and in you I am, yet I cannot reach you. You permeate me and envelop me, and I do not feel it.

St. Anselm, Proslogion 16

> Through all these creatures of yours let my soul praise you, O God, Creator of all; but let it not cleave too close in love to them through the senses. For they go their way and are no more; and they rend the soul with desires that can destroy it, for it longs to be one with the things it loves and to repose in them. But in them is no place of repose, because they do not abide. They pass, and who can

follow them with any bodily sense? Or who can grasp them firmly even while they are still here?

Be not foolish, my soul, nor let the ear of your heart be deafened with the clamor of your folly. Listen. The Word himself calls to you to return, and with him is the place of peace that shall not be broken, where your love will not be forsaken unless it first forsake ... Fix your dwelling in him, commit to God whatsoever you have: for it is from God. O my soul, wearied at last with emptiness, commit to Truth's keeping whatever Truth has given you, and you shall not lose any; and what is decayed in you shall be made clean, and what is sick shall be made well, and what is transient shall be reshaped and made new and established in you in firmness; and they shall not set you down where they themselves go, but shall stand and abide and you with them, before God who stands and abides forever.

St. Augustine, *Confessions* IV 10, 11

240. HE WHO IS

Holy, holy, holy is the Lord God Almighty, who was and is and is to come   *(Rev 4:8)*

1. God is the supreme Being; this is his foremost perfection, the one which distinguishes him radically from creatures. "I am who am" God said to Moses and added: "This is my name for ever, and thus I am to be remembered throughout all generations" (Ex 3:14-15). This name by which God called himself expresses his very essence, and tells us that he is Being itself, the eternally subsistent Being, who had no beginning and will have no end, the self-existent Being, who finds the cause of his Being in himself. St. John Damascene says: "God possesses Being itself as a kind of sea of substance, infinite and shoreless" (De fide orth 1:9). God revealed himself to St. Catherine of Siena under this aspect, when he said to her: "I am he who is, and you are she who is not." All creatures are nothing! "Lord ... my days are like an evening shadow; I wither away like grass"—chants the psalmist—"But you, O Lord, are enthroned forever" (Ps 102:11-12). The creature receives his being from God, while God is the cause of his own Being. A creature exists only so long as God maintains it in existence; God, however, is his own existence, because he possesses being by his very nature, and does not receive it from anyone. A creature is always a limited being in every aspect: vitality, strength, ability; God, on the contrary, is the infinite Being, who knows no limits, who has all power and virtue. A creature bears within himself the seeds of death and destruction; in God, all is life; he is life: "I am the life" (Jn 14:6), said Jesus.

Only God, the infinite Being, eternal life, can communicate

life, can give existence. Would it be too much, then, for us to consecrate our whole life and being to his service and glory? If we are living for God, we are living for life; if we live for ourselves, we are living for nothing, for death.

2. God is Being, the infinitely perfect Being who possesses all perfections, without defects and without limits. God is the infinitely good, beautiful, wise, just, merciful, omnipotent Being. All these perfections are not accidental qualities in him, as they are in us, who may be more or less beautiful, good or wise, without our ceasing to be human. In God, however, these perfections are essential: that is, they belong to the very nature of the divine Being, or rather, they are all one same thing. In order to speak of the divine perfections, we are obliged to enumerate them one after another, whereas, in reality, they are but one infinite perfection: goodness is identified with beauty; goodness and beauty, with wisdom; and these three, with justice; justice is identified with mercy, and so on. There is no multiplicity in God, but only one absolute unity. We need many words to speak of God, but God is not many things; he is the *One* Being, par excellence: one in the Trinity of his Persons, one in the multiplicity of his perfections, one in the variety of his works, one in his thought, will, and love.

Therefore, you also, who have been created to the image and likeness of God, ought to tend to unity. The divine commandment exacts it: "I am the Lord your God . . . you shall have no other gods before me" (Dt 5:6-7). We have received from God alone all that we are and have, and should depend only on him. Our life cannot and must not vacillate between two goals: our goal is one, because God is the Only One and permits no other gods beside him, no other dominions. "Hear, O Israel"—Scripture repeats—"the Lord our God is one Lord; and you shall love the Lord your God with all your heart, with all your soul, and with all your might" (Dt 6:4-5). This total subjection and adherence to God elevates rather than demeans us; it emancipates us from all earthly slavery, and enables us to find in "Him who is" that consistency, stability and unity which we would seek in vain in ourselves or in other created things.

> *I adore you, O my incomprehensible Creator, before whom I am an atom, a being of yesterday or an hour ago! Go back a few years and I simply did not exist; I was not in being and things went on without me: but you are from eternity; and nothing whatever for one moment could go on without you.*
>
> *And from eternity too you have possessed your nature; you have been—this awful mystery—the Son in the Father and the Father in the Son. Whether we be in existence, or whether we be not, you are one and the same always, the Son sufficient for the Father, the Father for the son—and all other things, in themselves, but vanity . . .*
>
> *O adorable mystery! Human reason has not conducted me to it,*

but I believe.

I believe because you have spoken, O Lord. I joyfully accept your word about yourself. You must know what you are—and who else? Not I surely, dust and ashes, except so far as you tell me. I take then your own witness, O my creator, and I believe firmly, I repeat after you, what I do not understand, because I wish to live a life of faith; and I prefer faith in you to trust in myself.

O my great God, from eternity you were sufficient for yourself. The Father was sufficient for the Son and the Son for the Father; are you not then sufficient for me, a poor creature, you so great, I so little!

J.H. Newman, *Meditations on Christian Doctrine*, VIII, 1-2

O Lord who make the sun shine upon the good and upon the bad, let the light of your countenance shine upon us. Light up your image in us, let your face shine upon us. You have imprinted your face upon us, made us in your image and likeness ... But your image should not remain in darkness; send forth a ray of your wisdom to dispel our darkness and let your image in us shine brightly. Make us grateful for all that we owe to your image ...

I dwell in the darkness of sin, Lord. Dispel my darkness with a ray of your wisdom and show me your face. And though through my fault this face may appear somewhat disfigured, do you restore it to what it was when you fashioned it.

St. Augustine, *In Ps. 66:4*

241.   FOURTEENTH SUNDAY OF ORDINARY TIME

YEAR A

"I will extol you, my God and King, and bless your name for ever and ever"   *(Ps 145:1)*

At the center of today's Liturgy is the Gospel passage (Mt 11:25-30), the precious pearl of St. Matthew's Gospel which enables us to cast a glance at the personal mystery of Christ and his intimate relationship with the Father. What is most striking is that this sublime revelation is reserved for the simple, that is, for the little ones, the humble, those who are despised by the wise of this world, while these latter are themselves definitely excluded. "I thank you, Father, Lord of heaven and earth, that you have hidden these things from the wise and understanding, and revealed them to babes" (ib. 25). God withholds himself from the wise who are puffed up with their own knowledge, convinced that they know everything, and reveals himself to the simple who open their hearts to him with the freshness of children, aware of their own ignorance. They are given a share in the sublime knowledge enjoyed by Jesus and his heavenly Father, which only God can communicate to men. "No one knows the Son except the Father, and no one knows the Father except the Son and any one to whom the Son chooses to reveal him" (ib. 27). The question here is of knowledge in the biblical sense, one that is vital and loving. The mutual knowledge by which the Father fully knows the Son, and the Son the Father, indicates that Jesus—the incarnate Son—is perfectly equal to the Father inthe depths of his being. It is perhaps this text of the synoptic Gospels that most clearly affirms the divinity of Jesus. Thus, while the wise—the scribes and Pharisees of his time and many learned ones of today—see Jesus as no more than a man, "the carpenter's son" (Mt 13:55), the simple of that time and of all times acknowledge him as the Son of God: "You are the Christ, the Son of the living God" (Mt 15:16). These are the souls to whom Jesus reveals himself and his Father.

Jesus does not stop here; he remembers the conditions of suffering in this world, and the distress with which the simple, the humble and the poor often have to struggle, and offers them his invitation: "Come to me, all you who labor and are heavy laden, and I will give you rest" (Mt 11:28). He will give them rest with his love, revealing to them the love of the Father, and teaching them to love him in return as his children. Jesus does not want to oppress us with burdensome laws, but gives us one single law, that of love for God and for our brothers, a law whose sole purpose is the accomplishing of his heavenly Father's will. This is a loving will because it is the love of a father, and, though demanding, is always lovable for anyone who knows how to embrace it as Jesus did: with love and gentleness and humility. "Take my yoke upon you and learn from me; for I am gentle and lowly in heart, and you will find rest for your souls. For my yoke is easy, and my burden is light" (ib. 29-30).

Jesus presents himself, under just this aspect, as the Messiah foretold by Zachariah (9:9-10; 1st reading): as a gentle and humble king who does not impose himself with ostentation and power as do the rich of this world, nor promote justice with the sword, but as a king who brings peace everywhere: "He shall command peace to the nations" (ib. 10). He teaches men how to behave like himself with mildness and humility, bending lovingly under the yoke of God's will, as he himself bent beneath the weight of the cross. In order to act in such a way, we need to mortify the inclinations of our flesh which rebels against injustice and suffering; instead, we must live according to the Spirit of Christ (2nd reading: Rom 8:9,11-13). It is possible for all the faithful to do this because, as St. Paul says: "You are not in the flesh, you are in the Spirit . . . Anyone who does not have the Spirit of Christ does not belong to him" (ib. 9). Obviously, in order to belong to Christ it is not sufficient to have received his Spirit in baptism; we also need to overcome our natural impulses so as to live according to his Spirit.

I will extol you, my God and King, and bless your name for ever and ever. Every day I will bless you, and praise your name for ever and ever.

Great is the Lord, and greatly to be praised, and his greatness is unsearchable. One generation shall laud your works to another, and shall declare your mighty acts. On the glorious splendor of your majesty, and on your wondrous works, I will meditate... (Men) shall pour forth the fame of your abundant goodness, and shall sing aloud of your righteousness.

Psalm 145:1-5,7

"I thank you, Father, Lord of heaven and earth, that you have hidden these things from the wise and understanding and revealed them to babes."

O Lord, to the wise and understanding who deserve to be laughed at, to the presumptuous who are apparently powerful but are in reality puffed up with themselves, you have contrasted, not the foolish and imprudent, but the little ones. Who are the little ones? The humble... O the way of the Lord! Why, O Lord, did you rejoice? Because it has been revealed to little ones.

O Lord, make us little; for, as a matter of fact, if we desire to be great, as if we were wise and intelligent, you will not reveal your mysteries to us. Who are great? The wise and understanding. By calling themselves wise, they have become foolish... And if I too, by calling myself wise, become foolish, Lord, make me call myself foolish, and then I shall be wise; but make me say this in the depths of myself and not in front of people.

St. Augustine, *Sermon 67:8*

YEAR B

Our eyes look to you, Lord, till you have mercy upon us (Ps 123:2)

Today's readings lead us to reflect upon the grave consequences of rejecting the word of God, and upon our obligation to receive his word even when it comes to us through humble and insignificant messengers.

The first reading (Ezek 2:2-5) records the incredulity of the children of Israel in regard to the prophet who was entrusted with announcing the destruction of Jerusalem as a punishment for their sins. God was acquainted with the obstinacy of that people, "impudent and stubborn" (ib. 4), which had been rebellious toward him for some time; yet he sent Ezekiel to them all the same. "Whether they hear or refuse to hear (for they are a rebellious house), they will know that there has been a prophet among them" (ib. 5). These are serious words which show how detestable rebellion against God is, for it hardens the heart and makes it obstinate against any summons. Still, God does not cease to enlighten us, nor to send us warnings through his prophets; in fact, their very presence and their admonitions make the sin of those who persist in incredulity the more serious. Sadly enough this situation is not an isolated one, but one that has been continually repeated throughout history even when God sent, not a prophet, but his divine Son. "He came to his own home, and his people received him not" (Jn 1:11).

This is what happened in Nazareth (Gospel of the day: Mk 6:1-6) when Jesus appeared at the synagogue to preach. Nazareth was his home, his country, where he had lived since his childhood, where he had relatives, and was well-known; all of which should have made his ministry easier there than elsewhere. Instead, it was an occasion for rejection. After a moment of amazement at his wisdom and his miracles, the Nazarenes incredulously reject him: "Is not this the carpenter, the son of Mary . . . ? And they took offense at him" (ib. 3). A secret, petty, mean pride prevented them from admitting that one of their own, who had grown up and practiced a humble trade in their midst, could be a prophet, even the very Messiah himself, the Son of God. Jesus' modesty and humility was the rock of scandal upon which they stumbled and which made them close their hearts to faith. Jesus observed sadly: "A prophet is not without honor except in his own country" (ib. 4). It was the lack of belief on the part of his own people that kept him from working there the great miracles he had performed elsewhere, for God is accustomed to exercise his omnipotence only in favor of those who believe. But there must have been some—probably among the most humble—who did believe, even in Nazareth, for Mark notes: "He laid his hands upon a few sick people and healed them" (ib. 5). It showed how ready Jesus always was to save anyone who accepted him as the Savior.

The second reading (2 Cor 12:7-10) interrelates with the themes of the other readings by outlining, in the words of St. Paul's confession, the way the prophet, or the apostle, must conduct himself. Although the prophet has been sent by God and gifted with special graces, he must always remember that he is still a weak man like every one else. Paul was very conscious of the "abundance of revelations" he had received, but humbly accepted that "thorn in the flesh"—which was perhaps some malady or temptation or apostolic tribulation—which had been sent by God to keep him from being too elated (ib. 7). Similar "thorns" are not lacking to any of us, and the apostle must use them to gain greater humility and faith in God: "I will all the more gladly boast of my weakness, that the power of Christ may rest upon me" (ib. 9). More than that, instead of being intimidated by the difficulties he meets, he must accept them as an indispensable component of his mission: "I am content with weaknesses, insults, hardships, persecutions, and calamities, for when I am weak, then I am strong" (ib. 10).

To you I lift up my eyes, O you who are throned in the heavens!
Behold, as the eyes of servants look to the hand of their master, as

the eyes of a maid to the hand of her mistress, so our eyes look to the Lord our God, till he have mercy on us.

Psalm 123:1-2

O Lord, dispel the darkness of this world and enlighten us with the light of faith; make us, who were condemned by the law, the children of your grace.

You came into the world to execute a judgment by which those who do not see, are called to see, and those who see become blind, in such a way that anyone who acknowledges the darkness of his errors receives eternal light and is freed from the shadow of sin. Those who boast of their personal merits, who are enveloped in pride and in their own kind of justice, never think of resorting to you, the divine physician who can save them—to you, O Jesus, who said: I am the gate for going to the Father.

Then come to us, O Jesus, to all of us who pray in your sanctuary, and heal us. We lay bare our wounds before your majesty; cure our infirmities. Come to our assistance, as you promised you would do for those who pray to you, O you have drawn us out of nothingness. Prepare a healing salve and anoint the eyes of our hearts and bodies, for fear that blindness may make us fall again into the darkness of error. We wash your feet with our tears; do not disdain our humiliation. O good Jesus who came to us in humility, we do not want to stray from your footsteps any longer. Listen to the prayer we all make: Dispel the darkness of our sins, grant us to contemplate the glory of your face in the blessedness of eternal peace.

cf *Eucharistic Prayers,* 90

YEAR C

O Lord of peace, give us peace at all times in all ways (2 Thes 3:16)

Peace stands out as the theme of today's readings, where it is presented in its multiple aspects.

The first reading (Is 66:10-14c) speaks of peace as a compound of good things—joy, security, prosperity, tranquility, consolation—promised by God to Jerusalem when it should be restored after the Babylonian exile. "Behold I will extend prosperity to her like a river, and the wealth of the nations like an overflowing stream . . . As one whom his mother comforts, so I will comfort you" (ib. 12-13). It seems clear from the context that we are dealing with a divine gift that is characteristic of the messianic age. Jesus will be the bearer of this peace which is at the same time grace, salvation and eternal happiness, not for individuals only, but for all the people of God coming together from every part of the world to the heavenly Jerusalem, the kingdom of perfect peace.

Then too, the Church, the new earthly Jerusalem, which already possesses the treasure of peace offered by Jesus to men of good will, has the duty of spreading it throughout the world. This was the mission which the Savior entrusted to the seventy-two disciples when he sent them to preach the kingdom of God (Gospel: Lk 10:1-12,17-20). "Behold I send you out as lambs in the midst of wolves" (ib. 3). Such a comparison indicates a mission of gentleness, goodness and peace, like that of Jesus, "the Lamb of God, who takes away the sin of the world" (Jn 1:29), who does not condemn sinners, but immolates himself, "and makes peace by the blood of his cross" (Col 1:20).

"Whatever house you enter, first say: 'Peace be to this house!' And if a son of peace is there, your peace shall rest upon him; but if not, it shall return to you" (Lk 10:5-6). It is not a question here of a simple greeting of good wishes, but of a divine blessing which of itself brings good things and salvation. Where the peace of Jesus, who has reconciled men with God and with each other, "comes down," salvation comes down. Those who welcome it are at peace with God and with their fellow men, they live in grace and love, and are saved from sin. This peace rests upon "the children of peace," that is, upon those who, after being called to salvation by God, correspond with his invitation by accepting its requirements; these are the fortunate heirs of Christ's peace, of messianic blessings. However, Jesus admonished us not to expect a peace like that offered by the world, an illusory promise of happiness exempt of all evil. He said: "Let not your hearts be troubled; neither let them be afraid" (Jn 14:27), because his peace is so deep that it can co-exist even with most severe tribulations. The world may scoff at and reject this peace, but his disciples, though hurt by this rejection, neither lose their interior peace, nor abandon their zeal for the "gospel of peace" (Eph 6:15). They are humble, poor, unpretentious, content with what suffices for the necessities of life (Lk 10:4,7-8); they continue Jesus' mission in the world by bringing "the good news of peace" (Acts 10:36) to all who are willing to welcome it.

St. Paul is the prototype in this (2nd reading: Gal 6:14-18). He sought no other support or glory in his apostolate save "in the cross of our Lord Jesus Christ" (ib. 14) by which he considered himself crucified to all that the world could offer: material benefits, glory, career. The world had no fascination for him who had been enchanted by the Crucified, and he was happy to bear on his body the "marks of Jesus" (ib. 17). Thus he had the right to be left in peace, in the peace of his Lord which he had implored for himself and for all who would follow his example: "Peace and mercy be upon all who walk by this rule" (ib. 16).

O God, who by the humiliation of your Son have raised a fallen world, give us your joy, that being freed from the oppression of sin, we may enjoy happiness without end.

Roman Missal, 14th Week Collect

O Lord Jesus Christ, all-powerful God, king of glory, you are the
true peace, eternal charity. We beg you to illuminate the depths of
our souls with the light of your peace, and to purify our consciences
with the sweetness of your love. Grant that we may be persons of
peace, who desire you, the prince of peace, and may be continually
protected and guarded by you from the world's dangers. Under the
shelter of your benevolence, help us seek peace with all the strength
of our hearts, so that you can welcome us into eternal joy when you
return to reward those who have merited it.

Lord Jesus Christ, you are the peace of every man; those who
find you, find rest; those who abandon you, are struck by the bit-
terest of evils. We beg you, Lord, never to let us give the kiss of
Judas; give us the peace that you commanded your apostles to
spread abroad. Throughout the course of our earthly life, let your
Church always find us to be men of peace, who praise your goodness
and may be able one day to share the happiness that knows no end.
Eucharistic Prayers 64a, 93

242. GOD, SUPREME SIMPLICITY

O Lord, that I may learn to seek you with sincerity of heart (Wis 1:1)

1. God is the unique simple Being because he is one in his
essence and in all his perfections. When St. Thomas speaks of
God's simplicity, he presents it as the absence of all that is com-
posite. In God there are not quantitative parts as there are in us
who are composed of body and soul. God is simple because in him
there is no matter; he is pure spirit. God is supreme simplicity
because in him essence and existence are not distinct; his essence
exists of itself, he is eternally subsistent. Neither do his innumerable perfections create any multiplicity. God is not composed of goodness, truth, wisdom, justice, but he is, at the same
time, goodness, truth, wisdom, justice par excellence. In God,
goodness and truth have met, justice and peace have kissed
(Ps 85:11). There is no distinction in him between substance and
quality, because all is substance; his infinite perfections are his
very substance. God contains in the one, unique and most simple
perfection of his divine Being, all the multiple perfections we find
divided among creatures and infinite other perfections beyond
these. God's simplicity is not, then, poverty, but infinite richness,
infinite perfection, which we ourselves ought to reflect.

God is rich in innumerable perfections and possesses them all
in the same degree. Man, on the contrary, is extremely poor in virtues, and if he has any at all, they are always limited and
restricted and mixed with faults; moreover, for one virtue we
possess in some slight degree, how many others we lack. God is
simple, we, on the other hand are so complicated. If we want to

simplify ourselves, we must contemplate the divine simplicity and try as hard as we can to imitate it by means of true simplicity of soul. "Seek the Lord with a simple heart," sacred Scripture advises; that is, with an upright heart that is incapable of subterfuge or ulterior motivation. No distortion escapes God, he knows our every sentiment. "I know, my God, that you try the heart, and have pleasure in uprightness" (1 Chron 29:17).

2. In God, being is not distinct from acting; there is no difference between potency and act. He is pure act, the act of an infinite intelligence which always subsists and desires the good. There is no admixture of error in God's eternal thought; there are no deviations toward evil in the eternal will of God. In God, there is no succession of thoughts, but only one single, eternal, immutable, subsistent thought which comprehends all truth. In God, there are no separate acts of the will which follow one another, but one single act, perfect and immutable, always willing the good with a most pure intention and if it permits evil, it does so only with a view to a greater good.

If we wish to approach in some way to divine simplicity, we must avoid every form of duplicity. We must avoid duplicity of mind by a dispassionate search for the truth, loving and accepting the truth even when it exacts sacrifice or if, by revealing our defects and errors, it is not to our credit. We must also cultivate the most candid sincerity, fleeing from every form of falsehood. Jesus said: "Let what you say be simply "yes" or "no" (Mt 5:37).

We shall avoid duplicity of the will by rectitude of intention: this will lead us to act solely to please God. Then even in the multiplicity of our acts, there will be simplicity and profound unity. Then we will not halt between two sides: between love of self and love of God, between creatures and the Creator, but we will walk on one road only, the straight road of duty, of God's will and good pleasure.

> *O God, in your unique and simple being, you are all the powers and grandeurs of your attributes. You are almighty, wise, and good; and you are merciful, just, powerful and loving, together with all the other infinite powers and attributes of which we have no knowledge. You are all of this in your simple being . . .*
>
> *O abyss of delight! You are so much the more abundant the more your riches are concentrated in the infinite unity and simplicity of your unique being, where one attribute is so known and enjoyed as not to hinder the perfect knowledge and enjoyment of the other; rather, each grace and virtue within you is a light for each of your other grandeurs. By your purity, O divine Wisdom, many things are beheld in you through one. For you are the deposit of the Father's treasures, the splendor of the eternal light, the unspotted mirror and image of his goodness.*
>
> St. John of the Cross, *Living Flame* III 2, 17

Give me, O Lord, that pure and perfect love that transforms the soul ... into your simplicity and purity. Then I shall see only you, and I shall find you everywhere without having to seek you, because I shall possess you and be everlastingly united to you. There will no longer be anything that really disturbs me or makes me suffer, because I shall find the savor of life in everything and shall rejoice in you, O my God ... O how beautiful is this life of love! ... O Holy Spirit, Spirit of Love, mutual and substantial Love of the Father and the Word, how I beg you ... to inflame me wholly, transform me completely, make your influence reach every least part of my being! ...

Teach me to utter only words that are inspired by you, make them reflections of the Word, directed only to the glory of the Father, without any human regard or respect, without false compassion, or natural indulgence, far removed from any adulation and any falsehood, but with great frankness and sincerity, without ever offending charity.

Sr. Carmela of the Holy Spirit

243. GOD DOES NOT CHANGE

O Lord, "your throne is established from of old; you are from everlasting"   *(Ps 93:2)*

1. All things created are subject to change, to variation, progress, decline and finally to death. Only God, uncreated life, remains eternally unchanged, without any shadow of alteration. "Heaven and earth will perish"—says the psalmist—"but you endure ... You are the same, and your years have no end" (Ps 102:26-27). St. Augustine puts it clearly: "Your years are as a single day; and your day comes not daily, but is today, a today which does not yield place to any tomorrow or follow upon any yesterday" (Conf XI 13). There is no succession of time in God, only an eternal now.

In God "there is no variation or shadow due to change" (Jas 1:17). God does not change and cannot change, because he is infinite and eternal. Being infinite, he possesses being and every perfection without limit; in him there is no limit, no beginning or end. Our souls, although created, will not die with our bodies; therefore, they are immortal, but not eternal, for they had a beginning; this, however, is not true in regard to God, who always was and always will be. Every perfection in man is subject to further development and progress; God, on the contrary, possesses every perfection in the highest degree, that is, in an absolutely infinite degree, to which nothing can be added.

Man, precisely because he is limited, is very much subject to change and variation; his opinions, tastes, desires, and his will, all change. In God there is nothing of all this: "I the Lord do not change" (Mal 3:6). His mind does not change because his infinite wisdom is immutable, embracing at once all truth, and only truth. His will does not change because it is an infinite will for good, always and indefectibly willing good, the greatest, absolute, infinite good.

How much we need to unite our inconstant and changeable will to the immutable will of God! The more we try to will only what God wills, to love only what he loves, the more will our will be freed from its inconstancy and become fixed in good.

2. St. Augustine says: "God was in the past, is in the present, and will be in the future. He *was* because he never was not; he *will be* because he will never cease to exist; he *is* because he always exists." This is a beautiful commentary on the well-known catechism answer: "God always was and always will be; he is eternal." God's eternity "is the possession of a full perfect life, an interminable life" (Boezio, De Cons. V 6). It is a full perfect life which subsists by itself with infinite power, vigor and perfection; an interminable life which has no beginning and no end, which is not susceptible to any succession, or mutation because God possesses the fullness of his infinite life *"tota simul,"* all simultaneously in an eternal now.

The immutability and eternity of God are not, then, something materially static and motionless, like fixed matter, which indicates negation rather than affirmation, but are characteristics of the greatest vitality. They are the fullness of an infinite, most perfect life in which there is no possibility of change or variation because it has in itself all possible perfection.

We, limited, changeable, mortal beings, live in time, and are subject to the succession of time, yet we are not created for time, but for eternity. God has destined us to share some day his divine immutability and eternity; therefore we must live oriented toward our eternal destiny, without letting ourselves be caught up in and detained by what is transitory and contingent. Vatican II exhorts: "On our Lord's advice, we must constantly stand guard. Thus when we have finished the one and only course of our earthly life, we may merit to enter into the marriage feast with him and to be numbered among the blessed . . . and may not be commanded to go into eternal fire . . . into the exterior darkness where 'there will be the weeping and gnashing of teeth' (Mt 22:13; 25:30)" (LG 48). For the Christian the purpose of time is to prepare for eternal happiness.

> *Your years, O Lord, endure throughout all generations! Of old you laid the foundation of the earth, and the heavens are the work of your hands. They perish, but you endure; they will all wear out like a garment. You change them like raiment, and they pass away; but you are the same, and your years have no end.*
>
> *Psalm* 102:24-27

Lord, you are always the same, and your years shall not fail. Your years neither go nor come, but our years come and go, that all may come. Your years abide all in one act of abiding; for they abide and the years that go are not thrust out by those that come, for none pass; whereas our years shall not all be, till all are no more. Your years are as a single day; and your day comes not daily but is today, a today which does not yield place to any tomorrow or follow upon any yesterday. Your today is eternity.

But now my years are wasted in sighs, and you, O Lord, my eternal Father, are my only solace; but I am divided up in time, whose order I do not know, and my thoughts and the deepest places of my soul are torn with every kind of tumult until the day when I shall be purified and melted in the fire of your love and wholly joined to you.

O Lord my God, how deep is the abyss of your secret, and how far from it have the consequences of my sins held me! Cleanse my eyes and let me rejoice in your light ... You are the immutable and eternal ... In the beginning you knew heaven and earth without any element of change in your knowledge; and similarly in the beginning you created heaven and earth without any element of change in your action. Let him who understands praise you, and let him who does not understand praise you likewise. You are the highest, and the humble of heart are your dwelling place. For you lift up them that are cast down, and those who do not fall have you for their high place.

St. Augustine, Confessions XI 13:16; 29:39; 31:41

244. HIS LOVE ENDURES FOREVER

I praise you Lord, for you are good, for your steadfast love endures
forever (Ps 106:1)

1. When Moses asked God to show him his glory, God replied: "I will make all my goodness pass before you" (Ex 33:19), as if to say that his glory is infinite goodness, the good that he possesses in such plenitude, that all good is in him and no good exists independently of him. God possesses good, not because he has received it from anyone, but because he himself is, by his nature, the sovereign good, because his Being is infinite goodness. If creatures are good, they are so, only because God has communicated to them a little of his goodness. Of itself, the creature cannot even exist, therefore it cannot possess any good of its own. That is why when the young man called him: "Good Teacher," Jesus said: "Why do you call me good? No one is good but God alone" (Mk 10:18). Only of God can it be said that he is good, in the sense that he is goodness itself, that goodness belongs to him by nature, as divinity belongs to him by nature; and just as it is impossible for his divinity to be lessened, so it is impossible for his goodness to be lessened. Heaven, earth, and the ages will pass away, but "his goodness endures forever" (Ps 106:1). Man's wickedness may accumulate sin upon sin, evil upon evil, but over all, God's goodness will remain unchangeable. The shadow of evil will not mar it; instead, God who is always benevolent, will bend over the evil to change it into good. Thus infinite goodness stooped over man, the sinner, and made an immensely superior good come from Adam's fall: the redemption of the world through the incarnation of his only-begotten Son. This is the distinctive character of God's goodness: to will the good, only the good, even to the point of drawing good from evil. Let us praise the Lord, "for he is good, for his steadfast love endures for ever!" (1 Chron 16:34).

2. "And God saw everything he had made, and behold, it was very good" (Gen 1:31). God, who is supremely good in himself, is also good in all his works; everything that has come from the hand of God bears the imprint of his goodness. The sun which illumines and warms the earth is good, the earth which brings forth flowers and fruit is good, the sea is good, the sky is good, the stars are good. "The works of God are all of them good" (Sir 39:33), because they spring from essential, infinite, eternal goodness.

But God has willed that among his creatures there should be some (such as man) who besides being good because he created them so, might also be good because of the adherence of their free will to that goodness which he has diffused in them. This is the great honor given by God to man: not only has he created him good, as he created heaven and earth good, but he has desired that man's goodness should result from the free concurrence of his will, as if God made him owner of the goodness he had placed in him. This is just why God has given man the great gift of liberty. We can understand, then, how far we withdraw from goodness when we use our free will to choose not good, but evil, and what an immense distance there is between God and us. God is infinite goodness to the extreme of drawing good even out of evil, whereas our profound malice is capable of making use of the good of our liberty to follow our egoism, our pride, our passions, and hence to offend God. Yet it would not be hard for us to be good if we adhered to that interior impulse toward good which God has placed within us, if we allowed the good he has infused into our hearts to develop.

God created us good; he desires us to be good. It is true that our malice—the consequence of sin—is great, but his infinite goodness immensely surpasses it. He can cure it or destroy it altogether, provided that we detest it. "You, O Lord, are good and forgiving, abounding in steadfast love to all who call on you" (Ps 86:5).

> *Your steadfast love, O Lord, extends to the heavens, your faithfulness to the clouds. Your righteousness is like the mountains of God, your judgments are like the great deep... How precious is your steadfast love, O God! Men take refuge in the shadow of your wings... With you is the fountain of life; in your light do we see light."*
>
> *Psalm 36:6-10*

> *My God, I adore you, as holy without, as well as holy within. I adore you as holy in all your works as well as in your own nature. No creature can approach your incommunicable sanctity, but you approach, and touch, and compass, and possess all creatures. And nothing lives but in you, and nothing have you created but what is good.*
>
> *I adore you, as having made everything good after its kind. I adore you, as having infused your preserving and sustaining power into all things, while you created them, so that they continue to live, though you do not touch them, and do not crumble back into nothing. I adore you, as having put real power into them, so that they are able to act, although from you and with you and yet of themselves.*
>
> *I adore you as having given power to will what is right, and your holy grace to your rational creatures. I adore you as having created man upright, and having bountifully given him an integrity of nature, and having filled him with your free grace, so that he was like an angel upon earth; and I adore you still more, for having given him your grace over again in still more copious measure, and with far more lasting fruits, through your eternal Son incarnate. In all your works you are holy, O my God, and I adore you in them all.*

You are holy in all your works, O Lord, and, if there is sin in the world it is not from you—it is from an enemy, it is from me and mine. To me, to man, be the shame, for we might will what is right, and we will what is evil. What a gulf there is between you and me, O my Creator! . . .

Your cross, O Lord, shows the distance that is between you and me, while it takes it away. It shows both my great sinfulness and your utter abhorrence of sin. Impart to me, my dear Lord, the doctrine of the cross in its fullness, that it may not only teach me my alienation from you, but convey to me the virtue of your reconciliation.

J.H. Newman, *Meditations on Christian Doctrine* XI

245. GOD'S GOODNESS IS DIFFUSIVE

I thank you, Lord, for your steadfast love, for your wonderful works to the sons of men   *(Ps 107:8)*

1. Goodness is not confined within itself; the greater the good, the more it tends to diffuse itself. God is the supreme good; therefore he diffuses himself sovereignly. He diffuses himself first in himself, in the bosom of the Blessed Trinity: the Father communicates to the Son all his divinity—essence, life, goodness and divine beatitude; the Father and the Son together communicate this to the Holy Spirit. The mystery of the Blessed Trinity, the intimate life of God, consists precisely in this essential, total, unceasing and absolute communication. In it we have the supreme expression of the axiom *"Bonum diffusivum sui."* Good is diffusive of itself.

But infinite goodness wills to pour itself out exteriorly also; thus God calls into existence an immense number of creatures to whom he communicates, in varying ways and degrees, some of his own goodness. God does not create creatures because he has need of them, for they can add nothing to his beatitude and essential glory. "He is from all eternity one and the same. In him "nothing can be added, or taken away" (Sir 42:21); he has no need of anything or anybody. In creation "God seeks only to communicate his own perfection, which is his own goodness. Only he is supremely generous, because he acts not for his own gain, but only out of his goodness" (St Thos 1,44,4). God wills creatures not because of any goodness or loveliness already in them, but because in creating them, he gives them a share in his own good and makes them lovable. God's goodness is so great that it can communicate itself to an infinite number of creatures without being diminished; it is so diffusive that it makes all it touches good. Confronted with this the psalmist exclaims: "O give thanks to the Lord of Lords . . . to him who alone does great wonders, for his steadfast love endures for ever" (Ps 136:3-4).

The goodness of God is the cause of our being and of our life: when we were created, it left its imprint on us, and it is always and unceasingly penetrating and enveloping us. Let us examine our heart to see if it has preserved the imprint of the divine goodness.

2. God's goodness is so gratuitous that it gives itself to creatures without any merit on their part; it is so liberal that it always precedes them and never fails to impart its light to them even when, by abusing their liberty, they show themselves unworthy of it: "He does not deal with us according to our sins, nor requite us according to our iniquities. For as the heavens are high above the earth, so great is his steadfast love toward those who fear him" (Ps 103:10-11). God has every right to requite man's sins by depriving him of life and all other good things, but his infinite goodness prefers to respond with new gifts, and new proofs of his kindness. Has he not said: "I have no pleasure in the death of the wicked, but that the wicked turn from his way and live" (Ex 33:11). The Book of Wisdom exclaims: "You spare all things because they are yours, O Lord and lover of souls" (11:26).

Anyone who compares his own goodness with that of God's is quickly aware how very weak, narrow, calculating and self-interested it is. How often we Christians are like those publicans of whom the Gospel speaks, who only love those who love them (cf Mt 5:46). We are good to those who will help us in return; but how many times we are hard and miserly with our gifts to those from whom we can expect no recompense. Does it not often happen that we are sweet and benevolent toward those who approve of us and share our opinions, but harsh and unkind toward those who oppose us? In the presence of coldness, ingratitude, insults, or even a trifling lack of consideration, our goodness closes up, and withdraws into itself and we are no longer capable of benevolence toward our neighbor.

See how infinitely dissimilar our goodness is to that of God's. See what need we have to meditate on the goodness of our heavenly Father: "Love your enemies and pray for those who persecute you, so that you may be sons of your Father who is in heaven; for he makes his sun rise on the evil and on the good, and sends rain on the just and on the unjust" (ib. 44-45).

> *Give thanks to the Lord, for he is good, for his steadfast love endures forever ... Give thanks to the Lord of lords, for his steadfast love endures for ever; to him who alone does great wonders, for his steadfast love endures for ever; to him who by understanding made the heavens, for his steadfast love endures for ever; to him who spread out the earth upon the waters, for his steadfast love endures for ever; to him who made the great lights, for his steadfast love endures for ever; the sun to rule over the day, for his steadfast love endures for ever; the moon and the stars to rule over the night, for his steadfast love endures for ever ...*

It is he who remembered us in our low estate, for his steadfast love endures for ever; and rescued us from our foes, for his steadfast love endures for ever; he who gives food to all flesh, for his steadfast love endures for ever.

Psalm 136:1-9; 23-25

O inestimable charity, sweet above all sweetness! Who would not be inflamed by such great love? What heart can help breaking at such tenderness? It seems, O abyss of charity, as if you were mad with love of your creature, as if you could not live without him, and yet you are our God who have no need of us. Your greatness does not increase through our good, for you are unchangeable, and our evil causes you no harm, for you are the supreme and eternal goodness. What moves you to do us such mercy through pure love, and on account of no debt that you owe us, or need that you have of us? We are rather your guilty and wicked debtors.

Can a wretch like me pay back to you the graces and the burning charity that you have shown and show with so much burning love in particular to me, beyond the common charity and the love that you show to all your creatures? No, but you alone, most sweet and amorous Father, are he who will be thankful and grateful for me, that is, that the affection of your charity itself will render you thanks, because I am she who is not, and if I spoke as being anything of myself, I should be lying ... because you alone are he who is. And my being and every further grace that you have bestowed upon me, I have from you, who give them to me through love, and not as my due.

St. Catherine of Siena, *Dialogue* 25;134

246. UNFATHOMABLE WISDOM

Lord, you are wonderful in counsel, and excellent in wisdom (Is 28:29)

1. "There is One [God] who is wise" (Sir 1:8); "his understanding is beyond measure" (Ps 147:5). In God wisdom is not distinct from being as it is in us; it is the very Being of God. Therefore, God's Being is supreme wisdom; it is a luminous, resplendent, eternally subsistent ray of intelligence which embraces and penetrates all the divine essence, and at the same time sees in it, as in their cause, all things which have existed or ever can exist. Divine wisdom, says sacred Scripture, "because of her pureness pervades and penetrates all things. For she is a breath of the power of God, and a pure emanation of the glory of the Almighty ... a reflection of eternal light, a spotless mirror of the working of God, and an image of his goodness" (Wis 7:24-26).

Divine wisdom is, before all, perfect knowledge of God. No

creature, not even the angels or the blessed in heaven, can know God to the point of exhausting the depths of the infinite greatness of his Being: God alone knows himself perfectly. Although we are incapable of knowing God as he really is, it is an immense joy for us to contemplate the divine wisdom which penetrates all the divine mysteries, and an immense comfort to invoke it that it may be our true light. "Lord of mercy, . . . give me wisdom . . . that may guide and guard me . . . Who has learned your counsel, unless you have given wisdom and sent your Holy Spirit" (Wis 9:1-11,17).

Divine wisdom sees all things; it "knows and understands all things" (Wis 7:23; 9:11). It can never be in error for it "is unfailing" (Wis 6:12). Nothing can be hidden from it, for it has created all things and penetrates their inmost essence; there is nothing new which it can learn because from all eternity it sees everything in an eternal present; nothing can escape its penetrating light. "Even the hairs of your head are all numbered" said Jesus (Mt 10:30). God knows us much better than we know ourselves; the most secret movements of our hearts, even those which escape our control, are perfectly manifest to him. Let us ask him for the grace to know ourselves in his light, in his eternal truth and wisdom.

2. Divine wisdom knows all things in God, in reference to him, who is their first cause. It sees all things as depending upon God and ordained by him to his glory; therefore, it does not judge them according to their outward appearances, but solely according to the value and meaning they have in God's eyes. Consequently, the judgments of divine wisdom are vastly different from our short human judgments which stop at the purely material aspect of things. "For as the heavens are higher than the earth"—says the Lord—"so are my ways higher than your ways and my thoughts than your thoughts" (Is 55:9). And St. Paul exclaims: "Oh the depth of the riches and wisdom and knowledge of God! How unsearchable are his judgments and how inscrutable his ways!" (Rom 11:33).

To know created things in their relation to God, and to esteem them according to the value they have in his eyes, is true wisdom which only God can give for "all wisdom comes from the Lord" (Sir 1:1). To judge creatures and events only from a human standpoint, basing our judgment solely on the joy or displeasure they give us "is folly with God" (1 Cor 3:19), precisely because it evaluates things according to their relation to man, and not in relation to God, judging them according to their appearances and not according to their reality. Only by accustoming ourselves to go beyond our human viewpoint will we be able to discover, in the light of faith, the significance and the value they have in the eyes of God. Then we will clearly see that everything that the world holds in high esteem—such as great talents, success, the respect of creatures, etc.—are as nothing in the eyes of divine wisdom, which deems the slightest degree of grace far superior to all the natural perfections of the universe (St. Thos. 1-2,113,9,2).

The humble consideration of our own foolishness should make us feel more keenly than ever the need of invoking divine Wisdom: "If any of you lacks wisdom, let him ask God, who gives to all men generously . . . and it will be given him" (Jas 1:5). Wisdom "renews all things . . . in every generation she passes into holy souls and makes them friends of God . . . for God loves nothing so much as the man who lives with wisdom" (Wis 7:27-28).

O divine wisdom, you are a breath of the power of God, and a pure emanation of the glory of the Almighty; therefore nothing defiled gains entrance into you. For you are a reflection of eternal light, a spotless mirror of the working of God, and an image of his goodness. Though you are but one, you can do all things, and while remaining in yourself, you renew all things; in every generation you pass into holy souls and make them friends of God and prophets; for God loves nothing so much as the man who lives with wisdom.

O God of my fathers and Lord of mercy, who made all things by your word, and by your wisdom formed man to have dominion over the creatures you have made, and rule the world in holiness and righteousness, and pronounce judgment in uprightness of soul, give me the wisdom that sits by your throne, and do not reject me from among your servants. For I am your slave and the son of your maidservant, a man who is weak and short-lived . . . For even if one is perfect among the sons of men, yet without the wisdom that comes from you he will be regarded as nothing . . .

For with you is wisdom, who knows your works and was present when you made the world, and who understands what is pleasing in your sight and what is right according to your commandments. Send her forth from the holy heavens, and from the throne of your glory send her, that she may be with me and toil, and that I may learn what is pleasing to you. For she knows and understands all things, and she will guide me wisely in my actions and guard me with her glory; then my works will be acceptable . . .

For what man can learn the counsel of God? Or who can discern what the Lord wills? For the reasoning of mortals is worthless, and our designs are likely to fail, for a perishable body weighs down the soul, and this earthly tent burdens the thoughtful mind. We can hardly guess at what is on earth, and what is at hand we find with labor; but who has traced out what is in the heavens? Who has learned your counsel, unless you have given wisdom, and sent your holy Spirit from on high?

Wisdom 7:25-28; 9:1-6,9-17

247. GOD IS LOVE

O God, who are love, make me know and believe in your love (1 Jn 4:16)

1. "God is love" (1 Jn 4:16), eternal, infinite, substantial love. Just as everything in God is beautiful, good, perfect, and holy, so everything in God is love: his beauty, holiness, wisdom, truth, omnipotence and even his justice are love. Love in God is the eternal act of his will, a most holy, perfect act, because it is always directed to the sovereign Good; this is the love with which God loves himself, precisely because he is the one supreme and eternal Good, to which no other good can be preferred.

The holy and infinite love which God has for himself has nothing in common with what we call self-love or egoism, that disordered love by which we prefer ourselves to God. We are selfish because we tend to love ourselves to the exclusion of every other affection; but God is so free from every shadow of egoism that, even though he loves himself infinitely and is wholly satisfied with his infinite good, he wills to diffuse his love and his good outside himself. It is thus that God loves creatures; his love is at the root of their being, for by loving them, he calls them into existence, by loving them he creates good in them. "The love of God"—says St. Thomas—"is the cause which infuses and creates good in creatures" (1,20,2). God loves with a love that is entirely gratuitous, free, and supremely pure, with a love that is at the same time benevolence which desires our good, and beneficence which does us good. By loving us God calls us to life, infuses grace in us, invites us to holiness, draws us to himself, and gives us a share in his eternal happiness. Everything we are and have is the gift of his infinite love. As Vatican II affirms: "Man would not exist were he not created by God's love and constantly preserved by it. And he cannot live fully according to truth unless he freely acknowledges that love and devotes himself to his Creator" (GS 19).

2. "I have loved you with an everlasting love; therefore I have continued my faithfulness to you" (Jer 31:3). We were nothing, but God already saw us and loved us and wanted us; his love has gone before him from all eternity. No creature could exist if God had not preceded it with his love: "You love all things that exist"—says sacred Scripture—"and loath nothing of the things which you have made; for you would not have made anything if you had hated it. How would anything have endured, if you had not willed it, or how would anything not called forth by you have been preserved?" (Wis 11:24-25). The story of our life is the story of God's love for us. This story, once begun, never ends because God's love has no end; sin alone, which is the rejection of divine love, has the sad possibility of interrupting it. But of himself, God loves with an infinite, eternal, immutable and most faithful love; he himself desired to express it most tenderly: "Can a woman forget her suckling child, that she should have no compassion on the son of her womb? Even these may forget, yet I will not forget you" (Is 49:15).

God loves us when he consoles us, but he also loves us when he afflicts us with sorrow; his graces and his consolations are love, so too are his trials and chastisements, "for the Lord reproves him whom he loves, as a father the son in whom he delights" (Prov 3:12). In all the circumstances of life, even the saddest and most painful, we are always encompassed by divine love, which can will nothing but good, and therefore God infallibly wills our good even when he leads us by the harsh rough road of suffering. Furthermore, it is not rare for God to strike hardest those whom he loves most, "for ... acceptable men [are tried] in the furnace of humiliation" (Sir 2:5). St. Teresa of Jesus writes: "See ... what [suffering] he gave to the one he loved most [Jesus] ... These are his gifts in this world. He gives according to the love he bears us: to those he loves more, he gives more of these gifts; to those he loves less, he gives less" (Way 32:7). Even when racked with pain, the true Christian does not waver in his faith, but repeats: "we know and believe the love God has for us" (1 Jn 4:16).

> I adore you Lord, in that infinite and most pure love of yourself, a love of your Son, and your Son's love for you, in which we conceive the procession of the Holy Ghost ...
> This, O Lord, is your ineffable and special blessedness. It is love, I adore you, O my infinite Love! And when you had created us, then you did but love more, if that were possible. You loved not only your own co-equal Self in the multiplied Personality of the Godhead, but you loved your creatures also. You were love to us, as well as Love in yourself.
> You were love to man, more than to any other creatures. It was love that brought you from heaven, and subjected you to the laws of a created nature. It was love alone which was able to conquer you, the highest—and bring you low. You died through your infinite love of sinners. And it is love, which keeps you here still, even now that you have ascended on high, in a small tabernacle, and under cheap and common outward forms ...
> O my God, I do not know what infinity means—but one thing I see, that you are loving to a depth and height far beyond any measurement of mine ... How can I help loving you with all my powers?
> J.H. Newman, *Meditations on Christian Doctrine* XI:1; X:1-3.

> O most gentle Jesus, the only good of my soul, although I may no longer feel your sweet love, I desire to love you more strongly with ever greater solicitude. But who am I to be worthy of being loved by so great and almighty a God? ...
> I desire to love you, O Lord, for you are my God, and you deserve to be loved eternally, just because of your own goodness. I want to love you because I have received from you my being and your likeness. Who was I, my God, before you made me? When I

reflect upon myself, I know that I was nothing, less than anything that is, even the tiniest worm on the ground. All the gifts I have received are from your Majesty . . . But how can I love you without love? I will love you, O Redeemer of my soul, by keeping your divine law . . . , and I will try to please you as much as I can in everything that is in harmony with your will.

St. Charles de Sezze, *Autobiography*, VII 30, Op. v.2

248. FIFTEENTH SUNDAY OF ORDINARY TIME

YEAR A

Lord, that our eyes may see, and our ears may hear (Mt 13:16)

The central theme of today's Liturgy is the power and efficacy of God's word. "As the rain and the snow come down from heaven, and return not thither, but water the earth, making it bring forth and sprout . . ."—says the Lord—"so shall my word be that goes forth from my mouth; it shall not return to me empty, but it shall accomplish that which I purpose" (Is 55:10-11; 1st reading). God's word always effects what it expresses: a simple "fiat" is enough to draw the entire universe out of nothing, and to give life to every creature. And when man rebelled instead of responding with love to the creative word, another word, the promise of the Savior, repeated through the centuries in a thousand ways, assured man of salvation, and directed him toward it. In the fullness of time God no longer sent mankind simply words, but his eternal Word, his Son. The Word took human nature, became man, was called Jesus Christ, and came to plant the word of God in men's hearts.

The subject of today's Gospel is the parable of the sower (Mt 13:1-23). "The sower . . . who went out to sow" (ib. 13) is, in actual fact, Jesus, and the seed that he sows "is the word of God" (Lk 8:11) that he—the uncreated Word—possesses within himself and expresses to men in human language. His word, then, is of divine power and efficacy, a most fertile seed which is capable of developing into salvation, holiness, and eternal life.

Yet—says the parable—this same seed produces abundant fruit in one plot of ground, and in another produces none at all. Here we see the mystery of man's freedom before the gift of God. Jesus sows his Word everywhere: he does not withhold it even from hardened sinners, from shallow and disinterested souls, nor from those immersed in their pleasures or engulfed in business matters; the parable compares these to the beaten path, the rocky or thorn covered ground; it all bespeaks the great mercy of the Lord. In fact in the spiritual order, even "stones can change and turn into fertile soil, the beaten path can be no longer trampled down and open to all who pass by, but may become a productive field; the thorns too can disappear and permit the wheat seed to grow and bear fruit in full freedom". If such a transformation does not take place in everyone, "the fault is not with the sower, but with those who have not been willing to change their life" (St. John Chrysostom, in Mt 44:3). It is a dreadful thing, but none the less true, that man can close himself to God's word, reject it, and thereby make it ineffective for himself. Then the Word will pour out its fecundity elsewhere with an extraordinary abundance of fruit, produced "in good soil", that is, in those who "hear the Word and understand it" (Mt 13:23), and consequently, put it into practice. But even in these cases the fruit will not be equal, but proportioned to the dispositions of each, yielding "in one case a hundredfold, in another sixty, and in another thirty" (ib.). Therefore, even before explaining the parable, Jesus reminded his disciples of what Isaiah had said of his contemporaries: "For this people's heart has grown dull, and their ears are heavy of hearing, and their eyes they have closed, lest they ... understand with their heart and turn for me to heal them" (ib. 15). It is truly something to reflect upon and pray about, that God's mercy may preserve his faithful from a like hardness. On the other hand, it is certain that whoever listens to the word of God with a willing heart will obtain fruit and enjoy the happiness proclaimed by the Lord: "Blessed ... are your eyes, for they see, and your ears for they hear" (ib. 16).

> "Behold the sower went out to sow". Whence did you go out, or how did you go out, Lord, for you are present everywhere and fill everything? When you came to us and took flesh, you certainly did not do it by passing from one place to another, but by assuming human nature and putting yourself in touch with us in a new contact. Since we could not enter there where God dwells, for our sins were like a wall that blocked our way, you came to us yourself. Why did you come?... You came to cultivate and care for this ground and to plant there the word of virtue and love ...
>
> O Jesus, you generously offered your word and your teaching to all. Just as the sower makes no distinction in the ground upon which he works, but simply broadcasts his seed everywhere, so you, in your preaching, make no distinction between the rich, the poor, the wise or the ignorant, the fervent, the lazy, the brave or the cowardly, but speak indiscriminately to all.
>
> Lord, make me listen attentively to your word, and constantly remember your teaching, so that I may put it into practice forcefully and courageously, despising riches and dismissing all the anxieties of worldly life ... Strengthen me on every side and help me to meditate upon your word, putting down deep roots and purifying myself of all worldly attachments.
>
> St. John Chrysostom, *Commentary on Gospel of St. Matthew* 44:3-4

YEAR B

Let me hear what God the Lord will speak, for he will speak peace to his people (Ps 85:9)

Fifteenth Sunday of Ordinary Time

The plan of salvation, which is set forth in today's second reading (Eph 1:3-14), can serve as a starting point for a meditation on the Liturgy of the Word. St. Paul goes back to the eternal call of the faithful to salvation, those who are blessed in Christ and "chosen in him before the foundation of the world" (ib. 4), predestined by God "to be his sons" (ib. 5). This magnificent design of mercy is accomplished "through Jesus Christ"; it is his blood that redeems us from sin and confers upon us "the riches of his grace" (ib. 7). But it also requires the cooperation of each individual: the faith and the personal pledge to "be holy and blameless before God in charity" (ib. 4). It is obvious that after having received so many benefits—"the word of truth, the gospel of ... salvation" (ib. 13)—we should be messengers among our brothers. No one should think that the call to salvation is completely answered by taking care of our personal welfare; that would no longer be Christian holiness, which is realized in the charity of Christ who gave his life for the redemption of the entire human race, in the love of his heavenly Father, which embraces all men. Every Christian is expected, though not all in the same manner, to spread "the gospel of salvation" to others.

However there are some who receive a special mandate: the prophets and the apostles, of whom both the first reading and the gospel passage speak (Mk 6:7-13). It is God who calls them, choosing them with absolute freedom from all categories of persons, with a marked preference for the simplest and humblest. Look at Amos, not chosen from among the professional prophets, but from the herdsmen. "The Lord took me from following the flock, and said to me: 'Go, prophesy to my people Israel' " (Amos 7:15). God sent him to a strange land to preach justice, for which he was hated by the priests of that place who would have liked to expel him. But Amos was not deterred, strong in the awareness of his divine calling which obliged him to speak out freely to all; he did not seek his own advantage, nor try to ingratiate himself with men, but only to bring them the word of God.

Look at the Apostles, chosen by Jesus from the humble folk of the nation, and made sharers in his mission and in his authority. "And he called to him the Twelve, and began to send them out two by two" (Mk 6:7), charging them to preach conversion, as well as empowering them to expel demons and to cure the sick. He required them to behave as simply and unselfishly as possible, to take nothing with them for their journey that was not strictly necessary, to reserve nothing for their own sustenance and instead, put their trust in the providence of the heavenly Father who would provide for them through the hospitality—more or less generous—that would be offered them at the places they would visit. Though the conditions and practices of modern society may not permit a literal adherence to these norms, it is still necessary to preserve a spirit of poverty and detachment. Because they are collaborators with him who came to preach the gospel to the poor, the apostles of all times must travel as he did, poor among the poor, rich only in the vocation they have received and in the grace and spirit of Christ. When the gospel is not preached in this way—unselfishly, with total dedication—it is not accepted, nor does it convince. On the other hand, those who hear the word of God also have a duty to accomplish: to accept this word readily, recognizing the prophet or apostle as God's messenger, and charitably providing for his needs, "for the laborer deserves his food" (Mt 10:10). Those who reject and will not listen to the Lord's ministers, resist grace and exclude themselves from the way of salvation.

God, you desire all men to be saved and to come to the knowledge of the truth; your harvest is ripe: watch over it, O Lord, and send laborers into it, that your Gospel may be preached to every creature; and that your people, gathered together by the word of life and made strong by your sacraments, may walk the way of salvation and love.

Roman Missal, *Mass for the Spread of the Gospel*, A

As for me, Father, almighty God, the first duty of which I am conscious, is that every word and thought of mine should express only you. The gift of speech comes to me from you. It cannot bring me any different or greater joy than that of serving you and of proclaiming to the world that does not know it, and to the heretic who denies it, that you are the Father, the Father of the only Son of God. This is my whole ambition.

For the rest, I beg your help, your mercy, so that it may unfurl the sails of our faith and of our Christian profession through the breath of your Spirit. Help us to open ourselves out, to be better able to make your message known, for your promise is unfailing: "Ask and you shall receive, seek and you shall find, knock and it shall be opened to you."

Therefore we turn to you in our poverty; we shall search the words of your prophets and apostles with persevering effort, and knock on all the closed doors of our understanding. It belongs to you alone to grant what we are asking, to make present what we are seeking, to open where we are knocking.

St. Hilary of Poitiers, *On the Trinity* I, 37

YEAR C

Lord, may your word be in my mouth and in my heart, so that I may do it (Dt 30:14)

God's law is the axis around which today's Liturgy revolves. "You will obey the voice of the Lord your God, keeping his commandments and his statutes" (Dt 30:10). God did not remain aloof from the life of man, but stooped down to him, set up a covenant with him, and made his will known in the law. It was not an abstract law, imposed solely from without, but inscribed in the heart of man from the first moment of creation; hence it was a law in harmony with his nature, responding to his essential needs, and suited to leading him toward full realization of himself according to God's purpose for him. "For this commandment which I command you this day"—says the sacred text—"is not too hard for you, neither is it far off ... But the word is very near you; it is in your mouth and in your heart, so that you can do it" (ib. 11:14). The word then became inexpressibly near to man when God's eternal Word, his only Son, was made flesh and came to set up his dwelling among men, revealing to them in the fullest way the divine will as set forth in the Commandments, teaching them how to practice these with perfection.

The Gospel of the day (Lk 10:25-37) shows us Jesus in conversation with a doctor of the law about the greatest commandment: love for God and for our neighbor. He questioned the Master, not from a desire to learn, but "to put him to the test" (ib. 25); he ended his inquiry by asking: "And who is my neighbor?" (ib. 29). Jesus did not answer with a definition, but with the story of a poor fellow who had been set upon by brigands, and robbed, and left half dead by the roadside. Two men passed him by—a priest and a Levite—they saw him, but went on their way without bothering to do anything for him; only a Samaritan took pity on him and stopped to help him. The conclusion is clear: we are not to make distinctions, either of religion or nationality, of friend or foe; anyone in need of help is our "neighbor" and must be loved as we each love ourselves. In addition the parable forced the doctor of the law to recognize that the law itself had been fulfilled, not by men who were especially learned in it like the priest and the Levite, but by a Samaritan whom the Jews looked upon as an unbeliever and a sinner; it was this very person who was being proposed as a model to those of pharasaic mentality who considered themselves just, sinless observers of the law. "Go and do likewise," Jesus told him. Indeed, it matters little if we know moral law perfectly and can discuss it and philosophize about it, if, in actual fact, we do not know how to put our most basic obligations into practice in cases that are as clear and urgent as the one brought out by the parable. The hardhearted and the selfish will always find a thousand excuses to shirk helping their neighbor, especially when doing so is inconvenient and requires sacrifice.

The second reading (Col 1:15-20) treats of an entirely different subject; it celebrates the greatness of Christ: his absolute supremacy over everything which had been created "through him and for him" (ib. 16), his sovereignty over men who are reconciled with God "through him" and redeemed "by the blood of his cross" (ib. 20). Yet we can see a relationship to today's Gospel: Jesus, "the image of the invisible God, the first-born of all creation," wishes to be acknowledged and loved by men in so humble and visible an image as our neighbor. "As you did it to one of the least of these my brethren, you did it to me" (Mt 25:40); this amounts to saying that a Christian must love his neighbor not only as himself, but as he is bound to love the Lord himself.

O God, you show the light of your truth to those who stray so they may be able to return to the straight way; grant that all of us who glory in the name of Christian, may reject whatever is contrary to this name, and may follow what is conformable to it.

Roman Missal, *Collect* (cf 15th Sunday)

O charity, you are that sweet and holy bond that joins the soul to its creator: you bind God to man, and man to God. O priceless charity, you held the God-man nailed to the wood of the holy cross; you overcome discord, unite the separated, and enrich those who are poor in virtue, because you give life to all the virtues. You give peace and put an end to war, you give patience, strength and long perseverance in every good and holy endeavor; you are never weary of nor diverted from the love of God and neighbor, whether by suffering or torture or insult or mockery or rudeness. You enlarge the heart that it may welcome friends and enemies and all creatures, because it is clothed with the affection of Jesus and follows him.

O Christ, sweet Jesus, grant me this priceless favor of persevering and of never being dissuaded, for whoever possesses charity is founded on you, the living stone; that is, he has learned from you how to love his Creator, by following your footsteps. In you I read the rule and the teaching that I must hold to, for you are the way, the truth, and the life; so by reading in you, who are the book of life, I shall be able to walk the straight path and attend only to the love of God and the salvation of my neighbor.

cf. St. Catherine of Siena, *Letter* 7, vol. 1

249. GOD MERCIFUL AND COMPASSIONATE

But you, O Lord, are a God merciful and gracious, slow to anger and abounding in steadfast love and faithfulness (Ps 86:15)

1. When God revealed himself to Moses, he called himself "merciful and gracious, slow to anger, and abounding in steadfast love and faithfulness; keeping steadfast love for thousands, forgiving iniquity and transgression and sin" (Ex 34:6-7). God's love for us assumes a very special character, adapted to our weakness: the character of mercy. Mercy is love bending over the miserable to relieve them, heal them, enrich them. God, who is infinite love, wishes to compensate for our indigence: by his goodness he wishes to cure our malice, by his wisdom our ignorance, by his purity our impurity, and by his strength our weakness. "As a father pities his children, so the Lord pities those who fear him. For he knows our frame, he remembers that we are

dust" (Ps 103:13-14). God hates sin, but although on its account he is forced to withdraw from us his friendship, that is, his grace, his mercy still knows how to find a way of continuing to love us. If he can no longer love us as friends he loves us as his creatures, the work of his hands; he loves us for the good that still remains in us, which gives hope of conversion. Then, when a sinner repents, God makes no delay in drawing him close with even greater affection. Turning to sinful Jerusalem, the Lord could say: "For a brief moment I forsook you, but with great compassion I will gather you. In overflowing wrath for a moment I hid my face from you, but with everlasting love I will have compassion on you" (Is 54:7-8). God's mercy is so immense that no sin, not even the most despicable, provided it is repented of, can exhaust it or halt it. Only man's own proud will which shuts him up in his own wretchedness, scorning divine mercy, has this sad power. The canticle of the Blessed Virgin recalls it to us for our warning: "The Lord ... has scattered the proud in the imagination of their hearts, he has put down the mighty from their thrones, and exalted those of low degree; he has filled the hungry with good things, and the rich he has sent away empty" (Lk 1:51-53).

"Let the wicked forsake his way ... let him return to the Lord, that he may have mercy on him" (Is 55:7). As long as we hate our sins, we shall always find mercy. God never rejects us because of our unfaithfulness, nor refuses us pardon, he does not reproach us for our offenses, not even when we fall again immediately after having been forgiven. Even when men condemn us, God absolves us and sends us away justified: "Go, and do not sin again" (Jn. 8:11). But infinite mercy can never be a pretext for falling into sin again with our eyes open, it is an invitation to acknowledge our sins with humility and to turn to God with complete confidence: "I did not hide my iniquity"—says the psalmist—"I said: 'I will confess my transgressions to the Lord'; then you forgave the guilt of my sin" (Ps 32:5). Then God's forgiveness comes down abundantly; it not only destroys the sin, but it gives back grace and restores divine friendship. "Bring quickly the best robe"—exclaims the father of the prodigal son—"put it on him, and put a ring on his hand ... and let us eat and make merry, for this my son was dead, and is alive again; he was lost, and is found" (Lk 15:22-24).

By his example and his teaching Jesus completed the revelation of God's infinite mercy; but he ended by saying: "Be merciful, even as your Father is merciful" (Lk 6:36). The measure of our mercy toward our neighbor will be the measure of God's mercy toward us, "for the measure you give will be the measure you get back" (ib. 38). In order to pour out the fullness of his mercy upon us, God does not require us to be sinless, but he does require us to be merciful to our neighbor. Only this way of acting gives us the right to trust completely in divine mercy; God will not be miserly with us, but will grant us the joy of that blessedness of which the psalmist speaks: "Blessed is he whose transgression is forgiven, whose sin is covered" (Ps 32:1).

> *O eternal mercy that covers the sins of your creatures! I do not wonder that you say of those who abandon mortal sin and return to you: 'I do not remember that you have ever offended me.' O ineffable mercy! I do not wonder that you say this to those who are converted, when you say of those who persecute you, 'I wish you to pray for such, in order that I may do them mercy.' O mercy proceeding from the Godhead, eternal Father who govern with your power the whole world, by your mercy were we created, in your mercy were we recreated in the blood of your Son. Your mercy preserves us. Your mercy caused your Son to do battle for us on the wood of the cross ... confounding death with life, and life destroying death.*
>
> *Your mercy gives life; it gives light by which your clemency is known in all your creatures, both the just and the unjust. In the height of heaven your mercy shines, that is to say, in your saints. If I turn to the earth, it abounds with your mercy. In the darkness of hell your mercy shines, for the damned do not receive the pains they deserve. With your mercy you temper justice; by mercy you have washed us in the blood, and by mercy you wish to converse with your creatures. O loving Madman! Was it not enough for you to become incarnate, that you must also die? ...*
>
> *O mercy! my heart suffocates in thinking of you, for wherever I turn my thought, on every side I find nothing but mercy. O eternal Father! forgive my ignorance, that I presume thus to speak to you, but the love of your mercy will be my excuse before the face of your loving-kindness.*

St. Catherine of Siena, *Dialogue* 30

250. THE LORD IS JUST

O Lord, give ear to my supplications. In your faithfulness answer me, in your righteousness! (Ps 143:1)

1. Addressing himself to God, the author of the Book of Wisdom declares: "You are righteous and rule all things righteously ... For your strength is the source of righteousness, and your sovereignty over all causes you to spare all ... You who are sovereign in strength judge with mildness" (Wis 12:15-18). To our limited human understanding, justice and strength seem opposed to goodness, clemency, and mercy; but in God, these attributes are so identified that it can be asserted that he is merciful because he is just, and that he is just because he is merciful. "It is because he is just"—writes St. Therese of the Child Jesus—"that God is also merciful" (Letters, 203). No one understands human weakness better than God; he knows the exact capacity of each of his creatures, and never demands anything that is beyond their strength.

Fifteenth Sunday of Ordinary Time

When sacred Scripture speaks of God's justice, it frequently couples it with his faithfulness and with his work of salvation. "Your righteousness is like the mountains of God, your judgments are like the great deep; man and beast you save, O Lord" (Ps 36:6-7). "His righteousness endures forever ... The works of his hands are faithful and just" (Ps 111:3,7). God's justice is directed not toward our perdition, but toward our good and our salvation, not so much to our earthly welfare as to our eternal good. For this reason God makes use of his justice to punish sin, so that we may amend our ways. "In fact, not to let the impious alone for long, but to punish them immediately, is a sign of great kindness ... [God] never withdraws his mercy from us. Though he disciplines us with calamities, he does not forsake his own people" (2 Macc 6:13-16). For as long as we live on earth, the purpose of God's justice is the triumph of mercy, that is, the conversion and pardon of the sinner. When God punishes, he tempers his justice with mercy, and always punishes much less than the sin deserves: "Though he cause grief, he will have compassion according to the abundance of his steadfast love; for he does not willingly afflict or grieve the sons of men" (Lam 3:32-33). It could be be said that God punishes unwillingly and really does so only as far as is necessary to bring his creatures back to good, and to assure them of eternal happiness.

2. "Every act of divine justice"—St. Thomas teaches—"always presupposes an act of mercy and is based upon this" (St. Thos. 1,21,4). For example, God would not have to provide for the necessities of human life—which is an act of justice—if he had not first created us—which is the action of mercy. Mercy is the chief source of every work of God and always accompanies it, since he gives each of his creatures much more than is due him in justice. "The Lord is good to all, and his compassion is over all that he has made ... You open your hand, you satisfy the desire of every living thing. The Lord is just in all his ways, and kind in all his doings" (Ps 145:9,16,17). All that is due to man by right is to be a simple creature, but God willed, instead, to elevate him to the dignity of a son and to call him to share in his eternal happiness. After sin, divine justice could have annihilated man, but, instead, God sought his salvation. One drop of Jesus' blood would have been sufficient to atone for sin and to redeem all mankind, but he desired to sacrifice his whole life and all his blood. "Where sin increased, grace abounded all the more, so that ... grace also might reign through righteousness to eternal life" (Rom 5:20-21). It is especially in the work of redemption that God's justice is infinitely surpassed by his mercy, which assumes unlimited and incredible proportions. "One will hardly die for a righteous man"—says St. Paul—"though perhaps for a good man one will dare even to die. But God shows his love for us in that while we were yet sinners Christ died for us" (ib. 7-8). The Son of God who became man and was crucified for the salvation of the world is the supreme and

most eloquent manifestation of how justice in God is fused together with mercy; they are two aspects of his eternal love. However, God's love demands a return, and, if he did not limit his love for us to what was due us, should we love him only out of justice? God saved us, "not because of deeds done by us in righteousness, but in virtue of his own mercy" (Tit 3:4). His infinite mercy must be answered by a boundless love.

> *You are righteous and rule all things rightly, deeming it alien to your power to condemn him who does not deserve to be punished.*
> *For your strength, Lord, is the source of righteousness, and your sovereignty over all causes you to spare all.*
> *For you show your strength when men doubt the completeness of your power and rebuke any insolence among those who know it. You who are sovereign in strength judge with mildness, and with great forbearance you govern us; for you have power to act whenever you choose. Through such works you have taught your people that the righteous man must be kind, and you have filled your sons with good hope, because you give repentance for sins.*
> Wisdom 12:15-19

> *O Lord, to me you have granted your infinite mercy; and through it I contemplate and adore your other divine perfections! All of these perfections appear to be resplendent with love, even your justice—and perhaps this even more so than the others—seems to me clothed in love. What a sweet joy to think that you, O God, are just, that is, that you take into account our weakness, that you are perfectly aware of our fragile nature. What should I fear then? Must not you, the infinitely just God who deigned to pardon the faults of the prodigal son with so much kindness, be just also to me who am with you always? (Autobiography A, p. 180)*
> *I know one must be most pure to appear before you, God of all holiness, but I know too that you are infinitely just; and it is this justice, which frightens so many souls, that is the basis of my joy and trust. To be just means not only to exercise severity in punishing the guilty, but also to recognize right intentions and to reward virtue.*
> *I hope as much from your justice, O God, as from your mercy, because you are compassionate and merciful, long-suffering and plenteous in mercy. For you know our weakness and you remember we are but dust.*
> St. Therese of the Child Jesus, *Letter* May 9, 1897

251. HE ORDERS ALL THINGS WELL

I trust in you, O Lord ... my times are in your hand (Ps 31:15-16)

1. The wisdom of God "reaches mightily from one end of the earth to the other, and orders all things well" (Wis 8:1). Divine

wisdom is thus identified with divine providence which orders, disposes, and directs everything toward the attainment of a well-defined end; the ultimate and supreme end which is the glory of God, and the proximate and secondary end which is the good and happiness of creatures. Nothing in the world exists without a reason nor happens by chance; everything is part of the magnificent plan of divine providence, since God "has arranged all things by measure and number and weight" (Wis 11:20).

If we sometimes fail to understand the reason for the existence of certain circumstances and creatures which cause us suffering, it is because we do not see the place they occupy in the plan of divine providence. At the same time it is certain that every event, even when sad and painful, is guided by God's loving providence. "Whatever the Lord commands will be done in his time ... No one can say: 'What is this? Why is that?' for everything has been created for its use ... Because of God all things come to a happy end; by his word all things hold together" (Sir 39:16,21; 43:26). Just because nothing escapes God's wise and fatherly government, there is nothing to be feared; even the most difficult and obscure situations, which upset our plans and interfere with our best laid schemes, and which, as far as we can see, appear to have no solution, will unfailingly be turned to good by God. "In everything"—says St. Paul—"God works for good with those who love him" (Rom 8:28). And St. Augustine, as if in comment, says: "The all-powerful God would not let any evil get into his works, if he were not so powerful and good that he can draw good even from evil" (Enchirid. 11). We need to be firmly convinced of this so as not to be scandalized by trials, nor harbor any doubts about divine providence. We can distrust ourselves, our goodness, and our faithfulness, but not God's, for his goodness is above the heavens, his fidelity beyond the clouds, his fatherly providence guides everything (Ps 108:5; Wis 14:3).

2. Having created the universe, God does not leave it to care for itself, he provides for every one of his creatures. "His care is for all things" (Wis 12:13), because he is the creator of all; but his providence is especially directed toward men, whom he loves as his children: "As one whom his mother comforts, so will I comfort you"—the Lord says to Israel—. "You whom I took from the ends of the earth, and called from its farthest corners ... fear not, for I am with you. Be not dismayed, for I am your God" (Is 66:13; 41:9-10). Each soul can in all truth consider these words as addressed to itself; God's providence is so immense that, while it embraces the whole universe, it takes care of each individual creature in a special way. Jesus gave us a clear picture of the providence of his heavenly Father when he said: "Not even one sparrow will fall to the ground without your Father's will ... Fear not, therefore; you are of more value than many sparrows" (Mt 10;29-31). Just as God did not create us wholesale, but creates each soul individually, so too, divine providence is not limited to helping us en masse,

but assists each one of us, knowing all our needs, our difficulties, and even our individual desires, fully cognizant of what is most suited to the true good of each of us. The most attentive mother may be unaware of some need of her child, she may forget, or make a mistake in providing for it, or may find it impossible to help at all, but this can never happen with God, whose providence knows, sees, and can do everything. "Consider the lilies of the field, how they grow; they neither toil nor spin; yet I tell you"—Jesus affirms—"even Solomon in all his glory was not arrayed like one of these. But if God so clothes the grass of the field, which today is alive and tomorrow is thrown into the oven, will he not much more clothe you, O men of little faith?" (Mt 6:28-30).

God's providence surrounds us on all sides; in it we live and move and have our being, and still we are so slow to believe in it, and so distrustful! What need we have to open our hearts to a greater and unlimited confidence, for divine providence has no limits!

> *O my God, you and you alone are all-wise and all-knowing! You know, you have determined everything which will happen to me from first to last. You have ordered things in the wisest way.*
>
> *You know what will be my lot year by year till I die. You know how long I have to live. You know how I shall die. You have precisely ordained everything, sin excepted. Every event of my life is the best for me that could be, for it comes from you.*
>
> *You bring me on year by year, by your wonderful Providence, from youth to age, with the most perfect wisdom, and with the most perfect love ...*
>
> *I know, O Lord, you will do your part towards me, as I, through your grace, desire to do my part towards you. I know well you never can forsake those who seek you, or can disappoint those who trust you. Yet I know too, the more I pray for your protection, the more surely and fully I shall have it. And therefore now I cry out to you, and entreat you, first that you would keep me from myself, and from following any will but yours. Next I beg of you, that in your infinite compassion, you would temper your will to me, that it may not be severe, but indulgent to me.*
>
> *Visit me not, O my loving Lord—if it be not wrong so to pray—visit me not with those trying visitations which saints alone can bear! Pity my weakness ... I leave all in your hands, my dear Savior—I bargain for nothing—only, if you shall bring heavier trials on me, give me more grace—flood me with the fullness of your strength and consolation, that they may work in me not death, but life and salvation.*
>
> J.H. Newman, *Meditations on Christian Doctrine* XII:2

252. ALL IS POSSIBLE TO GOD

Great and wonderful are your deeds, O Lord God the Almighty!
Just and true are all your ways (Rev 15:3)

1. In describing God's work of creation, Isaiah concludes: "Lift up your eyes on high and see: who created these? He who . . . calls them all by name, by the greatness of his might, and because he is strong in power, not one is missing" (40:26). God is the all-powerful One, he can do all that he wills, as he wills, and when he wills: "Whatever the Lord pleases, he does, in heaven and on earth, in the seas and all deeps" (Ps 135:6). Nothing can impede his action, nor oppose his will; nothing is difficult to him: "With God nothing will be impossible" (Lk 1:37). Even the simplest of our works require time, fatigue, material, and cooperation; but those of God, even the greatest, are accomplished in one instant by a simple act of his will. God is so omnipotent that with a single word he brought all things out of nothing: "For you spoke, and all your creatures were made . . . there is none that can resist your voice" (Jdt 16:14). Our words are empty sounds that disperse in the air; God's word is so effective that it produces whatever it expresses: "For he spoke, and it came to be" (Ps 33:9). God is so omnipotent that after creating us free, he rules and directs us according to his good pleasure, without prejudicing our freedom. God is so omnipotent that he can change us, the children of sin, into his adopted children called to share his divine life. God is so omnipotent that he can draw good even from evil. God's omnipotence is always active and working, without ever ceasing; and this marvelous, infinite, eternal omnipotence is completely at the service of his infinite goodness, or better, it is infinite goodness itself, which can do all the good it wishes. How sorely we need the help of this omnipotence, we who are so weak that even when we are willing the good, we are very often incapable of doing it!

2. "To him who by the power at work within us is able to do far more abundantly than all that we ask or think" (Eph 3:20), to him must we turn with trust and humility in order to find the help we need for our weakness and powerlessness. St. Paul warns us that we cannot "claim anything as coming from us: our competence is from God" (2 Cor 3:5). If there is something we can, and know how to do, it is only because God has shared his divine power with us. Left to ourselves, we could not even formulate a thought or utter a word. This radical powerlessness should keep us humble, but not discourage us, because God, infinite goodness, who called us to life, also gives us the capability and strength we need in order to live and to act; he communicates these gifts to us in greater measure the more humble we are, and the more trustingly we have recourse to him. "He gives power to the faint, and to him who has no might he increases strength. Even youths shall faint and be weary, and young men shall fall exhausted; but they who wait for

the Lord shall renew their strength ... they shall run and not be weary, they shall walk and not faint" (Is 40:29-31).

If it is painful to experience our powerlessness to its very depths, it is all the more encouraging to be able to rely on the power of God, who is pleased to choose "what is foolish in the world to shame the wise, ... what is weak in the world to shame the strong, what is low and despised in the world, even things that are not ..." in order to accomplish mighty works "so that no human being might boast in the presence of God" (1 Cor 1:27-29). The reason for so much of our failure in doing good lies in our not depending enough upon divine omnipotence, counting too much on our own capability and on human means. This is especially true for what concerns the salvation and sanctification of both ourselves and others, an enterprise that surpasses all human power. Yet we are obliged to undertake it with great zeal and confidence, continually imploring divine help, for "with men this is impossible, but with God all things are possible" (Mt 19:26).

> Yours, O Lord, is the greatness, and the power, and the glory, and the victory, and the majesty; for all that is in the heavens and in the earth is yours; yours is the kingdom, O Lord, and you are exalted as head above all. Both riches and honor come from you, and you rule over all. In your hand are power and might; and in your hand it is to make great and to give strength to all. And now we thank you, our God, and praise your glorious name.
>
> 1 Chronicles 29:11-13

> My Lord and Creator, you are my Lord who rule over all that is in heaven and on earth: such is your dominion that every created thing depends upon your infinite omnipotence. You are my absolute master, who can do with me anything that pleases you, whereas, O eternal wisdom, I was made by you from nothing, receiving being and sustenance from you who provide for my continual needs ...
>
> O most high God, I am ... the servant who has no way to repay you, for you are my master. I, O Lord, am that poor Lazarus, so infirm with the natural misfortunes that aflict the inferior part of man, and so poor that I am not conscious of having any virtue in me that would please you; but I do have a great desire to love you ...
>
> O my God, give me the wealth of your grace and make me rich with it, so that I may be able to offer you all the virtuous acts that it engenders; repentance for having offended you, resolution not to offend you again, a persevering spirit of imitating you in life and in death, in happiness and in suffering; and, finally, resignation to your will in all things, so that, in whatever may happen to me, whether pleasant or bitter to my spirit, I may always say: may your holy will be done in heaven and on earth.
>
> St. Charles da Sezze, *Autobiography* VII, 30

253. FAITH: THE GIFT OF GOD

Lord, enlighten the eyes of my heart (Eph 1:18)

1. "Without faith it is impossible to please God" (Heb 11:6). Faith is the foundation of our relations with God. For the man without faith, God has no meaning, no value, no place in his life. On the contrary, the more lively our faith is, the more God enters into our life, until finally he becomes our all, the one great reality for which we live, and the One for whom we courageously face sorrow and death. "If we live, we live to the Lord, and if we die, we die to the Lord" (Rom 14:8). Those who dedicate themselves to the spiritual life do not lack faith; but often our faith is not alive and concrete enough to make us always see God in everything, which would give us the sense of his fundamental, transcendent and eternal reality that infinitely surpasses all earthly realities.

Faith does not depend upon data received through the senses—on what we can see or touch—nor is it reduced to what the human intellect can understand about God, but going beyond all this, it makes us share in God's own knowledge of himself. It is the great gift God gives us, raising us to the status of divine sonship, thus making us share in his nature, and therefore in his life, which is a life of knowledge and of love. Faith allows us to share divine knowledge and charity, divine love. In baptism, together with sanctifying grace, we are given these virtues through which we become capable of sharing God's thought and God's love. Just as grace is a free gift, so also is faith: it is God who calls us to faith and who infuses faith. "For by grace you have been saved through faith"—states the Apostle—"and this is not your own doing; it is the gift of God" (Eph 2:8). And Vatican II declares that: "If this faith is to be shown, the grace of God and the interior help of the Holy Spirit must precede and assist, moving the heart and turning it to God, opening the eyes of the mind, and giving 'joy and ease to everyone in assenting to the truth and believing it' " (DV 5). In practice we do not reflect sufficiently on the truth that to be a believer is a pure gift of God, not due to any personal merit. God is both the object of faith and the giver of faith; it is he who infuses into us the desire to know him and to believe in him and who makes us capable of the act of believing.

2. Intelligence can give us only natural light on God and on creation, but faith, on the contrary, gives us supernatural light, which is a participation in the knowledge which God has of himself and of creatures. God in his great goodness was pleased to reveal himself to men; he revealed himself as he is and as he knows himself, which is not only as the Creator, but also as the Trinity, as the Father, as the Author of grace, as infinite love. This revelation took place gradually through the various stages of the history of mankind, becoming continually clearer and more complete until it reached its fullness in Christ, the great Revealer of the mystery

of God. "The deepest truth about God and the salvation of man is made clear to us in Christ, who is the Mediator and at the same time the fullness of all new revelation" (DV 2). Revelation is the foundation of faith. God has spoken and made himself known, and we believe upon his word. " 'The obedience of faith' must be given to God who reveals, an obedience by which man entrusts his whole self freely to God, offering 'the full submission of intellect and will to God' " (DV 5). God gratuitously infused the gift of faith into us at baptism, but this gift, which is offered and not imposed, expects the free adherence of will and intellect on our part. The act of faith of a child who is only beginning to know the Lord, must grow into the mature adherence of an adult who is really conscious of God's word, of divine Revelation, of holy Scripture, and of the teaching of the Church. Thus faith becomes an act of surrender to God: "I know whom I have believed, and I am sure ..." (2 Tim 1:12). Still this free and voluntary act always includes God's gift: "To believe"—St. Thomas teaches—"is an act of the intellect, which adheres to divine truth under the command of the will, moved by God through grace" (2-2.2.9). Realizing the poverty of our faith, let us humbly invoke divine help, begging God to bend our will and open our mind to his divine light.

Lord, I believe; I will to believe in you. O Lord, let my faith be complete, without reservations; make it penetrate into my thought and into my way of judging things, both divine and human;

O Lord, make my faith free; that is, accompanied by my own personal adherence to it, and accepting the renunciations and obligations that are involved, so that it may express the highest point of my personality: I believe in you, O Lord;

O Lord make my faith sure; sure through an exterior agreement of proofs and of an interior testimony of the Holy Spirit, sure in its encouraging light, its peace-giving conclusion, and its peaceful assimilation;

O Lord, make my faith strong, not fearing the contrariety of problems, which is the common experience of our life which is eager for light, not fearing the hostility of those who argue about faith, question it, reject it, or deny it; rather, strengthen it by the intimate experience of your truth ...

O Lord, make my faith joyful, giving peace and contentment to my soul, and making it able for prayer with God and for familiar converse with men, so that the interior blessedness of its happy possession may shine out in both holy and everyday conversation;

O Lord, make my faith productive and make charity the reason for its moral growth so that it may be a true friendship with you, and, in its works and sufferings and its yearning for the final revelation, a continuous search for you, a constant witness to you and a continual nourishment of hope;

O Lord, make my faith humble, not presuming to base itself on the experience of my own thought and feeling, but submissive to the testimony of the Holy Spirit, with no other guarantee than that of obedience to the tradition and the teaching authority of the Church. Amen.

Paul VI, Teachings v 6

254. HE WHO BELIEVES HAS ETERNAL LIFE

Eternal life is to know you, the only true God (Jn 17:3)

1. The rite of baptism insists upon faith in a very particular way, and especially upon the duty of parents to bring up their children in the faith. "Take care that your children who have been enlightened by Christ may always live as children of the light, that they may go out to meet the Lord who is coming with all his Saints to enter into the kingdom of heaven." Once the age of reason is reached, this becomes the personal and fundamental duty of every baptized person. In fact it is faith that introduces us to Christian life and opens the way to eternal life. Faith is not only a promise, it is the prelude to the gift of eternal life. Christ the Lord said: "Truly, truly I say to you, he who believes has eternal life" (Jn 6:47). Through faith we begin to know God as we shall know him one day in heaven; we already know in a hidden way here, in the truths that faith proposes for our belief, that same God and the same divine mysteries that we shall see unveiled in heaven in the light of glory. Faith and the beatific vision are two phases of the one knowledge of God: faith is initial knowledge, obscure and imperfect; the beatific vision is full, clear, and perfect. "Now"—St. Paul says—"we see in a mirror dimly, but then [we shall see] face to face. Now I know in part; then I shall understand fully, even as I have been fully understood" (1 Cor 13:12). In heaven faith will cease, because it will give way to the direct vision of God; but as long as we are pilgrims on earth, there is no other way to know God and to put ourselves into contact with him than by faith. Besides, faith is the only way to attain to the beatific vision. St. Thomas therefore teaches that "faith is an intellectual habit, through which eternal life begins in us" (2-2,4,1). It is an intellectual habit, that is, an habitual disposition, a virtue infused by God into the mind of man to make him capable of knowing God supernaturally, of believing in him.

"This is eternal life"—said Jesus in his prayer to the Father—"that they may know you, the only true God, and [him] whom you have sent" (Jn 17:3).

2. St. John of the Cross uses an original comparison to make us understand that faith already contains the germ of the beatific vision. He refers to the scriptural narrative of Gideon's soldiers who carried "lamps in their hands, yet did not see the light because the lamps were hidden in darkness within earthenware jars; but when these jars were broken, immediately the light appeared". The Saint comments: "Faith, typified by those clay jars,

contains the divine light. When faith has reached its end and is shattered by the ending and breaking of this mortal life, the glory and light of the divinity, the content of faith, will at once begin to shine" (Asc. II 9:3).

But eternal life is not simply vision, it is also communion with God, a communion which springs from the vision. It is analagously the same in regard to faith. God does not reveal himself to men only to make himself known, but also to give himself to them and to "invite and take them into fellowship with himself" (DV 2). Supernatural knowledge of God through faith is the indispensable basis of this wonderful fellowship which is perfected by charity, and reaches its fullness in heaven. Here we see the inexpressible grandeur of the gift of faith, which, by putting us on the level of divine knowledge, prepares us for friendship and communion with God, and for the eternal possession of God. "This is the will of my Father"—Jesus said one day—"that everyone who sees the Son and believes in him, shall have eternal life" (Jn 6:40).

Just as eternal life surpasses all earthly life, so faith surpasses any natural knowledge of God. One act of supernatural faith is worth immensely more than all human knowledge, not excluding that of theological study. It is faith that justifies and saves. How grateful we should be to God for this gift which has been lavished upon us so gratuitously, and how much we need to preserve it and make it grow! How fittingly Vatican II urges the faithful to grow daily "more conscious of the gift of faith" (GE 2), and to endeavor by prayer and act to communicate "to others this gift of faith which they have freely received" (AG 41).

O Lord, I shall begin to arrive at vision through faith: I am already on the way as I run in search of my homeland. During this journey, my soul keeps saying: my every desire is before you, and my groaning is not hidden from you. But in the promised land, I shall no longer need to pray, but only to give praise, for there, nothing is lacking. Here I believe, but there I shall see; here I hope, there I shall possess; here I ask, there I shall receive! (Ser. 159:1).

Now I pay attention to what I see, and I believe what I do not see. O Lord, you have not abandoned me by calling me to believe; even when you command me to believe what I cannot see, you have still not left me without sight of things that help me to believe what I do not see ... Although it was impossible to see your divinity, I could see your humanity very well; indeed this is the reason you became man, that, in one single person, I might have an object of vision and an object of faith (Ser. 126:5).

St. Augustine

O faith of Christ my Spouse, I address myself to you because you contain and hide the image and the beauty of my Beloved. You are pure and strong and clear, cleansed of errors; you are the spring from which flow the waters of all spiritual goods. O Christ, when

you spoke with the Samaritan woman, you called faith a "spring",
declaring that in those who believed in you, you would make a foun-
tain whose waters would leap up unto life everlasting (cf Sp. C.
12:1-3).

O faith, you alone are the only proximate and proportionate
means to union with God. For the likeness between you and God is
so close that no other difference exists than that between believing
in God and seeing him. As God is infinite, you propose him to us as
infinite; as there are Three Persons in the one God, you present him
to us in this way; and as God is darkness to our intellect, so do you
dazzle and blind us. Only by your means, in divine light, light ex-
ceeding all understanding, does God manifest himself to the soul.
Oh then, Lord, increase my faith, for the more intense my faith is,
the closer is my union with God (Asc. II 9:1).

St. John of the Cross

255. SIXTEENTH SUNDAY OF ORDINARY TIME

YEAR A

You, Lord, are good and forgiving (Ps 86:5).

Today the Liturgy of the Word is like a hymn to God's mercy
leading the faithful to reflect upon this consoling divine attribute
so as to nourish their faith in the Lord, and to incite them to imitate him in their own conduct. The first reading (Wis 12:13,16-19)
introduces the theme: "For your strength is the source of
righteousness, and your sovereignty over all causes you to spare
all . . . You who are sovereign in strength judge with mildness, and
with great forbearance you govern us . . . Through such works you
have taught your people that the righteous man must be kind"
(ib. 16,18-19). With men might often destroys justice and stifles
forbearance; such is not the case with God whose power is equally
the source of justice and of mercy, and is identified with them.
Thus he tempers just punishments with a clemency that is
waiting to give me the chance of "repentance for sins" (ib. 19). The
same theme is illustrated in concrete form in the gospel parable of
the weeds (Mt 13:24-43). The narrator is no longer the author of
the Book of Wisdom, but Jesus, incarnate Wisdom: "The kingdom
of heaven may be compared to a man who sowed good seed in his
field" (ib. 24). Then during the night an enemy came and sowed
weeds, which quickly invaded the wheat, but when the servants
suggested uprooting the weeds, the owner forbade it: "No, lest in
gathering the weeds you root up the wheat along with them. Let
both grow together until the harvest" (ib. 29-30). A farmer would
not reason in this way: he would cultivate the wheat to free it from
the weeds. But here we are not being given a lesson in agriculture,
but rather are being shown how God deals with the good and the

bad. In the explanation of the parable we are told that the field is the world where Jesus, the Son of man, sows the seed of the kingdom of heaven. "The good seed means the sons of the kingdom; the weeds are the sons of the evil one, and the enemy who sowed them is the devil" (ib. 38-39).

In this world, the kingdom of heaven is in a state of development, of growth, and therefore there is not a clear distinction between the good and the bad; God does not want that; in fact, he allows them to live side by side with each other, both to test the former and strengthen them in virtue, and to give the latter time for conversion. Also there cannot be excluded the possibility that at some point the good seed can degenerate into weeds. Just as in this life no one is definitively a son of the devil, because one can always withdraw from sin, so it is also true that no one is definitively a son of the kingdom, because unfortunately one can be perverted. Hence, the parable contains a call to vigilance for all of us, not to let the hour of grace pass in vain, but to keep ourselves ever ready for the harvest, because "just as weeds are gathered and burned with fire, so will it be at the close of the age". Then "all evildoers" will be thrown into the furnace of fire", while "the righteous will shine like the sun in the kingdom of their Father" (ib. 40-43). God's merciful forbearance will one day change into irrevocable judgment for those who have been obstinate in evil. Meanwhile, the "children of the kingdom" are called to imitate the heavenly Father's mercy by accepting patiently the hardships that arise from living among the enemies of good, and by treating these with brotherly kindliness in the hope that, conquered by love, they will change their ways. Moreover we should have recourse to prayer that God will stem the tide of evil and defend his children from its contagion; but we must always leave the way of doing this to him. The words of St. Paul are appropriate here (2nd reading: Rom. 8:26-27): "We do not know how to pray as we ought" (ib.); but the Holy Spirit knows it; we must entrust the cause of the good to him who intercedes "for the saints according to the will of God" (ib.).

> *O Lord, you are merciful to all, for you can do all things, and you overlook men's sins that they may repent. For you love all things that exist and feel loathing for none of the things which you have made, for you would not have made anything if you had hated it. How would anything have endured if you had not willed it? Or how would anything not called forth by you have been preserved? You spare all things for they are yours, O Lord, who love the living. For your immortal spirit is in all things.*
>
> *Therefore you correct little by little those who trespass, and remind and warn them of the things wherein they sin, that they may be freed from wickedness and put their trust in you, O Lord.*
>
> *Wisdom 11:23-26; 12:1-2*

How badly we repay your friendship, O Lord, since we turn so quickly into mortal enemies! Indeed, how great is your mercy! Where would we find a friend so patient? And even if a friend commits only one fault, it is never erased from the other's memory, nor do the two manage to have a friendship as trusting as before. On the other hand how often we fail in our friendship with you, O Lord, and how many years you wait for us! May you be blessed, Lord, my God, for you show us so much pity that it seems you forget your greatness so as not to punish—as would be right—a betrayal as treacherous as this!

St. Teresa of Jesus, *Meditations on the Song of Songs* 2:19

YEAR B

The Lord restores my soul; he leads me in paths of righteousness (Ps 23:3).

The theme of God as shepherd, and therefore of the Messiah as shepherd, which was so dear to the Old Testament, recurs frequently in the renewed Liturgy which freely uses the prophetic texts to introduce the gospel excerpts which are attuned to this topic.

Speaking through Jeremiah (23:1-6) in the first reading, God condemns the conduct of evil shepherds: "Woe to the shepherds who destroy and scatter the sheep of my pasture" (ib. 1). Instead of gathering the sheep—the people of God—they have scattered them; instead of guarding them, they have let them perish; therefore God will punish them. He himself will "gather the remnant of his flock" (ib. 3), and will entrust them to worthier shepherds; much more even, he will raise up from David's descendants "a righteous branch" (ib. 5), the Messiah, the shepherd-king, under whose rule the scattered sheep of Israel will finally be gathered together, and will enjoy security, justice, and peace. When we read the responsorial psalm with Christian eyes, we find that it exactly delineates the figure of Christ as the good shepherd and expresses the joy of the faithful who find every good in him: "The Lord is my shepherd; I shall not want" (Ps 23:1). He assists his flock with solicitude, defending it from danger and nourishing it with the rich food of his word, his flesh and his blood.

The Gospel (Mk 6:30-34) gives a brief sketch of the activity of Jesus the shepherd. His first care is for the Apostles, the chosen portion of his flock, whom he gathers around himself after the fatigue of their first mission. "Come away by yourselves to a lonely place, and rest a while" (ib. 30). A fruitful apostolate is impossible without such refreshing pauses beside the Master, which are intended to reinvigorate not only their physical forces, but their spiritual ones as well: pauses for prayer, for interior recollection, in order to plumb the depths of the words of the Lord and to translate them ever more meaningfully into their own lives. Then the Gospel presents Jesus' intense activity for the people, who cling closely to him without leaving him a moment's respite: "For many were coming and going, and they had no leisure even to eat" (ib. 31). And when the Lord and the Twelve set off in a boat to find a little solitude, the people went before them to meet them, so that when he landed, he was again surrounded by the crowd. St. Mark points out that seeing this: "He had compassion on them, because they were like sheep without a shepherd; and he began to teach them many things" (ib. 34). Completely forgetful of himself, Jesus gave himself wholly to the care of the flock which the Father had confided to him; at that time he instructed them, and later, he would redeem them on the cross. He is the good Shepherd who gives his life for his sheep, and he teaches those who represent him to do the same. Although only bishops and priests are official shepherds of the people of God, in a more modest and indirect way those who occupy a position of responsibility in the family or school or society, also participate in this office. In order to fulfill their duty, they all need to look at Jesus, and to model themselves upon him.

The second reading (Eph 2:13-18) completes the theme with a picture of the universal salvation brought about by Christ. He drew to himself the far-away sheep—the pagans—and made them into one single flock with the sheep of Israel who were nearer to him because they already belonged to the people of God. He made a single people of the two—pagan and Jewish—"to reconcile them both to God . . . through the cross, thereby bringing the hostility to an end" (ib. 16). In fact it is through his death that all men have become brothers to one another and children of the heavenly Father. For through him "both have access in one Spirit to the Father" (ib. 18). A single Shepherd and a single Father, a single flock and a single sheepfold: this is the fruit of the life Jesus offered for his sheep.

O good Shepherd, you are all we need. You know what we need and you give it to us at the time that pleases you; we are your poor sheep, give us the pasture that we need as we need it. Sometimes you console us to keep us from being discouraged, sometimes you let us feel the confusion in our souls in order to give rise to humility, which is truth. We are in good hands. Your heart never ceases watching over us, you love us infinitely, and behold us incessantly, and are all-powerful. Oh, prepare for us a blessed eternity by whatever means you know are best; make us work hard when, like the little children we are, we would like to stop and rest.
cf Charles de Foucauld, *Letter* 5,4,1909

O Lord, through the loving disposition of your providence, you have wished to call yourself a shepherd. You are not only concerned about me, but went searching for me; you not only found me, O

worker of wonders, but in the indescribable goodness of your love,
you carried me on your shoulders to give me new life, and made me
share with the heavenly band in the heritage of your Father.

O you who are powerful, the source of life, blessed, full of succor
and compassion and mercy . . . now open to me again the depths of
your mercy and the outpouring of your goodness.

St. Gregory of Narek, *Le livre des prieres*

YEAR C

My Lord, I beg you . . . do not pass by your servant (Gen 18:3)

God's dwelling among men and the hospitality men offer him
is the thought-provoking theme of today's Gospel.

In the first reading (Gen 18:1-10a) we have the remarkable appearance of Yahweh to Abraham in the guise of three mysterious
personages, the visible representatives of the invisible majesty of
God. The exceptional concern with which Abraham welcomed
them and the sumptuous banquet that he prepared for them
reveal the patriarch's intuition of an extraordinary divine event.
"My Lord"—he said, prostrating himself to the ground—"if I
have found favor in your sight, do not pass by your servant" (ib.
3). Much more than a simple invitation, these words were a
supplication expressing his keen desire to be host to the Lord, to
welcome him into his own tent, to keep him near. Abraham also
showed himself here "the friend of God" (Is 41:8) who treated with
the Lord with the greatest respect, and at the same time with
humble confidence and a lively desire to serve him. At the end of
the meal, the promise of a child, in spite of the advanced age of
both Abraham and Sara, clearly revealed the supernatural nature
of the three personages, one of whom spoke as God himself would
speak (ib. 13). Ancient Christian tradition saw this apparition—of
three men greeted by Abraham as a single son—as a symbol of the
Trinity. In any case, the truth is that "the Lord appeared to
Abraham by the oaks of Mambre" (ib. 1), spoke with him, and
dealt familiarly with him, even sitting down at his table.

Today's Gospel also shows God sitting at table with men, but
this time with an absolutely new concreteness, for God's Son had
taken flesh, and come to live among men. The scene took place at
Bethany, in the home of Martha, where Jesus was given hospitality with a concern that was very much like that of Abraham for his
visitors. Like him, Martha busied herself in preparing a very
special dinner; but her solicitude was not shared by her sister who,
in imitation rather of Abraham's eagerness to linger in God's
presence, took advantage of the Master's visit to sit at his feet
and listen to him. In reality, although Martha's intentions were of
the very best, and all her preparations were an expression of her
love, there was a still better way to welcome the Lord; as he
himself declared, it was the one Mary chose. In fact when God

visits man, it is above all to bring him his gifts and his word, and man must not think that busying himself in work is more important than listening to the word of the Lord. Whatever God does and says to men is always worth more than what they can do for him. "Martha, Martha, you are anxious and troubled about many things; one thing is needful" (ib. 41-42). This one thing is so necessary that without it there is no salvation, for the word of God is the word of eternal life, and to listen to it is an absolute necessity. A man is saved, not by the multiplicity of works, but by the word of God heard with love, and lived with faithfulness. "Mary has chosen the good portion" (ib. 42). Such a choice is not to be left only to contemplatives; every Christian ought, at least to some extent, make it his own, not presuming to devote himself to activity without having first thoroughly examined the word of the Lord in prayer. Only in this way will he be able to live the gospel even when doing so is arduous and entails sacrifice. St. Paul could say joyfully: "In my flesh I complete what is lacking in Christ's afflictions for the sake of his body, that is, the Church" (Col 1:24; 2nd reading); because he had meditated at length upon the gospel and had understood the mystery of Christ, he had found the strength to relive it within himself.

> Listen, O Lord, to my inner voice, which my intense desire sends up to your ears. Have mercy on me and hear me. My heart had said to you: I have sought your face. I have not made a display of myself before men, but in secret, where you alone hear, my heart has said to you: I have sought from you no reward apart from yourself, but only your countenance. Your face, O Lord, will I seek. Upon this search I will persistently persevere. Not anything of small value will I seek, O Lord, but your countenance, that I may love you freely, since I can find nothing more precious.
>
> St. Augustine, *In Ps* 26, I 7-8

> O Lord, give me a passion for listening to you. Sometimes this desire to be silent is so strong that the only thing I long to do is to remain like Magdalen at your feet, O my adored Master, eager to hear everything and to penetrate deeper and deeper into the mystery of charity that you came to reveal to us. Grant that in action, even when I seem to be fulfilling the office of Martha, my soul may remain buried like Magdalen in her contemplation, remaining at the source like one athirst. That is how I understand the apostolate, O Lord; I shall then be able to radiate you, to give you to souls, if I remain always at these divine springs. Grant that I may draw very near to you, my beloved Master, enter into communion with your soul, identify myself with its every disposition, and then go forth like you to do the will of the Father.
>
> cf Elizabeth the Trinity, *Letter* 133, February 24, 1903

256. UNHESITATING FAITH

Lord, let me resist, being firm in my faith   (1 Pet 5:9)

1. The great value of faith, which we never appreciate enough, is that it places us on the level of divine knowledge. It means knowing, thinking, and judging beyond human short-sightedness, in the way that God knows, thinks, and judges; certainly not in so exhaustive a manner, but as a participation in the divine light. Just because such knowledge infinitely surpasses the possibilities and the limits of the human mind, faith is certain though not visible. "Faith"—says St. Paul—"is the assurance of things hoped for, the conviction of things not seen" (Heb 11:1). The baptized person possesses eternal life in embryo, but does not see it; divine revelation makes us know that such a life exists, but does not show it to us; it tells us that God is Triune, but it does not show us the Trinity. The truths that faith proposes for our belief are more real than those which our senses perceive, yet they are not subject to our control. Confronted by an evident truth such as that two and two make four, our intellect cannot refuse to accept it, nor is the concurrence of my will needed in order to accept it. But in the presence of the truths of faith, the intellect remains free to acquiesce or not, and cannot give its assent without the concurrence of the will, which makes the decision: "I will to believe," and does so, relying solely on the infallible authority of God who reveals it.

"The act of faith is of its very nature a free act. Man ... cannot give his adherence to God revealing himself unless the Father draw him to offer to God the reasonable and free submission of faith" (DH 10). The "attraction" of God which inclines us to believe is the gift of faith, and the "reasonable and free submission" to God who is revealing himself is our response to this gift, a response which constitutes the act and the merit of faith. There is no merit in admitting evident truths. On the other hand there is much merit in believing truths which remain in great part obscure, because this presupposes an act of humble submission and of full trust in him who reveals it. Only God is worthy of this homage, the homage of unhesitating faith.

2. "By faith"—St. Paul says—"Abraham obeyed when he was called [by God] ... and he went out, not knowing where he was to go ... By faith, Abraham, when he was tested, offered up Isaac ... his only son, of whom it was said: 'through Isaac shall your descendents be named.' He considered that God was able to raise men even from the dead" (Heb 11:8,17-19). This is a magnificent example of heroic faith exercised in circumstances that were as obscure and contrary as they could be to what God himself had promised; it was this that made Abraham the father and prototype of our faith.

The mystery that envelops supernatural truths and the lack of evidence for the divine promises can generate doubts and perplexities. We should not be dismayed: it is natural for our intellect to doubt what it does not see and cannot understand. Moreover, God himself may permit, as he did in the case of Abraham, certain situations in which we must go ahead in darkness without knowing where we are headed, supported only by the word of him who said: "Heaven and earth will pass away, but my words will not pass away" (Mt 24:35). This obscure side of faith is painful for us, who by nature love to base ourselves on evident facts, while where the mysteries and ways of God are concerned, the more sublime they are the more dark and obscure they are for our intellect, which is incapable of grasping the infinite. Yet we must react to any kind of doubt by a leap into the darkness and plunge ourselves into believing, believing at any cost and against every proof to the contrary, because God is God, and "he remains faithful, for he cannot deny himself" (2 Tim 2:13). Sacred Scripture repeatedly praises the perfect faith of Abraham, who was faced with situations which seemed to offer no way of solution; "no distrust made him waver concerning the promise of God, but he grew strong in the faith as he gave glory to God, fully convinced that God was able to do what he had promised" (Rom 4:20-21). Unshakeable faith in adverse circumstances gives strength to man and glory to God.

At the time of her bitter trial against faith, St. Therese of the Child Jesus wrote: "While I do not have *the joy of faith,* I am trying to carry out its works at least. I believe I have made more acts of faith in this past year than all through my whole life" (Auto C, p. 213). Through trials like this, faith grows purer, more supernatural and meritorious.

O abyss! O eternal Godhead! O deep sea!... with your light you have made me know your truth: you are that light above all light which illuminates the eye of the intellect, clarifying the light of faith so abundantly and so perfectly that I see my soul is alive, and in this light, receives you, O light.

By the light of faith I have acquired wisdom in the wisdom of the word of your Son; in the light of faith I am strong, constant and persevering. In the light of faith I hope; suffer me not to faint by the way. This light without which I should still walk in darkness, teaches me the road, and for this, O eternal Father, I said that you have illuminated me with the light of holy faith. Truly this light is a sea, for the soul revels in you, O peaceful sea, eternal Trinity. The water of the sea is not disturbed, and causes no fear to the soul, for it knows the truth; it is distilled and manifests secret things, so that where the light of your faith abounds, the soul is certain of what it believes...

Clothe me, O eternal Truth, clothe me with yourself, that I may run my mortal course with true obedience and the light of holy faith, with which light I feel my soul is becoming enraptured.
St. Catherine of Siena, *Dialogue* 148

O blessed faith, you are to me certain but also obscure. You are obscure because you bring me to believe divinely revealed truths which transcend every natural light and infinitely exceed all human understanding. Your excessive light is darkness to my soul, for a brighter light eclipses and suppresses a dimmer one; the sun so obscures all other lights that they do not seem to be lights at all when it is shining, overwhelming my power of vision...

You are a dark night for the soul; indeed the more darkness you bring upon it, the more light you shed... You were foreshadowed in that cloud that separated the children of Israel, just before their entry into the Red Sea, from the Egyptians... That cloud, dark in itself, could illumine the night!... so you, O faith, a dark and obscure cloud to the soul, illumine and pour light into the darkness of the soul... Consequently "darkness is as light with you" (Ps 139:12) which amounts to saying: Your night, O blessed faith, will be my guide in the delights of my pure contemplation and union with God.

cf St. John of the Cross, *Ascent* II 3:1,4-6

257. INCREASE OUR FAITH

Lord, I believe, help my unbelief   *(Mk 9:24)*

1. Jesus has said: "All things are possible to him who believes" (Mk 9:23); it would seem that before an act of living faith, blind, unconditional faith, God does not know how to resist and considers himself almost obliged to heed our requests. The gospel tells us this on every page; before Jesus performed a miracle, he always asked for an act of faith: "Do you believe that I am able to do this?" (Mt 9:28); and when faith was sincere, the miracle took place immediately: "According to your faith be it done to you" (ib. 29), he said to the two blind men; and to the woman suffering from a hemorrhage: "Take heart, daughter; your faith has made you well" (ib. 22). Jesus never said: my omnipotence has saved you and healed you, he says *your faith*, as though to make us understand that faith is the indispensable condition that he requires for benefiting from his omnipotence. Jesus, always omnipotent, will use his omnipotence only for the benefit of those who believe firmly in him. This is the reason the divine Master refused to work in Nazareth and Capharnaum the many miracles he performed elsewhere. The more lively our faith, the more powerful it is, with the very power of God. Jesus affirmed: "Truly I say to you, if you have faith as a grain of mustard seed, you will say to this mountain: 'Move from here to there,' and it will move; and nothing will be impossible to you" (Mt 17:20). Like all the words of the gospel, these also are true, literally true. If they are not effectual for us, it is only because our faith is weak. We

often encounter difficulties in life which seem to us immovable mountains. Faults we cannot overcome, virtues we cannot seem to acquire, trials we cannot accept, or other kinds of difficulties . . . All this brings on discouragement and lack of confidence. Only a little faith is needed, only as much as a mustard seed, provided that faith is living and capable of sprouting and growing like the mustard seed.

Sometimes the Lord delays in coming to our help because he does not find in us a faith that is alive and certain. He asks us: "Do you believe that I am able to do this?" and we do not know how to answer: "Yes, Lord!" (Mt 9:28) with strength and determination. Every Christian should have the faith of the two blind men of the Gospel, or that of the Canaanite woman who was told: "O woman, great is your faith! Be it done for you as you desire" (Mt 15:28).

2. Great faith does not come of a sudden: it is the result of the seed that has fallen "on good soil," that is, of the gift of faith entrusted to those who, "hearing the word, hold it fast in an honest and good heart, and bring forth fruit with patience" (Lk 8:15). Just as a baby grows and becomes an adult, so also faith must pass from the state of infancy to a maturity which requires deep convictions capable of influencing and inspiring Christian life. Vatican II reminds us that the believer "is bound by a grave obligation . . . ever more adequately to understand the truth received from Christ, faithfully to proclaim it, and vigorously to defend it" (DH 14). Although the truths of faith go beyond human understanding, this does not excuse us from studying its basic principles, from knowing what divine Revelation and Church doctrine teach. "Learning"—writes St. Teresa of Jesus—"is a great thing, because learned men teach and enlighten us who know little; and when brought before the truths of sacred Scripture, we do what we ought. May God deliver us from foolish devotions!" (Life 13:16). We must have an illuminated faith, so we may understand the truths we believe. Therefore we must know and study and meditate upon the divine Scriptures which "the Church has always regarded, and will ever regard . . . as the supreme rule of faith; inspired by God . . . they impart the word of God himself without change" (DV 21). The sacred text contains all that God has revealed of himself to men, and all that has to do with our eternal salvation. The word of God contains in itself a very particular grace for nourishing faith: it is its light, its source, its guide, and its support. The Church therefore exhorts her children to come "freely" to her, ever mindful "that prayer should accompany the reading of sacred Scripture, so that God and man may talk together, for 'we speak to him when we pray, we hear him when we read the divine sayings' " (DV 25). May the prayer that accompanies our reading be especially, "Lord, increase our faith!" (Lk 17:5).

*If you can believe, everything is possible for you who believe."
O Lord, make me believe and I shall have found. Indeed to believe
means to have found. We know through faith that you dwell in our
hearts. What could be closer than this? Then let me seek without
fear, with love and with trust. You are good, Lord, to the soul that
seeks you. Make me seek you with desire, follow you with deeds,
find you through faith. What is there that faith will not find? It
reaches inaccessible realities, discovers the unknown, embraces the
immeasurable, takes possession of the eternal, and finally, in a certain manner, contains eternity itself with its vast expanse. I can say
boldly: I believe in you, eternal and blessed Trinity that I do not
understand; and while I am not capable of containing you with my
mind, I embrace you with my faith.*

St. Bernard, *In Cantica Cant.* 76:6

*O Lord, I confess your great power. If you are powerful, as you
are, what is impossible for you who can do everything? . . .
Although I am miserable, I firmly believe you can do what you
desire. And the more I hear of your greater marvels and consider
that you can add to them, the more my faith is strengthened; and I
believe with greater determination that you will do this. What is
there to marvel at in what the Almighty does?*

St. Teresa of Jesus, *Soliloquies* IV 2.

*Lord, let my life be one of faith, made concrete in thoughts,
words, and acts that are based entirely on the teachings of faith,
based on your words and your example, and all entirely for supernatural motives of faith; in the silencing of all undue suggestions of
human reason and experience, no matter how reasonable they may
seem, as soon as they disagree, not just with the dogmas of the
Catholic faith, but even with anything that faith asks us to think,
say, or do.*

cf C. de Foucauld, *Meditations on the Gospel*

258. THE JUST MAN LIVES BY FAITH

*O Lord, by your power fulfill my every good resolve and work of
faith*   *(2 Thes 1:11)*

1. "He who through faith is righteous shall live" (Rom 1:17).
For a Christian, faith ought to be the light that illuminates not only the times of prayer, but the whole of life. During prayer it is not
difficult to say: "I believe in God the Father almighty"; but a few
minutes afterwards, when faced with some difficult task, a
tiresome person, or some circumstance that is painful or upsets
our own plans, we easily forget that all this has been arranged by
God for our sanctification; that God is our Father and is more con-

cerned about the welfare of each of us than we are ourselves, even though we are the interested parties; that God is all-powerful and can help us in every difficulty. If we lose sight of the light of faith, we shall get lost in merely human considerations and protests, or in discouragement, like that of people who have no faith. We believe in God the Father almighty, but we do not believe strongly enough to recognize his will or at least his permission in every event, nor do we turn to him in every circumstance. Until the light of faith so penetrates us that it makes us see all things in relation to God and as dependent on him, it cannot be said that faith enlightens our entire life. Certain areas still remain in the shadows and still escape the true light. God never lets go of those who live by faith; in whatever situation they may be they can turn to their Creator and find in him their rock of refuge (Is 17:7-10). When Abraham was in obscure and extremely difficult circumstances, he believed unhesitatingly in God, and merited through faith to be called the "friend of God" (Jas 2:23); friendship means a continuous relationship, trusting recourse, unreserved self-surrender.

Those who live by faith, says Sr. Elizabeth of the Trinity, "never deal with secondary causes, but only with God ... Then nothing is ever trivial, not even performing the most ordinary actions, because we are not living in these things but go beyond created things" (Letters 268). Over and above all earthly circumstances and involvements, one who lives by faith perceives the hand of God, attends to his plans, welcomes his invitations, and adheres to him.

2. The just man lives his faith not for himself alone but for others as well. "Nor do men light a lamp and put it under a bushel, but on a stand, and it gives light to all in the house" (Mt 5:15). The light of faith which is enkindled in each Christian on the day of baptism, must be held high, above every human thought and reasoning, so that for each of us, it may illuminate our whole house: the interior dwelling of our soul, and the exterior house of our surroundings and of the society in which we live. "Let your light so shine before men"—exhorts the Lord—"that they may see your good works and give glory to your Father who is in heaven" (ib. 16). Of what good is faith without works? "Show me your faith apart from your works"—says St. James—"and I by my works will show you my faith" (2:18). The great duty of every believer is to give witness to faith through his actions. "The split between the faith which many profess and their daily lives deserves to be counted among the more serious errors of our age" (GS 43). Such behavior as this discredits the gospel, and is a cause for confusion and scandal. In pointing out this danger, Vatican II insists upon the necessity for a "living and mature faith, namely, one trained to see difficulties clearly and to master them ... This faith needs to prove its fruitfulness by penetrating the believer's entire life, including its worldly dimension" (ib. 21), that it may give proof of an entirely Christian life. This obligation is incumbent on the or-

dinary faithful, for they too are called to "share in Christ's prophetic office and to spread abroad a living witness to him, especially by living a life of faith and charity" (LG 12); they must accomplish their social apostolate "through a life in harmony with their faith, so that they can become the light of the world" (AA 13). Words do little to convince the modern world; it demands the testimony of deeds, and only this will induce it to accept the message of the gospel. Only those who "steadfastly join their profession of faith to a life springing from faith" become effective "heralds of the faith" (LG 35).

O Lord, grant that my will, upheld by grace, may keep far from all that is worldly and always run to you and receive everything from your hands with faith. The only true life of the soul lies in forgetting self in order to think of you and to be occupied only with your interests. Make me understand that in a life of faith nothing is capable of hindering love; that, instead, everything becomes a means, and even the obscurity of this faith is strong, substantial food for love.

My God, I run to you because I am in love with you; in love with you in faith and through faith. Grant that I may always will as you will, so that I can live of your life, and be transformed into you. Make my will continually run toward you without pause, and my soul see only you so that it may always be hastening toward you.

You penetrate everywhere with your goodness, with your love which is at once personal and infinite, and with your omnipotence. O Lord, give me a faith so simple that, without any reflection, my soul will seek refuge in it as if by instinct, and will enjoy in peace the good things that flow from this truth as from an abundant spring. Grant that moved by simple faith I may rest in this truth as in an inner refuge of repose, where nothing can harm me as long as I remain well hidden there. I must resolutely consider your goodness as above every goodness, your love above every love, your omnipotence above every power; and I must dwell and hide and live in this love and clothe myself in it; above all I must believe, because the just man lives by faith. Lord, make me believe and so surrender blindly to you.

cf Bl. M. Therese de Soubiran

O Lord, what good would it do me to have believed with my heart in order to obtain justification, if I hesitate to profess in word what I have received in my heart? You see the faith within, but that is not enough . . .

O Christ, my Lord, let me never be ashamed of your name, but, rather, allow me to be insulted because I believe in one who was crucified and put to death; without the shedding of your blood my sins would still be in existence.

St. Augustine *Sermon* 279:7-8.

259. CALLED TO HOPE

O God of hope, may hope live in me by the power of the Holy Spirit
(Rom 15:13)

1. "Every person should walk unhesitatingly according to his own personal gifts and duties, in the path of living faith which arouses hope, and works through charity" (LG 41). This is the dynamism of the Christian life when it is entirely founded upon the theological virtues. Hope is born of living faith. Faith not only makes us certain of the existence of God, but assures us that God is goodness, beauty, wisdom, providence, and infinite love which wants to give itself to us as our good, our possession, and our eternal happiness. Thus there is enkindled in the heart the desire of possessing this God who is so great and good. Is that possible? Yes, because it is God himself who made himself our final end, our highest good. Even in our status as simple creatures, our end is God, though only on a natural plane. By complying with the laws imprinted upon creation, we could attain to a certain natural enjoyment of God; however we could never aspire to possess God in himself nor enter into the current of his intimate life, nor participate in his Trinitarian life. Only the theological virtue of hope, gratuitously infused into us "by the power of the Holy Spirit" (Rom 15:13), confers this right upon us. Hope corresponds to a definite call which is due to God's liberality. "You were called to the one hope that belongs to you all" (Eph 4:4), says St. Paul, to the hope of an initial possession of God, already here on earth, through grace and the theological virtues, and of the full eternal possession of God in the blessedness of heaven. Every Christian is called to the theological virtue of hope, which has God as its object, and through this virtue is enabled to attain to such a lofty goal. What a wonderful condescension of God, who created us for himself, who wanted us to be his children, and who made us share in his divine nature, precisely in order that he might be the object of our hope, the final end of our life, and our eternal happiness. This is why an authentic Christian lives "awaiting our blessed hope, the appearing of the glory of our great God and Savior Jesus Christ, who gave himself for us to redeem us from all iniquity" (Tit 2:13-14).

2. "For in this hope we were saved"—St. Paul affirms—"Now hope that is seen is not hope. For who hopes for what he sees?" (Rom 8:24). Salvation, eternal happiness, and the eternal possession of God are objects of hope, precisely because we do not yet possess them. Just as what we see is not an object of faith, so also what we possess cannot be an object of hope. The movement of hope—even purely human hope—is all the more intense the less we possess its object and the less satisfied we are with what we have. "If something were possessed"—says St. John of the Cross—"there could no longer be hope for it" (Asc II 6:3). One who

has his fill of worldly goods, and of the conveniences and pleasures these offer him, is closed to any hope outside this world. So also one who feels himself "rich" enough from either a moral or spiritual point of view is at the opposite pole from hope. Such was the position of the Pharisee in the Gospel: he had nothing to ask of God, and expected nothing from him, because he was puffed up and satisfied with his "justice." Only one who has a spirit of true "poverty," who acknowledges his spiritual indigence, his frailty, and his moral weakness can open himself fully to hope, while awaiting salvation from God. Poverty of spirit and humility are the fertile soil in which the precious seed of theological hope develops.

Holy Scripture is filled with the cry of hope which rises from the hearts of the "poor of Yahweh": "But I am poor and needy; hasten to me, O God! You are my help and my deliverer; O Lord, do not tarry!" (Ps 70:5). "Whom have I in heaven, but you? And there is nothing upon earth that I desire besides you. My flesh and my heart may fail, but God is the strength of my heart and my portion for ever" (Ps 73:25-26).

To hope in our own power or capacity, in men and wealth and worldly resources is a fallacy without any stability; only God, who kindled in us the yearning for infinite happiness, "meets the deepest longings of the human heart . . . which is never fully satisfied by what this world has to offer" (GS 41).

> *My God, it was your supreme blessedness in the eternity past, as it is your blessedness in all eternities, to know yourself, as you alone can know you . . . O my God, what am I that you should make my blessedness to consist in that which is your own! That you should grant me not only the sight of you, but to share in your very own joy! O prepare me for it, teach me to thirst for it.*
>
> *O my God, shall I one day see you? What sight can compare to that great sight? Shall I see the source of that grace which enlightens me, strengthens me, and consoles me? As I came from you, as I am made through you, as I live in you, so, O my God, may I at last return to you, and be with you for ever and ever.*
>
> J.H. Newman, *Meditations on Christian Doctrine* XX:3; XVII:3

> *Living hope in God imparts such courage and valor and so elevates the soul to the things of eternal life that in comparison with these heavenly hopes all earthly things seem—as they truly are—dry, withered, dead, and worthless.*
>
> *A person is thus divested of all worldly garments and does not set his heart on anything of what there is, or will be, in the world; he lives clothed only in the hope of eternal life . . . he raises the eyes to look only at God . . . hoping for nothing from any one else . . . "as the eyes of a maid to the hand of her mistress, so our eyes look to the Lord our God, till he have mercy on us who hope in him (Ps 123:2) . . . Let me always gaze upon you, looking at nothing else and*

*not be content save with you alone, and so please you that it is true
to say that the soul obtains from you all that it hopes to receive from
you.*

St. John of the Cross, Dark Night II 21:6-8

260. CHRIST OUR HOPE

All my trust is in you, O Christ Jesus our hope   (1 Tim 1:1)

1. "Remember what you were at that time . . . having no hope
and without God in the world" (Eph 2:12), wrote St. Paul to the
Ephesians, referring to the time when they were still living in
paganism. What sadness comes from being "without hope!" The
one unfailing hope of man is God, the true God who from the
beginning of mankind has revealed himself as the God of the Promise, the Savior of his people. To the deceitful serpent who led
man into sin, he foretold the defeat that would be inflicted by the
"seed of the woman," that is, by her descendant (Gen 3:15): this
first promise already gives a glimpse of the Messiah. The promise
is renewed to Abraham: "And I will make you a great nation, and
I will bless you . . . I will make you exceedingly fruitful . . . And I
will establish my covenant between me and you and your
descendants . . . an everlasting covenant to be God to you and to
your descendants after you" (Gen 12:2; 17:6-7). When, humanly
speaking, all hope seemed lost, the totally unthought of birth of
Isaac began the promised line of descent: here was the people that
God was choosing as "his people," whom he will shield against
idolatry, and save from war, slaughter, and slavery and lead
through all the vicissitudes of the centuries to the fulfillment of
the promise: the birth of the Redeemer. The whole history of Israel
was stretched out toward the hope of the fulfillment of the promise, and found therein its purpose. The Church, founded by
Christ the Redeemer, is the new Israel, the new people of God, the
heir of the promise. St. Paul's exhortation is based upon this concept: "Let us hold fast the confession of our hope without wavering, for he who promised is faithful" (Heb 10:23). The foundation
of our hope is God's promise, his faithfulness; it is his helping omnipotence, which he has put at our disposal in order to lead us to
salvation. More fortunate than ancient Israel, the new People of
God has in Christ the highest proof of God's fidelity. While
Israel's hope proceeded somewhat gropingly because the promise
was still veiled, and was being fulfilled gradually, Christian hope
is now well defined and oriented decisively toward "Christ Jesus
our hope" (1 Tim 1:1).

2. "Christ redeemed us . . . having become a curse for
us . . . that in him the blessing of Abraham might come upon the
Gentiles, that we might receive the promise of the Spirit through

faith" (Gal 3:13-14). In Christ, who redeemed us by his death on the cross, we receive the blessing God promised to Abraham. In Christ the promise is fulfilled, and in him we have the pledge and the means of our redemption: the forgiveness of the sins "that he himself bore in his body on the tree" (1 Pet 2:24), and the grace, which by justifying us, makes us his brothers, sons of the same Father, and therefore "heirs, heirs of God and fellow heirs with Christ, . . . that we may also be glorified with him" (Rom 8:17). And not only this, for through the mediation of Christ, the new promise, too, is carried out: the sending of the Holy Spirit, for, since we are "sons, God has sent the Spirit of his Son into our hearts, crying, 'Abba, Father!' " (Gal 4:6).

Christian hope is not based on personal merit, nor upon good works, nor good intentions, for all these are too transitory, and too utterly disproportionate to the attainment of God; rather, our hope is based upon God himself, upon Christ the one Mediator and Savior. For hope not to become rashness, it must obviously be accompanied by personal effort and diligence; still we must be convinced that all our good will and good works are always insufficient; only God can sanctify us, only God can raise us up to himself and give us himself as our possession. Only God, the object of our hope, is also the support of hope, its buttress, its fulcrum. With this in mind St. Therese of the Child Jesus wrote: "Sanctity does not consist in this or that practice; it consists in a disposition of the heart which makes us humble and little in the arms of God, conscious of our weakness, and confident to the point of audacity in the goodness of our Father" (Novissima Verba, p. 129).

Since God has blessed us and predestinated us in Christ, we find in Christ the immediate basis of our hope: he is our way, our Mediator before the Father, the "living bread" (Jn 6:51), the viaticum for our journey.

You, O Lord, are my hope. Whatever I must do or give up, endure or desire, you are my hope . . . This is the sole reason for my expectation. Others may allege their own merits, boasting that they bear the burden of the day and the heat, saying that they fast twice on the sabbath, and finally glory that they are not like other men; instead, for me, it is good to adhere to you and to put my hope in you, Lord God. Let others put their hope in other things; some trusting in knowledge or in worldly astuteness, and others relying upon their nobility or their rank, or some other vanity; but, thanks to your love, I look upon all these things as loss, and esteem them as refuse, since you, O Lord, are my hope. Let him who wishes, rely on the uncertainty of riches; I, though still far from you, do not even trust in what is necessary for life, confiding simply in your word, for on the strength of that, I have renounced everything: Seek first the kingdom of God and his justice and all these other things will be added for you . . . If I am promised rewards, I shall hope to obtain them through your goodness; and if battles are waged against me, if the world grows cruel, if the devil fumes with rage, if my flesh itself rebels against the spirit, I will hope in you.

St. Bernard, *In Psalmum "Qui habitat"* 9:5

O hope, sweet sister of faith, you unlock eternal life with the keys of your blood. You guard the city of the soul against the enemy's confusion; you never slacken your steps, so that the devil may not confound the soul with despair because of the weight of sins committed; but fearlessly, you persevere in virtue, putting the price of blood upon the balance scale. You crown with victory the head of whoever perseveres, because you expected this by virtue of your blood; it is you who bind the devil of confusion with the cord of living faith; you defeat the subtle deceit that he uses against the soul to keep it in continual darkness and affliction.

St. Catherine of Siena, *Letters* 343, v.5

261. THE HOPE OF GLORY

Lord, you are my portion; therefore I will hope in you (Lam 3:24)

1. "May the Father of glory . . . have the eyes of your hearts enlightened that you may know what is the hope to which he has called you, what are the riches of his glorious inheritance in the saints" (Eph 1:17-18). Only God can make us understand the greatness of our Christian calling to hope, which decisively directs us to "the inheritance of God among the saints," that is, to the beatific possession of God in eternal life in fellowship with the whole Church triumphant. A Christian is a person journeying toward a goal beyond this world; we have not here a lasting dwelling-place, our hearts are not anchored to the goods of earth, but go beyond them because in hope we have "a sure and steadfast anchor of the soul, a hope that enters into the inner shrine behind the curtain [heaven], where Jesus has gone as a forerunner on our behalf" (Heb 6:19-20), to prepare a place for us in his glory.

When hope enters deeply into a Christian's life it unifies every aspiration and desire, and directs him toward God. Then there is no longer any room for so many little worldly hopes: for the esteem and the applause of men, an easier and more comfortable life, and a desire for the first place. A Christian does not despise earthly realities, but utilizes them and values them with an unfettered heart; rather than being an object of attachment, they become a springboard for leaping always further ahead toward the conquest of God. Thus life takes on the pace of a voyage that has no definite stops here on earth. It acquires a sense of expectation, of a vigil filled with longing. There is no time to lose, there can be no laziness or indolence for those who yearn to reach God: each day should mark a step forward toward eternity. "So we are always of good courage,"—writes St. Paul—"we know that while we are at home in the body we are away from the Lord—we are of good courage, and we would rather be away from the body and at home with the Lord" (2 Cor 5:6-8). This is the cry of Christian hope, impatient to reach God, a cry that does not end in sighs, but in busy deeds to attain its purpose. "Whether we are at home or away, we make it our aim to please him" (ib. 9).

2. Writing about the witness of the laity in this connection, Vatican II says: "They show themselves to be children of the promise, if, strong in faith and in hope, they make the most of the present time, and with patience await the glory that is to come. Let them not, then, conceal this hope in the depths of their hearts, but even in the framework of secular life let them express it by a continual turning toward God and by wrestling 'against the world-rulers of this darkness, against the spiritual forces of wickedness' (Eph 6:12)" (LG 35). Our conduct as Christians should make it plain that our hope is not shut up in the narrow confines of earthly life, that we are not satisfied, either for ourselves or for others, with bread, home, work, profession, or bettered social structures, but that our hope goes beyond all this, fixing itself on God above every earthly good. "Always be prepared to make a defense to anyone who calls you to account for the hope that is in you" (1 Pet 3:15), wrote St. Peter to the early Christians. The principal response is always that given by deeds. If someone is eager to amass worldly goods in order to enjoy them selfishly, how can he demonstrate that his hope lies above all in eternal life?

"If for this life only we have hoped in Christ, we are of all men most to be pitied," St. Paul said rightly (1 Cor 15:19). But in the risen and glorified Christ the hope of the Christian reaches heaven. It is this very hope that infuses the courage to confront not only the ordinary adversities of life, but also, should it be necessary, persecution and even martyrdom. This would be the moment, then, to put St. Peter's exhortation into practice, not concealing our hope, but openly justifying it to anyone who asks. Threats, dangers, and adversities do not intimidate those who have put all their hope in God, for they know that God can give them strength with his own strength, and that "the sufferings of the present time are not worth comparing with the glory that is to be revealed to us" (Rom 8:18).

My God you want me to love you more than your creatures, and eternal things more than those of this world, as is written: Seek first the kingdom of God and his justice, and all these things will be added ... Make me understand that my purpose is eternity, and that temporal things are given me to be used ... Often, instead, when I am seeking temporal goods, I pay no attention to eternal rewards ... But if I sought heavenly things, my labor would already be fruitful; indeed, when during prayer the soul yearns for your beauty, O my Creator, inflamed by divine desires, it is united with heavenly realities, and detached from lower things; in the joy of its fervor it is enlarged to understand better, and, understanding, becomes inflamed. To love heavenly things is already a leap upward, and when a man is aspiring to heavenly things with great longing, he already begins to have in a wonderful way the very things he is asking to receive.

St. Gregory the Great, Morals XV, 53.

O Lord, here on earth you are my hope, but here on earth you are not my inheritance, although certainly in the land of the living. This is in truth the land of the dying: we must leave it, but what counts is where we are going. Here on earth, the evil man goes his way, and the good man goes his way; it is not that the good man passes on and the evil one remains here, or that the evil man passes on and the good one stays; they pass on together, but they are not headed toward the same end ... Different places will receive them for different merits accompany them ...

From the moment that hope nourishes our life here on earth, our perfect life is none other than that which is promised us. Meanwhile, here, there are still lamentations, still temptations, still anxieties, still grief, still dangers ... because we are exiles far from you, O Lord. If indeed, to be united with you is life, then to go far from you is death. What comforts us? Hope.

Lord, let us live in hope; from hope will blossom our praise, our hymn to you ... in our toilsome pilgrimage, amid the wickedness and snares of the enemy, troubled on all sides by the temptations of the world, and destined to live in weariness and suffering, do not let us be abandoned by hope!

St. Augustine, In Ps. 145:7,9.

262.   SEVENTEENTH SUNDAY OF ORDINARY TIME

YEAR A

Lord, I pray you, make the spirit of wisdom descend upon me
(Wis 7:7)

The wisdom that comes from God and is directed toward salvation constitutes the message of today's Liturgy. The first reading (1 Kg 3:5,7-12) gives us Solomon's beautiful prayer to God, who had appeared to him in a dream and told him to ask whatever he wished. Very wisely the king asked for "a kind heart" for governing his people, one that would be "able to discern between good and evil" (ib. 9). In substance he was asking for wisdom: this pleased the Lord, and he granted it, together with other blessings. Unfortunately, the great king's end was not equal to his beginning; yet his wise request lives on to point out that true wisdom is worth more than all earthly treasures, and that only God can grant it.

The Gospel of the day (Mt 13:44-52), relates the last parables of the kingdom, and shows Jesus—Wisdom incarnate—teaching men the wisdom that is needed in order to conquer the kingdom of heaven. His teaching in parable form is particularly vivid and suited to impress both mind and heart, and hence to impel to action. Jesus compares the kingdom of heaven to "a treasure hidden in a field, which a man found and covered up; then in his joy he goes and sells all that he has and buys that field" (ib. 44). Or else, "it is like a merchant in search of fine pearls" (ib. 45), who, when he finds one of great value, "goes, sells all he has, and buys it" (ib. 46). In both cases there is the discovery of a treasure: in the first it is found by chance; in the second, sought for on purpose; in both, the finder hurries to sell all that he has in order to acquire it. The kingdom of heaven—the gospel, Christianity, grace, and friendship with God—is the treasure which is hidden and still present in the world; many have it close at hand, yet do not discover it, or having discovered it, do not value it as much as it deserves; and so they neglect it, preferring, instead, the earthly kingdom, that is, the pleasures, riches, and satisfactions of life in this world. Only those who are docile of heart can be taught to understand "the difference between good and evil" (1 Kg 3:9), between the eternal and the transitory, between substance and appearance; only these will make the decision to "sell all they possess" in order to acquire this precious treasure. Jesus does not ask only a little of us for attaining to the kingdom, he asks us for everything; but it is also true that he does not promise us a little, he promises everything: eternal life in eternal and beatifying communion with God. If a man is ready to lose all his earthly belongings in order to save his earthly life, why will he not do as much and more to assure himself of eternal life? The parable of the net, filled with all kinds of fish, which are going to be sorted out at the end of the day and the bad ones thrown away (Mt 13:47-48), leads to the same conclusion. It is not the temporary situations that are of value, but the final ones, the definitive, eternal ones; nevertheless these latter are prepared for now, in time, by those who act with true wisdom. In order to learn this, it is not enough just to listen to the parables; we need to understand them. "Have you understood all this?" (ib. 51), Jesus asked his listeners. He meant "understood" not only in an abstract, indefinite sense, but in concrete relationship with self, with life, with personal circumstances. One who understands in this manner becomes the disciple that Jesus compared to "the housholder who brings out of his treasure what is new and what is old" (ib. 52), that is, one who is able to find in the gospel, what is new, and in the Old Testament, what is old, for the wise standard of conduct. Then neither the renunciations required for attaining the kingdom, nor the adversities of life will dismay us, because we shall have understood that what counts is not happiness in this world, but eternal happiness, and we shall be convinced that "in everything God works for good with those who love him" (Rom 8:28; 2nd reading).

O God, our strength and our hope, without whom nothing is holy, nothing has value: pour out your mercy upon us, so that, upheld and guided by you, we may use the good things of this passing world, while holding firmly to everlasting realities.
Roman Missal, Collect

Lord, help me to direct myself to everything in an ordered love, diverting my gaze from the world, and turning it toward heaven, making use of this world as though I used it not, and distinguishing, through an intimate tasting of my mind, the things that I should make use of and that I should enjoy, so that I may concern myself with transitory things only provisionally and only as far as necessary, but may embrace eternal realities with an eternal desire.

O Truth, the homeland of exiles, and the final end of their exile! I see you but cannot enter you: the flesh holds me prisoner; I am not worthy to be admitted for I bear the mark of sin. O Wisdom, reaching from end to end mightily, ruling all things with power, and sweetly disposing all things to satisfy and regulate our affections, direct our actions according to the needs of our temporal life, and govern our affections according to the demands of your eternal truth, so that each one of us may glory in you without fear, and say: Lord, you have set charity in order in me. You are indeed the strength of God and the wisdom of God; O Christ, bridegroom of the Church, our Lord, God blessed above all things throughout all ages.
St. Bernard, In Cantica Cant. 50:8.

YEAR B

You open your hand, Lord, you satisfy the desire of every living thing   *(Ps 145:16)*

God's providence, which satisfies all man's needs, is the recurring theme of the day. In the Second Book of Kings (4:42-44), we read of the multiplication of the loaves worked by Elisha, a symbol and a prelude of the one accomplished some eight centuries later by Jesus of which we read now in the Gospel of John (6:1-15). A man with "twenty loaves of barley" was presented to the prophet Elisha, who ordered him to distribute them to the hundred men who were present. The servant objected that the supply was insufficient, but Elisha repeated his order in God's name: "Thus says the Lord: 'They shall eat and have some left' " (2 Kg 4:43). The miracle was repeated—in a much more imposing way—on the grassy slopes of Galilee—when Jesus, who had gone up the mountain with his disciples, saw himself surrounded by "a multitude that was coming to him" (Jn 6:5). Just as Elisha had taken care of his disciples' hunger, so Jesus provided for the crowd that had followed him in order to hear his words. But while in the first case twenty loaves had satisfied a hundred men, here only five loaves and two fishes were enough for around five thousand; in both cases there were fragments—a full twelve baskets in the gospel account—to demonstrate that God is not stingy in providing for the needs of his creatures. "You open your hand"—sings the responsorial song—"you satisfy the desire of every living thing" (Ps 145:16). Then why are there so many hungry people in the world today? That is something to think about. The two miracles here were not performed out of nothing, but from a small, in fact a very small, supply: the twenty loaves offered to Elisha by the man from Baal Shalisha, the five loaves and two fishes given to Jesus by a boy who had brought them along. Almighty God can make everything from nothing, but when he is dealing with his free creature, man, he normally does not act without man's concurrence. Whatever we can do is always little, but God wants that little, in fact requires it as the condition of his intervention. And although there are so many people today who cannot get enough bread to satisfy their hunger, may this not perhaps be because those who are rolling in wealth cannot find it in their hearts to offer to their brothers at least what they do not need themselves. The man who brought the first of his loaves of bread to Elisha in a time of scarcity, and the boy who gave up the little he had so that Jesus might multiply it, do not have many imitators even among believers. When we do our part, God—ever merciful and omnipotent—does not fail to intervene by making our good works bear fruit. Saints like Cottolengo or Don Guanella experienced this even to the miraculous. Jesus, who was moved and concerned about the hungry crowd, reminds the faithful of the need for a practical understanding of the needs of others; one not limited to kind words, but extending to concrete help.

Just as Elisha's miracle was a figure of the multiplication of the loaves performed by Jesus, so this latter miracle is itself a preparation for, and a figure of, a still more striking miracle, that of the Eucharist. It was not by chance that the account of the Lord's actions—"Jesus took the loaves, and when he had given thanks, he distributed them" (Jn 6:11)—anticipates almost to the letter the actions and words of the institution of the Eucharist. After having provided so liberally for the hunger of the body, Jesus will provide in a divine and ineffable manner for the hunger of the spirit. Nourished by one bread, the Body of the Lord, the faithful form one body, the Mystical Body of Christ. This truth is the basis of the obligation of charity and of the Christian solidarity of which St. Paul speaks in the second reading (Eph 4:1-6), as he urges the faithful to "maintain the unity of the Spirit in the bond of peace," because there is "one body and one Spirit . . . one Lord, one faith" (ib. 4-5).

> *All your works shall give thanks to you, O Lord, and all your saints shall bless you! . . . The eyes of all look to you, and you give them their food in due season. You open your hand and satisfy the desire of every living thing. The Lord is just in all his ways, and kind in all his doings.*
>
> Psalm 145:10, 15-17

> *Lord, when you saw the hungry multitude in the desert, you said: "I feel compassion for this crowd;" you, who with five loaves of bread satisfied the hunger of five thousand persons, look kindly upon your famished children . . . and after satisfying their bodily hunger, be good enough to satisfy the hunger of their souls also, with the heavenly food of your teaching, you who live and reign as God for ever and ever. Amen.*
>
> Paul VI, *Teachings*, v.4

> *My God, you are careful and tender to each of the beings that you have created, as if each were the only one in the whole world. For you can see every one of them at once, and you love every one in this mortal life, and pursue every one by itself, with all the fullness of your attributes, as if you were waiting on it and ministering to it for its own sake . . .*
> *All your acts of providence are acts of love. If you send evil upon us, it is in love . . . And you turn that evil into good. You visit men with evil to bring them to repentance, to increase their virtue, to gain for them greater good hereafter. Nothing is done in vain, but has its gracious end . . . I acknowledge with a full and firm faith, O Lord, the wisdom and goodness of your Providence, even in your inscrutable judgments and your incomprehensible decrees.*
>
> J.H. Newman, *Meditations on Christian Doctrine* XIX 1,2

YEAR C

> *Lord, your steadfast love endures forever. Do not forsake the work of your hands*   *(Ps 138:8)*

Man's prayer and God's merciful acquiescence are the interwoven themes of today's readings. In the first place we are given the touching yet daring prayer of Abraham on behalf of the two sinful cities (Gen 18:20-32 1st reading), a magnificent expression of his confidence in God and of his concern for the salvation of others. God had revealed to him his plan for the destruction of Sodom and Gomorrah, which were corrupt in the extreme, and the patriarch sought to ward off this punishment for the sake of the just who might be found in the midst of the sinners. But he was forced to come down gradually from his first suggestion of fifty just men to the much lesser number of ten: "Oh, let not the Lord be angry, and I will speak again but this once. Suppose ten are found there" (ib. 32). Neither the benevolent acquiescence of God who each time accepted the smaller number, nor Abraham's heartfelt entreaty succeeded in saving the city, because of its general perversion; only Lot's family was to be saved to give testimony to divine mercy and to the powers of Abraham's intercession. This episode remains forever a proof of the terrible consequences of obstinancy in evil and of the saving power of good through which only ten just men—if they had been found—would have been able to prevent the destruction of the two cities.

But notice in the New Testament how there opens a new and wonderful page in God's mercy: a single just man, "the Servant of Yahweh," already foretold by the prophets, is sufficient to save not two cities, nor a country, but the whole of humanity. God has forgiven all the sins of men in virtue of Christ's passion, "having canceled the bond which stood against us with its legal demands: this he set aside, nailing it to the cross" (Col 2:14; 2nd reading). St. Paul's imaginative sentence gives a good explanation of how the enormous weight of the sins of the whole human race has been canceled by Christ's death. Nevertheless, not even his superabundant expiation will be of use to individual souls if these do not cooperate with their own personal renunciation.

The Gospel again takes up a full treatment of the topic of prayer. At the request of his disciples, Jesus teaches them how to pray: "When you pray, say: 'Father hallowed be thy name; thy kingdom come'" (ib. 2). Abraham, the friend of God, used to call him "my Lord"; the Christian, on the authority of Jesus, calls him "Father," a name that gives his prayer an entirely new filial tone, so that he is now free to pour out his heart into the heart of God by declaring his needs in the simplest and most spontaneous form, such as that indicated in the "Our Father." Besides, through the parable of the importunate friend, Jesus teaches us to pray with perseverance and insistency—as Abraham did—without fear of being indiscreet: "Ask, seek, knock." There are no inopportune times for God: he is never vexed by the humble and confident prayer of his children; on the contrary, he is pleased by it: "For everyone who asks receives, and he who seeks finds, and to him who knocks, it will be opened" (ib. 10). And if we do not always get everything we want, it is nevertheless certain that our prayer is never going to be wasted because our heavenly Father always responds with his love and his favors, even though it may be in a hidden way or in one that is different from what we expect. The important thing is not to receive this or that favor, but that we may never lack the grace to be faithful to God every day of our lives. This grace is assured to anyone who prays without tiring: "If you, then, who are evil, know how to give good gifts to your children, how much more will the heavenly Father give the Holy Spirit to those who ask him!" (ib. 13). In the gift of the Holy Spirit are included all the supernatural blessings that God wishes to grant his children.

> *Oh, what a difficult thing I ask you, my true God: that you love someone who does not love you, that you open to one who does not knock, that you give health to one who likes to be sick and goes about looking for sickness. You say, my Lord, that you come to seek sinners; these, Lord, are real sinners. Do not look at our blindness, my God, but at all the blood your Son has shed for us. Let your mercy shine upon evil that has so increased; behold, Lord, we are your handiwork. May your goodness and mercy help us!*
>
> St. Teresa of Jesus, *Soliloquies* 8:3

> *O Jesus, we believe that you can do all things, and that you will grant us all that we ask for in faith; you will do this because you are infinitely good and omnipotent; you will grant us still more because you have plainly promised it. You will give us either what we are asking or something better. Although you may make us wait, and although we may receive it late, or even never, we are sure that waiting is the best thing for us, and that to receive it late or even never is better for us than to receive it at once.*
>
> C. de Foucauld, *Meditations upon the Gospel*

263.   HOPE DOES NOT DISAPPOINT

You are good, Lord, to those who wait for you, to the soul that seeks you   *(Lam 3:25)*

1. "In hope [Abraham] believed against hope, that he should become the father of many nations" (Rom 4:18). The theological virtues are deeply connected: faith enkindles hope, and hope sustains faith. And just as a Christian gives proof of the solidity of his faith by persevering in it in spite of its obscurities, he also gives proof of the solidity of his hope by not ceasing to hope in adverse circumstances. Indeed these very obstacles make his hope grow stronger. For this reason St. Paul can say: "We rejoice in our sufferings, knowing that suffering produces endurance, endurance produces character, and character produces hope." He concludes: "And hope does not disappoint us" (Rom 5:3-5). Christian hope never disappoints, not even when adversity afflicts us. For every creature that is dear to God relives in some manner the story of Job, who was tested in his material goods and in his sons, abandoned by his wife and his friends, reduced to the most squalid wretchedness and loneliness, and covered with leprosy from head to foot. Why does God permit his friends to suffer so much? "God

did not make death"—says Scripture—"and he does not delight in the death of the living. For he created all things that they might exist . . . But ungodly men by their words and deeds summoned death" (Wis 1:13-14,16). Death and suffering are the result of sin, not only as a punishment, but also as a purification, as a saving expiation for self and for others in union with Christ's passion. Viewed in this light it is not difficult to realize the necessity and the function of sorrow; but when we are groaning under such blows, the divine plan—which is one of love and salvation—is far from evident to us, and we cannot escape the painful feeling of being abandoned by God. This is the moment to hope against all hope, to remember that "hope does not disappoint," because we are counting on God's love, and this love has already been poured into our hearts "through the Holy Spirit which has been given to us" (Rom 5:5). The love of God, his grace, and still more, the Holy Spirit, are the pledge of the eternal life which awaits us, and for which suffering is preparing us.

2. "Man can never love God as much as he should be loved, neither can he ever believe and hope in him as much as he ought" (St Thos 1-2,64,4co). This is why we can truly say that the measure of hope in God is to hope without measure. When we sincerely try to do all we can on our part to please God, we need not fear that we are being too bold in our hope. Blind, limitless hope in the Lord is so pleasing to him, that the more we hope, the more God helps us, and overwhelms us with his graces. "The more a soul hopes, the more it attains," St. John of the Cross declares (Asc III 7:2), and St. Therese of the Child Jesus, elaborating on this thought, writes: "We can never have too much confidence in God, so powerful and so merciful. We obtain from him as much as we hope for" (cf *Story of a Soul,* Taylor).

Sometimes, the consciousness of sins committed, of infidelities, and of failures in the practice of virtue, can discourage us and clip the wings of our hope. Then we must remember that God loves us not because we are without sin, but because he has infused his grace into us and made us his children. He wants our salvation and our sanctification more than we do; if we are seeking him with all our heart and trusting in him with all our strength, he himself will sanctify us in spite of the failures of the past, and the wretchedness and weaknesses of the present.

A genuine Christian is a person of unconquerable hope, and also a sower of hope. The modern world, immersed in religious indifference, imprisoned in materialism, and not infrequently tempted to despair, has an extreme need of opening itself to the expanding influence of Christian hope. There is need to arouse in men throughout the world "a lively hope, the gift of the Holy Spirit, that they will finally be caught up in peace and utter happiness" (GS 93). This was St. Paul's wish for the Romans: "May the God of hope fill you with all joy and peace in believing, so that by the power of the Holy Spirit you may abound in hope" (Rom

15:13). It must be the Christian's work to bring it to all the world.

O Lord, our God, let us hope in the shadow of your wings. Guard us and bear us up. Yes, you will uphold us: uphold us when we are little, and when we have grown old you will still sustain us; for our strength is strong when it rests upon you, but weakness when it depends upon ourselves. Our good is always alive when it is near you, and when we are averted from you we are perverted. O Lord, let us return to you again that we may not be swept away, for our unfailing good is with you and is identified with you; nor are we afraid of not finding again on our return the place from which we fell. Our house is your eternity, which will not fall down while we are absent.
St. Augustine, *Confessions* IV 16:31

Let us hope! We are among those, O Jesus, whom you have come to save just because we are perishing . . . because without you we are continuously perishing . . . Let us have hope!
Whatever our faults may be, O Jesus, you want to save us. The worse sinners we are, the closer we are to death, the more desperate the state we are in both as to body and to soul, the more you want to save us, O Jesus, because you have come to save that which is about to perish . . . Do not let us ever be discouraged, make us always hope! We are on the edge of the abyss, we are about to perish, we deserve to perish, we ought justly to perish after all our ingratitude, we are perishing; we are precisely the ones you came to save, O Jesus. You came to save those who are perishing. You are infinitely good and infinitely powerful; this is true until the last moment, as long as there is a breath of life, for anyone who hopes in you!
C. de Foucauld, *Meditations on the Gospel*

264. THE FATHER'S LOVE

Blessed are you, O God, who in your love have destined us to be your sons   *(Eph 1:3-5)*

1. In the Old Testament God revealed himself as the supereminent Being: "I am who am" (Ex 3:14); in the New, he revealed the deep intrinsic nature of his being: "God is love" (Jn 5:16). God is love in his intimate life, and is for this very reason the Trinity: he is the Father who begets the Son by giving him his entire nature and his divine life; he is the Son who in turn gives himself totally to the Father; he is the Holy Spirit who proceeds from the love and the mutual gift of the Father and of the Son. God is love outside of himself also, in his works: he is love in the creation of all the beings that he freely calls to life, and above all in the creation of man, whom he forms in his image and likeness (Gen 1:26). But God demonstrates his love yet more by raising man from the status of

a simple creature to that of his son: "See what love the Father has given us, that we should be called children of God; and so we are" (1 Jn 3:1). It is not a case, here, of an honorable, symbolic term, or of a "manner of speech," but of a great reality, of a new "manner of being," by which man is profoundly transformed, and made a participant in the nature and the life of God, that is, of God's being, which is love. Man enters thus into being a part of God's family: he is loved by God his Father, and is capable of returning that love as a son, because God has infused his love into him. "For you did not receive the spirit of slavery"—exclaims St. Paul—"but you have received the spirit of sonship. When we cry 'Abba! Father!' it is the Spirit himself bearing witness with our spirit that we are children of God" (Rom 8:15-16). A son cannot have a nature different from that of his father; God is love, and for that reason he has infused his love into man in order that man, too, might be love. God "tells us how he wants to be known: that he is love; and how he wishes to be honored and served by us: that love is our supreme commandment" (Paul VI, Eccl suam 41).

2. " 'God is love, and he who abides in love abides in God, and God abides in him' (1 Jn 4:16). God pours out his love into our hearts through the Holy Spirit who has been given to us. Thus the first and most necessary gift is that charity by which we love God above all things, and our neighbor because of God" (LG 42). The virtue of charity is created participation in the infinite love by which God loves himself; that is, in the love by which the Father loves the Son, the Son loves the Father, and they love each other in the Holy Spirit. Through charity a Christian is called to "abide in God" (1 Jn 4:16), to enter into the circle of the eternal love that unites the three Persons of the most holy Trinity to each other. Faith, which makes us share in the knowledge God has of himself, has already given us entry into the intimacy of divine life, while hope makes us confident of sharing one day in eternal happiness; but charity impels us still further by introducing us even here below into that movement of ineffable love that is the life of the Most Blessed Trinity. Through charity the Christian abides in God to the point of being associated with the Father's love for the Son, and the Son's love for the Father, loving the Father and the Son in the love of the Holy Spirit.

And since divine love does not remain shut up in the bosom of the Trinity, but is poured out upon us from the Trinity, charity produces a similar impulse in those who open their hearts to the love of all their brothers. Only through the charity which makes us a sharer in God's love do we become capable of "loving God above all things, and of loving our neighbor on account of our love for God." Charity is completed only when it goes out from God to embrace all creatures with him, in him, and for him. Love in God is one: in his intimate life and in his relations with men; charity in the Christian is one and indivisible in the impetus toward God and the impulse toward neighbor. "This commandment we have from him, that he who loves God should love his brother also" (1 Jn 4:21).

O charity, you have been able to make God a man. For a little while, you separated from his immense majesty this God become small ... You prepared the holy cross for the salvation of the world which by that time was lost. You made death vain by teaching God to die. When God, the Son of God almighty was killed by men, it was because of you, O charity, that neither of the two, neither Father nor Son, was moved to anger.

You sustain the life of the heavenly people when you assure peace, preserve faith, protect innocence, honor truth, love patience, and restore hope. You make a single body and a single spirit of men who are different in customs, age, and power, but endowed with the same nature. You do not let the glorious martyrs be dissuaded from confessing themselves Christian by any torment, or new kind of death, or reward, or friendship, or feeling of affection, which tortures more cruelly than any executioner ...

You join heavenly mysteries to human ones, and the human to heavenly. You preserve the divine secrets. In the Father you govern and command. In the Son you obey yourself. In the Holy Spirit you rejoice. And since you are one in three Persons, you can in no way be divided; no trick of human curiosity can disturb you. You spring from the source that is the Father, and you flow fully into the Son: but even though you flow fully into the Son, you are not separated from the Father. You are rightly called God, because you alone direct the power of the Trinity.

St. Zeno of Verona, *De spe, fide, et caritate* 9

Thanks, thanks to you, O eternal Father, for you have not despised me, the work of your hands, nor have you turned your face from me nor despised my desires ... Your wisdom, your goodness, your clemency, and your infinite good have overlooked all the endless evils and faults that are in me, and through your light you have given me light. In your wisdom I have understood the truth, in your clemency I have found your charity and love of neighbor. What has constrained you? Not my virtues, but only your charity ... Grant that my memory may be capable of remembering your benefits, that my will may burn in the fire of your charity ...

I confess, and do not deny, that you loved me before I existed, and that your love for me is ineffable, as if you were mad with love for your own creature.

St. Catherine of Siena, *Dialogue* 148

265.   HE FIRST LOVED US

Lord, you have loved me with an everlasting love   (Jer 31:3)

1. "We love because he [God] first loved us" (1 Jn 4:19). Man, as a simple creature, is capable only of human love, which can be

affection, sympathy, sentiment, or even passion; and this can even reach the point of total dedication to the person loved, as that of a mother for a son. All this is noble and beautiful, but it is infinitely distant from charity, which is "a participation in the infinite charity which is the Holy Spirit" (St Thos 2-2,24,7), and hence in the love of God himself.

From the point of view of charity, we cannot take any initiative; this can come only from God. In fact, God loved us "first," and by loving us has poured his divine love into us, so that we can love him in return with his very love. Our capacity for affection, however great it may be, cannot reach nor produce even the least degree of divine love. "Charity"—St. Thomas teaches—"is not to be found in us by nature, nor to be acquired by natural powers; rather, it is due to the effusion of the Holy Spirit, who is the love of the Father and of the Son, and the participation in this which is offered us is precisely created charity" (ib. 2). The holy Doctor does but comment upon and amplify the famous Pauline statement: "God's love has been poured into our hearts through the Holy Spirit which has been given to us" (Rom 5:5).

God's love has preceded us without waiting for us to be worthy of it; by loving us he made us worthy. "In this is love"—explains St. John—"not that we loved God, but that he loved us and sent his Son to be the expiation of our sins" (1 Jn 4:10). For divine love to be able to reach us, God had to knock down the barrier that had been set up by sin; he did it, not through patriarchs or prophets, but by means of his divine Son. This is the greatest initiative and at the same time the greatest proof of God's love for us.

2. The love which originates from God is absolutely gratuitous and spontaneous; we have not done, nor would we have been able to do, anything to deserve it. Indeed, on our part, we have done nothing else than be unworthy of it, not only through the sin of our first parents, but also by our personal sins. God's love is not directed to the innocent and the just, but to sinners: "If we say we have no sin, we deceive ourselves" (1 Jn 1:8). Yet God's love is not stopped. He had already announced it to the chosen people through Hosea: "When Israel was a child, I loved him, and out of Egypt I called my son. The more I called them, the more they went from me . . . yet it was I who taught Ephraim to walk, I took them up in my arms; but they did not know that I healed them . . . My heart recoils within me, my compassion grows warm and tender . . . I will not again destroy Ephraim; for I am God and not man" (Hos 11:1-3;8-9). Israel's history is prolonged in the history of every one of us. God preceded us with his love, but we do not understand: instead of accepting the divine gift we turn our back to him and go in search of worldly loves; we become slaves of our own passions and of those of others. But God pursues us, not to destroy us for he has too much compassion; he is God, "not man;" he is Love, and wants to conquer with love. "But God who

is rich in mercy"—says St. Paul—"out of the great love with which he loved us, even when we were dead through our trespasses, made us alive together with Christ . . . that in the coming ages he might show the immeasurable riches of his grace in kindness toward us in Christ Jesus" (Eph 2:4-7). Through his beloved Son God reaches man the sinner, redeems him, and pours out his love upon him. If we think about it, we might say that God has not only desired to put us in a position to love him, but in a position where it would be impossible not to love him. Yet, we have still not understood the mystery of the "great love" with which God has loved us, and like Israel we go in search of strange gods, of wealth, of an easy life, of an honorable position, of worldly pleasures. If we knew the gift of God and who it is that loves us, we would not cease to call upon his love.

O Lord Jesus Christ, you invite us, you enrapture us, you draw us to your love by anticipating ours, so great is the force of your affection. Indeed, no invitation to love is more insistent, no compulsion and no allurement so strong as being already loved beforehand, for a heart which has been slumbering is roused when it feels the first stirring of love; if it was already burning, it becomes all the more inflamed when it sees that it is loved and forestalled in love.

Even though you were loving me beyond all that words can describe, O most beloved Lord Jesus Christ, still, ungrateful sinner that I am, with a heart of stone within me . . . I did not recognize your burning love in my icy heart. And even though I might wish that the affection which you were so freely offering me should permeate me through and through, still I did not wish to give you my love in exchange.

Oh, then, deign to help me, O most loving Lord Jesus Christ, who am not able not to love; and by the vehemence of your most gentle love, force my rebellious heart to love you, so that I may serve you in peace and attain to an eternal life of love.

R. Jourdan, *Contemplations* 5

"God is love, and whoever abides in love abides in God, and God dwells within him." We dwell within each other: the one who contains and the one who is contained. I dwell in you, my God, but in order to be held by you; you dwell in me in order to hold me, and not let me fall . . . You are medicine for the sick, guidance for the wicked, light for the blind, and home for the abandoned. So everything is being offered me. Make me understand that it is not I who give to you, when I come to you, not even the possession of my very self . . .

O Lord, you have no need of my goods . . . You are the true Lord who seek nothing from me, and woe to me if I do not seek you. If there was a single lost sheep, you found it, and all joyfully brought it back upon your shoulders. Did the shepherd need that sheep, or was it not rather that the shepherd was needed by the sheep? . . . O God, confirm the gift of your charity in me, and help me to live well.

St. Augustine, *In 1 Io* 8:14

Seventeenth Sunday of Ordinary Time

266. THE FRIEND OF MAN

Praise be to you, God of mercy, for the great love with which you
have loved us (Eph 2:4)

1. Holy Scripture repeatedly presents God as the friend of man. We read in Exodus: "The Lord used to speak to Moses face to face, as a man speaks to his friend" (Ex 33:11). God himself called Abraham his friend (Is 41:8), and the Jews appealed to this friendship to implore divine protection: "Do not take away your mercy from us for the sake of Abraham, your friend" (Dan 3:35D). In a more general sense, the Old Testament declares that those who possess divine wisdom have "obtained friendship with God"; in fact it is the duty of wisdom to "make friends for God" (Wis 7:14,27).

In truth, all Revelation attests that God has made use of every kind of ingenuity to win men to his friendship, to "invite and take them into fellowship with himself" (DV 2). The divine plan reaches its very highest point when God himself, the eternal Word, uncreated wisdom, takes human flesh, is seen upon earth, pitches his tent among men, and converses with them" (Bar 3:38 Douai). Friendship presupposes a certain equality and community of life, whereas between God and men there is a supreme and limitless distance. But for the very purpose of making friendship possible between himself and men, God became man and shared his divinity with man. "The Word became flesh and dwelt among us" (Jn 1:14), so that we might become "partakers of the divine nature" (2 Pet 1:4). The foundation of friendship, of communion, was established.

Friendship demands reciprocal love. God has loved us first; our love can be only a reponse: "We love, because he first loved us" (1 Jn 4:19). We return God's love, first of all by accepting it, by opening our heart to him, and letting ourselves be loved. The very love which God has infused into us becomes the beginning of our response, of our love. "Love is from God" (ib. 7), it can come only from him, and moreover we cannot love God supernaturally except with God's very love. If we correspond, there will be perfect friendship, because it will be based on equality of love.

2. The mystery of the friendship between God and mankind is based entirely upon the nature of charity, which is not human love, but divine love, by which we become capable of loving divinely. Jesus spoke many times about this divine love lavished upon mankind, but he did so in a special way in his discourse at the Last Supper. "As the Father has loved me, so have I loved you; abide in my love" (Jn 15:9). Again, addressing himself to his Father: "May the love with which you have loved me be in them, and I in them" (Jn 17:26). The itinerary of divine love is indicated: from the Father to the Son, from the Son to men. We are urged to "abide," that is to live in this love in order to share in the life of infinite

charity that is in God and also to love God in return with a love worthy of him, that is, with his very own love. It is the communion of friendship. Then what is our part in the exchange of divine friendship? Jesus has told us: "You are my friends if you do what I command you.—If you keep my commandments, you will abide in my love" (Jn 15:14,10). The fellowship required by friendship calls for a communion of affections, of desires, and of the will. A friend desires that which his friend desires. We are God's friends if we will and do what God wills: if we keep his commandments, if in every thing we seek not our own will, but God's will. Thus we can understand why Abraham has been called the friend of God, for he was always ready to follow the divine will, even to the point of abandoning his native land, his home, his people, even to raising the knife to sacrifice his son.

God's free gift of love, preceeding man, desires to be returned with that love of friendship by which man gives himself totally to God, wanting only what he wants. This response on man's part will invite new outpourings of love from God: "He who loves me will be loved by my Father, and I will love him.—For the Father himself loves you, because you have loved me" (Jn 14:21;16:27). So charity grows in the heart of man, as he becomes ever more capable of loving; his friendship with God becomes deeper, and prepares him for eternal friendship.

> O most sweet fire of love, you fill the soul with all sweetness and gentlenss! For no suffering or bitterness can affect one who burns with so sweet and glorious a fire . . .
>
> O sweetness of love, how can the heart of your bride not love you, considering that you are the spouse of life? Eternal God, you created us in your image and likeness through love alone, and when we had lost grace because of our wretched sin, you gave us the Word of your only-begotten Son; you gave us life and punished our iniquities on his body, paying off the debt that he had never incurred. Oh, miserable creatures that we are! We are the thieves, and he is hanged [crucified] for us. Oh, shamed be the bride, who is ignorant and hard-hearted and blind, for not loving, when she sees herself so much loved by you, O God; and there is so much delight in this sweet and gentle bond.
>
> St. Catherine of Siena, *Letters* 217, v.3

> Love is a great thing only if it returns to its first principle, if it has been restored to its source, if having flowed back to its fountain-head, it draws from thence the power to flow on for ever. Out of all the motions of the soul, those of the senses as well as those of the affections, it is love alone in which the creature can make a return to the Creator, although not on equal terms . . .
>
> You who are love ask only a return of love and fidelity. Let the creature, therefore, return love for love . . . How could love not be loved?

With good reason renouncing all other affections the soul gives itself wholly to love alone—for in reciprocating love it is constrained to make a return of love to him who is love itself. For when the soul has poured out its whole being in love, what is this in comparison with the unceasing flow of the fountain of love? The waters of love do not flow with equal copiousness from the lover and from him who is Love . . . from the Creator and the creature. You might as well compare one who is thirsty and the fountain from which he drinks. What then? . . . The aspirations of one who sighs with longing, the ardor of one who loves, the trust of one who abounds in confidence—will they cease? . . . Assuredly not. For although a creature loves less because he is less, yet if he loves with his whole being, there can be nothing wanting.

St. Bernard, *In Cantica Cant.* 83:4-6

267. THE MORE EXCELLENT WAY

Lord, direct my heart to the love of God (2 Thes 3:5)

1. After St. Paul had mentioned in detail the charismatic gifts granted by God to the faithful of Corinth, he concluded: "You earnestly desire the higher gifts. But I will show you a still more excellent way" (1 Cor 12:31), and he immediately sings his famous hymn to charity, raising it far above all charisms and all virtues. "If I speak in the tongues of angels, but have not love, I am a noisy gong or a clanging cymbal . . . so faith, hope, love abide, these three: but the greatest of these is love" (ib. 13:1,13). Why? The most complete answer is the one St. John gives: "He who loves is born of God" (1 Jn 4:7); and he who loves passes from death to life (ib. 3:14). Only love makes us children of God, makes us pass from the death of sin to the life of grace. Where there is no charity there is no grace; there is no life. "He who does not love abides in death" (ib.), and contrariwise, he who loves "abides in God, and God abides in him" (ib. 4:16).

Faith and hope, as also all the charismatic graces, are not sufficient for man to pass from death to life. Both the one and the other can also exist in those who have not yet received sanctifying grace, or who have lost it; not so with charity. Charity is so vital that it cannot co-exist with the death of sin: it is so vital that it is inseparable from grace, the two are, as it were, indivisible. It cannot be otherwise, since grace makes us participate in the divine life, and this is a life of love.

Furthermore, charity "never ends" (1 Cor 3:8), and will remain imperishable for all eternity. "As for prophecies, they will pass away; as for tongues, they will cease" (ib.); even faith and hope will cease, giving place to vision and the beatific possession of God, whom we shall see "face to face" in heaven, but charity [love] will remain, the eternal bond of the union of man with God. Here on earth, we always have the unhappy possibility of losing charity, but in heaven we shall be established indefectibly with no such fear; we shall be fixed in love and shall abide for ever in God and God in us.

2. Faith and hope are incomplete virtues, because without charity they lack the power to unite us with God and to produce the works of eternal life. The faith and hope of the sinner, who has lost charity, are inactive and inoperative; they remain in him, but they are as if dead. Faith "apart from works is dead" (Jas 2:26), and only "faith working through love" (Gal 5:6) has merit. St. Paul goes so far as to say: "If I have all faith, so as to remove mountains, but have not love, I am nothing" (1 Cor 13:2). The power to perform miracles in the name of God is nothing compared to the least degree of charity. It is charity that gives the warmth and strength of eternal life to faith and hope; it is charity that perfects these virtues. Only one who loves is capable of believing and hoping in God without condition, and without measure.

The same holds true for the moral virtues, which can make us honest and virtuous, but can in no way bring us into friendship with God, nor give us the possibility of meriting eternal life. Without the life-giving breath of charity, everything is dead, sterile, and cold; without charity we remain confined to the natural level, we cannot be children of God, we cannot be his friends, we cannot live in the company of the divine Persons. It is a truly impressive thought: not even the greatest of works, such as the renunciation of all our possessions, and the sacrifice of life itself, have any value without charity. "And if I give away all I have, and if I deliver my body to be burned, but have not love, I gain nothing" (1 Cor 13:3). But when charity intervenes, everything is completely changed: even the lowliest works, the most secret acts of virtue, performed out of love for God, acquire value for eternal life. This is the miracle worked by charity, which St. Thomas defines as the "form and mother" of the other virtues. It is the form because it orders their works toward their ultimate end; it is the mother because it conceives these deeds out of desire for the ultimate end. (St Thos 2-2,23:8). Vatican II states on this point: "Charity . . . rules over all the means of attaining holiness, gives life to them and makes them work" (LG 42).

"Love alone is what gives value to all things, and a kind of love so strong that nothing hinders it is the one thing necessary" (T.J., Exclamations 5:2).

O Lord Jesus Christ, your love, your charity: this is the most direct way . . . to reach you! It is a short way without weariness; a level road without detours; a clear, unclouded road; a safe road without danger; a joyful road, together with a good friend, that is, with you, O Lord, most loving guide! This is the path for reaching eternal delights, which does not let the traveler swerve to the right into prosperity, nor to the left into adversity.

This road of love, O Lord Jesus Christ, eternal guide of lovers, is the true road, without pretense or deceit; a road that is traveled with the heart, not with idle talk; a fruitful way without idleness; a way that is not so much of words, but of deeds; a cautious way without surprises; prudent, not foolish, where the beloved is loved and sin is rejected . . .

O Lord Jesus Christ, most constant of lovers, if anyone wants to reach his heavenly country quickly, he must travel by the road of love, of charity, since he who loves the more ardently runs the faster and arrives the sooner . . . In your loving mercy, give me so great a grace of loving you that abandoning every vain affection, that is not pleasing to you, I may love you above all things with a love that is constant and not just at intervals; and that I may never be separated from your love, but may abide in it throughout eternity.

R. Jourdan, *Contemplations* 17

O Lord, you give me once and for all a short commandment: Love and do what you will. If you are silent, be silent through love; if you speak, speak through love; if you correct, correct through love; if you forgive, forgive through love. O Lord, let the root of love be in me, since from this root nothing can proceed save good.

St. Augustine, *In 1 Io* 7:8

268. ROOTED IN CHARITY

O Lord, let my heart be rooted and grounded in love (Eph 3;17)

1. "Blessed be the God and Father of our Lord Jesus Christ, who has . . . chosen us in him before the foundation of the world, that we should be holy and blameless before him" (Eph 1:3-4). God wants us to be holy in love, and this cannot be otherwise because he, the holy one, is love. By pouring out his love into us, God shares his holiness with us. God sanctifies us by making us more and more like him, and this is tantamount to rooting us more and more in charity. To the extent that we open our heart to the gift of divine love and assist its development, we become holy by the holiness of God himself. "Therefore be imitators of God, as beloved children; and walk in love," St. Paul urges (Eph 5:1). Children must become like their Father: "You must be perfect as your heavenly Father is perfect" (Mt 5:48). If the holiness of the Father is love, that of his children must be the same.

However, charity must be understood in all its fullness: love of God and love of neighbor, devotion to God and devotion to our neighbor.

We cannot give ourselves holiness, only God can sanctify us; and it is clear that the more we are united to him, the more God will share his sanctity with us. The power that unites us to God is precisely charity: "Charity"—says St. Thomas—"makes us tend toward God by joining our affection to him, so that we live no longer for self, but for God" (2-2,17:6). But before this, charity brings about something much deeper: it makes God abide in man and man in God: "If a man loves me . . . my Father will love him, and we will come to him and make our home with him" (Jn 14:23). And when God is present in us by dint of his charity and grace, it is always charity which allows us to unite ourselves with him to the point of no longer living for self, but for God. St. Paul's burning cry: "It is no longer I who live, but Christ who lives in me" (Gal 2:20), is the extreme expression of the charity that intimately unites us to the One who said: "Abide in me, and I in you . . . abide in my love" (Jn 15:4,9).

2. Just as faith enters thoroughly into the understanding and makes it capable of supernatural knowledge of God, so charity invades the will and makes us capable of loving God, the infinite Good. Even in the sphere of human affection, love consists essentially in an act of the will, which *wishes good* to someone; however, given the psychology of the human person, such an act also involves a movement of feeling. The same thing happens in the sphere of theological charity, which transforms human affections, but does not change their dynamism. Nevertheless, theological charity is not grafted on feeling but on the will. Therefore, emotional feelings must not be confused with charity, and still less be substituted for it.

God asks us to love him with all our strength, hence "with all our heart" (Mk 12:30) also. He does not scorn the creature's feelings of affection, in fact he desires them, and sometimes arouses them, in order to make the practice of charity easier for those who need to be encouraged with a little attraction that can be felt. But all this is but an echo of charity; it is not charity. St. John of the Cross writes: "No delightful feelings can be adequate means for the union of the will with God, but only the will's operation, which is love." Only through this operation can the will be united with God and terminate in him "who is love" (Letter 12). Jesus himself said: "Not everyone who says to me: 'Lord, Lord' "—as an expression of feeling—"shall enter the kingdom of heaven, but he who does the will of my Father" (Mt 7:21), and this is the act of charity. God, a most pure spirit, cannot be reached by feeling, but only by the will, transformed by his love. There can be great love for God without any resonance in feeling. God often leads his friends along an arid road, deprived of joy to self, in order to make their love purer and more supernatural, more like his own, and hence more sanctifying. God has chosen us "to be holy in love:" in *his* love, which is the infinite, eternal act of his will, with which the full, whole-hearted act of our wills must correspond.

O Love, O God, you are the consummation and end of all good;
all whom you have chosen, you love unto the end; whatsoever comes

into your hands, you will not cast out, but will keep for yourself with exceeding care. Come, appropriate me to yourself by right of everlasting possession.

O Love, O God, who have created me, in your love re-create me. O Love who have redeemed me, fill up and redeem for yourself in me whatever part of your love has fallen into neglect within me. O Love, O God, who to make me yours, have purchased me in the blood of your Christ, sanctify me in your truth. O Love, O God, who adopted me as a daughter, fashion and foster me after your own heart. O Love, who have chosen me as yours and not another's, grant that I may cleave unto you with my whole being. O Love, O God, who have first loved me, grant that I may love you with my whole heart with my whole soul and with my whole strength.

St. Gertrude, *Exercises 5.*

O Lord, "put me as a seal upon your heart, as a seal upon your arm, for love"—the act and work of love—"is as strong as death, and emulation and importunity endure as long as hell"... Grant, O Lord, that I may in no way seek consolation or satisfaction either in God or in anything else; neither do I desire or ask favors of you, for I have already received many. Let all my care be directed toward how I may give you some pleasure and render you some service because of what you deserve and the favors you have bestowed on me, even though the cost may be high...

Ah, my Lord and my God, how many go to you looking for their own consolation and gratification, your favors and gifts, while those who want to give you pleasure and something at a cost to themselves, setting aside their own interests, are so few! (Dk Night II 19:4)

My Beloved, all that is rugged and toilsome, I desire for myself, and all that is sweet and delightful I desire for you. (Maxims on love 52)

St. John of the Cross

269.   EIGHTEENTH SUNDAY OF ORDINARY TIME

YEAR A

Lord, the eyes of all look to you, and you give them their food in due season   *(Ps 145:15)*

The theme of God's Providence bending lovingly over the needs of men reappears in today's Liturgy. The starting point is a passage of Isaiah (55:1-3) which contains God's pressing invitation, given to the exiled Hebrews in Babylon, not to delay in returning to their homeland, lest they find themselves in distress. God will provide liberally for their needs: Let "everyone who thirsts, come to the waters; and he who has no money, come, buy and eat! Come, buy wine and milk without money and without price" (ib. 1). But over and above the material food and drink, it is easy to see anticipated here the blessings of the Messiah, which the Old Testament often symbolizes in an abundance of water, wine, milk, and fat. This is expressed still more clearly in the lines that follow: "Incline your ear, and come to me; hear, that your soul may live, and I will make you an everlasting covenant, my steadfast, sure love for David" (ib. 3). Yes, God provides for our material needs but much more for those that are spiritual; then, there is the great promise reserved for those, who heeding his invitation, go to him: God will establish an eternal covenant with them, which will again its fruition in Jesus, the Messiah.

The Gospel of the day (Mt 14:13-21), in a very picturesque setting, shows us the actualization of the promise. Jesus had disembarked in a lonely place and found himself surrounded by a crowd of poor people who had followed him there, carrying their sick with them, in the secret hope of finding in him that understanding and that assistance of which they had such need. The Lord "had compassion on them, and healed their sick" (ib. 14). He cured them without being asked, for their having brought the sick to that distant place was itself more than a prayer and was also a tacit expression of faith. Meanwhile it was getting toward evening and his disciples were worried and said to him: "This is a lonely place, and the day is now over; send the crowds away to go into the villages and buy food for themselves" (ib. 15). This, to them, was the simplest and most natural solution for providing for the hunger of those people; but Jesus had another, infinitely more simple and compassionate, which only he was in a position to offer: not to send them away to buy something, but to provide personally for them; his disciples hear themselves invited to attend to it: "You give them something to eat!" (ib. 16). They have only five loaves and two fish; they need only to hand them over to Jesus, to see them multiplied not a hundred, but a thousand times: "He blessed and broke and gave the loaves to the disciples, and the disciples gave them to the crowd. And they all ate and were satisfied" (ib. 19-20). Even if, on account of our own limitations and poverty, we can do little to benefit our brothers, God wants us to do this little that we can do, fully and wholeheartedly; he himself will take care of multiplying it.

The hope with which the crowd had been following Jesus, heedless of their own hunger, was not disappointed; the words of Isaiah were verified in their regard: "Buy and eat without money;" and this was not only in the physical sense, for while Jesus was multiplying the loaves to feed their bodies, he was dispensing his word to nourish their souls. Those who follow Christ resolutely find in him everything they need, both for their life on earth and for their eternal one. But they must follow him with an unshakeable faith which rests upon the certainty of his love. Then we can undersand the Apostle's impassioned cry: "Who shall separate us from the love of Christ? Shall tribulation, or distress, or persecution, or famine, or nakedness, or peril, or the sword?" (Rom 8:35; 2nd reading). Neither the adversities of personal life nor the toils to be faced in the apostolate can tear the disciple from his Master, because he is convinced that in the Master's love, he, the disciple, will find the strength to overcome every difficulty.

> *O Jesus, let us also learn to keep united to you, but not because of any material favors you grant us ... Make us seek heavenly bread, and when we have obtained it, banish from our hearts all preoccupation with earthly life. If that multitude forsook their homes, their towns, their relatives, and everything else, in order to go away into a desert place, and did not return even when hunger tormented them, so much more we who approach your divine table ought ... to love spiritual realities, and only after these should we concern ourselves with the things of sense ...*
>
> *O Lord, make us love the great gifts of the Spirit; then you will give us the rest as well, in abundance ... Let us not place our desires on temporal goods, but rather be completely indifferent either to possessing them or to losing them; ... Let us learn to use temporal riches wisely, helping those in need ... The one who taught us this is you yourself, O Christ, and your Father: "Be merciful"—you say—"like your Father in heaven" ... What is the purpose of our learning this? Heaven, and the good things of heaven, that is, ineffable glory, spiritual nuptials, shining lights, eternal life together with you, O divine Spouse, and all the other good things which no mind is able to conceive and no words can describe.*

St. John Chrysostom, *Commentary on Gospel of St. Matthew* 49:3-4

YEAR B

Lord, you are the bread of life; whoever comes to you shall not hunger   *(Jn 6:35)*

Today the Liturgy of the Word—and also of the three following Sundays—centers upon Jesus' discourse on the "bread of life," recounted in the Gospel of John immediately after the multiplication of the loaves (cf preceding Sunday); the discourse treats of two important subjects: faith and the Eucharist.

As usual, the main point of the Gospel is introduced by a passage from the Old Testament. Today we read in Exodus (16:2-4, 12-15) the story of the murmuring of the Jews in the desert, when they saw themselves deprived of food and water, and they longed for the pots of meat that had been left behind in Egypt. Although their complaints were excessive, God intervened once again in their favor: "Behold I will rain bread from heaven for you" (ib. 4). Thus manna began to fall upon their camp in the morning, and meat—quail—in the evening, for the nourishment of all. As soon as we are in trouble, we seem always ready to murmur against Providence and to regret what has been left behind. The ancient people acted thus, and the new people continue to do so today, forgetting the many beneficial interventions of God in their life and demonstrating the poverty of their faith. St. Paul's admonition is appropriate here: "Now this I affirm and testify in the Lord, that you must no longer live as the Gentiles do, in the futility of their minds—You did not so learn Christ!" (Eph 4:17,20; 2nd reading). It is spiritual vanity to complain about Providence, to mourn for temporal goods, to have little confidence in God on account of the difficulties of life, and to seek God not for himself but for one's own interests.

Jesus reproved the crowd about similar errors, for after he had multiplied the loaves, they had pursued him around the lake: "You seek me not because you saw signs, but because you ate your fill of the loaves. Do not labor for the food which perishes, but for the food which endures to eternal life" (Jn 6:26-27). St. Augustine comments: "How many seek Jesus only for temporal favors! . . . It is hard to seek Jesus for his own sake" (In Io 25:10). An unselfish search for Jesus presupposes faith; and this is precisely the point on which Jesus insists in his debate with the Jews: "This is the work of God, that you believe in him whom he has sent" (Jn 6:29). The first and most important work that God asks of men is that they believe in him, and in what he does for them in Christ Jesus. Only those who believe that Jesus is the Son of God, sent to save the world, go to him with confidence, surrendering completely to his redeeming action. The Jews who did not have this faith exacted "signs" from Jesus, like that of the manna sent down from heaven. Jesus, endeavoring to raise them to more spiritual thoughts corrects them: "It was not Moses who gave you the bread from heaven; my Father gives you the true bread from heaven. For the bread of God is that which comes down from heaven, and gives life to the world" (ib. 32-33). But, referring always to physical food, and perhaps hoping for a miracle that would prolong the multiplication of the loaves, they said to him: "Lord, give us this bread always" (ib. 34). This way of thinking and responding was similar to that of the Samaritan woman, who was thinking of material water when she said to Jesus: "Sir, give me this water" (Jn 4:15). To these, as before to her, Jesus wanted to make the true meaning clear, and he expressed himself to them in much the same words as he had used to the Samaritan woman: "I am the bread of life; he who comes to me shall not hunger, and he who believes in me shall never thirst" (Jn 6:35). Misunderstanding was no longer possible: the bread of life, the bread of God sent down from heaven to give life to the world, is Jesus; whoever goes to him and is nourished by him—by his word and by the Eucharist—with a living faith, will hunger or thirst no more.

Give me yourself, Lord, and it is enough; for without you no comfort is of any avail. Without you I cannot exist; and without your visitation I am unable to live. Therefore I must often come to you, and receive you as the medicine of my salvation, lest I perhaps faint on the way, should I be deprived of this heavenly food. For so you, O merciful Jesus, when you had been preaching to the people and curing their various ills, once said: I will not send them fasting to their homes, lest they faint on the way. Deal with me, therefore, in like manner, for you have left yourself in this Sacrament for the comfort of the faithful.

O Lord my God, illuminate my eyes to behold so great a mystery, and strengthen me to believe it with an undoubting faith. For it is your work and not man's power; your sacred institution, not man's invention . . .

Lord, in the simplicity of my heart, with a good and firm faith, and at your command, I come to you with hope and perseverance; and I believe truly that you are present in this Sacrament, both God and man. You will, then, that I receive you and unite myself to you in charity; therefore I beseech your clemency and beg you to give me a special grace: that I may be wholly dissolved in you, and overflow with your love, and no more concern myself about any other kind of consolation.

Imitation of Christ IV 3:2; 4:1-2

YEAR C

Come, let us sing to the Lord, . . . the rock of our salvation (Ps 95:1).

The theme presented in this Sunday's readings treats of the value of worldly realities—life, work, riches, etc—and the Christian's conduct in regard to these. The first reading (Eccles 1:2;2:21-23) explains vanity, that is the inconsistency of the things of the world which pass with the swiftness of wind: "Vanity of vanities. All is vanity". Man's life is short, destined to perish; his labor and his wisdom can, at the most, procure him a sizable estate, but he will one day be forced to give it up. Then why all this bustle? "What has a man from all the toil and strain with which he toils beneath the sun? (ib. 2:22). Of what use are his days, tormented with grief and worry? And his sleepless nights? The brief passage does not give the answer, but limits itself to the observation that life in the world, lived for itself, disconnected from God and from a higher purpose, is frustrating indeed. Already in the Old Testament, and especially in the Book of Wisdom which speaks of man's immortality, we find the solution to this painful problem. But only the New Testament gives us a definite answer: all worldly realities are of value in relation to God when they are used in the manner he has ordained.

The second reading also refers to this (Col 3:1-5,9-11) in the well-known sentence of St. Paul: "If then you have been raised with Christ, seek the things that are above . . . set your minds on things that are above, not on things that are on earth" (ib. 1-2). As Christians reborn through baptism to a new life in Christ, we know that our destiny is not closed within earthly horizons, and that, even while we must attend to the duties of this present life, our heart must be directed toward our final goal: eternal life in eternal fellowship with God. Therefore we do not expect from earthly life the happiness which it cannot give us, and which we can find only in God. Consequently we shall be moderate in our use of earthly goods, and shall know how to mortify ourselves—in our passions, in corrupt desires, in cupidity (ib. 5)—and to die to sin, which separates us from God, in order to live, instead, "with Christ in God" (ib. 3).

But the direct answer to the first reading is in the Gospel of the day (Lk 12:13-21); it is introduced by Jesus' resolute refusal to intervene in the division of an inheritance. He had come to bring *eternal life,* not to occupy himself with temporal goods, which can offer no stability to our existence. "Take heed and beware of all covetousness"—said the Lord—"for a man's life does not consist in the abundance of his possessions" (ib. 15). He immediately added the parable of the foolish rich man, which gave a practical demonstration of the wisdom of his warning. This man had reaped such an abundant harvest from his land that he did not know where to store it. But while he was planning to build new granaries, intending to enjoy his wealth for a long time, he was called by God to render an account and heard him say: "The things you have prepared, whose will they be?" (ib. 20). The stupidity and sin of this man consisted in his having accumulated wealth for the sole purpose of selfishly enjoying it: "My soul . . . take your ease, eat, drink, be merry" (ib. 19), with no thought of the needs of his neighbor nor of his obligations toward God. God was entirely absent from his plans, as if his life, instead of depending on God, depended on his material wealth: "You have ample goods laid up for many years" (ib.). But that very night his life is cut short, and he finds himself empty-handed before God, lacking in the good works necessary for eternity. The parable concludes: "So is he who lays up treasure for himself, and is not rich toward God" (ib. 20).

All below heaven changes: spring, summer, autumn, each has its turn. The fortunes of the world change; what was high, lies low; what was low rises high. Riches take wings and flee away; bereavements happen. Friends become enemies, and enemies friends. Our wishes, aims, and plans change. There is nothing stable but you, O my God! And you are the center and life of all who change, who trust you as their Father, who look to you, and who are content to put themselves into your hands.

I know, O my God, I must change, if I am to see your face! I must undergo the change of death. Body and soul must die to this world. My real self, my soul, must change by a true regeneration. None but the holy can see you ... Let me day by day be molded upon you, and be changed from glory to glory, by ever looking towards you, and ever leaning on your arm. I know, O Lord, I must go through trial, temptation, and much conflict, if I am to come to you. I know not what lies before me, but I know as much as this. I know, too, that if you are not with me, my change will be for the worse, not for the better. Whatever fortune I have, be I rich or poor, healthy or sick, with friends or without, all will turn to evil if I am not sustained by the Unchangeable; all will turn to good if I have Jesus with me, yesterday and today the same, and for ever.

J.H. Newman, *Meditations on Christian Doctrine* IX 2-3

270. THE GREAT AND FIRST COMMANDMENT

Lord, your commandment is exceedingly broad. Oh, how I love your law! (Ps 119:96-97).

1. "Hear, O Israel: the Lord our God is one Lord; and you shall love the Lord your God with all your heart, and with all your soul, and with all your might" (Dt 6:4-5). Thus did Moses proclaim the precept of the love of God. And when Jesus was questioned about the first commandment of the law, he simply repeated Moses' words: "You shall love the Lord your God with all your heart, and with all your soul, and with all your mind, and with all your strength" (Mk 12:30).

God, who is infinite love, eternally happy in himself, does not need our love. Yet he wants it. It was God who by loving us created love in us, a love that was a sharing in his own infinite charity. This love is "his", it belongs to him; he is jealous of it, wishes it, protects it, commands it. The love that has come down to us from God should rise again to God from us. This is the reason Jesus presented the precept of love as not only the first commandment, but as the greatest of them all: "There is no other commandment greater than this" (ib. 31). Greater in respect to what is due to God and greater also in respect to man's happiness. We live by God's love: his love has created us, maintains us in existence, and "calls us to communicate in life and glory with himself. Out of pure generosity God has generously poured out his divine goodness and does not cease to do so ... procuring at one and the same time his own glory and our happiness" (AG 2). We have an extreme need of God's love, of being loved by him, and of loving him in return: It is a question of life, of our eternal happiness. "You have made us for yourself, O Lord, and our hearts are restless until they rest in you" (St. Augustine, Conf. I, 1:1). Nothing glorifies God so much as the voluntary love of his creature; at the same time nothing so ennobles man and makes him happy as the love of his God. The commandment to love is at the center of Christian life; much more than the pious Israelite, the Christian must carry it stamped upon his heart, thus fulfilling the words of Scripture: "You shall teach [these words] diligently to your children, and shall talk of them when you sit in your house, and when you walk by the way, and when you lie down, and when you rise" (Dt 6:7).

2. Treating of the call of everyone to holiness, Vatican II states precisely: "All the faithful, of whatever rank or status, are called to the fullness of the Christian life and to the perfection of charity" (LG 40). In actual fact, there is no fullness of Christian life without fullness of charity, because growth in grace is simultaneous and correlative to growth in charity. A stronger and more generous love supposes a more intense and invading grace.

Moreover, charity is not a counsel, it is a commandment imposed on all without distinction, and is absolutely necessary for salvation: "He who does not love does not know God" (Jn 4:8). But up to what point do we have to love God? St. Bernard answers: "The reason of loving God is God himself; the measure of loving God is to love him beyond measure" (On the Love of God I 1:2). No matter how much we love God, we can never love him as much as his infinite lovableness demands; for this reason the precept of love excludes by its very nature every limitation. The life of a Christian is a continuous journey toward God, our last end. Upon this road, St. Thomas teaches, "The more we advance, the closer we come to God; we draw nearer to him not with bodily steps, but with the affections of the soul" (2-2,24,4). The steps of love lead us to God, and charity unites us to him. If these steps stop, if charity does not grow, we cannot reach our end. St. Paul wrote to the Philippians: "It is my prayer that your love may abound more and more" (1:9), and, speaking of himself, said: "Not that I have already obtained this or am perfect; but I press on to make it my own" (3:12). The precept of charity calls for this continuous pressing onward, this continuous straining toward God, the infinite Good. The very phrasing of the precept: "you shall love with *all* your heart, with *all* your soul, and with *all* your strength" indicates totality and generosity without pause and without reservation. But as charity comes only from God, so only God can increase it. And God, who is infinite power, can increase it without limit; to do this he asks only a will that is docile, available, and generous.

You know, O my God, I have never desired anything but to love you, and I am ambitious for no other glory. Your love has gone before me, and it has grown with me, and now it is an abyss whose depths I cannot fathom. Love attracts love, and, my Jesus, my love leaps toward yours; it would like to fill the abyss which attracts it, but alas! it is not even like a drop of dew lost in the ocean! For me to love you as you love me, I would have to borrow your love, and then only would I be at rest.

See, O Jesus, all that you lay claim to from us; you have no need of our works, but only of our love, for you are the same God who declared that you had no need to tell us when you are hungry and did not fear to beg for a little water from the Samaritan woman. You were thirsty ... but when you said: "Give me to drink", it was the love of your poor creature that you, the Creator of the universe, were seeking. You were thirsty for love. Ah! I feel it more than ever before, you are parched, O Jesus, for you meet only the ungrateful and indifferent among your disciples in the world, and among your own disciples, alas, you find few hearts who surrender to you without reservations, who understand the real tenderness of your infinite love.

St. Therese of the Child Jesus, *Autobiography*, C p. 256; B p.189

Your love, O Lord Jesus, is the fount of life, and a soul cannot live unless it drinks of it, nor can it drink of it unless it is present at its very source, that is, yourself, who are the fountainhead of all love.

O spring of true love and immense sweetness, which never fails, but is constantly renewed, here am I, a miserable sinner, overwhelmed by the heavy burden of my sins; see how parched I am for love, for I have gone too far away from you, its living source. Deign then to look mercifully upon me, and to lead me back to you, O Spring of love and delight, so that I may drink the water of your boundless love; may drink of it and be refreshed by it, and may savor its sweetness and its taste; let my soul be washed and cleansed from every stain of sin, so that, purified of all guilt, I may be pleasing to you and serve you and live with you in love, throughout all ages to come.

R. Jourdan, *Contemplations*

271. THE SECOND IS LIKE TO THE FIRST

O God, let me imitate you as a true son, and walk in love (Eph 5:1)

1. Immediately after speaking of the love of God, "the great and first commandment", Jesus added: "And the second is like it: 'You shall love your neighbor as yourself'. On these two commandments depend all the law and the prophets" (Mt 22:38-40). The great innovation by Jesus was his uniting and almost fusing into one the commandment of the love of God and that of the love of neighbor, showing that these were the foundation for all the others. Charity is one in its source, which is God; and it is one also in the Christian, into whom it is infused in baptism as a created participation in the infinite love with which God loves himself, the

supreme Good, and men, the creatures of his love. "The Lord Jesus"—affirms the Council—"sent the Holy Spirit upon all men that he might inspire them from within to love God with their whole heart and with their whole soul, with all their mind and all their strength, and that they might love one another as Christ loved them" (LG 40). Implicit in love for Christ is love for the Father, for the one and triune God.

Charity is the same activity in the Christian as it is in God: love for God and love for men. It is impossible to separate the charity due to God from that which is due to men; to do so would be to destroy it. St. John, the apostle-theologian of charity, states it in his rapid, clear-cut, striking style: "He who does not love his brother . . . is not of God; . . . if anyone says 'I love God', and hates his brother, he is a liar, for he who does not love his brother whom he has seen, cannot love God whom he has not seen" (1 Jn 3:10;4:20). Man is the living image of God; his entire being bears God's imprint; anyone who disdains man, disdains God. The very fact that man exists tells us that God wanted him, that he has loved him, and does love him; every human being—even the poorest, the most miserable, the most unworthy—is the creature of his love; and to shut our heart to a man, even to one single man, is to reject God. The consequence follows inevitably: the commandment to love God is not being observed unless we are also, at the same time, observing that of the love of neighbor.

2. The commandment of the love of neighbor has its deep-seated motive in God, and more directly in his love for men. "He loved us and sent his Son"—St. John repeats—"to be the expiation for our sins. Beloved, if God so loved us, we also ought to love one another" (1 Jn 4:10-11). The line of reasoning is very simple and clear. If God loved men so much that he sacrificed his own Son for their salvation, men are bound, in their turn, to love each other. When we are moved by the thought that God has loved us from all eternity and has chosen us and redeemed us in Christ, and has made us his adopted children, we should realize that this love and these privileges are not an exclusive possession, nor reserved only for so-called "practicing believers", but are intended for all men. The heavenly Father's love is for all without distinction; and it is really his love that causes us to be brothers, by creating the sacred bonds of charity and solidarity between us. "God, who has fatherly concern for everyone"—Vatican II teaches—"has willed that all men should constitute one family, and treat one another in a spirit of brotherhood. For having been created in the image of God, . . . all are called to the one and same goal, namely, God himself. For this reason, love for God and neighbor is the first and greatest commandment. Sacred Scripture, however, teaches us that the love of God cannot be separated from love of neighbor" (GS 24). If "God shows no partiality" (Acts 10:34), but calls everyone to be his children, offers to all his salvation, his love, and his pardon, and opens his heart and his house to all, how can we,

children of God, limit our love to a determined category of persons? As a father suffers when his children are in discord with one another, so God is wounded in his love when we, in our turn, do not love each other, when even a single one is rejected by his brothers.

St. Paul says in praise of the Thessalonians: "But concerning the love of the brethren, you have no need to have anyone write to you, for you yourselves have been taught by God to love one another" (1 Thes 4:9). By extending his fatherhood to all men, God himself is showing them how to love; God makes them ready for universal charity by pouring his own love into them.

> *O charity, you seek nothing for yourself, but only the glory and praise of God's name in the salvation of souls; and you do not seek your neighbor for yourself, but only for God. You are a mother who nourishes at her breast the children of the virtues, for without you no virtue can have life ... You love what God loves, and hate what God hates. Therefore, whoever possesses you, puts off the old man and clothes with the new ... who is Christ, sweet Jesus, whom he binds to himself by following Christ's doctrine ...*
>
> *Anger never overcomes you, for you bear patiently the faults of your neighbor; you are not irate, but are kind ... you serve your neighbor with great care, showing him the same love that you have for God. We cannot be of any profit to God, but, using the means he has given us, let us do our best to be of service to the one he has loved so much, that is, to his rational creature. You are sweet indeed, O mother of charity: no bitterness comes from you; rather you always bring joy to the heart of one who possesses you.*
>
> St. Catherine of Siena, *Letters* 357, v 5

> *O most merciful God, grant that I may love you above all things as you command, and in addition, as is right, love my neighbor no less than myself, as you also command. In fact, it is most just and fully reasonable that we should love you above all things, and also more than ourselves, since you loved us before we were, by loving us you created us, and after creating us were anxious to make us know your holy name; truly we have nothing except from you, not even the capacity for loving you nor any other blessing.*
>
> *Justly then, you command us to love our neighbor as ourselves ... since you created us all with equal love. Impelled by one identical love, you went to your passion for us all, and you prepared eternal life for us all without any distinction.*
>
> *O most merciful Father, grant that those who have the true faith may live rightly and holily, and may not deviate in the least thing from your commandments; and to those who do not yet believe in you, grant that before they die they may have faith and love for your most holy name, and may preserve these gifts whole and inviolate to the end.*
>
> St. Anselm, *Prayers* 28

272. THE FOUNDATION OF THE LAW

Lord, enlarge my heart, that I may run the way of your commandments (Ps 119:32)

1. "On these two commandments depend all the law and the prophets" (Mt 22:40). Jesus did not say that everything is based upn the commandment to love God, but upon it together with and completed by that of the love of neighbor. St. Augustine said: "Love and do what you will" (In Io 7:8). One who truly loves God and his neighbor spontaneously observes all the other commandments, because love by its own nature leads us to desire the good of the person loved and to do his will. Besides, every commandment is directed toward love, and has the specific purpose of safeguarding love and of assuring its practice in relation to God and to neighbor. The first place always belongs to God: absolute preference is due to him above every creature. "He who loves father and mother more than me is not worthy of me" (Mt 10:37). It is not lawful, for the love of a creature, even the dearest, to offend the Creator or to take from him any of the love owed to him. God demands absolute primacy, he must be loved more than parents, more than children, more than oneself and one's own life, at no matter what cost or sacrifice. "He who does not take his cross and follow me is not worthy of me ... and he who loses his life for my sake will find it" (ib. 38-39).

But nothing is taken away from God when we love our neighbor in conformity with him as his image and his child, and when we love our neighbor as God loves him, seeking his true good and his true happiness. Only theological charity can love in this way, going beyond the ties of flesh and blood, beyond all likes and dislikes, and every passion or interest or seeking of personal satisfaction. Love of neighbor then becomes the surest guarantee and the most certain proof of our love of God. "No man has ever seen God; if we love one another, God abides in us and his love is perfected in us" (1 Jn 4:12). Now we can understand why love of neighbor can and must be considered the foundation of the law.

2. "Owe no one anything, except to love one another, for he who loves his neighbor has fulfilled the law. The commandments 'You shall not commit adultery, You shall not kill, You shall not steal, You shall not covet' and any other commandment, are summed up in this sentence: "You shall love your neighbor as yourself' ... Love therefore is the fulfilling of the law" (Rom 13:8-10). It almost seems as if St. Paul is displacing love for God by making the fulfillment of the law consist solely in fraternal charity. In reality, if a Christian loves his neighbor as the gospel teaches and as Christ himself did, there can be no doubt of his love for God. This is so true, and fraternal charity is so pleasing to God, that when Jesus spoke of the last judgment he gave no other

reason for justification or condemnation than the love, or lack of it, shown to one's neighbor. "Come, O blessed of my Father, inherit the kingdom prepared for you from the foundation of the world; for I was hungry and you gave me food . . . I was a stranger and you welcomed me, I was naked and you clothed me . . ." (Mt 25:34-36). Christ not only considers men his brothers, but almost identifies himself with them, especially with the very poor, the destitute, and those bereft of help; he says: "As you did it to one of the least of my brethren, you did it to me" (ib. 40). This is a very consoling truth, but it is counterbalanced by another very serious one. Jesus, infinite goodness and mercy, does not hesitate to pronounce a sentence of eternal condemnation against those who have denied a neighbor the help of fraternal charity, for to act in that way is the same as having denied it to Jesus. "Depart from me, you cursed, into the eternal fire . . . for I was hungry and you gave me no food, I was thirsty and you gave me no drink" (ib. 41-42). Men belong to Christ; they are his. He has bought them back at the price of his blood, he has engrafted them into himself as members of his Mystical Body; whoever strikes a man, any man, strikes him, and whoever does not love a man does not love him. When St. Paul wrote: "Charity is that which fulfills the law", he certainly had in mind the Lord's teaching and the mystery of his Mystical Body, of which Paul himself was the herald.

"I give you this command: that you love one another" . . . O Lord, you yourself have given us this reciprocal love, you who chose us when we were fruitless, not yet having chosen you. You chose us, and you formed us so that we might bear fruit, that is, that we might love one another: without you we could not bear this fruit, just as branches cannot produce anything without the vine. Our fruit, then, is charity, which . . . is born of a pure heart, of a good conscience, and of a sincere faith. It is this charity that allows us to love one another, and to love you, O Lord. Make me understand that this reciprocal love would not be genuine without your love, and that if we are able to love our neighbor as ourselves it is only by our loving you . . . In these two precepts of charity are summed up the whole law and the prophets: this is our fruit . . .

"The fruit of the spirit is charity"; . . . all the other fruits are derived from charity and are closely linked to it . . . And in truth, how can joy be well ordered if we find our joy in what is not good? How can we be truly at peace, if we are not at peace with the one we sincerely love? Who can be long-suffering and ever perserving in the good, except one who loves ardently? How can we call a person kind, who does not love the one he is helping? Who is good, but one who becomes so by loving? Who can be a believer in a healthy sense, unless by faith that operates through charity? Of what use is it to be meek, if the meekness is not inspired by love? And how can a person remain virtuous in the midst of corruption except by loving what ennobles him?

*With good reason, then, O good Teacher, do you insist so strong-
ly upon love, considering this one commandment to be enough.
Make me understand that without love all the rest serves no purpose, whereas love is not conceivable without the other good
qualities, thanks to which we become good.*

St. Augustine, In Io 87:1

273. WHO IS MY NEIGHBOR?

Lord, may I increase and abound in love to all (1 Thes 3:12)

1. "You have heard that it was said: You shall love your
neighbor and hate your enemy. But I say to you: Love your
enemies and pray for those who persecute you, so that you may be
sons of your Father who is in heaven, for he makes his sun to rise
on the evil and on the good, and sends rain on the just and the unjust" (Mt 5:43-45). According to Mosaic law love of neighbor did
not go beyond the ties of blood and the borders of their country.
With one stroke Jesus renewed the law; he extended the commandment of love to every person whatsoever, not excluding
enemies, the unjust, and foreigners, and modeled the love of a
Christian upon the infinite love of his heavenly Father.

When a doctor of the law asked him: "Who is my neighbor?"
(Lk 10:29), instead of giving a theoretical answer, the Master at
once put forward a concrete example: the parable of the good
Samaritan. There was no need of a discussion in order to know
who is or is not our "neighbor"; all men are. The essential thing is
for us to become a neighbor to everyone, that is, to draw near to
everyone, especially to one in need, without paying attention to
what his ideas or political party or religion might be, just as the
Samaritan had done. Christ's words are easy to understand, but to
put them into practice involves turning our way of thinking up-
side down, a profound conversion in order to conform ourselves to
the law of love as renewed by Christ. Even a Christian is too much
tempted to love those who love him, who belong to his circle or his
party, and to go right on past all others. "For if you love those
who love you, what reward have you? . . . And if you salute only
your brethren, what more are you doing than others? Do not even
the Gentiles do the same?" (Mt 5:46-47). A pagan spirit makes an
attempt at charity and in doing so, destroys it. The motive for
charity is not in the neighbor, nor in his affection, not in his good
services, nor in his good qualities; it is not even in the sympathy
we may feel toward him, nor in ties of blood; the motive for charity
rests solely in God, whose child every person is. It is God who
wishes to be discovered and loved in every person, even if sin has
disfigured the divine image, and if, in order to find it again, we
have to dig through the coarseness of an ungrateful nature, or
through error and the debris of evil.

2. "The aspect under which our neighbor is to be loved, is God," says St. Thomas, "since what we ought to love in our neighbor is that he may be in God" (2-2,25:1), which is equivalent to loving his belonging to God as a creature and as a child; also to acknowledging and loving his right to share in the redemption, to belong to the Mystical Body of Christ, to possess eternal life and blessedness. By the simple fact that every man is a creature of God, he is called to enjoy these blessings, and if he is not yet enjoying them, then theological charity loves him in view of them, and takes steps that he may attain them. Charity is never only sympathy and human affection or pure philanthropy; it is loving from the motive of God and in line with his command. Only in this way can it be universal, extending itself even to those who are not deserving or welcome, to those who cause suffering, who are ungrateful, and sometimes even treacherous. Is this not the way God has loved us? "God shows his love for us in that while we were yet sinners Christ died for us" (Rom 5:8). God did not wait to love us until we were without sin, nor did Christ wait for us to be his friends before he gave his life for us.

Even though baptized, a Christian is not a child of the heavenly Father nor a brother of Christ, unless he is living the charity of the Father and of the Son. God's charity is this: that "he first loved us" (1 Jn 4:19). Therefore, Christian charity will always take the first step, not waiting for it to be preceded by some act of kindness, or to be entreated with some proof of esteem or with an attitude of deference or congeniality. Christ's charity is "that he laid down his life for us; and we ought to lay down our lives for the breathren" (ib. 3:16). Will it be too much to benefit, help and serve those who do not love us, and to sacrifice even to the point of giving—there is no need to exclude it—our very lives for them, since Christ gave his life for us, when we were dead through sin, and perhaps have never been completely his friends?

> *To love our neighbor with the love of charity is to love you, my God, in man, and man in you; it is to love you alone for the love of yourself, and to love the creature for love of you ... O God of Goodness! When we look at our neighbor, created in your image and likeness, should we not say to one another: see how much this creature resembles the Creator? Should we not embrace him ... and weep with love over him? Should we not give him many blessings? And why? For love of him? Certainly not, for we do not know if he of himself is worthy of love or of hatred. For your sake, O Lord, who created him to your image and likeness, and made him capable of participation in your goodness, grace, and glory ... Therefore, O divine Love, you have not only commanded us many times to love our neighbor, but you produce it and infuse it yourself into our hearts ...; therefore just as man is your image, so also man's holy love for man is a true image of man's heavenly love for you.*
> St. Francis de Sales, *Treatise on the Love of God* X 10, v2

O Lord, help us to be merciful, bending our hearts over all distress, that of the body and even more, that of the soul...

You offer your whole body for us to love, O Jesus; all your members deserve equal love from us, because all are yours. But some are healthy, and some are sick: Although they must all be equally loved, the sick members call out much more for our care, a thousand times more than the others. Before we anoint the others with perfume, show us how to cure the wounded, the bruised, the sick, that is, all those who are needy in body and soul, especially the latter, and more especially still, sinners... Bring us to believe that we can do good to every one without exception with our prayers, our penances and our personal sanctification.

C. de Foucauld, *Meditations on the Gospel*

274. AGAIN, THE NEIGHBOR
Teach me, O Lord, to progress further in charity (1 Thes 4:9-10)

1. "You shall love your neighbor as yourself" (Mt 22:39). This commandment which was reaffirmed by Jesus, already existed in Hebrew law where it was expounded with surprising shrewdness. For example: "You shall not reap your field to its very border, neither shall you gather the gleanings after your harvest; you shall leave them for the poor and for the sojourner". Also, "the wages of a hired servant shall not remain with you all night until the morning" (Lev 19:9-10,13). We could ask ourselves if we reach this level of sensitivity in full Christianity. And still again: "You shall not hate your brother in your heart ... you shall not take vengeance or bear any grudge against the sons of your own people" (ib. 17-18). It is a genuine prelude to the charity of the gospel. The Christian, too, has cause for reflection, all the more because the gospel requires this behavior of him not only toward his brothers and his fellow-citizens, but toward all men. The Book of Tobit has a very noteworthy exhortation: "What you hate, do not do to anyone" (4:16). This is a negative interpretation of the precept of loving the neighbor as oneself; and it goes far. But Jesus goes further, and immediately gives it a positive interpretation: "Whatever you wish that men would do to you, do so to them" (Mt 7:12). It is not enough for a Christian not to hate, not to harbor a grudge, not to take revenge; it is not enough not to do evil; we must do good: we must do for our neighbor all the good which we desire for ourselves. The field is almost without limit. Anyone who passes over this commandment, thinking that it is something elementary, something already taken into account, makes it evident that he has thought about it too superficially. The good that each of us desires for ourself is so great that if we could really succeed in desiring just as much for our neighbor, the problem of fraternal charity would be solved: every person would be a sincere, generous, faithful friend to his fellowman. It would be a most noble friendship because it would be founded on God, and

rooted in his love. This is exactly the example of Christian life that Vatican II desires of every believer, that they "be joined . . . by esteem and love to those among whom they live" (AG 11) or whom they meet along their way.

2. Jesus insisted upon the positive side of love of neighbor: "Do good to those that hate you, pray for those who abuse you . . . From him who takes away your coat do not withhold even your shirt. Give to everyone who begs from you . . ." (Lk 6:27-30). We would like to say that this is too much! But who of us would not want to be treated in this way, even if we had behaved badly, or had offended some one, or found ourself in need? In actual fact, when others are good and generous toward us, it never seems to us that it is excessive, but when we have to act in this way toward others, it does seem excessive. Self-love is the great enemy of evangelical charity; at its urging even Christians often distort the Lord's commandment: they want a very large measure of love for themselves, while content to use a much smaller measure for others, and even while negligent and stingy in disseminating love, think they are doing too much. This happens almost unconsciously, and can become such a habit that we are not conscious of the enormous difference that exists between our conduct and the commandment to love our neighbor as ourselves. We use the motive of prudence and of proper moderation as a pretext, or excuse ourselves by thinking that it is not necessary to take the gospel literally, as long as we follow its spirit. Yet the spirit of the gospel is precisely this: do good to all, sacrificing self, giving what is ours, even at the cost of being thought a fool. The spirit of the gospel is revolutionary: it gives no peace to self-love, but wants to drive it out completely, and is the declared enemy of a comfortable, mediocre Christian life; it demands generous, concrete, timely charity.

Vatican II "lays stress on reverence for man; everyone must consider his every neighbor, without exception, as another self . . . In our times a special obligation binds us to make ourselves the neighbor of absolutely every person and to help him actively when he comes across our path: whether he be an old person, abandoned by all, a foreign laborer . . . a refugee, a child born of unlawful union . . . or a hungry person who disturbs our conscience by recalling the voice of Our Lord: 'As you did it to one of the least of these my brethren, you did it to me' (Mt 25:40)" (GS 27). This is the authentic gospel.

As you, O God, have created man to your image and likeness, so you have commanded us to love men with a love similar to that due to your divinity. The reason why we love you, O Lord, is your sovereignly high and infinite goodness, . . . and the reason why we love men is because they have all been created to your image and likeness, so that we love them as holy, living images of your divinity.

... We love ourselves with the love of charity because we are created to your image and likeness; and because all men have this dignity, for this reason we love them as ourselves, that is, as most holy and living images of your divinity. The same charity with which we love you, O Lord, is the source of the acts with which we love our neighbor. One same love holds for you, my God, as for our neighbor; it elevates us to the union of our spirit with you, my God, and it brings us back to loving society with our neighbor, but in such a way that we love him because he is created to your image and likeness, created to share in your divine goodness, to participate in your grace and to enjoy your glory.

St. Francis de Sales, *Treatise on the love of God* X 10,v2

You made me understand, O Jesus, that charity must not remain hidden in the bottom of the heart. You said: "No one lights a lamp and puts it under a bushel basket but upon the lamp-stand, so as to give light to all in the house." It seems to me that this lamp represents charity which must enlighten and rejoice not only those who are dearest to me, but "all those who are in the house" without distinction.

Charity seems, but is not difficult, for your yoke, O Lord, is sweet and light. When we accept it, we feel its sweetness immediately and cry out with the psalmist: "I have run the way of your commandments when you enlarged my heart". It is only charity which can expand my heart. O Jesus, since this sweet flame consumes it, I run with joy in the way of your new commandment. I want to run in it until that blessed day when, joining the virginal procession, I shall be able to follow you in the heavenly courts, singing your new canticle which must be love.

St. Therese of the Child Jesus, *Autobiography* C, p 220,225,226

275. AS I HAVE LOVED YOU

Lord Jesus, may we love one another as you have loved us (Jn 15:12)

1. The final touch that perfects fraternal charity and brings it to its highest expression was given by Jesus in his farewell address to his disciples. He was about to leave them: "Where I am going you cannot come" (Jn 13:33). But something of *himself* was to remain among them so as to prolong his presence. "A new commandment I give you, that you love one another; even as I have loved you, that you also love one another" (ib. 34). The love he has shown his disciples must remain among them and manifest itself in their mutual love. He will soon say: "Abide in my love" (Jn 15:10); abide in it not so much to enjoy it individually, as to live this love in their mutual relationships. This will be the unmistakable mark which will cause them to be recognized: "By this all men will know that you are my disciples, if you have love for one another" (Jn 13:35); it will also be the truest evidence of their

adherence to Christ.

The formula for the love that was in force in the Old Testament: "You shall love your neighbor as yourself," which Christ confirmed and was completing, was, in fact, substituted by a new formula: "Love one another as I have loved you." The old wording was already surpassed when Jesus presented the love of the Father as the model and foundation of fraternal love. But this love, although manifested in so many ways through creation, providence, and the redemption, was less accessible to men who needed to understand divine love through a human heart. So Christ pointed to his own heart: "Love one another, even as I have loved you". Christ's love, which translates into human form and expression the Father's infinite love, becomes the norm of the new law: the *new* commandment, *his* commandment. "This is my commandment, that you love one another as I have loved you" (Jn 15:12). Now, no longer will a human measure govern fraternal charity, but a divine one, that is, Christ's love. Limits disappear; there is no longer any measure applicable. The more deeply a Christian enters into the mystery of Christ's infinite love, the more he understands how far he must go in loving his brothers.

2. The new people of God "has as its law the new commandment to love as Christ loved us" (LG 9). To make this possible "the Christian, conformed to the likeness of that Son, who is the first-born of many brothers, receives 'the first fruits of the Spirit' (Rom 8:23), by which he becomes capable of discharging the new law of love" (GS 22). Vatican Council II repeatedly insists upon the obligation of each member of the faithful to love as Christ loved. There is but one way: to open oneself to the action of the Holy Spirit, who, in making the baptized person like to Christ, pours his love into him. Without this divine gift, the new commandment would be absolutely impracticable and Jesus would not have been able to propose it. But the gift was made, the way is clear: every Christian can and must emulate the Savior's love.

St. Therese of the Child Jesus reflected upon this precept and wrote: "How I love it . . . since it gives me the assurance that your will, O Lord, is to love in me all those you command me to love" (Auto. C, p. 221). For a Christian who "abides" in the love of Christ, it is really Christ who loves in him, forgives in him, and saves through him. This is the mystery of his Mystical Body, by which he, the glorious divine Head, continues to act through his members. It is urgent that we make room for him, and put ourselves entirely at his disposal, so that, through the heart of his disciple, Christ can continue to manifest his love to the world.

"Greater love has no man than this, that a man lay down his life for his friends" (Jn 15:13). Jesus explains his commandment by what he was about to do for mankind. We must follow him even here. "He laid down his life for us"—says St. John—"and we ought to lay down our lives for the brethren" (1 Jn 3:16). This is the great reality that so many genuine Christians—the saints—have lived to the letter. The new law of love is sealed with the blood of Christ and must also have the seal of his disciples' blood. So much will not be asked of everyone, but everyone is asked to spend his own life in an engagement of brotherly charity which will be a living testimony of the love of Christ.

> *O kindly Lord, you have given us a kind commandment. For you said: "A new commandment I give you, that you love one another, even as I have loved you". You who have loved us and purified us from our sins in your blood, gave us a commandment of love.*
>
> *O good, sweet, delightful commandment of life and eternal salvation! In it is summed up all the law and the prophets ... Charity is the precious pearl, for which your bride, once she has found it, sells everything in order to buy it. It is the ladder which appeared to Jacob in a dream, which he saw reaching to the sky ... In fact, just as the angels come down by its means, so we ascend to the angels, since without this ladder no one can mount to the kingdom of heaven ...*
>
> *O Lord, who give us the commandment to love our brothers, you are the very one who desires to be wholeheartedly loved by your servants. Yet it is not as important that the servant love his lord, as that he be loved by his lord.*
>
> Bl. Oglerio, *Sermon* 5:1

> *When you commanded your people to love their neighbor as themselves, you had not as yet come upon the earth. Knowing the extent to which each one loved himself, you were not able to ask of your creatures a greater love than this for the neighbor. But when you gave your apostles a new commandment, your own commandment ... it was no longer a question of loving one's neighbor as oneself, but of loving him as you, Jesus, loved him, and will love him to the consummation of the ages.*
>
> *Ah! Lord, I know you don't command the impossible. You know better than I do my weakness and imperfection; you know very well that never would I be able to love my sisters as you love them, unless you, O my Jesus, loved them in me. It is because you wanted to give me this grace that you made your new commandment. Oh! how I love this new commandment since it gives me the assurance that your will is to love in me all those you command me to love. Yes, I feel it, when I am charitable, it is you alone, Jesus, who are acting in me, and the more united I am to you, the more also do I love my sisters.*
>
> St. Therese of the Child Jesus, *Autobiography* C, p. 220-221

276. NINETEENTH SUNDAY OF ORDINARY TIME

YEAR A

Lord, save me! (Mt 14:30)

The first reading (1 Kg 19:9a, 11-13a) tells of Elijah, the prophet of fire, who exhausted by struggles and persecution, climbed Mount Horeb seeking a little comfort in the place where God had revealed himself to Moses. And upon that holy mountain, God revealed himself to Elijah also: "Go forth"—he was told—"and stand upon the mount before the Lord". Immediately, "a great and strong wind rent the mountains"; then an earthquake followed, and then a fire, "but"—the sacred text repeats it three times—"the Lord was not in the wind ... he was not in the earthquake ... he was not in the fire" (ib. 11-12). When all was calm, behold "a still, small voice" in which Elijah sensed the presence of God, and immediately, as a sign of respect, "he wrapped his face in his mantle" (ib. 13). God himself had preceded, and as it were, announced himself by the powerful forces of nature, indications of his omnipotence; but when he desired to reveal himself to his discouraged and weary prophet, he did so in the gentle murmur of a light breeze, which, while expressing his mysteries spiritually, also indicated his delicate kindness toward man's weakness, and the intimacy with which he wished to communicate with his creature. Our account stops here without relating the dialogue between God and his prophet, but it is enough to show how God intervenes to support one who seeks refuge in him when oppressed by life's difficulties.

In quite a different context the Gospel (Mt 14:22-23) presents a substantially similar episode. On the evening of the multiplication of the loaves, Jesus commanded his disciples to cross the lake and to precede him to the other shore, while he dismissed the crowd and went along to the mountain to pray. It was night and, because of the violence of the waves and the high winds, the boat of the Twelve was in trouble and they "were making headway painfully" (Mk 14:27). Toward dawn they saw Jesus coming toward them "walking on the sea", and thinking they were seeing a ghost, they cried out in terror. But the Lord's word reassured them: "Take heart, it is I; have no fear" (Mt 14:27); and Peter said boldly: "Lord, if it is you, bid me come to you upon the water" (ib. 28). The apostle had no doubt that Jesus possessed such power; at his word he got out of the boat and walked upon the waves. But a moment later, frightened by the violent wind, he was about to sink, and cried out: "Lord, save me!" (ib. 30). This contrast between Peter's faith and his instinct of fear was so human; like Elijah he was full of zeal and courage for his Lord, and yet, still exposed to fears and discouragement and in need of his Lord's intervention to support him. Upon Horeb, God had made his presence known to the Prophet; he had revealed himself, and spoken to him, but had remained the Invisible One. But on the lake God let himself be recognized in the reality of his human-divine person; his disciples did not cover their faces before him, but fixed their gaze upon him because he had himself veiled his divinity under human flesh. He had made himself man, a brother;

for this reason the disciples, and especially Peter, dealt with him with so much familiarity. With equal familiarity Jesus encouraged them, and rebuked and calmed the wind, and held out his hand to Peter, taking hold of it and saying: "O man of little faith, why did you doubt?" (ib. 31).

It is insufficiency of faith that makes a Christian fearful in danger and discouraged before difficulties, and hence sometimes on the point of foundering. But where faith is alive, where there is no doubting of Jesus' power and his continual presence in the Church, there will be no foundering, because the hand of the Lord will be invisibly stretched out to save the ship of the Church and of each individual member of the faithful.

> *"Have no fear!": you say to your disciples ... Oh! how good you are, my God, to speak these words to us! I am so weak, so wretched, such a sinner, so continually buffeted by the wind of temptation, that I am like a ship that is taking in water on every side ... since it is not so much that the temptation is strong as that I am weak ... Ah! I recognize that you do not let me be much tempted, and I constantly feel your hand upon me to protect me from any serious temptation ...*
>
> *How good you are, my God, to tell me who am rowing without making any progress and who feel myself all tossed about by the sea and powerless to move ahead: "Have no fear!" ... How good you are, not only to say this to me, but also to permit me to glimpse the hope that there will perhaps come a day when you yourself will step into my poor boat, and then it will at once find itself near the shore toward which it is now straining without ever making headway. That shore is the fulfillment of your will, which I would so like to reach in this life, and it is also the blessed eternity to which I beg you let my boat arrive, O dear divine pilot, O good Jesus!*
>
> C. de Foucauld, *Meditations on the Gospel*

YEAR B

"O taste and see that the Lord is good! Happy is the man who takes refuge in him!" (Ps 34:9)

Jesus, the living bread come down from heaven, is at the center of today's Liturgy of the Word, which is entirely directed toward the Eucharist. The first reading (1 Kg 19:4-8) is a most fitting introduction: it gives us the picture of Elijah fleeing into the desert to save himself from the fury of Queen Jezebel and throwing himself upon the ground beneath a bush, lamenting: "It is enough; now, O Lord, take away my life; for I am no better than my fathers" (ib. 4). After having struggled to the limit in defense of the worship of the true God, the prophet was experiencing that he was a poor man like every other, and he begged for death. Then, falling asleep, he heard said to him: "Arise and eat" (ib. 5,7); the angel of the Lord had put beside him a little hearth cake and some water; whereupon, at his invitation Elijah "arose and ate and drank, and went in the strength of that food forty days and forty nights to Horeb, the mount of God" (ib. 8). The despondency of the prophet reflects the experience of one who, after accomplishing great enterprises—even apostolic ones—and having perhaps believed himself better than the rest, finds himself at some point on the ground, deprived of all strength; it is a most valuable experience for it situates a man in the reality of his shortcomings, and of his essential and continual need of God. The divine food which reinvigorated Elijah and gave him the strength to support the long march to the holy mountain is a clear figure of the Eucharist, the viaticum of the Christian on his journey to eternity of which the Gospel of the day speaks (Jn 6:41-52), taking up again the theme of the preceding Sunday.

The Jews murmured because Jesus had declared that he was the bread come down from heaven; was it possible that bread could take the form of a man? And that man—Jesus—was he not "the son of Joseph, whose father and mother we know?" (ib. 42). Not having faith, they were unable to go beyond a material interpretation of our Lord's words. And besides, faith is a gift: "No one can come to me unless the Father who sent me draws him" (ib. 44). The Father attracts, but man must let himself be attracted and taught by him: "everyone who has heard and learned from the Father comes to me" (ib. 45). The sin of the Jews was always that of stubbornly rejecting the word of God brought to them through Christ. Christ is the sacrament of the Father, and anyone who rejects him, cannot go to the Father, nor can he have eternal life; only "he who believes has eternal life" (ib. 47). It was a fearful thing, this resistance to the Savior on the part of his contemporaries who, no less than his disciples, had seen his miracles and listened to his teaching. But Christ is also with his Church today, and everyone can find him in the Eucharist; yet how many believe in this "mystery of faith"? Not for nothing did Jesus, before proclaiming the Eucharist, insist so strongly on the need of faith. For anyone who believes, the Lord's words leave no doubt: "I am the living bread which came down from heaven; if anyone eats of this bread, he will live forever; and the bread which I shall give for the life of the world is my flesh" (ib. 51). The Jews who ate manna are now dead; Elijah, revived by the food offered him by the angel, had had the strength to climb the holy mountain where the Lord revealed himself to him in a mysterious theophany; the Christian who eats the flesh of Christ "will live forever", and will be admitted to face to face vision with his God. He is not alone in this journey toward the eternal vision, but is intimately united and makes one body with his brothers, who also are nourished by the Eucharist, the sacrament of love, the sacrament of unity. In this manner he becomes capable of "walking in love" (Eph 5:2; 2nd reading), imitating the charity of God who so loved him that he gave his only Son, and imitating the charity of Christ who gave himself for his creature, even to dying on the cross, even to giving his own flesh as food.

O sweetest Bread, heal the palate of my heart so that I may taste the sweetness of your love. Cure it of every weakness, that I may taste no other sweetness save you, may seek no other love and love no other beauty save you. O purest Bread, containing in yourself every delight and the savor of every sweetness, who are always refreshing us without ever taking anything away from yourself, nourish my heart with yourself and fill the depths of my soul with your sweetness. The angel finds his full sustenance in you; let pilgrim man be also sustained by you according to his capacity, so that strengthened by such food he may not faint by the way.

O holy Bread, living Bread . . . who come down from heaven and give life to the world, come into my heart, and cleanse me of every impurity of the flesh and of the spirit; come into my soul and sanctify me inwardly and outwardly. Be the continual salvation of my soul and body. Keep far from me the enemies who set snares for me: may they flee from your powerful presence so that, strengthened by you from within and without, I may reach your kingdom by the straight path, where we shall see each other, face to face, no longer veiled in mystery as in this life . . . Then you will fill me with yourself with a wonderful satiety, in such a way that I shall not be hungry or thirsty for all eternity.

St. Anselm, *Prayers* 29

YEAR C

"Let your steadfast love, O Lord, be upon us, even as we hope in you" (Ps 33:22)

Today's Liturgy sums up the life of faith in expectation of the heavenly homeland. It begins with a short passage from the Book of Wisdom (18:6-9), which records the prophetic night of the liberation of the chosen people. It was a night of grief and slaughter for the Egyptians who saw their first-born perish, because they had rejected the word of God which Moses had announced to them; for the Hebrews it was a night of joy and deliverance, for they had believed in the divine promises and were spared, and began their march of liberation toward the desert where God was awaiting them in order to draw up his covenant with them. The presence or absence of faith decided the fate of the two nations, and while ruin cut down the unbelieving, salvation was given to those who believed. The whole history of the Jewish people whom God had chosen as "his" people is interwoven with the thread of faith.

The theme is continued in the second reading (Heb 11:1-2,8-19), where St. Paul sketches out with masterly effectiveness the great figure of Abraham, the father of believers. The patriarch's entire life is in rhythm with his wonderful faith. Through faith Abraham obeyed God, left his country, and set out for a destination that was not yet made clear. Through faith he believed that although by that time he was enfeebled with age, he would have a child by Sara who too was already old. Through faith he did not waver, after the divine command to sacrifice Isaac, his only son, from whom he had hoped to have the descendants God had promised. Abraham believed against all evidence and all hope, for "he considered that God was able to raise men even from the dead" (ib. 19). His conduct clearly showed that "faith is the assurance of things hoped for, and the conviction of things not seen" (ib. 1). With unshakeable faith, he awaited the fulfillment of the divine promises even when the last spark of hope was about to be extinguished; he awaited without flinching because he did not set his hope on earthly values, but "looked forward to the city . . . whose builder and maker is God" (ib. 10).

The day's Gospel (Lk 12:32-48) likewise invites us to confidence: "You also must be ready" (ib. 40); ready in faith and hope in expectation of the day of the Lord, of the heavenly city. The gospel passage begins with a promise expressing a tenderness that is more than paternal: "Fear not, little flock, for it is your Father's good pleasure to give you the kingdom" (ib. 32). Although the disciples of Jesus were few in number and scattered in the midst of an unbelieving world, they must not fear: the Father has made them heirs of the kingdom, and their certitude of reaching it one day is based upon him. But, like Abraham, they must renounce worldly security and accept living as poor men, detached, uprooted, wholly stretched out toward the true treasure which is not on earth, but in heaven. Therefore they must have no excessive preoccupation nor anxiety over temporal things; rather, they should deal with these with "loins . . . girded and . . . lamps burning, . . . like men who are waiting for their master . . . so that they may open to him at once when he comes and knocks" (ib. 35-36). The parable of the faithful steward follows, for the purpose of stressing the grave responsibility of those who are entrusted with providing for their brothers. Woe to them if, while waiting for their master, who "delayed in coming" (ib. 45), they should take advantage of their position at the expense of those who had been entrusted to their care. A protracted delay cannot authorize any negligence or intemperance.

When will the Lord come? When and how shall we be brought into his eternal kingdom? This is God's secret. Christians too, like Abraham, must wait in faith and hope without knowing when or how the divine promises will be fulfilled.

Lord, I beg of you a new, lively, deep faith . . . My soul is harder than stone, more insensible than steel, and drier than the desert, but it is eager to drink great drafts of this ocean of faith and love . . . since it is faith I need and love—charity—for my soul is cold; the

*Blessed Virgin, the consoler of sinners, will give me this enthusiasm
and this faith ... Thus I shall be raised to the highest ranks of Christianity ... with strong faith and a pure heart, like a Christian of
Stephen's time.*

*This I ask, Christ Jesus, nothing else: faith, a fullness of faith,
and a pure desire to serve you and your Church.*

G. Canovai, Suscipe Domine

*O Lord, you do not reveal the day of your coming in order to
make us vigilant and always ready, always prepared for battle, and
constantly dedicated to virtue. You want us to live in continual expectation and to be always fervent: this is why you leave the end of
each of us in uncertainty. Since we know you will surely come, make
us watchful and ready, so that we may escape being taken by surprise.*

*O Lord, you demand faithfulness and prudence of your servant.
You call him "faithful" because he appropriates nothing for himself,
and does not uselessly waste his master's property; you call him
"prudent" because he knows how to administer advantageously
what has been entrusted to him. Lord, make us also faithful and prudent servants, so that we will not appropriate to ourselves anything
that belongs to you, and will distribute your goods wisely.*

cf St. John Chrysostom, *Commentary on the Gospel of St. Matthew*
77:2-3

277. CONQUER EVIL WITH GOOD

Teach me, O Lord, always to seek to do good to all (1 Thes 5:15)

1. "You have heard that it was said, 'An eye for an eye, and a
tooth for a tooth', but I say to you: Do not resist one who is evil.
But if anyone strikes you on the right cheek, turn to him the other
also, and if anyone would sue you and take your coat, let him have
your cloak as well" (Mt 5:38-40). Faced with an insult or an act of
violence, we are always ready to react and not only defend
ourselves, but take revenge as well. Jesus obliges his followers to
struggle constantly against this instinct. Evil is not to be fought
nor conquered with evil, but with its opposite: good, and with the
example of Christ who conquered sin, not by condemning us but
by loving us even to dying for us. When the duty to defend others
does not enter the picture, and the evil affects ourselves only, the
rule is plain: "Do not be overcome by evil, but overcome evil with
good" (Rom 12:21). One who lets himself be drawn into disorderly
reactions is conquered; but the one who responds to evil with good
is the conqueror. The Lord's teaching had been deeply assimilated
by the early Church, and it constantly surfaces in the writings of
the Apostles. "Repay no one evil for evil ... Love does no wrong
to a neighbor" (Rom 12:17;13:10), and he says to the Thessalonians: "See that none of you repays evil for evil, but always seek

to do good to one another and to all" (1 Thes 5:15). Addressing the first Christians who had to undergo insult and persecution at the hands of the pagans, St. Peter wrote: "It is God's will that by doing right you should put to silence the ignorance of foolish men" (1 Pet 2:15). Such conduct will not always achieve its purpose; it may also be the cause of further insults and sufferings, but the Christian must not change his course: "If when you do right and suffer for it you take it patiently, you have God's approval. For to this you have been called, because Christ also suffered for you, leaving you an example, that you should follow in his steps" (ib. 20-21). The example of the crucified Christ, imprinted on our minds and hearts, gives us the strength to overcome evil with good, to be good and generous even at our own expense. "For it is better to suffer for doing right, if that should be God's will, than for doing wrong" (ib. 3:17).

2. St. Paul writes to the faithful of Corinth who in their daily disputes were accusing each other before the civil courts: "To have lawsuits at all with one another is defeat for you. Why not rather suffer wrong? Why not rather be defrauded?" (1 Cor 6:7). The Apostle does not investigate whether these lawsuits are provoked or unexpected, but simply condemns all such litigation between those who have the precept of loving one another as Christ has loved them. It is far better to suffer injustice than to contend with one's brothers. He presents this way of conduct not as an heroic act, but as the simple duty of every Christian.

"The teaching of Christ"—Vatican II recalls—"even requires that we forgive injuries ... What does most to reveal God's presence is the brotherly charity of the faithful who are united in spirit, ... and who prove themselves a sign of unity" (GS 28,21). One of the things that most scandalizes the world is precisely division among good people, discord among the faithful, and contention among religious persons. The Church invites all her children to renew themselves on this point: "The new commandment of love is the basic law of human perfection and hence of the world's transformation. To those, therefore, who believe in divine love, he gives assurance that the way of love lies open to all men and that the effort to establish a universal brotherhood is not a hopeless one. He cautions them at the same time that this love is not something to be reserved for important matters, but must be pursued chiefly in the ordinary circumstances of life" (GS 38).

Only the love of God can transform the world and "achieve universal brotherhood"; Christians must carry the example of it everywhere; it is their duty and obligation. May "all of you"—St. Peter urges—"have unity of spirit, sympathy, love of the brethren, a tender heart and a humble mind. Do not return evil for evil, or reviling for reviling; but on the contrary bless, for to this you have been called, that you may obtain a blessing" (1 Pet 3:8-9). Blessed by God in Christ, we are called to pass on to others, the blessing we have received from God, speaking well of everyone, wishing and doing good to all, just as God blessed each one of us.

> *How good you are, my God! ... Loving Father, you desire an unchangeable love among all your children, and that, in order to preserve this peace, they endure with mildness and patience, and without any resistance, every form of violence or insult, even death itself ... O God of love, good Father, what love you wish to see among us, what peace, what living unity among your children! ...*
>
> *Our brother is unjust ... teach us, O Jesus, to let ourselves be despoiled, to yield in everything, and "not to resist evil", ... help us to convert him through brotherly correction, as you have taught us, after we have tried to convert him through our gentleness ... In the family of your children, O my God, the least increase in charity between men is worth a thousand times more, and is thousands of times more important than all the material wealth in the world ...*
>
> *This is your commandment, O Jesus, and it is also the example that you yourself gave us, letting yourself be despoiled of everything and dying naked upon the cross without offering any resistance, praying for those who despoiled you and made you die.*
>
> C. de Foucauld, *Meditations on the Gospel,* op. sp.

> *Truly, O charity, the injuries that you undergo are a scandal for the weak. In fact, you neither take offense nor show contempt when you are offended. In truth, you cannot deny yourself, nor be divided within yourself. Rather, you know how to unite within yourself what is divided, but not how to divide what is united. You love peace, you rejoice in unity. Truly only you generate, stabilize and preserve ... unity in the bond of peace. You knock at the door of a friend with full confidence without the least thought of being refused, because you know you are the mother of all friendship ... O charity, how true and sincere you are, you love your neighbor's good as you do your own ...*
>
> *When I love you, Lord Jesus, I possess the love of God and the love of my neighbor; in fact you are my neighbor, because you made yourself man and showed me mercy, and you are no less God, blessed above all things through all ages.*
>
> Anonymous (sec XIII), *De Charitate* 5:27

278. CHARITY IS MAGNANIMOUS

Lord, forgive me my debts, as I also have forgiven my debtors (Mt 6:12)

1. "Love is patient and kind" (1 Cor 13:4); love is magnanimous. Magnanimity is the first quality which St. Paul attributes to it. Charity makes the soul big, generous, free from the calculations and pettiness of selfishness.

When St. Peter asked if it were enough to forgive his neighbor seven times—which perhaps seemed to him the utmost possible—he was answered: "I do not say to you seven times, but seventy times seven" (Mt 18:22). This was tantamount to saying: always, without any limit, really as God does, "for he will abundantly pardon" (Is 55:7). The whole of our life is sustained by God's pardon. We have scarcely opened our eyes to existence, when God gives us new life in grace and welcomes us into his forgiveness, by which he redeems us from original sin. Then, from our first use of reason until death, there is a constant succession of divine pardons. How could a Christian live in grace, persevere and grow in friendship with God, and be nourished with the Body of Christ without the continual, renewed pardon of the heavenly Father? This is how the magnanimity of the Father must become the norm of the magnanimity of his children: "Be merciful, even as your Father is merciful" (Lk 6:36). After Peter had experienced the forbearance of the Master's forgiveness, whom he had denied, he had no further need of calculation to know how many times he should forgive his neighbor. Perhaps he was thinking of the forgiveness so abundantly granted him when he wrote that anyone who does not love his brother "is blind and shortsighted, and has forgotten that he was cleansed from his old sins" (2 Pet 1:9). Just because we live by God's forgiveness, we must know how to forgive our brothers. The embrace of forgiveness which God gives us again and again with untiring magnanimity must not end in us; it is our duty to pass it on to our neighbor. This is so important in God's eyes that he inverts the roles and measures the liberality of his forgiveness against the generosity that we each show in our forgiveness of others. "Forgive, and you will be forgiven ... for the measure you give will be the measure you get back" (Lk 6:37-38).

2. Charity is magnanimous toward others because "it is not irritable or resentful" (1 Cor 13:5). What cools fraternal charity is the thought of wrongs done to us, which is something we find very hard to forget. God's forgiveness not only pardons debts incurred, but so consumes them as to wipe out their memory. "None of the transgressions which [man] has committed shall be remembered against him" (Ezek 18:22). Furthermore, together with his pardon, God gives back his friendship intact. The pardon we give is not complete, unless we aim at forgetting the harm received to the point where we will deal with the offender with the heart and action of a friend. St. Paul insists: "Be kind to one another, tenderhearted, forgiving one another as God in Christ forgave you" (Eph 4:32). If our resolution of forgiveness is not lived with generosity and constancy, we pronounce our own condemnation when we appear before the heavenly Father in prayer: "And forgive us our debts, as we also have forgiven our debtors" (Mt 6:12). What would happen to man if God became, like him, stingy with his forgiveness? Perhaps the mediocrity of so many who were

once fervent and generous in the service of God, can be explained by the scantiness of their own forgiving, which has paralyzed their spiritual life. "He who sows sparingly will also reap sparingly" (2 Cor 9:6). He who sows a meager and miserly forgiveness cannot expect a generous magnanimous pardon from God, nor an abundance of grace and love.

"Give, and it will be given to you"—repeats the Lord—"good measure, pressed down, shaken together, running over will be put into your lap" (Lk 6:38). Charity is not complete unless it is magnanimous in its every aspect. All men live by God's gifts, and all should exchange with one another the gifts they have received: the spiritual gifts of love, benevolence and forgiveness, and the physical gifts that are necessary for life. "If your enemy is hungry, give him bread to eat; and if he is thirsty, give him water to drink" (Prov 25:21). "But if anyone has the world's goods and sees his brother in need, yet closes his heart against him, how does God's love abide in him? Little children, let us not love in word or speech, but in deed and in truth" (1 Jn 3:17-18).

> *Forgive us, Lord! Oh, that like the sinful woman I may hear from you the sweet and consoling words: "Your sins are forgiven, because you have loved much; those who are forgiven more, love more, and those who are forgiven less, love less." These are your words, O eternal Truth! Forgive me, then, and make me love you as much as I have need for your pardon ...*
>
> *And in order that nothing should be lacking to perfect charity, there is also fraternal love. Nothing must hinder union with our brothers, since not even offenses can stand in the way. We forgive them, Lord, just as we wish to obtain pardon for ourselves, with the same sincerity. We hold no resentment, just as we desire you not to hold any. We restore our love to them, just as we want you to share yours with us.*
>
> J.B. Bossuet, *Meditations upon the Gospel* III 51, v.1

> *Is there anyone, Lord, who is not in debt to you, unless he be without any sin? Is there anyone who does not have some brother as his debtor, unless he be one who was never offended by anyone? ... Every person is a debtor, and yet, in turn, has someone indebted to him. Therefore, Lord, in your justice you have established that your rule of conduct toward me, your debtor, should be that which I follow toward the one who is debtor to me.*
>
> *There are in fact, two works of mercy that set us free, of which you yourself briefly made note in your gospel: Forgive and it will be forgiven you; give and it will be given to you ... I want to be pardoned for my sin, Lord, so it follows that I have something which I can be forgiven ... The poor man borrows from me, and I am your beggar, Lord. Indeed when we pray we are all your beggars: we are standing before the door of the great father of the family, rather we are prostrate before you, begging and weeping from our longing to*

receive something, and this something is you, O Lord! What does a poor man ask of me? Bread. And what do I ask of you, if not yourself who said: "I am the living bread come down from heaven? To obtain forgiveness, I will forgive; I shall pardon others, and I shall be pardoned; wishing to receive, I shall give, and it will be given to me.
St. Augustine, *Sermon* 83,2

279. CHARITY IS KIND

Lord, may my heart be blameless in your statutes (Ps 119:80)

1. Kindliness is the fruit of a good, charitable heart which, in imitation of God, desires and seeks only the good of the brethren: "Always seek to do good to one another and to all" (1 Thes 5:15) urges St. Paul. If the heart is good, then the thoughts are good, and the judgments also are well-disposed.

"Why do you see the speck that is in your brother's eye, but do not notice the log that is in your own eye?" (Mt 7:3). The poorer a man is in virtue, the more trifling his own faults seem to him and the graver those of others, particularly if they impinge on his sensitiveness. Then he is tempted to set himself up as his neighbor's judge, a way of acting that makes the insufficiency of his love evident. It is all too easy for a certain amount of this critical spirit to be harbored even by those who devote themselves to piety and perhaps live in the shadow of the sanctuary. But this injures the spiritual life in its source since it wounds charity which is its foundation. If God is present where charity and love reign, he does not willingly dwell where charity and love run short, for then there is no, or almost no, communion with him, and only the external framework of a life of piety remains.

Judgment belongs solely to God, for only he searches the heart. "Man looks on the outward appearance, but the Lord looks on the heart" (1 Sam 16:7). Since no man knows the intentions and the cicumstances of another's actions, a judgment by man—unless it is a duty of his office—is always rash and usurps the rights of God. St. Paul cries out: "Who are you to pass judgment on the servant of another? It is before his own master that he stands or falls" (Rom 14:4). God is the master, and we shall all appear at his tribunal for judgment: "Each of us shall give an account of himself to God" (ib. 12). Intransigent judgment is condemned by Jesus, who applies to it the rule for forgiveness: "Judge not, that you be not judged. For with the judgment you pronounce, you will be judged" (Mt 7:1-2). Instead of judging our neighbor, charity fosters feelings of mercy for him, busying itself to excuse rather than to condemn.

2. When the workers of the first hour were complaining because those who had come last were paid at the same rate as themselves, the owner of the vineyard said: "Am I not allowed to do what I choose with what belongs to me? Or do you begrudge

my generosity?" (Mt 20:15). If the eye is evil, the heart is not well-disposed toward the neighbor, and consequently the well-being of others gives rise to discontentment, jealousy, and envy. On the contrary, charity "is not jealous" (1 Cor 13:4); in fact it rejoices in the good of others, promotes it, and procures it, even if doing so causes a personal loss. "Rejoice in the good of others as if it were your own"—says St. John of the Cross—"desiring that they be given precedence over you in all things . . . Try to practice this more with those who least attract you" (Cautions 13).

A Christian's conduct toward his neighbor should reflect God's kindliness and love, for we have been saved through his goodness (Tit 3:4); kindliness in our feelings, thoughts, words, and deeds, as sacred Scripture continually exhorts. St. Peter urges us to put away "all envy and slander" (1 Pet 2:1). St. James recommends: "Do not speak against one another, brethren. He that speaks evil against a brother or judges his brother, speaks evil against the law" (Jas 4:11). To act thus injures the law of charity which Christ left to his disciples, and consequently our friendship with Christ is weakened and chilled. How can we forget his words: "You are my friends if you do what I command you" (Jn 15:14)? Now the commandment that is dearest to him is precisely that of mutual love. St. Paul, too, insists: "Do all things without grumbling or questioning, that you may be blameless and innocent, children of God without blemish" (Phil 2:14-15). We must be without blemish in practicing a kindly, pure charity which seeks the good of others and not the gratification of our own heart or our own advantage.

Finally charity is kindly in affable, courteous ways, kindly in spreading goodness everywhere, and also where this goodness is lacking. In every person, even the wicked, there is good, for it is the mark of God who made him. It is the work of goodness to discover this good and make it come to the surface again. The goodness of a Christian must be like the goodness of God, who creates good in those whom he loves.

Help me, Lord, always to look at the virtues and good qualities which I find in others and cover their defects with the thought of my sins. In this way I shall gradually gain a great virtue, that is: considering all others better than myself. I shall begin to acquire this virtue with your help for that is always necessary, and when it is lacking, all my efforts are useless. I beseech you to give me this virtue, for you will not refuse it to anyone who does his best.
cf St. Teresa of Jesus, *Life* 13:10

O Lord, in order that your judgment may be favorable or rather that I be not judged at all, I want to be charitable in my thoughts towards others at all times, for you said: "Judge not, and you shall not be judged".
When the devil tries to place before the eyes of my soul the

*faults of such and such a sister ... help me to hasten to search out
her virtues, her good intentions ... Even if I have seen her fall once,
she could easily have won a great number of victories which she is
hiding through humility, and even what appears to me as a fault can
very easily be an act of virtue because of her intention.*

St. Therese of the Child Jesus, Autobiography C p. 222, 221

*Doing good means bearing worthy witness to you, O Jesus, Son
of God and Son of Mary, universal Teacher and Savior of the world.
There is no learning or wealth, there is no human power that is more
effective than a good nature: a heart that is gentle, friendly, and patient. The good-hearted man may suffer mortifications and opposition, but he always wins through in the end because goodness is
love, and love conquers all ...*

*Lord, do not let me fall into the error of thinking that kind-
ness—affability—is a minor virtue. It is a great virtue because it
means self-control and a disinterested intention, with a fervent love
for justice; it is the expression and the splendor of brotherly love. By
your grace, O Jesus, it is the touch of human and divine perfection.*

cf John XXIII, *Prayers and Devotions,* Dec. 6

280. LOVE IS NOT BOASTFUL

*Teach me, Lord, to seek not that which puffs up, but the charity
which builds up (1 Cor 8:2)*

1. "... Love is not ... boastful, it is not arrogant or rude" (1
Cor 13:4). Vainglory seeks its own glorification, whereas charity
acts "not to please men, but to please God" (1 Thes 2:4). Vainglory
puts self at the center of life; charity puts God and the neighbor
there. Vainglory is puffed up with the little it has; love empties
itself of whatever it has in order to give it to others. Vainglory
seeks self; charity dedicates self to God and to the neighbor. Love
and pride point in opposite directions, and cancel each other. "A
soul enkindled with love"—says St. John of the Cross—"is a gentle, meek, and humble soul" (Sayings of Light 1:27).

The deeper our charity is, the more we give ourselves to
others, serve our neighbor, and give to anyone in need with
simplicity and tact, without putting any value on our services;
rather, we try to let them pass unnoticed. "Beware of practicing
your piety before men in order to be seen by them", said Jesus (Mt
6:1). Charity does not sound a trumpet to make its good works
known. "When you give alms, do not let your left hand know what
your right hand is doing, so that your alms may be in secret, and
your Father who sees in secret will reward you" (ib. 3-4). Charity
does not give with arrogance, but puts itself on an equal level.
Brother gives to brother, rejoicing in sharing what he has, and
does not consider his superiority, because he is convinced he has
none. "For if anyone thinks he is something, when he is nothing,

he deceives himself" (Gal 6:3). Charity comes from God, and God is truth; therefore where charity is sincere, there can be no deceit or vainglory.

"Let him who boasts, boast of the Lord", says St. Paul (2 Cor 10:17). The Christian's glory is to love and to help his neighbor, not to be conceited over it; instead, he is grateful to his neighbor for giving him the opportunity and to God for sustaining him with grace for doing right.

2. "Let us have no conceit, no provoking of one another, no envy of one another" (Gal 5:26). The ambitious have no regard for others, they put themselves ahead of everyone else, they want to be first, and to make themselves respected. Their conduct disgusts and provokes their neighbor, who sees himself injured in his rights; whence come dissension, jealousy, and antagonism. Charity, on the other hand, "is not arrogant or rude" (1 Cor 13:5) to anyone, and rather than compete with others or prefer itself to anyone chooses the last place for itself. Charity inspires sensitivity of feeling toward the neighbor, despises no one, respects and honors everyone. "Love one another with brotherly affection; outdo one another in showing honor," St. Paul wrote to the Romans (12:10); and to the Philippians he suggested: "In humility count others better than yourself" (2:3). Instead of getting embroiled in petty quarrels, taking turns in putting each other down, Christians, as true brothers, should vie in yielding honor and precedence to the other.

In order to encourage humility in their relationships with one another St. Paul offered the faithful Christ's own sublime example: "Have this mind among yourselves, which is yours in Christ Jesus, who, though he was in the form of God, did not count equality with God a thing to be grasped, but emptied himself, taking the form of a servant" (Phil 2:5-7). The Son of God loved and saved us by making himself like us, one of us. He pointed out the way: in order to love our neighbor efficaciously, we must put aside all ambition and make ourselves little and humble, putting ourselves on a level with everyone, so that all may feel themselves brothers. This is the one way, not only for fraternal charity, but for every apostolate. "Respect and love"—Vatican II teaches—"ought to be extended also to those who think and act differently than we do in social, political, and also religious matters. In fact the more deeply we come to understand their ways of thinking through such courtesy and love, the more easily will we be able to enter into dialogue with them" (GS 28). But let no one fool himself into thinking that he knows how to love and respect those who are far distant from him, if he does not love and respect those who live near him.

"If our hearts do not condemn us, we have confidence before God"... Lord, let my heart reply to me in full truth that I love my brothers, that my brotherly love is sincere, not feigned, the kind that

seeks a brother's good without looking for any return from him but only his salvation.

"We have confidence before God, and receive from him whatever we ask, because we keep his commandments". O Lord, grant that this may be so, not before men, but in my heart where you see me ... What are your commandments? ... "I give you a new commandment, that you love one another". Charity is precisely the commandment of which you are speaking and upon which you insist so strongly here. Oh, give me a brotherly love that is visible to you; when questioning my heart in straight-forward judgment, make it able to answer that there is in me the root of that brotherly love from which come the fruits of goodness. Then I shall trust in you and you will give me all that I ask, because I am keeping your commandments.

St. Augustine, In Io 6:4

O God our Creator, you so arrange things that anyone who might become proud over some gift of his, is humbled because of something he does not have; while you lift up some one by granting him a favor, you subject him to another in something else ... You arrange things in such a way that each thing may belong to all, and, by reason of charity, everything may belong to each one, and that each one may possess in another what he has not received directly, and humbly give over to others what he has received from you.

O Lord, help us to administer well your multiform grace; that is, make us convinced that the gifts given to us belong to others, since they are given to us for their benefit ... Make us of service to each other, through charity. In fact, charity frees us from the yoke of guilt when it makes us mutually serve each other out of love; thus we may hold that the gifts of others are also ours, and we offer ours to others as if they were theirs.

St. Gregory the Great, Morals XXVIII,22

281. CHARITY IS NOT SELFISH

Lord, may I not seek my own advantage but that of others (1 Cor 10:33)

1. "Love does not insist on its own way" (1 Cor 13:5). Being sensitive to the needs of others and ready to respect and serve the neighbor is no justification for expecting a like return. Charity gives itself wholeheartedly to others, without claiming anything for itself. "Do good, and lend, expecting nothing in return, and your reward will be great, and you will be sons of the Most High; for he is kind to the ungrateful and the selfish" (Lk 6:35). Charity is not a giving in order to get, but a giving without counting the cost or self-interest; it considers itself fully repaid by the honor of being able to serve and love God in the neighbor. He whose heart is full of charity loves, serves, and gives prodigally for the

pleasure of loving and serving God in his creatures, for the joy of imitating his infinite prodigality and of knowing himself God's son. What greater reward is there than to share with Jesus the title "son of the Most High" (Lk 1:32)? In order to have this unique reward, a Christian flees all worldly recompense and seeks to benefit most of all those from whom he can expect no return. "When you give a dinner or a banquet, do not invite your friends or your brothers . . . or rich neighbors, lest they also invite you in return, and you be repaid. But when you give a feast, invite the poor, the maimed, the lame, the blind, and you will be blessed, because they cannot repay you" (Lk 14:12-14). The logic of the Gospel is at an immense distance from that of calculation, but there are very few who have the courage to follow it to the full.

"Keep your life free from love of money" the Apostle urges (Heb 13:5), and he recommends that we live in charity "by looking not only to (our) own interests, but also to the interests of others" (Phil 2:4). It is always the seed of selfishness that makes us avaricious and self-interested even when doing something good; the seed lies hidden and wreaks havoc even in the hearts of devout people; it makes charity sterile, hardens the spirit, and extinguishes compassion for the needs and sufferings of others. Then there may well be repeated here the episode of the Levite and the priest who, with no thought for the injured man they met along the road, went straight ahead, attending to their own affairs.

2. "Through love be servants of one another" (Gal 5:13). While selfishness shuts a man up in himself within the narrow circle of his own interests, charity impels him to forget himself in order to make him available to his neighbor's needs, and to put him at his neighbor's disposal. Charity frees a man from the slavery of selfishness to engage him in a generous service of his neighbor. It was Jesus who gave the world the supreme example of service; he who was God became a servant and said: "I am among you as one who serves" (Lk 22:27). At the same time he also gave this precept: "Whoever would be first among you must be your slave . . . even as the Son of man came not to be served, but to serve, and to give his life as a ransom for many" (Mt 20:27-28). Service is not a secondary or optional element of the following of Christ; it is an essential one, so essential that, according to Our Lord's word, a Christian's greatness will be in proportion to his generosity in "making himself a servant". Such service does not degrade, but ennobles, because it is the fruit of love and because we cannot fully realize our potential "except through a sincere gift of ourselves" (GS 24). This kind of service elevates us, making us like Christ, and leads us to a dedication like his.

This disinterested gift of self on the part of the faithful should be witness to the world of the value of Christian charity, and should bring to every soul an echo of Christ's love and of that of his heavenly Father. "The presence of Christian faithful in human society"—states Vatican II—"should be characterized by that charity with which God has loved us, and with which he wills that we should love one another. Christian charity truly extends to all ... without looking for either gain or gratitude. For just as God has loved us with a spontaneous love, so also the faithful in their charity care for the human person by loving him with the same affection with which God sought out man" (AG 12).

O God, your goodness and your eternal will neither seek nor will anything but our sanctification; you permit the devil to make us suffer and be persecuted by men, only to exercise us in the virtues of love and true wisdom, so that imperfect love may come to perfection.

Teach us, O God, to love you for yourself, because you are supreme, eternal goodness and are worthy of being loved; and to love our neighbor for your sake, not for our own profit, whether for the delight or the pleasure we find in him, but because he is a creature loved and created by you, supreme eternal goodness, and we serve and help him since we cannot be of service to you. Thus since we cannot really be useful to you, teach us how to be so for our neighbor.

Give us the perfection of love. When love is thus perfect, it does not cease loving nor serving, neither on account of injuries nor insults done to it, nor because it does not find pleasure and joy in the neighbor, but it attends only to pleasing you.

St. Catherine of Siena, *Letters* 151

O Lord, just as you have always preferred us to yourself, and do so still every time you give us yourself in the Blessed Sacrament, making yourself our food, so you wish us to have such great love for each other that we always prefer our neighbor to ourselves. Just as you have done all you could for us—except for sin which you neither would nor could do—so you want us to do everything we can for each other, except sin. Grant then, Lord, that without giving you any offense, my love for my neighbor may be so firm, cordial and strong that I will never refuse to do or endure anything for his sake.

Teach me to show my love through my deeds, obtaining for him all the good I can, to pray for him and to serve him lovingly whenever I have the opportunity. Make me quick to spend my life for my brothers, and to pledge myself to them without any reservation. Not only this, but that I may let myself become involved according to the will of others and out of love, since this is what you taught us yourself, O most loving Savior, by your death on the cross.

cf St. Francis de Sales, *Maxims* 4:2,9

282. CHARITY IS NOT RESENTFUL

Grant us, O Lord, a love that is "peaceable, gentle, open to reason, and full of mercy" (Jas 3:17)

1. When James and John were angry at the Samaritans for not having welcomed the Master, they said: "Lord, do you want us to bid fire come down from heaven and consume them?" and Jesus "turned and rebuked them" (Lk 9:54-55). Since he came to save, not to damn, to heal the sick of soul and body, and to redeem sinners, he would not use violent means, but presented himself to the world as the true "Servant of Yahweh" who does not cry aloud, nor break the bruised reed, nor quench the smoldering wick (Mt 12:19-10). He steals into our hearts with infinite gentleness, instructs, admonishes, and points out the way of salvation; to us and to all who follow him, he repeats: "My yoke is easy, my burden is light" (Mt 11:30).

Mildness is the flower of charity; it is a participation in the infinite sweetness with which God guides and governs all things. No one has so strong a desire for our well-being as God, yet there is no harshness in his desire, no rigidity nor violence; his desire is accompanied by gentleness, respecting his creature's freedom. He sustains our efforts and, with infinite forbearance, awaits our acceptance of his grace. Jesus gave the world a most convincing example of this, particularly in his passion, for when "he was reviled, he did not revile in return; when he suffered he did not threaten" (1 Pet 2:23). Peter was an eyewitness of this and when the Master was captured heard him say: "Put your sword back into its place" (Mt 26:52); he was so struck by this that ever afterwards he kept control of his fiery temperament. His frequent exhortations to evangelical mildness are a proof of this. He recommends to servants that they be subject to their masters, "not only to the kind and gentle, but also to the overbearing" (1 Pet 2:18); and to wives that they be submissive to their husbands, with "a gentle and quiet spirit, which in God's sight is very precious" (ib. 3:4); he counsels all to defend themselves "with gentleness and reverence" (ib. 16), even when unjustly harrassed. St. James echoes this advice: "The wisdom from above . . . is peaceful, gentle, open to reason, and full of mercy" (Jas 3:17). Both these apostles had learned from Christ the language of charity.

2. Charity "is not resentful" (1 Cor 13:5), and therefore St. Paul recommends: "Let all bitterness and wrath and anger and clamor and slander be put away from you, and all malice" (Eph 4:31). All these are vices opposed to charity, and originate in uncontrolled passions which, under the impact of opposition, break through all restraint. Uncontained anger is the source of ill-advised and violent words and deeds, which forcibly disturb fraternal relationships. One who loves his neighbor prefers doing violence to himself in the effort to dominate his rising anger, rather than hurt others with bitter acrimony and violence.

All the same, charity does not exclude, and sometimes even demands, a just firmness when evil needs to be corrected or put down, particularly when God's rights are in question, or those of the little and the weak. Even Jesus was roused to anger against those who were profaning the temple and he hurled harsh invectives against the Pharisees who were oppressing and deceiving the people with their hypocrisy and false interpretation of the law. But whereas indignation in Christ was perfectly controlled by reason and will, this is not the case in us, because of the disorder brought about by sin. Therefore, it is always dangerous to give anger an opportunity: "Be angry, but sin not"—says the Apostle—"do not let the sun go down on your anger and give no opportunity to the devil" (Eph 4:26-27). If, through human frailty, a spark is lit, we should hurry to put it out, lest it work havoc in our own heart and in that of others and of giving an occasion for sin. The devil makes use of anger to stir up grudges and discord, which break charity. In the book of Proverbs we read: "A soft answer turns away wrath, but a harsh word stirs up anger—A hot-tempered man stirs up strife, but he who is slow to anger quiets contention.—Pleasant words are like a honeycomb, sweetness to the soul and health for the body" (15:1,8; 16:24). Meditation upon these sayings, which are full of wisdom because they are inspired by the Holy Spirit, is very useful for learning how to control ourselves and how to conform ourselves to the meekness of Christ who said: "Learn from me; for I am gentle and lowly in heart" (Mt 11:29).

> *O unspeakable charity of our God! ... What have you taught me, O uncreated Love? You have taught me that I should bear patiently, like a lamb, not only harsh words, but even harsh and hard blows, and injury, and loss. And with this you will that I be innocent and spotless, harmful to no one of my neighbors and brothers; not only in the case of those who do not persecute us, but in that of those who injure us; and you will that we pray for them as for special friends who give us good and great gain. And you will that I be patient and meek not only in injuries and temporal losses, but, universally, in everything that may be contrary to my will: as you did not will your own will to be done in anything, but the will of your Father* ...
> *O my sweetest love, Jesus, make your will always be fulfilled in us, as it always is in heaven by your angels and saints.*
> St. Catherine of Siena, *Letters* 132

> *O charity, you do not seek your own interest nor get angry ... instead of the evil you have received you overwhelm with blessings ... O charity, you endure everything, you ignore, you wait, when someone blunders you do not let him fall; O charity, because you are kind, you attract, you will over, you dissuade from error. O kind charity, you love even those whom you have to bear with and you love them warmly. Yes, you weep, but for love, not out of grief; you weep with desire, you weep with those who weep.*
> *O charity, good mother, whether you are supporting the weak or spurring on the skillful or calming the uneasy, however differently*

*you act with different persons, you love them all as your children!
You are mild when you scold, unaffected when you caress; when you
have to be harsh it is only with compassion, you are soothing
without deceit, and know how to be angry with patience and to accept offense with humility; when provoked you do not let yourself
feel hurt, when disdained you call again. You are really the mother of
men and of angels. Not only have you made peace in affairs of this
world, but in those of heaven as well. By appeasing God towards
man, you have reconciled man with God.*

Anonymous (sec. XIII), De Charitate 5:26-7

283. TWENTIETH SUNDAY OF ORDINARY TIME

YEAR A

*"Let the peoples praise you, O Lord; let all the peoples praise you"
(Ps 67:4)*

From the earliest times, God chose Israel as his people and
assigned them a privileged place in the history of salvation; the
first fruits of the gifts of salvation were to be reserved for them.
But in the fullness of time, through Israel, a priestly people, salvation was to be extended to all nations without distinction. This
plan, which had been announced by the prophets, is recalled today
in the first reading (Is 56:1,6-7). Through the words of Isaiah God
assures his merciful kindness to any of the gentiles who believe in
him and serve him by fulfilling his law: "These I will bring to my
holy mountain, and make them joyful in my house of prayer . . .
My house shall be called a house of prayer for all peoples" (ib. 7).
Thus the choice of Israel does not signify any rejection of other
peoples, but is rather ordained toward their salvation.

St. Paul enlarges upon this thought in the second reading
(Rom 11:13-15,29-32). Although the Apostle was saddened by the
resistance of his countrymen to the gospel of Christ, he did not
give up trying in every way possible to bring them to the faith and
dedicated himself zealously to the conversion of the gentiles, with
the secret hope of "making his fellow Jews jealous, and thus saving some of them" (ib. 14). God, indeed, does not repent of his
gifts: the promises made to Israel and its vocation "are irrevocable" (ib. 29). If the Jews would acknowledge their errors,
God was ready to forgive them. Just as the pagans who once were
disobedient to God were being received into his mercy, so too the
Jews, who were disobedient to God when they rejected Christ, will
be once again the object of divine mercy when they return to him.
Moreover, as St. Paul explains, inasmuch as Israel's refusal of
Christ had caused the gospel to be preached to the pagans so that
they might find mercy, the conversion of these will one day be the
occasion for the repentance of the chosen people. In fact, God who
wishes to "have mercy on all men" (ib. 32), turns the very perversi-

ty of the one to good, that is, to the conversion of the other. Though sin is always a cause of ruin for the one who obstinately persists in it, it cannot upset the plan of universal salvation which God has willed.

In the Gospel (Mt 15:21-28), Jesus himself confirmed the mysterious order of the divine plan by his conduct toward the Canaanite woman. She cried out: "Have mercy on me, O Lord, Son of David", imploring help for her daughter, who was "severely possessed by a demon" (ib. 22). The fact that this pagan woman turned to Jesus and called him the "Son of David", a Messianic term that not even the Jews accorded him, is not without significance; it shows that God does not deny his light to any people or class. The disciples acted annoyed at the insistence of this foreigner, and Jesus himself did not seem to be encouraging her: "I was sent only to the lost sheep of the house of Israel" (ib. 24). It was, in fact, the Father's will that he keep his activities within the borders of Palestine; only when he had gathered together the stray sheep of Israel and made them a united flock would these in their turn be sent out to carry the gospel to all people; but this would come about after his ascension. Meanwhile the woman continued her entreaty, and Jesus answered with deliberate harshness: "It is not fair to take the children's bread and throw it to the dogs" (ib. 26). But she was not discouraged; in fact she seized upon his words and came back again to retort: "Yes, Lord, even the dogs eat the crumbs that fall from their master's table". The Lord was conquered, and his mercy, held back until then, burst out to the full: "O woman, great is your faith! May it be done for you as you desire" (ib. 27-28). Belonging to a privileged people or class is of no account; what does count is faith.

May God be gracious to us and bless us, and make his face shine upon us, that your way may be known upon earth, your saving power among all nations.

Let the peoples praise you, O God; let all the peoples praise you. Let the nations be glad and sing for joy, for you judge the peoples with equity and guide the nations upon earth.

Psalm 67:2-5

O God, our Creator, you have opened the eyes of our heart, that we may know you who alone are Highest among the highest and Holy reposing among the holy; who humble the pride of the haughty, destroy the designs of the heathen, who raise up the lowly and humble the lofty. You make rich and make poor, slay and bring to life; who alone are the benefactor of spirits and God of all flesh. You gaze upon the deep, you behold the works of men, the Helper in danger, the Savior in despair, the Creator and Watcher of every spirit. You multiply the nations upon the earth, and from all you have chosen those that love you through Jesus Christ, your beloved Son, through whom you have instructed, sanctified and honored us.

We beg you, O Master, to be our helper and protector: deliver those of us who are in distress, raise up the fallen, show your face to those in need, heal the infirm, bring back the erring of your people, feed the hungry, ransom our prisoners, set the infirm upon their feet, comfort the fainthearted; let all the nations know that you are the only God, that Jesus Christ is your Son, that we are your people and the sheep of your pasture.

St. Clement of Rome, 1 Corinthians 59

YEAR B

Grant that by eating you, I may live because of you (Jn 6:57)

In line with the preceding Sundays, the theme of the "bread of life" (Jn 6:51-59) is continued and explained in explicitly sacramental terms: the flesh and blood of Christ given as food to men. The first reading (Prov 9:1-6) gives a kind of preview of the figure in a sumptuous banquet prepared by wisdom, personified as a rich matron who invites everyone to her feast, especially the most unprovided for, such as immature youth and the ignorant. "Come, eat of my bread and drink of the wine I have mixed" (ib. 5). In this context bread and wine are synonymous with wise and prudent counsel freely given by wisdom. But this does not hinder the Christian reader from seeing in it—as the day's Liturgy suggests—a foreshadowing of the eucharistic bread and wine offered by Christ to all believers.

When Jesus said: "The bread which I shall give for the life of the world is my flesh" (Jn 6:51), he was making known his intention of carrying his gift of self to men even to leaving his flesh and blood to them for food. Thus the Eucharist is manifested not only in immediate relationship to the Lord's death, but also to his incarnation, almost as a mystical prolongation of it. The flesh which the Word assumed in order to offer it to the Father upon the cross continues to be mystically sacrificed in the eucharistic Sacrament, and offered to the faithful as food. The Jews reacted violently against such an unheard-of proposal: "How can this man give us his flesh to eat?" (ib. 52). It is a justifiable complaint; what ordinary man would not shudder at the idea of having to eat the flesh of another man like himself? Yet Jesus neither withdrew nor attenuated what he had said; on the contrary he strongly reaffirmed it, putting even more stress on the necessity of this "eating": "Truly, truly I say to you, unless you eat the flesh of the Son of man and drink his blood, you have no life in you; he who eats my flesh and drinks my blood has eternal life . . . For my flesh is food indeed, and my blood is drink indeed" (ib. 53-55). Our Lord gives no explanation to make the mystery more understandable; one who does not believe in him will not accept any. He wants faith. But believers, those who have received the gift of faith, how far and in what manner do they believe in the wonderful mystery?

The modern world is perhaps so skeptical about the Eucharist precisely because it too often treats this Sacrament with a superficial and easy-going attitude that is frightening. We need to fall down on our knees, to ask pardon, beg for a lively faith, delve more deeply into our Lord's words through prayer, adore his Sacrament, and partake of it with trembling and love. Then we shall understand other sublime statements of Jesus: "He who eats my flesh and drinks my blood abides in me, and I in him. As the living Father sent me, and I live because of the Father, so he who eats me will live because of me" (ib. 56-57). The Eucharist is intended to nourish the Christian so that he may be an ever more living branch of Christ, a creature made in the likeness of its Lord, immersed and abiding in him in such a way that the Christian's being and behavior will make obvious the presence of the One who, by nourishing us with his own flesh and blood, makes us more like himself. Our conduct should make it evident that we no longer live for ourselves, enclosed within narrow earthly horizons, but for Christ, open to the immense horizons of eternity; and that our works already bear the imprint of the eternal life with which the Eucharist nourishes us. Only in this way can we who believe be living witnesses to the world of the ineffable reality of the eucharistic mystery.

> *Eternal God, highest and eternal purity, constrained by the ardor of your charity, you united yourself to us as food . . . You are the food of the angels, O highest and eternal purity; therefore you ask and desire so great purity in the soul that receives you in this sweetest sacrament . . . How is the soul purified? In the fire of your charity, washing its face in the blood of your only-begotten Son . . .*
>
> *I will take off my stinking clothing, and in the light of holy faith . . . I shall understand how you, eternal Trinity, are food and table and servant to us. Eternal Father, you are that table that gives us the food of his teaching which nourishes us in your will, or in the sacrament which we receive in Holy Communion, which feeds and comforts us while we are pilgrims and travelers in this life. The Holy Spirit is like a servant to us, because he administers your teaching to us, enlightening the eye of our intellect, and inspiring us to follow it. He also gives us love for our neighbor, and hunger for the food of souls and for the salvation of the entire world, for your honor, O Father.*
>
> St. Catherine of Siena, *Prayers*

YEAR C

Lord, may I resist even to shedding my blood in my struggle against sin (Heb 12:4)

When the service of God is taken seriously, it does not offer a comfortable and tranquil life, but often exposes us to risk, struggle, and persecution. This is the theme of this Sunday's Liturgy, set out in the first reading (Jer 38:4-6,8-10). Because Jeremiah preached without any human respect, he became "a man of strife and contention to the whole land" (Jer 15:10). In order to be delivered of him the military leaders accused him of wanting to remove the king, and having gotten possession of him, they threw him into a slimy cistern where he sank into the mire. He would certainly have perished if God had not come to his aid through an unknown person who succeeded in wresting permission from the king to extricate him from that place of death. The responsorial psalm of today expresses Jeremiah's situation very well: "I waited patiently for the Lord; he inclined to me and heard my cry. He drew me up from the desolate pit, from the miry bog" (Ps 40:1-2).

In the second reading (Heb 12:1-4), St. Paul speaks of the intrepid faith of the ancient patriarchs and prophets and encourages Christians to emulate them: "Let us also ... run with perseverance the race that is set before us, looking to Jesus, the pioneer and perfecter of our faith" (ib. 1-2). From the Old Testament the Apostle directs the Christian toward Jesus, of whom even the greatest figures of antiquity, Jeremiah included, are but weak symbols. He is the divine exemplar upon whom we are to model ourselves, he is the supreme fighter for God's cause, who in order to be faithful to God's will "endured the cross, despising the shame' ' (ib.). By basing our faith on him who is its author, its cause, its support, we must not be afraid to resist "to the point of shedding (our) blood in the struggle against sin" (ib. 4) and against anything that might divert us from full fidelity to God.

In today's Gospel (Lk 12:49-53), Jesus, who had proclaimed peacemakers blessed, and left his peace as a heritage to his disciples, openly declares that he has come not to bring peace, but division (ib. 51). Although disconcerting at first glance, this statement neither contradicts nor nullifies all that he had said elsewhere; rather it makes it clear that interior peace, the sign of harmony between God and man and hence of adherence to his will, does not exempt us from struggle, or from war against all that is opposed to God's will or that threatens faith or hinders us in the service of the Lord, whether the obstacles be within us—as our passions, our temptations, our sins—or in our surroundings. In such circumstances the most peaceful of Christians must become a courageous, fearless fighter, afraid of neither danger nor persecution, after the example of Jeremiah and, still more, of Christ who fought against sin even to bloodshed and the ignominy of the cross. But for this struggle to be legitimate and holy, no human or personal motive or purpose should be mixed with it; it should be roused only by that fire of love which Jesus came to cast upon the earth (ib. 49), with the sole purpose of blazing everywhere for the glory of the Father and the salvation of men. Because of this fire of love Jesus anxiously desired the bloody baptism of his passion (ib. 50); because of this fire of love the Christian must be prepared to resist even the persons who are dearest to him, even to separating himself from them, if they impede his professing his faith or carrying out his vocation or accomplishing God's will. Such sorrowful separations are truly very painful crosses, but they are directed—like Jesus' own cross—toward the salvation of these very ones who are being abandoned for the sake of his love.

> *I waited patiently for the Lord; he inclined to me and heard my cry. He drew me up from the desolate pit, out of the miry bog, and set my feet upon a rock, making my steps secure. He put a new song in my mouth, a song of praise to our God.*
> *Blessed is the man who makes the Lord his trust.*
>
> Psalm 40:1-4

> *O Jesus, sweet Captain, as you raise the emblem of your cross you lovingly tell me: "Take the cross I am giving you, and however heavy it may seem to you, follow me and do not hesitate." In order to correspond with your invitation, I promise you, my heavenly Bridegroom, never more to resist your love. But I already see that you are on the road to Calvary, and here is your bride following promptly ... Always do with me whatever pleases you most, because I am content with everything, provided I may follow you on the road to Calvary; the more thorny I find it, and the heavier the cross, the more I shall be consoled, for I want to love you with an enduring love ... a firm and undivided love.*
> *Willingly I offer my heart as prey for afflictions and sadness and labor. I rejoice at not rejoicing, for fasting in this life must precede the eternal banquet that awaits me.*
> *My Lord, you are on the cross for me, and I for you. Oh, if it could be understood even once how sweet and of how great value it is to suffer and be silent for your sake, O Jesus! O dear, suffering, good Jesus!*
>
> St. Teresa Margaret Redi, *La Spiritualita*

284. CHARITY AND JUSTICE

You are righteous, Lord, you love righteous deeds; the upright shall behold your face (Ps 11:7)

1. Charity not only "does not rejoice at wrong" (1 Cor 13:6), but is grieved by it and does everything it can to defend and promote justice. Jesus presented his mission as a work of salvation and justice, especially on behalf of the poor, of prisoners, and of the oppressed, freeing them from the slavery and blindness of sin, and also from the injustice of the great and the proud (Mt 12:18-20). He came to establish the kingdom of love and justice, open to all without any distinction; and if there was to be any

preference it was really for the humble, the needy, the oppressed. The Church follows the same course: "founded on the Redeemer's love, she contributes to the wider application of justice and charity" throughout the world (GS 76); she concerns herself with "instructing the faithful in love for the whole Mystical Body of Christ, especially for its poor and sorrowing members, and for those who are suffering persecution for justice' sake" (LG 23).

Without justice there can neither be charity nor true Christian life. St. James forcefully reprehended those faithful who, in their gatherings, saved a place of honor for the rich, and neglected the poor. "Has not God chosen those who are poor in the world to be rich in faith and heirs of the kingdom which he has promised to those who love him? But you have dishonored the poor man . . . If you show partiality you commit sin" (lJas 2:5-9). This is the sin of injustice, something with which Christian charity should never be stained. "He who oppresses a poor man insults his maker," says the book of Proverbs (14:31). Vatican Council II has inculcated these principles with much insistence, and desires them to penetrate "the believer's entire life, including its worldly dimensions, by activating him toward justice and love, especially regarding the needy" (GS 21). This was strongly felt in the early Church, in which the faithful put their belongings together in common in a spontaneous impulse of charity, so that "there was not a needy person among them" (Acts 4:34). In the letter to the Hebrews, St. Paul recommends that they persevere in this spirit: "Do not neglect to do good and to share what you have, for such sacrifices are pleasing to God" (13:16).

2. To the Pharisees who had reduced religion to ritual observances, such as the purification of utensils, Jesus said: "Give for alms those things which are within; and behold, everything is clean for you" (Lk 11:41). Acts of worship are of little or no value if they are not accompanied by charity and justice, since only these virtues purify man's heart from selfishness and greed, and incline him to honor God with sincerity and to love his neighbor not in word, but by deed. "If a brother or sister is ill-clad and in lack of daily food, and one of you says to them: 'Go in peace, be warmed and filled', without giving them the things needed for the body, what does it profit?" (Jas 2:15-16). Without good works, religion and love are useless.

Help for the poor must not be thought of as simply an act of charity that is more or less optional, but also as a strict obligation of justice. "God"—says the Council—"intended the earth and all that it contains for the use of every human being and people . . . Therefore man should regard his lawful possessions not merely as his own, but also as common property, in the sense that they should accrue to the benefit of not only himself, but of others" (GS 69). This is what St. Paul was proposing to the Church at Corinth when he urged it to assist the Church at Jerusalem. "I do not mean that others should be eased and you burdened. but that as a matter of equality, your abundance at the present time should supply their want" (2 Cor 8:13-14). If all men are brothers because all are God's children, their very brotherhood requires that while some are rolling in wealth, others should not be perishing in destitution. The Church therefore teaches that "men are obliged to come to the relief of the poor, and to do so not merely out of their superfluous goods ... It is the duty of the whole people of God, following the word and example of their Bishops, to do their utmost to alleviate the sufferings of the modern age. As was the ancient custom in the Church they should meet this obligation out of the substance of their goods, and not only out of what is superfluous" (GS 69,88). Gifts offered to the poor are "a sacrifice acceptable and pleasing to God" (Phil 4:18).

> *O charity, you open the heart to the love of God and to affection for the neighbor... You are kindly and peaceful, not hot-headed; you do not seek what is unjust, but things that are just and holy, and since you seek them, you preserve them within you, and your heart is like a shining pearl of justice...*
>
> *O charity, you love everyone with a compassionate love as your children... You are a mother who conceives in her soul the fruits of virtue, and gives birth to them for the honor of God in your neighbor.*
>
> *Enlightened by prudence, you know how to give according to each one's readiness to receive; you correct with mercy, becoming infirm with the infirm, both coaxing and correcting depending on whether justice or mercy is needed.*
>
> St. Catherine of Siena, *Letters* 33

> *"I was hungry and you gave me to eat."* O Lord, here you give us the true motive for almsgiving, the strongest reason of all. There are others: the need to give in obedience to your many times repeated order; the need to obey in order to imitate you who give yourself so generously;... the need to give because your love obliges us to pour out the love we have for you upon men, for they are your beloved children; the need to give out of goodness, simply to practice and cultivate this virtue that should be loved in itself, since it is one of your attributes, one of your divine beauties, one of your perfections, and consequently your very self, O my God.
>
> *But among all our motives for giving the one that impels us most, the one that ... inflames us more than anything else, is that everything we do for our neighbor is done to you, O Jesus: that is enough to change and reform our whole life, and to re-direct all our actions, our words, and our thoughts. Whatever we do for our neighbor, we do for you, O Jesus!*
>
> C. de Foucauld, *Meditations on the Gospel*

285. CHARITY AND TRUTH

Lord, give me a sincere love for my brothers, that I may love them
earnestly from my heart   *(1 Pet 1:22)*

1. Love "does not rejoice at wrong, but rejoices in the right" (1
Cor. 13:6). Here are two qualities which cannot be separated,
because justice supposes truth, and vice versa, while where there
is injustice there is deceit, or fraud, or at least a false impression of
the truth.

Charity and truth are absolutely identical in God in the most
absolute way, because in him all is love and all is truth. John
shows us the Word as "the true light that enlightens every man"
(1.9); not a cold light, but light that is a flame of charity, because
"God is love" (1 Jn 4:16). The true light, that is, divine truth, has
been brought into the world by the Son of God through the
ministry of his love.

God puts man in the truth because he loves him, and leads
him toward the good. Our love and good will toward our neighbor
"must in no way render us indifferent to truth and goodness. Indeed love itself impels the disciples of Christ to speak the saving
truth to all men" (GS 28). This teaching of Vatican II focuses
upon the obligation of never betraying truth under the pretext of
charity. Besides, love would not be true love, if it did not lead to
truth. At the same time, truth cannot be imposed by force; rather,
we need to be patient with indulgent charity, and gradually open
up, through love, a passage for light to enter. We also have "to
distinguish between error, which always merits repudiation, and
the person in error, who never loses the dignity of being a person,
even when he is flawed by false or inadequate religious notions"
(ib.).

St. Paul exhorts us to "speak the truth in love" (Eph 4:15); the
defense of truth must never involve a lessening of charity. Also
when there is a difference of opinions, the faithful should "always
try to enlighten one another through honest discussion, preserving mutual charity, and caring above all for the common good"
(GS 43). It is not always easy to harmonize charity and truth, considering our human limitations, but it is a goal toward which we
must aim, keeping our eyes fixed upon God, who is truth and love,
and who leads man by means of love to truth and to good.

2. "Putting away falsehood, let everyone speak the truth with
his neighbor, for we are members one of another" (Eph 4:25).
Falsehood is a sin, not only against justice, but also against charity, for since Christians are brothers, members of one body, we owe
each other the truth. Falsehood does not foster brotherly unity,
but harms and destroys it; no one who feels he has been deceived
can think that he is loved. St. Peter, too, suggests that the faithful
put aside "all malice, all guile, all insincerity" (1 Pet 2:1), which in-

dicates that he, quite as much as St. Paul, considers the renunciation of every kind of falsehood a characteristic of a Christian reborn to new life in Christ; he should be like a newborn babe (ib. 2), and should "put on the new nature, created after the likeness of God in true righteousness and holiness" (Eph 4:24). Everything that comes from the hand of God has the brightness of truth and the warmth of love. Falsehood and Christian life are contradictory, just as falsehood and charity are.

"Let love be genuine; hate what is evil, hold fast to what is good" (Rom 12:9). Love cannot follow twisted paths which apparently lead to good, but which secretly pursue evil. Courtesies, compliments, and favors poured out to gain ambitious aims or profit, or words which feign affection and esteem, but really disguise ulterior motives and soon change to complaints and calumnies, are actions unworthy of a Christian, who should always behave with complete candor and sincerity.

Charity must be so fond of truth, that when circumstances require, it will also know how to expose and renounce evil, in order to defend the weak and the guileless from being the victims of fraud. St. Paul indicates that the profession of truth in charity is the great means of growing up "into him who is the head, into Christ" (Eph 4:15). In actual fact, a Christian, a member of Christ, cannot live and cannot grow in him except by sharing in his very life, a life of truth and of love, a life which attests to and promotes the true through works of charity.

O Lord, if I see my neighbor committing sin, I shall make an excuse for him on the grounds of his intention, which being hidden cannot be seen, and even if I see plainly that his intention was distorted and evil, help me to know how to make allowance for the temptation, which is something from which no mortal is excluded.

And if some one should come to speak to me of my neighbor's faults, I do not want to listen, and I shall answer that I will pray for him and ask the Lord to let me first amend myself. Besides, it will be easier for me to speak to my erring neighbor himself about his fault than to talk about it with others, because instead of remedying that fault, many others, much more serious, may be committed than those that are being discussed.

St. Mary Magdalen de Pazzi, *The Probation*

Lord, may I love and compassionate the sinner, not loving the sin in him, but pursuing the sin out of love for him. When I love a sick man I fight his fever, for if I spared the fever, I would not be loving the sick man. So I will tell my brother the truth without evasion. Yes, with frank openness I will tell him the truth; but I will be patient with him about correcting himself. While the just man chides the sinner, he caritably tolerates his sins, since charity endures all things (Ser. 4:20).

Yes, Lord, I will reprove; but though I am stern for charity's sake, do not let my heart lose its gentleness. Who is more merciful than the doctor who uses his instruments? He deplores having to cut, but he cuts, deplores having to cauterize, but he cauterizes. This is not cruelty. He is merciless to the wound so that the person may recover, for to coddle the wound would be to destroy the patient. O Lord, grant me also to love my sinful brother in every kind of way, and not drive out charity toward him from my heart, but at the same time make me know how to correct him if that is necessary. (Ser 83:8).

cf St. Augustine

286. CHARITY BEARS ALL THINGS

Lord, may I not grow weary in well-doing toward all   *(Gal 6:9-10)*

1. "Above all hold unfailing your love for one another, since love covers a multitude of sins" (1 Pet 4:8). Charity makes amends for and covers over our own sins, and also those of others. In the book of Proverbs we read: "Love covers all offenses" (10:12). And Jesus said of the sinful woman: "Her sins, which are many, are forgiven, for she loved much" (Lk 7:47). Charity does something similar for the sins of the neighbor. Above all, charity seeks, as much as possible, to excuse our neighbor's faults, just as a mother seeks, as much as possible, to excuse her children's mistakes. "Father, forgive them, for they know not what they do" (Lk 23:24), was Jesus' plea on the cross for all those who had collaborated in his passion. There were excluded from this prayer neither the traitorous apostle who from living so intimately with him knew only too well his kindness and his greatness, nor the judges who had condemned him although convinced of his innocence, nor the people who had listened to his teaching and been benefited by his miracles, yet had willed his death. Instead of pointing the finger at others' responsibilities, charity makes us solicitous and ingenious in seeking to minimize them. The diligence which each of us spontaneously uses to excuse our own mistakes, is what charity teaches us to use also in regard to the mistakes of others.

Covering up the faults or defects of our neighbor also means not talking about them unnecessarily, not drawing others' attention to them, nor being curious to know the whole story. "Never listen to talk about the faults of others"—says St. John of the Cross—"and if someone complains of another, you can tell him humbly to say nothing of it to you" (Maxims 2:68).

But charity is not satisfied with this; it wants to do something more positive: to make reparation, to expiate in imitation of Christ who "bore our sins in his body on the tree" (1 Pet 2:24). To shoulder the faults of our brothers as though they were our own, to atone for them in ourselves by prayer and penance is the duty of one who desires to live the charity of the Savior to the point of sharing in his vicarious expiation. Then such a one can rightfully say: "Father, forgive them."

2. "If your brother sins against you, go and tell him his fault,

between you and him alone. If he listens to you, you have gained your brother" (Mt. 18:15). Charity makes no connivance with evil. Excusing the faults of others does not mean tacit indulgence, or silent permissiveness through a desire to live in peace or through cowardice. There are cases—wrongs which may infringe on the common good or entice others into evil—where charity imposes the duty of fraternal correction. It is a question then, as the gospel puts it, of gaining one's brother, and for this it is necessary to act in such a way that instead of feeling himself humbled and reproved, he should feel himself loved, and hence warned for his own good. Fraternal correction is, and must show itself as, a true act of charity. "Brothers"—St. Paul informs us—"if a man is overtaken in any trespass, you who are spiritual should restore him in a spirit of gentleness" (Gal 6:1). How blameworthy they are, who out of cowardice neglect the duty of fraternal correction, and those also who allow themselves to be carried away by indiscreet, sharp, abrasive zeal. "Look to yourself"—says the Apostle—"lest you too be tempted" (ib. 2). He who warns must not do it haughtily, but by putting himself on the same level as the guilty person in humble consciousness of his own weakness, since temptation could surprise him from one moment to the next and without the help of grace he could very well end up lower than his brother. "Let anyone who thinks that he stands, take heed lest he fall" (1 Cor 10:12).

Love "bears all things, believes all things, hopes all things" (ib. 13:7). In the matter of fraternal correction this means having confidence in the guilty one, believing in his willingness to amend himself, not being exasperated if he falls again, nor tired of extending a hand to him in fraternal kindness. If, because of his obstinacy in evil, as the gospel refers to it, this brother must be separated from the rest, charity will not cease to follow him with a loving heart, always working and waiting for some sign of repentance. "Be at peace among yourselves," says St. Paul, and he adds immediately: "And we exhort you, brethren, admonish the idlers, encourage the faint-hearted, help the weak, be patient with them all" (1 Thes 5:13). Peace among brothers is not in opposition to the duty of fraternal correction; both are fruits of evangelical charity.

"I give you a new commandment: that you love one another" . . . *This commandment of yours, O Christ, is called love, and by virtue of this love sins are done away with.*

O Lord, fill me with a fullness of charity that I will be ready not only not to hate my brother, but to die for him . . . You have given us an example of this charity by dying for all and by praying for those who were crucifying you when you said: "Father, forgive them because they know not what they are doing" . . . This is perfect charity . . . Is charity, perhaps, perfect from the moment it is born? It has begun its existence, but it needs perfecting; therefore, Lord, nourish it in me, and make it grow strong until it reaches perfection.

Lord, help me to love; then I shall be able to do only good. Perhaps I shall have to rebuke someone? It will be love operating in me, not resentment. Must I administer corporal punishment to someone? It will be to teach him. Love that is charity will not permit me to neglect the unruly ... Teach me, Lord, to pay no attention to the words of those who flatter, and to the apparent severity of those who reprove; make me wise enough to consider the source, to look for the root from which such an attitude springs. The one flatters in order to deceive, the other reprimands to correct.

O charity, your rule, your strength, your flowers, your fruit, your beauty, your attractiveness, your food, your drink, your nourishment, your embrace—these know no satiety. If you fill us with delight now while we are still pilgrims, what will our joy be in our eternal home?

St. Augustine, *In I Io* 5:2,4; 10:7

287. CHARITY ENDURES ALL THINGS

Teach me, Lord, to endure all things for the sake of your elect
(2 Tim 2:10)

1. "Bear one another's burdens, and so fulfill the law of Christ" (Gal 6:2). Everyone has his own burden to bear: physical and moral weaknesses, duties, responsibilities, fatigues and sufferings which weigh heavily on our shoulders; and everyone feels the need of a friendly hand to help him carry his burden. The "law of Christ," which is the law of brotherly love, exacts this mutual assistance through which the Christian has his heart always open to others, ready to neglect himself in order to offer his brethren some help and comfort. "Rejoice with those who rejoice, weep with those who weep," says St. Paul (Rom 12:15).

Charity leads us to become "all things to all men" (1 Cor 9:22). To adapt ourselves not only to the needs of our fellowmen, but also to the mentality, the character, tastes, and personality of each one, to love our neighbor because of God, recognizing in each person the image, the creature, the child of the heavenly Father, does not mean so to denude charity as to reduce it to a kind of cold, stereotyped love which embraces everybody as a whole, without regard for the individual person. It is certain that Jesus loved all men with a divine love; yet throughout the pages of the gospel we can observe how his love took on different shades and ways according to the person he was dealing with. His was not a standardized love which was indifferent to the particular needs of each. Consider for example, the difference in the way he treated each disciple, or his friends in Bethany: he did not treat Peter like John, nor Martha like Mary. Charity makes us alert to dealing with each person according to the concrete reality of his individual situation—temperament, sensitivity, character and limitations—so as to make him feel the warmth of an affection which tries hard to conform to his person and to lighten his burdens. St. Paul writes: "May the God of steadfastness and encouragement grant you to live in such harmony with one another, in accord with Christ Jesus ... Welcome one another, therefore, as Christ has welcomed you, for the glory of God" (Rom 15:5-7).

2. Love "bears all things" (1 Cor 13:7). Particularly in living together, the faults, weaknesses, deficiencies, and the more or less happy or pleasing temperament of each person can be a real mutual burden, which we must do our best to bear with love. Given each one's limitations, it is impossible to live together without one being a burden to the other, even if it is in a way that is completely involuntary. This is a condition no one can avoid and which has to be resolved by "forbearing one another in love" (Eph 4:2), with the humble knowledge that if each has something to suffer, it is at the same time a cause of suffering to others. The strong may make the weak uneasy, the active upset the indolent, the courageous the timid, and vice versa. On the other hand, one who has greater resources is the more bound to restrain himself and to be compassionate and to adapt himself to the situation. St. Paul says: "We who are strong ought to bear with the failings of the weak, and not to please ourselves; let each of us please his neighbor for his good, to edify him. For Christ did not please himself" (Rom 15:1-3). Just as Christ adapted himself to man even to becoming a man, so the Christian studies how to adapt himself to others, renouncing himself.

During the last months of her life, St. Therese of the Child Jesus would write: "I understand now that perfect charity consists in bearing with the faults of others and in not being surprised at their weaknesses" (Auto p.220). If at the beginning we endure, fuming and clenching our teeth, little by little, charity will teach us to endure with kindliness and understanding, as a mother puts up with her child's mischief. Charity teaches us to bend our back willingly to take on the burden of others, not even avoiding those who annoy us. "If anyone forces you to go one mile, go with him two miles. Give to him who begs from you, and do not refuse him who would borrow from you" (Mt 5:41-42). This inculcates a generous renunciation of our own needs and even our own rights, so that we may second our neighbor with a fully dedicated love.

O Lord, how far I yet am from true charity and humility ... You show me that it is no great thing to associate with the good and gentle, for this is naturally pleasing to all, and every one prefers peace and loves best those that have like sentiments. But to be able to live peacefully with the hard and the perverse, or with the undisciplined and those who contradict us, is a great grace, and a highly commendable and manly thing.

If all were perfect, what then would we have to bear with from others for your love, O God? But now you have thus ordered it that we may learn to bear one another's burden; for no one is without a fault, no one but has a burden; no one is sufficient for himself, no one is wise enough for himself; but we have to support one another, comfort one another, and admonish one another.

Imitation of Christ II 3:2, I 16:3-4

O Lord, if I willingly share with my brothers the gifts I have received from you, and show myself obliging to everyone, kindly, grateful, friendly, and humble, I shall be able to spread abroad the fragrance of mercy. Make me able not only to bear patiently the physical and moral weaknesses of my neighbors, but beyond that bring to them as far as is possible the help of my services, the comfort of my words and good counsels.

Give me a heart of mercy that I may be kind and generous not only toward relatives and friends, or toward those who treat me well and from whom I may look for some benefit, but to everyone, so that, for your love, I will never deny the charity of material or spiritual help even to an enemy. Then I shall be rich in the best of ointments, and shall pour it out not only upon your head and feet, but upon your whole body, which is the Church.

cf. St. Bernard, *In Cantica Cant.* 12:5,7

288. THAT THEY MAY BE ONE

Lord, help me to pursue what makes for peace and mutual upbuilding *(Rom 14:19)*

1. When Jesus left his followers his new commandment, he said: "As the Father has loved me, so have I loved you, abide in my love" (Jn 15:9). The love which flows from the Father into the Son, through the Son reaches the disciples who are invited to "abide" in this love by behaving in the way suited to its divine requirements. These requirements are indicated immediately: "If you keep my commandments you will abide in my love" (ib. 10); and Christ puts "his" commandment first among these: "That you love one another as I have loved you" (ib. 12). The disciples are to love each other mutually with a love that is a prolongation of the love with which Christ has loved them, and is at the same time a proof of their love for Christ, recognized and loved in each of the brethren. They are to be blended and united in this love and made one single body, such as the Lord will ask for them in his priestly prayer. "Holy Father, keep them in your name ... that they may be one, even as we are one" (Jn 17:11). The wickedness of the world will assault the disciples' unity, and muster all its astuteness to divide them by breaking the bond of their mutual love. Jesus foresaw this and prayed that their unity might be so perfect and supernatural that it would be a reflection of the indissoluble union which exists between himself and the Father. Jesus begged for this same unity both for the little group of disciples who lived with him and for all the believers who would

come after them, for the entire Church. "I do not pray for these only, but also for those who believe in me through their word, that they may all be one ... that they may be one even as we are one" (ib. 20-22). Quoting this text, Vatican II says: "The Lord Jesus ... opened up vistas closed to human reason, for he implied a certain likeness between the union of the divine Persons, and the union of God's sons, in truth and in charity" (GS 24). It would be impossible to propose a more sublime ideal of unity. It is the goal toward which we must always tend, living one single truth: faith in Christ and in his gospel, and one single charity: the charity of Christ and of the Father.

2. "Even as you, Father, are in me, and I in you, may they also be one in us, so that the world may believe that you have sent me ... I in them and you in me, that they may become perfectly one, so that the world may know that you have sent me" (Jn 17:21,23). The spectacle of perfect union among men is something so rare and so difficult that it constitutes the most valid reason for belief in the divinity of Christ and the truth of his teaching. It was in this precise aspect that Jesus had appealed for perfect unity among his own. The world, so divided and torn by selfishness, will be more convinced by the miracle of a charity which is capable of overcoming all the diversities of temperament, mentality, civilization, race, and interests, than by the preaching of the gospel message. Considering human limitations, such an undertaking would be impossible if Christ had not left to his faithful, together with his commandment, his Body and Blood, the viaticum of love and concord. "We who are many are one body, for we all partake of the one bread" (1 Cor 10:17). The Eucharist is the bread that unites all the faithful in Christ, and makes them find in him the principle of mutual union and the strength necessary for overcoming all individualism.

"I beg you"—St. Paul writes—"to lead a life worthy of the calling to which you have been called ... eager to maintain the unity of the Spirit in the bond of peace. There is one body and one Spirit ... one hope ... ; one Lord, one faith, one baptism, one God and Father of us all, who is above all and through all and in all" (Eph 4:1-6). The Apostle appeals to all the motives for unity in order to stimulate Christians to remain united "in the bond of peace." From this it follows that every baptized person is responsible both for his personal sanctification and for the good of the Church, and also for the witness that he should give the entire world. The faithful divided against each other are an occasion of scandal, and an obstacle to the spread of the gospel. While the feeling of solidarity among mankind is more than ever increasing, it is urgent that to give it the example of a solidarity that is stable because it is founded on evangelical charity. This is the duty of every believer; once he has received the grace of charity in baptism, he must be the yeast of concord, unity, and peace in the world.

We fall on our knees before you, Lord, and implore you ... to have mercy on us and be reconciled to us and restore us to the venerble and holy practice of brotherly love. This alone is the holy gate which opens out into life ... There are many open gates, therefore, but only this holy gate is yours, O Christ. Blessed are all those who enter it and walk the straight path in holiness and observance of the law ...

Who will ever be able to explain the binding power of your love, O my God? The radiance of your beauty, who can voice it to satisfaction? The sublimity to which love leads up is unutterable; love unites us to you; love covers a multitude of sins, love endures all, is long-suffering to the last. Love creates no schism, love does not quarrel, love preserves perfect harmony; in love all your elect reached perfection and apart from love nothing is pleasing to you.
St. Clement of Rome, 1 *Corinthians* 48-49

O God, Father, Son, and Holy Spirit! I recognize myself in all and through all that is made to your image, since even the unity you wish to establish among us men is the imperfect image of your perfect unity. O charity! Grow and increase to infinity in us, since the pattern of union and fellowship which you are proposing is a model whose perfection we could never otherwise attain.

O Jesus, since you are ceaselessly instilling this unity into us, grant that we may direct all our thoughts, all our desires, and all our efforts toward establishing it in our hearts ... Grant that we may try on our part to be one even with those who do not wish to be one with us ... may we really suffer at not being able to share sufficiently with others all that we have and are ...

O charity! O love, compassion, indulgence, patience! Generosity, almsgiving, consolation, sympathy, brotherly peace in God and our Father, and in Jesus Christ—I desire you with all my heart and do not wish to desire anything else. Amen.
J.B. Bossuet, *Meditations on the Gospel* II 26, v. 2; 61

289. THE SURE SIGN

May I walk in love as Christ loved me and gave himself up for me
(Eph 5:2)

1. The Christian who lives for God and wishes to love him with all his strength feels the need to be sure that his love for God is not an illusion; but how can he be sure? The apostle John answers: "If we love one another, God abides in us and his love is perfected in us" (1 Jn 4:12). The great criterion which characterizes true love of God is the love of our neighbor. This is an infallible standard because theological love is unique, and though difficult to test in relation to God, it is easily verifiable in relation to the neighbor. We do not need much discernment to perceive whether our love of neighbor is a matter of words, or is a concrete reality, proved in

deed. St. Teresa of Jesus teaches her daughters: "We cannot know whether or not we love God, although there are strong indications for recognizing that we do love him; but we can know whether we love our neighbor. And be sure that the more advanced you are in love for your neighbor, the more advanced you will be in the love of God" (IC V 3:8). When fraternal love is sincere and heartfelt and shown by deed, there can be no doubt that God's "love is perfected in us" (1 Jn 4:12). The Apostle goes still further and says: "We know that we have passed out of death into life, because we love the brethren. He who does not love remains in death" (ib. 3:14). We share in the life of God to the extent that we abide in love, "for God is love" (ib. 4:8).

To live in love and to live in God are the same thing. To deny love is to deny life; to shut ourselves off from love is to shut ourselves off from God. To refuse love to a brother is enough to break the bond of love and consequently of life in God. "Anyone who hates his brother is a murderer, and you know that no murderer has eternal life abiding in him" (ib. 3:15). Life in God, in love, and in grace, are three correlated realities and one cannot exist without the others. Love toward our neighbor is a sure sign of our love for God, and therefore of life in God, a life of grace that is a prelude to eternal life.

2. Jesus, too, has given love for our brethren the value of a sign: "By this all men will know that you are my disciples, if you have love for one another" (Jn 13:35). However, love for neighbor has the value of a distinctive sign of the disciples of Christ and guarantees the truth of their love for God, only to the extent that it is a theological love. No one has taught us to love one another more than Christ has, but our love must be one which is rooted in God and is ordered toward him: "Love, so that you may be sons of your Father who is in heaven" (Mt 5:44-45); and he urges us to carry out this duty of fraternal love in the same way as we give alms to the poor, doing it first of all for the honor of God, and seeking only his approval. Jesus summed up the whole law in the one precept of charity, but before mentioning the love of neighbor, he spoke of the love of God: "You shall love the Lord your God with all your heart, and all your soul, and with all your mind" (Mt 22:37), and introduced the second commandment only upon this foundation of total dedication to God, declaring the second to be like the first. The value of the second commandment lies in its being based upon the first, and on being like to it; but if the first is set aside, the second has nothing to stand on and can no longer be spoken of as like to the precept of love for God. Jesus declared that when anyone is in conflict with his neighbor, before going to worship he must make peace with his neighbor: "Leave your gift there before the altar and go; first be reconciled to your brother, and then come and offer your gift" (Mt 5:24). This is not because love for neighbor is in itself more important than the worship due

to God, but because every act of worship must express a love that is true and complete, and this is not the case if brotherly love is impaired.

Hence it is not possible to speak of Christian charity solely on a horizontal plane; this would simply be a form of humanism that does not flow from the gospel. Besides, Jesus established that we should love one another as he himself loved us. He has loved us in relation to the Father, in order to fulfill his will and to lead us to him: "I lay down my life for the sheep ... This charge I have received from my Father" (Jn 10:15,18). It all culminates in the love and the glory of the Father: "I have glorified you on earth, having accomplished on earth the work which you gave me to do" (Jn 17:4).

> *O Lord, the most certain sign as to whether or not we are observing these two laws of love is whether we observe well the love of neighbor ... The love you have for us is so great that to repay us for our love of neighbor you will in a thousand ways increase the love we have for you.*
>
> *Give me, O Lord, this perfect love of neighbor ... You will give me more than I know how to desire if I am striving and making every effort to do what I can about this love. I shall force my will to do the will of my Sisters in everything even though I lose my rights; I shall forget my own good for their sakes no matter how much resistance my nature puts up and when the occasion arises I shall strive to accept work myself so as to relieve my neighbor of it. But I must not think that it won't cost me anything or that I shall find everything done for me. Besides, I see what your love for us cost you! To free us from death, you died that most painful death of the cross.*
>
> St. Teresa of Jesus, *Interior Castle* V 3:8,12

> *How sweet it is! At each step I meet you, O Lord. Owing to the wonder of our divine incorporation with your holy Person, I cannot make a movement that is not perceived by you.*
>
> *If I turn my eyes within, you are there; if I look towards my neighbor, you are there also; I am surrounded by living tabernacles, if I only have eyes to recognize them! ... We are joined in fact, or at least potentially, to Jesus Christ and through him share in the divine life. Because we are all living, or ought to be living, the same divine life in you, O Christ Jesus, there should be a strong bond of charity joining us together. Once we have grasped this truth we are not surprised that you, O Lord, should have chosen brotherly love as the special mark of a true Christian which should differentiate your followers from the worldling: "Love one another." By this sign you will know that we are your disciples.*
>
> R. Plus, *Christ in His Brethren* pp 42,43

290. TWENTY FIRST SUNDAY OF ORDINARY TIME

For though you are high, Lord, you regard the lowly, but the
haughty you know from afar (Ps 138:6)

The episode of Jesus' appearance at night upon the lake, when Peter went to him, walking upon the water, ended with his disciples' spontaneous declaration: "Truly you are the Son of God!" (Mt 14:33). But at Caesarea Philippi (Mt 16:13-20), Jesus evoked another response, more complete and official. He questioned the disciples as to what the people were saying about him, in order to make them reflect and go beyond public opinion because of their more direct and intimate knowledge of him as a person. Among the people, some were taking him to be "John the Baptist, others say Elijah, and others Jeremiah" (ib. 14); they could not think of any more illustrious personages. Yet between these and the Messiah there was an immense distance that no one dared to bridge. But Peter did so and answered at once without hesitation in the name of his companions: "You are Christ, the Son of the living God" (ib. 16). The disciples understood. They were the simple to whom the Father was pleased to reveal his mystery. And just as Jesus had once exclaimed: "I thank you, Father . . . that you have hidden these things from the wise and understanding, and revealed them to babes" (Mt 11:25), so he now replied to Peter: "Blessed are you . . . for flesh and blood has not revealed this to you, but my Father who is in heaven" (Mt 16:17). Without an interior illumination on God's part, such an explicit act of faith in the divinity of Christ would not be possible. Faith is always a gift. To Peter who opened himself to this gift with singular promptness, Jesus foretold the great mission which would be entrusted to him: "You are Peter, and on this rock I will build my church, and the powers of death shall not prevail against it" (ib. 18). The humble fisherman would become the steady rock upon which Christ would build his Church, like to a building so solid that no power, not even a diabolical one, could undermine it. He said even more: "I will give you the keys of the kingdom of heaven, and whatever you bind on earth shall be bound in heaven" (ib. 19). In biblical language keys indicate power: "I will place on his shoulder the key of the house of David," says the first reading today (Is 22:19-23), referring to Eliakim, the superintendent of the royal palace. The power conferred upon Peter is of an immensely higher nature: to him are given the keys not of an earthly kingdom, but of the kingdom of heaven, namely, of the kingdom which Jesus came to establish in his Church, in which Peter has the power "to bind and to loose", that is, to condemn and to absolve, to exclude and to welcome, not only people, but doctrines and customs as well. It is a power so great that his decisions are to be ratified "in heaven" by God himself. To confer such a power upon a man is bewildering, and would be inadmissible if, in entrusting it to Peter, Christ had not assured him of special assistance. In such a way did Jesus will to establish his Church and in such a way is the Church to be accepted, accepting at the same time the primacy of Peter, which, equally with the Church, is of divine institution. Although this can be questioned by a society which is excessively rationalistic and intolerant of all authority, the true Christian acknowledges—most gratefully—what Christ has established for making the way of salvation more certain for mankind. Besides, there is no area in which man can presume to judge God's plans or ways of acting; rather, he must repeat with St. Paul: "How unsearchable are his judgments and how inscrutable his ways!" (Rom 11:33; 2nd reading).

> *By your light and with your grace, O Father in heaven, Peter has proclaimed the ineffable nature of your only beloved Son, and has merited to become the rock against which the gates of hell will not prevail.*
> *O Lord, you chose the blessed Peter above the other Apostles, as leader in the faith and foundation of your Church. Through his prayers, O Christ, have mercy on us.*
>
> cf *Eucharistic Prayers* . . . 120

> *I cry to you today, O my love, Eternal God, to have mercy on this world and to give it the light to recognize your Vicar with the purity of faith with which I beg you, my God, to endow him; give him light, so that the whole world may follow him. Grant him supernatural light; from the moment you endow your Vicar with a fearless heart, let him be adorned with your holy humility, for I shall never cease to knock at the door of your kindness, my love, that you may exalt him. So reveal your virtue in him that his brave heart may always burn with your holy desire and be clothed in your humility, and by thus acting with your kindliness and charity and purity and wisdom may draw the whole world to himself.*
>
> St. Catherine of Siena, *Prayers*

YEAR B

"Lord you have the words of eternal life, and we have believed"
(Jn 6:68-69)

The theme of the first and third readings today is that of choosing God and being loyal to him.

When the Hebrews had crossed the Jordan and were about to enter the promised land, Joshua confronted them with a difficult choice: either to fraternize with idolators or to choose Yahweh. In other words: either God or idols. The response was unanimous: "Far be it from us that we should forsake the Lord to serve other gods . . . We will serve the Lord for he is our God" (ib. 16,18). In practice, however, Israel continued as in the past to waver between faithfulness to God and idolatry; but in theory, the choice had been made: the people acknowledged that Yahweh was their God; and if many, even most, would subsequently fail him, there would always be a "remnant" who would remain faithful. It is a warning that should make us reflect; it is not enough to choose God once for a lifetime, for we must renew our choice every day, remembering that it is impossible to serve God and at the same time serve the theories, the vanities, and the whims of the world, which are as so many idols.

At the conclusion of his long discourse on the "bread of life" (Jn 6:61-70), Jesus also imposed a choice on all who were listening to him.Either follow him by accepting the mystery of his flesh and blood, given as food to man, or separate from him. It was not only the Jews who were scandalized by his words, "many of his disciples" also murmured: "This is a hard saying; who can listen to it?" (ib. 60). Instead of softening his words, Jesus reminded them of the need for faith: "It is the Spirit that gives life, the flesh is of no avail; the words that I have spoken to you are spirit and life. But there are some of you that do not believe" (ib. 63-64). Consequently, do not be scandalized or engage in discussion, but believe. Without faith, without the Holy Spirit who enlightens and gives life, even the mystery of the Body of Christ can remain simply "flesh" which is of no benefit to the spirit, and which gives no life. Without faith, man can hear about Christ's flesh and blood, can see the bread and wine, but not grasp the great reality hidden in these words and signs. We should not readily condemn those who do not believe; but rather excuse and pray for them, that they may open their hearts to the gift of faith, which God is so ready to grant, and not reject it by preferring their own limited human reasoning. After this rejection "many of his disciples drew back and no longer went about with him" (ib. 66). It is striking to observe that our Lord did nothing to hold them back, but turning to the Twelve asked: "Do you also wish to go away?" (ib. 67). The mystery of Christ is one and inseparable: either we accept him wholly, or by rejecting one aspect, we deny him completely. Not even compassion for unbelievers nor the desire to attract distant brothers can justify any reduction in what Jesus has said about the Eucharist. No one loved men more nor desired their salvation more than Jesus did, yet he preferred to lose "many" disciples rather than modify a single one of his words. Anyone who has chosen Christ can but answer with Peter: "Lord, to whom shall we go? You have the words of eternal life; and we have believed, and have come to know, that you are the Holy One of God" (ib. 68-69). We have need to remember with trembling fear that Judas broke away from the Master on just this ocasion: the proclamation of the Eucharist was the touchstone of the genuineness of the choice of Christ, not only on the part of the people but also for the disciples and apostles. Thus through the centuries, faith in this mystery will continue to distinguish the true followers of Christ.

O God, who make the faithful to be of one mind and will, grant that your people may love what you command, and desire what you promise, so that amid the changing things of this world, our hearts may be set where true joy is found.

Roman Missal, Collect (4th Sunday after Easter)

We are united to you, O Lord, through our faith; through the understanding we are enlightened. Grant that we may first be united to you through faith so that we can be enlightened through understanding. Whoever is not united to you, resists you, and whoever resists you, does not believe. And how can anyone who resists you be enlightened? Such a one is turning his back to the ray of light which should be enlightening him: he does not divert his gaze, but closes his mind ... Lord, make me believe and open myself to you; make me open myself that I may be enlightened.

If we turn away from you, to whom shall we go? "You have the words of eternal life ... " You give us eternal life by offering us your body and your blood. "And we have believed and have understood ... " We have believed in order to be able to understand; in fact if we had wanted to know before believing, we would not have succeeded either in knowing or in believing. What have we believed and understood? "That you are the Christ, the Son of God," that is, that you are eternal life itself, and in your flesh and blood you give us what you are. St. Augustine, *In Io* 27:7,9

YEAR C

O Lord, great is your love for us, and your faithfulness endures forever *(Ps 117:2)*

The theme of salvation is presented by this Sunday's Liturgy with a universal breadth. The first reading (Is 66:18-21) relates one of the most magnificent prophecies about the call of all peoples to the faith. "I am coming to gather all nations and tongues"—says the Lord—"and they shall come and shall see my glory" (ib. 18). Just as division among men is a sign of sin, so their unification is a sign of God's saving power and of his love for all. He will send the survivors of Israel, who had remained faithful to him, to far-distant lands to make his name known. Not only will the pagans be converted, but they will lead back the dispersed Jews to Jerusalem "as an offering to the Lord" (ib. 20), and from these same converted pagans God will choose his priests (ib. 21). It is the supreme overcoming of the division between Israel and the other nations; an overcoming which the prophets had many times foretold, but which had been very little understood and which only Jesus will achieve, preparing the way with his preaching and uniting the nations with the blood of his cross.

The Gospel of the day (Lk 13:22-30) directly refers to Jesus' teaching on this subject, which was provoked by the question: "Lord, will those who are saved be few?" (ib. 23). Jesus goes beyond the question and concentrates on the main point: all can be saved because salvation is offered to all, but to attain it, each one must hurry to be converted before it is too late. Jesus is concerned with breaking down the Jews' restricted mentality and declares that on the day of final reckoning it will be of little worth to have belonged to the chosen people or to have been intimately connected with them; therefore, it will be useless to say: "We ate and drank in your presence, and you taught in our streets" (ib. 26). If faith and works do not accompany these privileges, even the children of Israel will be excluded from the kingdom of God. "They will come from east and from west, and from north and south, and will sit at table in the kingdom of God. And behold, some are last who will be first, and some are first who will be last" (ib. 29-30). Although they were the first to be called to salvation, if they are not converted and do not accept Christ, the Jews will find themselves replaced by other peoples who were called last. Likewise it must be said of the new people of God: the privilege of belonging to the Church does not lead to salvation unless it is accompanied by full adherence to Christ and his gospel. The faithful, then, cannot shut themselves up in their privileged position, for it really only makes it more incumbent on them to reach out to all their brethren to draw them to the faith. Privileges do not count with God, but only the humility that eliminates all presumption, the love that opens the heart to seek the good of others, the spirit of renunciation which gives the courage to "enter by the narrow door" (ib. 24), overcoming every form of self-seeking.

At this point the second reading (Heb 12:5-7,11-13), interjects St. Paul's warm exhortation to endure the battle of life with a stout heart. Through trials and suffering God puts his children to the test, for he wishes to correct them, to purify them and to make them "share in his holiness" (ib. 10). Nevertheless, it is true that "for the moment all discipline seems painful rather than pleasant; later it yields the peaceful fruit of righteousness" (ib. 11), that is, of virtue, of greater closeness to God. God is a father who corrects and tries us only in view of a higher good: "For the Lord disciplines him whom he loves, and chastises every son whom he receives" (ib. 6). To accept our trials is to enter "through the narrow door" which Jesus has pointed out.

O Father, who won for yourself a multitude of children by the one sacrifice of Christ, grant us in your Church the gift of unity and peace.   (Secret)

O God, bring the work of your mercy to completion: renew us to the very depths and make us fervent in your love, so that we may be able to please you throughout our lives. (Post-Communion)
Roman Missal

O God, to you a single soul is like an entire world, and the whole universe like a single soul. You created us, one by one, and you also govern us, one by one, individually. You think of and love each one of us as if each were the only creature in the world ...

O eternal Shepherd, before you walked on at the head of your cherished sheep, even before you took flesh in order to show us the way, indeed, before you led us out of that blessed sheepfold which is the sanctuary of your thoughts and of your loving will, before you brought us forth in time and put us on the way to our destiny, you called each of us, one by one, by name. You say: "The good Shepherd calls his own sheep, and leads them out. He goes before them, and the sheep follow him, for they know his voice" (Jn 10:3-4).

C. Gay, *Christian Life and Virtues* 2:22, vol 1

291. MY LORD AND MY GOD!

You are the Lord, my God. I shall have no other gods before you (Dt 5:6-7)

1. Jesus said: "Render to God the things that are God's" (Mt 22:21). What does man have that is not from God, that he has not received from him? Natural and supernatural life, understanding, and will, every gift of nature and of grace, every resource and capability, the universe that surrounds him and all that is required for his existence, the wonders and riches of creation: all comes from him who is Creator, Lord, and Father.

"I am the Lord your God" (Dt 5:6). This solemn statement, which begins and punctuates the entire Ten Commandments, should penetrate our hearts and give us a profound sense of God's sovereign dominion, whose every right must be acknowledged. No matter how much we do, we shall never be able to give God all the homage, reverence, adoration, and love that are due him. We shall always be infinitely wanting in what we owe the divine Majesty. Even when we consecrate our whole life to God, we are but giving back to him what we have received from him, and always in a way that is less perfect and generous. Even when we consume all our strength and substance in serving him, we can only conclude in the words of the gospel: "We are unworthy servants" (Lk 17:10). Giving God what is God's, which is the essential duty of the virtue of religion, means acknowledging his absolute sovereignty by our way of life, offering him not such or such an act of homage, but the total homage of the spirit, of the heart, of life itself. The deeper our religious sense, the more aware we are of our radical insufficiency for rendering God a homage that is worthy of him; while, on the other hand, we feel driven to give him our utmost, and hence to strive with all our strength to praise, adore, and love our God, in generous and perfect obedience to his law and his will. The virtue of religion thus places us in an attitude of subjection to God that knows no reserve and of interior worship which, recognizing him as the only Lord, makes us true worshipers "in spirit and truth" (Jn 4:24).

2. "How long will you go limping with two different opinions? If the Lord is God, follow him!" (1 Kg 18:21). The words of Elijah, burning with zeal for his God, are the spontaneous cry of the faith that is deeply rooted in the heart of man. God's dominion is to be truly acknowledged in the concreteness of everyday life. "You shall have no other gods before me ... For I, the Lord your God, am a jealous God" (Dt 5:7,9), say the Ten Commandments. Jesus makes it crystal clear: "You shall worship the Lord your God and him only shall you serve.—No one can serve two masters" (Mt 4:10;6:24). The Christian has one only God, one only Master, one only Lord. Who doubts this in theory? But in practice it is all too easy to admit into daily life the concurrence of more masters. Self, money, and pleasure are masters which even a Christian is not uncommonly tempted to serve.

"You will be like God" (Gen 3:5): the ancient suggestion of the serpent is still heard; pride tempts us to set ourselves up, at least in some areas, as unconditional masters of our own lives in rivalry with God and his sovereign rights. But it is impossible for this compromise to last; at some point or other, a choice has to be made. "He who is not with me is against me," said Jesus (Mt 12:30). Everything in our life that does not correspond to the requirement of being with Christ, of giving God the primacy that is due him, is against Christ, against God.

To make our choice a stable one and to protect God's rights in us, we must renounce self in our whole way or conduct, and everything else—large or small,—which in little or in much draws us away from God's dominion. This is the great petition included in the first commandment, the key to the observance of the whole Decalogue. Only in this way is it possible to love God "with all your heart, with all your mind, and with all your strength" (Mk 12:30). Only in this way are we truly sincere, when, prostrate in adoration, we say: "My Lord and my God!" (Jn 20:28).

What shall I render to you, O Lord, for all these things? Reason as well as natural justice impels the infidel to surrender his whole self to him from whom he has received all that he is, and reminds him that he is bound to love him with his whole self. To me, faith reveals that you should be loved the more and to the degree that I understand you are to be esteemed above myself; I, indeed, who hold that you are the bestower not only of myself, but even of your very self as well ... If I owe you my whole self for being made, what more shall I give now in return for being re-made, and re-made in such wise? ... In the first work, you gave me myself; in the second, yourself; and when you gave me yourself, you restored me to myself again ... I owe it as a twofold debt. What shall I render to God in return for himself? For even if I were able to give myself back a thousand times, what am I in your sight, O God?

I will love you, O Lord, my strength, my support, my refuge, and my deliverer, and whatever of mine that can be said to be the object of my desires and of my love. My God, my help, I shall love you according to your gift to me and after my own manner—which is less, to be sure, than justice demands, but clearly not less than I am able to give; I, who although I cannot give as much as I owe, cannot, however, give beyond what I am able. I shall be able to give more when you deign to give me more: but never according to your worth. You have seen my imperfect being; but nevertheless in your book all shall be written—they who do what they are able to do, although they are not able to do what they ought to do.

St. Bernard, On the Love of God 15,16 p. 24-28

"My God and my all! To have you is to have everything I can have. O Lord, give me yourself. I dared not have made so bold a request, it would have been presumption, unless you had encouraged me. You have clothed yourself in my nature, you have become my brother, you have died as other men die, only in far greater bitterness, that instead of my eyeing you fearfully from afar, I might confidently draw near to you ... My God and my all, what could I say more than this, if I spoke to all eternity! I am full and abound and overflow, when I have you, but without you I am nothing—I wither away, I dissolve and perish.

O my Savior, you shall be my sole God!—I will have no Lord but you. I will break to pieces all idols in my heart which rival you. I will have nothing but Jesus, and him crucified. It shall be my life to pray to you, to offer myself to you, to keep you before me, to worship you in your holy Sacrifice, and to surrender myself to you in Holy Communion.

J.H. Newman, Meditations on Christian Doctrine VI 2:1,3

292. FATHER!

Lord, morning by morning, waken my ear to hear you and serve you with love   *(Is 50:4)*

1. Christ Jesus "is he whom God made our wisdom, our righteousness and sanctification and redemption" (1 Cor 1:30). In him we find not only our salvation and our personal justification, but also what we need to satisfy our debts to God and to pay him a homage that is worthy of him. In fact, the Son of God took flesh not only to redeem the human race, but above all to render to God, in the name of all creation, worship worthy of his infinite majesty.

Thus the Christian religion has in Christ Jesus its inspiration, its model, its one and highest prototype: he who fulfills it in himself at the most perfect level. We are religious in the genuine sense of the word to the extent that we try to reproduce in ourselves the essential characteristics of Christ's religiousness by associating ourselves with his attitude toward his heavenly Father.

In relationship with the Father, Jesus is essentially son; the Son who lives solely for the Father from whom he has existence: "The living Father sent me, and I live because of the Father" (Jn 6:57); the Son who has no other ideal except the will of the Father, to which he adheres with every impulse of his heart: "My food is to do the will of him who sent me" (Jn 4:34); the Son who in every action seeks but the approval of the Father: "I always do what is pleasing to him" (Jn 8:29). Jesus, the only Son of God by nature, has willed to make us share through grace in his divine sonship and has involved us in the current of his filial feelings toward his Father. More than any other, Jesus acknowledges and adores God as the supreme Being, the Lord and absolute Master of the entire universe; more than any other he understands and lives under the rule of the Almighty; and at the same time more than any other he has the right to call God by the name of Father and to deal with him with the heart of a son. Through grace he shares this privilege "with all who believe in his name" (Jn 1:12); to these he reveals the mystery of God's fatherhood and teaches: "Pray then like this: Our Father who art in heaven" (Mt 6:9).

2. Jesus, the only-begotten Son of God, willed to be foretold in prophecy as the "Servant of Yahweh" (Is 42). Son and servant: two words which seem the antithesis of each other, but really are not when the one who personifies them serves his father with the love of a son and loves him by serving him with full dedication. This is fulfilled in Jesus, whose life is wholly pledged to a loving service of his Father: "Did you not know that I must be in my Father's house?" (Lk 2:49). In the words of the boy Jesus we find all the yearning of the heart of a son to hurry to be of service to his Father.

Our religious sense as Christians should lead us to the same line of conduct: To pledge our whole heart and our whole life to the service of God. This is true devotion, which St. Thomas defines as "the will . . . to dedicate oneself promptly to the things which pertain to the service of God" (2-2,82,1). This is devotion in the generic sense of the word, which embraces the whole of life and orients it toward the service of the Lord; devotion in the specific sense which concerns itself with all the acts of interior and exterior worship. In each case this devotion is not a feeling, but the fruit of the will; it is a firm, constant, and generous decision to give ourselves to God. Thus there can be true devotion even in a person who, instead of finding comfort in serving God, experiences aridity, coldness, and perhaps even repugnance, whether in prayer or in the practice of virtue. What counts is the decision of the will;

and the profoundly filial attitude by which we serve God not with
the heart of a mercenary, but with that of a son. The mercenary
does only what is strictly necessary to receive his pay; he is lazy
and avaricious and takes as much care of himself as possible. On
the other hand, a son puts himself at his father's disposal without
calculation or reservation; he is conscientious, generous, does not
measure his self-denial; he seeks only to make his father happy
and is glad to repeat to him at every moment: "Lo, I have come to
do your will" (Heb 10:9). Such is the conduct of a Christian, who
sums up in himself the feelings of the humility and reverence of a
servant of God and those of the love and disinterested devotion of
a son of the heavenly Father.

*Father, I turn to you ... with quiet, gentle confidence. Your Son
has taught me that you are my father, and that I need not call you
by any other name. You are entirely father. Father, I come to tell
you in all simplicity that I am your son, and I say this with the
greatest sincerity.*

*Father, do what you want with me; I am here, ready to do your
will. I know that you will is for me to become like your Only-
Begotten, the elder Brother who has taught me your name, and to
travel on his same road; I know this, and with what love I accept it!
O Father, I am not strong enough for this, yet I accept it! You see
me here: work in me, cut and take away, comfort me or leave me all
alone, I shall never insult you by being afraid or by thinking that
you are forgetting me; if I find my cross very heavy, I will at least be
able to repeat to you continually that I believe in your love, and accept your will.*

*But I desire to drink from the same chalice as your Son; O
Father, do not refuse me this ... You will not refuse it, because I
know that this is your will ... Lord God, here is my life for you to
make of it what you wish, for you to make of it the life of Jesus
Christ. But wherever you may wish to send me, whether I am happy
or sad, sick or well, satisfied or humiliated, you will not be able to
prevent the spirit in me from crying out impetuously to you, urgent-
ly appealing to your love, for those brothers of mine who do not
know that you are the father. O Father, here is my life, but give me
my brothers, so that I may give them to you.*

P. Lyonnet, *Spiritual Writings*

*Father, I surrender to you, do with me as you please. Whatever
you may do with me, I thank you for it ... I am ready for everything,
I consent to everything, I give you thanks for everything, if only
your will may be accomplished in me ... if only it may be accomplished in all your creatures, in all your children, and in all those
whom your heart loves. I want nothing else, my God.*

*I put my soul into your hands, I give it to you, my God, with all
the love of my heart, because I love you. For it is a need of my love to
give myself, to commit myself to your hands without limit ... with*

infinite trust, because you are my Father.

C. de Foucauld, *The Prayer of the Poor*

293. I WILL ADORE THE LORD MY GOD

"To the only God be honor and glory for ever and ever" (1 Tim 1:17)

1. "The hour is coming"—said Jesus to the Samaritan woman—"when neither on this mountain nor in Jerusalem will you worship the Father" (Jn 4:21). The coming of the Savior marked the beginning of a new kind of worship, bound neither to Garizim where the Samaritans prayed, nor to the temple of Jerusalem, which was the center of worship for the Jews. All national cults were to cease and to be replaced by the worship which the Son of God made man had come to establish, in which all men should be associated. "The hour is coming, and now is, when the true worshipers will worship the Father in spirit and truth, for such the Father seeks to worship him" (ib. 23). Jesus himself is the first, in fact the only true worshiper of the Father: he alone knows him perfectly and he alone is in a position to adore him perfectly "in spirit and truth," because he is the Truth and possesses the fullness of the Spirit. By his divinity Jesus has full knowledge of God's infinite dignity and is capable of divine actions; at the same time he is also true man and can prostrate himself in adoration before the Father and, in so doing, draw all humanity with him. This is the only adoration worthy of God, one in which the chief worshiper is Christ and the One who inspires is the Holy Spirit, while man, led by Christ, contributes what is proper to him: the acknowledgement of his nothingness in order to exalt the all of God. "In Christ"—recalls Vatican II—"we received the means for giving worthy worship to God," and having been reborn in him through baptism, we receive "the spirit of adoption as sons, by virtue of which we cry: 'Abba, Father' (Rom 8:15); and thus become those true worshipers whom the Father seeks" (SC 5:6).

It is deeply significant that in his explanation of the new worship, Jesus presents God as Father. He whom he adores, and whom his disciples are to adore, is not only the Most High, the Lord of heaven and earth, upon whom everything depends, he is also the Father who loves mankind even to the point of giving up his only-begotten Son for their salvation (Jn 3:16). The Christian's worship is reverent homage to the sovereignty of God and joyous admiration of his fatherhood.

2. "O come, let us worship and bow down, let us kneel before the Lord, our Maker! For he is our God, and we are the people of his pasture and the sheep of his hand" (Ps 95:6-7). This call to worship, so often repeated in the Liturgy, emphasizes the concept that God is the Creator and that all men belong to him as his people and his flock. The magnificent vision of the Creator is completed by that of the loving Shepherd who feeds "his flock from his own hand."

Jesus will say much more: "Our Father, who art in heaven, hallowed be thy name. Thy kingdom come, thy will be done" (Mt 6:9-10). In these lines we are permitted to glimpse something of Christ's adoration of the Father, that true adoration to which he wishes to introduce his disciples; above all, the recognition of God's paternity: through it the Father eternally begets the Son, "God from God, Light from Light, true God from true God; begotten, not made; of one substance with the Father" (Creed). The eternal divine fatherhood is the root, in time, of God's fatherhood of men. Accompanying it is the recognition of his sovereign majesty, for God is he "who is in heaven," infinitely different from and above every created being. From this there follows the exaltation of the Father's holiness; the strong desire of the Son that his Father's holiness be recognized and glorified by all creatures. This is the primary desire of the only-begotten Son, the essential motive of his incarnation, and it should be the first aspiration of all those who in him will be adopted children. Finally, God's universal kingship is proclaimed with the desire that his kingdom may be spread throughout the earth. In order that this may come to pass, we pray that his will be done, the one holy and sanctifying will which is capable of bringing about the Kingdom and the salvation of creatures. In homage to this will, Christ will suffer agony and sweat blood. Worship reaches its highest peak in the supreme sacrifice of the creature.

Indeed, it is easier to adore in silence than to express our adoration in words; and the only words which can possibly express its depth of meaning are those which Jesus taught his disciples.

> *I call upon you, my God, I call upon you who are near to those who call upon you, to those who call upon you in truth . . What else is it to call upon the Truth in truth, than to call upon the Father in the Son? . .*
>
> *What can be sweeter than to entreat the Father in the name of his Only-Begotten, and to move the Father to mercy by reminding him of his Son? . . O all-powerful Father, I beg you through the charity of your all-powerful Son . . . ; indeed, I do not know what other mediator to offer you in my favor except him who is the propitiation of our sins, who sits at your right hand to intercede for us.*
>
> St. Anselm, *Orationes, 2*

Our Father *most holy, our Creator, our Redeemer, our Savior, our Consoler.*

Who art in heaven, *in the angels and in the saints: you enlighten them that they may know you, because you, Lord, are the Light; you make them burn that they may love you, because you, Lord, are love; you dwell in them and fill them, that they may possess all happiness, because you, Lord, are the supreme good, the eternal good, from which comes every good, and outside of whom no good exists.*

Hallowed be thy name: *that we may know you clearly so as to com-*

prehend the breadth of your gifts, the extent of your promises, the height of your majesty, the depths of your judgments.

Thy kingdom come: *so that you may reign in us with your grace and enable us to reach your kingdom, where we shall see you with our love for you made perfect, in blessed companionship with you, enjoying you eternally.*

Thy will be done on earth as it is in heaven. *Grant that we may love you with all our heart, thinking of you without ceasing; with all our soul, desiring you always; with all our mind, directing every intention toward you and seeking your glory in everything; with all our strength, using every energy and power of our soul and body in the service of your love alone.*

St. Francis of Assisi, from *Il Padre nostro spiegato dai Padri*

294. LET US GIVE THANKS TO GOD

Lord Jesus, let everything be done in your name, giving thanks to God the Father through you (Col 3:17)

1. "Give thanks to God in all circumstances, for this is the will of God" (1 Thes 5:18). Since we are powerless to pay our debts to God in any adequate way, we must at least try to compensate with gratitude. Even the most miserable wretch who has nothing to give in return for the alms he has received has, nevertheless, the power to show himself grateful to his benefactor. Such is our situation before God: we possess nothing of our own, all that we are and have is his gift; and there is no way for us to make a return for his infinite generosity except to use his very gifts to show him our gratitude. God, who blesses us with supreme generosity, has the right to expect the homage of gratitude. "Whatever you do"—repeats St. Paul—"do everything in the name of the Lord Jesus, giving thanks to God the Father through him" (Col 3:17). Yet this, which is a spontaneous need for sensitive hearts, is a duty which is often neglected even by good people, even by the ones who have received most. When Jesus had healed ten lepers, and only one came back to thank him, he complained: "Where are the nine? Was no one found to return and give praise to God except this foreigner?" (Lk 17:17-18). The ungrateful ones were, in fact, nine Jews, the Savior's own countrymen, who were in a privileged position compared to the foreigner. Often the very ones that Jesus has called to live closer to him by giving them a privileged vocation, are the least appreciative. It almost seems as though the very multiplicity of the graces they have received dulls their sensitivity; and they seem to heed neither the greatness nor the total gratuity of the divine gifts, all of which makes the spontaneous flow of gratitude dry up in their hearts. "Ah"—exclaims St. Teresa of Jesus—"how the greatness of your favor harms those who are ungrateful!" (Solil. 3:2). Ingratitude always results in personal disadvantage, as was the case with the nine lepers; because

they did not return to give thanks for having been healed, they did not share with their grateful companion the joy of hearing from Jesus: "Your faith has made you well" (Lk 17:19).

2. "In everything, by prayer and supplication with thanksgiving, let your requests be made known to God" (Phil 4:6). Although our needs are many, the divine gifts we enjoy without even realizing it are still more numerous; that is why the prayer of petition always goes hand in hand with thanksgiving. "What have you that you did not receive? If then you received it, why do you boast as if it were not a gift?" (1 Cor 4:7). Ingratitude, so often the result of pride, is a tacit way of boasting, because one who does not give thanks is considering what he possesses not as a gift freely bestowed by God, but as something of his own, gained through his own abilities. There are also those whose thanks are only on their lips, for in their heart they attribute to their own merits the graces they have received or the good deeds they have accomplished. "God, I thank you that I am not like other men" (Lk 18:11); it is evident from the context of the Gospel that the Pharisee is far from attributing to God the good that is in him.

Gratitude acceptable to God is that which comes from a humble heart that is convinced that only God arouses us "to will and to work" (Phil 2:13). Such is the gratitude of which the Church sings everyday in the name of all men to supply for the ingratitude of the many and to implore the salvation of all. "It is truly meet and just, right and availing to salvation, that we should at all times and everywhere give thanks to you, O holy Lord, Father almighty, everlasting God" (RM). The Church defines thanksgiving as "right and availing to salvation"; to thank God for his countless favors is to beg for the accomplishment of his work of mercy for our own salvation and for that of the entire world. But this result is assured only when thanksgiving is carried out "through Christ our Lord," in union with him and through his infinite merits. This comes to pass in the eucharistic Sacrifice, which is pre-eminently the act of giving thanks, in which Christ, Priest and Victim, is a living thanksgiving to the Father in the name of the whole human race. "Father, calling to mind the death your Son endured for our salvation ... we offer you in thanksgiving this holy and living sacrifice" (Euch Pr III).

I praise you, I glorify you, I bless you, my God, for the countless favors you have granted me in spite of my unworthiness; you have helped me in my times of uncertainty and lifted me up from hopelessness.

I praise your indulgence that waited so long for me and the sweetness that was your revenge; your pity that called me and your kindliness that welcomed me; your mercy that pardoned my sins; your goodness that revealed itself far beyond my merits; your patience which did not remember my abuses; your self-abasement whereby you comforted me, and the patience with which you protected me; the eternity that will preserve me; the truth which will give me my reward.

What then shall I say, O my God, of your inexpressible generosity? In fact, you call me back when I flee, welcome me when I return, help me in uncertainty, arm me in combat, and crown me triumphant; you despise not the sinner who has done penance, and do not remember the insults you have received . . .

I am utterly incapable of giving you the praise you deserve for all these favors: so I give thanks to your majesty for the abundance of your immense goodness, because in me you multiply, preserve, and always reward grace.

St. Thomas Aquinas, Prayers

All powerful, most holy, high and supreme God, you who are the highest good, every good, all that is good, who alone are good, I give you all praise, all glory, all thanks, all honor, and all blessing, and always attribute all good to you.

Since I, wretched and sinful, am not worthy to name you, I entreat you that our Lord Jesus Christ, your beloved Son, in whom you are well pleased, together with the Holy Spirit, the Comforter, may give you thanks that is pleasing to you, for me and for all: he who always satisfies you in everything, and through whom you have given us so much.

St. Francis of Assisi, Sayings

295. ASK AND IT SHALL BE GIVEN YOU

"Lord, teach us to pray" (Lk 11:1)

1. "Ask and it will be given you; seek and you will find; knock and it will be opened to you" (Mt 7:7). Jesus taught us not only to adore and give thanks to our Father in heaven, but also to turn to him with childlike trust in every necessity. The prayer of petition is much more than a selfish request; it is a practical recognition of the creature's total dependence on God. Its center is not so much man's need, as God's fatherly providence which is the sole source of life and of all that ministers to life's preservation, whether on the natural or supernatural level. Disclosing our needs to God is equivalent to acknowledging that everything comes from him and testifies to our faith in his goodness and fatherhood. Even among men, a son does not hesitate to ask his father for what he needs, for the precise reason that he knows he can count on his father. "Or what man of you, if his son asks him for bread, will give him a stone? Or if he asks for a fish, will give him a serpent? If you, then, who are evil, know how to give good gifts to your children, how much more will your Father who is in heaven give good things to those who ask him!" (ib. 9-11). Jesus descends to such practical examples in order to encourage us to have recourse to our heavenly Father with confidence. There is no doubt that he will listen and will provide much more for us than the best of earthly fathers can do. Our confidence honors God, just as adoration and thanksgiving honor him, and it particularly honors his providence and his fatherhood.

While Jesus repeatedly insisted upon this confidence,—we need only recall the parable of the importunate friend (Lk 11:5-8), and that of the judge and the widow (Lk 18:1-7)—he advised us not to "heap up empty phrases as the Gentiles do; for they think they will be heard for their many words," because "your Father knows what you need before you ask him" (Mt 6:7-8). What is important is not the number of words, but the interior intensity of our prayer, the intensity of our reliance on God, which can well be expressed in a simple cry of the heart.

2. While the first part of the "Our Father" is the perfect model for the prayer of worship and praise, the second part is the model for the prayer of petition. All man's basic needs are summarized in three short petitions, which are presented to the heavenly Father with fundamental simplicity and brevity.

"Give us this day our daily bread" (Mt 6:11); bread represents all that we need for earthly life. It is not unseemly to speak of this with God, who is "our Father", because physical life is also his gift, and only by sustaining it is it possible to attend to serving him. But Jesus teaches us to be sparing, not to ask for more than is necessary and hence to be content with what suffices for each day's life. This is in perfect harmony with his admonition: "Do not be anxious about tomorrow, for tomorrow will be anxious for itself" (ib. 34).

"And forgive us our debts, as we have forgiven our debtors" (ib. 12). God's forgiveness is even more necessary for us than bread, not only because of our sins, but also because our whole life is nothing but a great debt owed to him who created us and redeemed us, and who every day preserves the gifts he gave us. Who of us can say that we make sufficient use of the abilities we received? Who can say that we love God with all our heart and with all our strength? Still, our Father is ready to grant generous pardon for every debt we owe him, provided that we are willing, in our turn, to forgive one another each and every wrong. Asking for forgiveness is thus among the most compromising and binding of petitions.

"And lead us not into temptation, but deliver us from evil" (ib. 13). The worst evil that we can fall into is sin, and for that reason, Jesus teaches us to ask not so much to be free from all temptation, but that we may not yield to temptation. It is what he said to his Apostles on the night of his betrayal. "Watch and pray that you may not enter into temptation" (Mt 26:41). Just as a child seeks help from his father in the face of danger, so a Christian, when confronted with temptation, seeks refuge in the heart of God. He is his son, and can count on his Father in heaven. As long as his prayer is inspired by this teaching of Jesus, he can venture to ask anything.

O my Lord, how does anyone who has so poorly served you and so poorly known how to keep what you have given her dare to ask for favors? What can be entrusted to one who has so often been a traitor? What, then, shall I do, Consoler of the destitute and Cure for anyone who wants to be cured by you? Would it be better, perhaps, to keep still about my needs, hoping you will provide the remedy for them? Certainly not: for you, my Lord and my delight, knowing the many needs there must be and the comfort it is for us to rely on you, tell us to ask you and that you will not fail to give.

St. Teresa of Jesus, Soliloquies 5:1

Lord, you will give me everything that I ask of you, as long as I ask with faith, and with the confidence of receiving it, on condition, however, that I do not ask for anything harmful to me ... You are always a father, as almighty and wise as you are infinitely good and loving. You speak to this child of yours, who is so little and scarcely able to stammer, and who can walk only if you hold him by the hand, still you say to him: I will give you whatever you ask of me, provided you ask with confidence. Then you give it, most readily ... when his requests are reasonable, especially when they correspond with your desires ... If he asks for playthings that could hurt him, you refuse them out of your goodness to him while comforting him by giving something else that is sweet but harmless ... you take him by the hand to lead him not where he wants to go, but where it is better for him to go.

C. de Foucauld, The Prayer of the Poor.

296. BE SOBER AND BE WATCHFUL

Lord, unite me with you in death, that I may be united with you in your resurrection (Rom 6:5)

1. "Wisdom teaches self-control and prudence, justice and courage; nothing in life is more profitable for men than these" (Wis 8:7). The Old Testament considered wisdom as the source of all virtue; the New, instead, identifies the source as charity. When charity is actually alive, it impels us toward the good in every area, regulating our life also in its earthly dimension and in its social relationships, in such a way that nothing obstructs its flight toward God. It is in this sense that St. Augustine explains the cardinal virtues as particular aspects of love. "Temperance is the love that keeps itself whole and pure for God; fortitude the love that endures everything easily for God; justice is the love that serves God alone, and by so doing fittingly governs all that is subject to man; prudence is the love that distinguishes clearly what helps to lead us to God from what would impede us" (De mor. Eccl. 25). Charity, which is "the bond of perfection" (Col 3:14), gives life and form to all the moral virtues, while these dispose us toward charity, making it easy and assuring our practice of it. If we must love God with all our heart, it is clear that we must be temperate and must moderate those instincts, those passions, which lead us

astray and divide our energies, and thus impede us in directing ourselves wholly to God. This is the particular work of temperance.

In his first letter, St. Peter repeats this admonition a full three times: "Be sober" (1:13; 4:7; 5:8). In his second, after recommending flight from "the corruption that is in the world because of passion", he invites us to "make every effort to supplement faith with virtue" (1:4-6); and among the first virtues he indicates we find temperance in its function of charity. Faith and charity are the essential content of Christian life, but faith cannot become operative in charity (Gal 5:5) unless concupiscence is restrained by temperance. A temperate person controls and dominates his instincts and passions, and is vigilant lest they give encouragement to the devil to lead him into sin. "Be sober, be watchful. Your adversary the devil prowls around like a roaring lion, seeking someone to devour" (1 Pet 5:8).

2. "For the grace of God has appeared for the salvation of all men, training us to renounce irreligion and worldly passions, and to live sober, upright, and godly lives in this world" (Tit 2:11-12). God's grace, which comes to us through Christ the Savior, requires us to learn to reject worldly avidity, that is, the unrestrained attractions of the senses, which, on account of the disorder brought about by original sin, seek their satisfaction over and above the bounds of reason and of every law. "For the mind that is set on the flesh is hostile to God; it does not submit to God's law" (Rom 8:7); and by flesh he means all uncontrolled passion. Through his baptism a Christian has died to the world of the flesh; and the life of grace, which is the life of the spirit, supposes his remaining in this state of death through the assiduous practice of temperance. "We were buried therefore with [Christ] by baptism into death, so that as Christ was raised from the dead by the glory of the Father, we too might walk in newness of life" (Rom 6:4). When we mortify the attractions of the senses, by restraining our instincts and passions, refusing them illicit pleasures and moderating them in lawful ones, we are but living our baptism, making our death in Christ actual in order to direct our new life of grace and love. Thus we can understand that Christian temperance is a requirement of baptism; it is the concrete actualization of that "putting on the new man" which cannot take place without the corresponding divesting of "the old man" (Col 3:9-10), who is the slave of concupiscence. Temperance thus becomes like continence, chastity, modesty, sobriety; virtues which have not just a negative aspect, stemming from the necessity of mortifying all that is disorderly, but also a positive one which bespeaks freedom, serenity, internal and external order, through which we can rejoice in our new life in Christ and can love God and our neighbor with a heart that is pure and free.

Grant, O Lord, that I may be established in true and perfect charity, for such charity is the mother and nurse of all the virtues...

O charity, you are not imprudent, but make use of everything with great prudence. You are just, for you give each one his due: to God you give glory, and praise his name with holy virtues, and to your neighbor kindness... You are strong: for neither adversity can weaken you through impatience, nor prosperity through inordinate cheerfulness... You clothe the soul with the vestment of grace in its full strength, so that no blow can humiliate us; rather, it returns upon him who launched it. If our neighbor assails us with insult, we bear it patiently; ... if the world assails us with pleasure, and its situations, we receive them with regret ... If impurity seeks to strike us we strike back with the fragrance of purity. Such purity and continence make the soul angelic and the dear daughter of charity.

St. Catherine of Siena, *Letters* 289

O my God, since seeking you demands a heart, naked, strong, and free from all evils and goods which are not purely you, help me not to gather the flowers I see along the way, nor pay heed to the gratifications, satisfactions, and delights which may be offered to me in this life, and which may hinder me on the way.

I will not set my heart on the richs and goods the world offers, neither will I tolerate the delights of my flesh, nor pay heed to the satisfactions and consolations of my spirit in a way that may detain me from seeking my Love in the mountains of virtues and trials. And finally, if it be possible, grant, O Lord, that my soul may be truly loving, esteeming you above all things, trusting in your love and friendship.

St. John of the Cross, *Spiritual Canticle* 3:5,8

297. THE BLESSED TRINITY

Sunday after Pentecost

YEAR A

"He has shown that he loves us" (Entrance Antiphon)

"Blessed be God the Father and his only-begotten Son and the Holy Spirit: for he has shown that he loves us." The entrance hymn of the Mass leads us immediately to the consideration of the great mystery of the Blessed Trinity, stressing its essential aspect: love. Love illuminates the mystery of the Trinity in which God is love, always in the act of begetting, of giving himself, of communicating himself. From all eternity the Father begets his Word—the Son—in whom he expresses his entire self, communicating his entire divinity; the Father and the Son each give each other and possess each other in an act of infinite love, in a perfect substantial communion that is the Holy Spirit. Yet God's love does not remain circumscribed within the Trinity, but bursts forth into creation. All that man is and has is a gift of the Holy Trinity, of the love of the Father and of the Son and of the Holy Spirit, for "great is his love for us".

When divine love addresses itself to man, it takes on the special character of mercy: "A God, merciful and gracious, slow to anger, and abounding in steadfast love and faithfulness" (1st reading: Ex 34:4b-6, 8-9). This touching declaration was God's answer to Moses' grieving entreaty, when he was begging forgiveness for the infidelity of the people who had adored the golden calf. When God found repentance and prayer, he pardoned, he renewed his covenant with Israel, and kept it in his grace, even consenting to a new request: "O Lord, I pray you, go in the midst of us" (ib. 9). As a matter of fact, God had always "gone" with his people during their long wanderings in the desert, making himself present in the cloud that guided them, or in the tent of meeting; God would not deprive Israel of this privilege, the highest expression of his mercy, when they returned to him repentant.

But in the fullness of time, God would do still more: he would come in person to live among men, sending his Son to save the world: "God so loved the world that he gave his Son" (Gospel: Jn 3:16-18). With the incarnation of the Son, which came to pass through the will of the Father and the work of the Holy Spirit, God's love for man was manifested in the most eloquent way, and at the same time God is revealed in his Trinitarian mystery. Man had sinned, but God would not let him perish: he was saved by the Father's mercy, the blood of the Son, and the outpouring of the Holy Spirit. In order to enter into the orbit of salvation, we must believe in the love of God as Trinity; we must acknowledge it in Christ who is its incarnation, and who was sent "so that whoever believes in him should not perish, but have eternal life" (ibid). To believe in Christ is to believe in the Trinity: in the Father who sent him, in the Holy Spirit who guided him in accomplishing his mission. The mystery of the Trinity is the source of the mystery of Christ, of universal salvation, and of the Christian life.

Then we understand the beautiful Trinitarian formula with which St. Paul closes his second letter to the Corinthians: "The grace of the Lord Jesus Christ, and the love of God, and the fellowship of the Holy Spirit be with you all" (2 Cor 13:14; 2nd reading). The Apostle wishes to all the grace of salvation merited by Christ, the love of the Father which is its cause, and the fellowship of the Holy Spirit through whom grace and love are poured into the hearts of the faithful who are going to be taken into fellowship with the Father and the Son. Thus, by means of Christ, we enter into the rhythm of the life of the Trinity, a life of love and communion with the three divine Persons dwelling within us. Not only that: we are invited to express our personal communion with the Trinity in our relations with our neighbor through sincere love, which is the wellspring of peace, of harmony, of fellowship with all.

> *God, our Father, you sent your Word to bring us truth, and your Spirit to make us holy. Through them we come to know the mystery of your life. Help us to worship you, one God in three Persons, by proclaiming and living our faith in you.*

Roman Missal, *Collect A*

> *O eternal Trinity, O Godhead! This Godhead gave value to the blood of your Son. O eternal Trinity, you are a deep sea, into which the deeper I enter the more I find, and the more I find the more I seek; the soul cannot be satiated in your abyss, for it continually hungers after you, the eternal Trinity, desiring to see you with light in your light. As the heart desires the spring of living water, so my soul desires to leave the prison of this dark body and to see you in truth. How long will your face be hidden from my eyes?*
>
> *O eternal Trinity, fire and abyss of love, melt at once the cloud of my body. The knowledge which you have given me of yourself in your truth constrains me to long to abandon the heaviness of my body and to give my life for the glory and praise of your name, for I have tasted and seen with the light of the intellect in your light, the abyss of you, the eternal Trinity, and the beauty of your creature.*

St. Catherine of Siena, *Dialogue* 148, p. 343

YEAR B

"Glory to the Father, and to the Son, and to the Holy Spirit" (Alleluia)

We have been considering all the mysteries of salvation from the birth of Christ to Pentecost, and now the Church directs our attention to the primordial mystery of Christianity, the Blessed Trinity, the source of every gift and every good. She invites us to sing in praise: "Glory to the Father, and to the Son, and to the Holy Spirit; to him who is, who was, and who is to come" *(Alleluia)*.

The revelation of the Trinity belongs to the New Testament; the Old was wholly intent on proclaiming and exalting the unity of God: there is only one Lord. We read in today's first lesson (Dt 4:32-34; 39-40): "Know therefore . . . and lay it to your heart, that the Lord is God in heaven above and on the earth beneath; there is no other." Israel was living in contact with pagan peoples, and needed to be constantly reminded of this truth in order not to fall into idolatry. The Old Testament exalts the greatness of Yahweh, the one only God: he is the Creator of the entire universe, the absolute Lord; but it also praises his condescension toward man: he is the Shepherd who goes in search of his creatures in order to help them, to protect them from harm, and to draw them to himself. Israel had great experience of this, for God made them his chosen people, he freed them from slavery in Egypt by wonderful miracles, he offered them his covenant, and granted them the privilege of hearing his voice, and of enjoying his presence. "Ask now . . . since the day that God created man upon the earth, whether such a great thing as this has ever happened or was ever heard of?" (ib. 32).

Yet the new people of God—the Church—enjoys still greater privileges, the fruit of the incarnation of the Son of God, of his passion-death-resurrection. With the coming of Christ, God reveals himself to the world in the mystery of his inner life and of the perfection and fecundity of his knowing and loving, through which he is Father who begets the Word, and communion from which the Holy Spirit proceeds. Most wonderful of all, God now enters into relationship with men, not only as their one Lord and Creator, but also as the Trinity: he is a Father who loves them as sons in his only Son and in communion with the Holy Spirit. This privilege is not reserved to a single people but is extended to everyone who accepts the message of Christ. In fact, before Jesus ascended into heaven he gave his Apostles the mandate of preaching the gospel to all nations and of baptizing them "in the name of the Father, and of the Son, and of the Holy Spirit" (Gospel: Mt 28:16-20). Each of us enters into a special relationship with the Trinity through baptism; through it, we are born again into a new life, becoming children of the Father who decreed our regeneration, brothers of Christ who merited this for us through his blood on the Cross, temples of the Holy Spirit who infuses into us the spirit of adoption. In God's eyes one who is baptized is not just a creature, but a son introduced into the intimacy of his Trinitarian life in order that he may live in the company of the divine Persons who dwell in him.

The second reading (Rom 8:14-17) particularly stresses the action of the Holy Spirit in this divine sonship of the faithful: "You have received the spirit of adoption. When we cry: 'Abba! Father!' it is the Spirit himself bearing witness with our spirit that we are children of God" (ib. 15-16). The Holy Spirit has been sent to us in order to transform us interiorly and to make us children in the image of the Son. This intimate regeneration, this real spiritual rebirth is attributed to the Holy Spirit; he is its author and also its witness, who by infusing into us an intimate conviction that we are sons of God, encourages us to love and to call upon God as Father. But for the Holy Spirit to accomplish his work, we must let ourselves be led by him to the imitation of Christ, who was moved by the Spirit in every action. "All who are led by the Spirit of God are sons of God" (ib. 14). There is no more beautiful way of honoring and bearing witness to our love for the Trinity than by living the gifts of the Trinity to the full and opening ourselves to the action of the Holy Spirit by behaving as children of the Father and as brothers of Christ.

It is always fitting that we give thanks everywhere to you, O holy Lord, Father almighty, everlasting God. With your only-begotten Son and the Holy Spirit, you are one God, one Lord; not in the oneness of a single Person, but in the Trinity of one substance. For that which we believe from your revelation concerning your glory, that same we believe of your Son, that same of the Holy Spirit, without difference or separation. So in confessing the true and everlasting Godhead, we adore the Trinity of Persons, oneness in being, and equality in majesty.

Roman Missal, Preface

Eternal Father, prostrate in humble adoration at your feet, we consecrate our whole being to the glory of your Son Jesus, the Word Incarnate. You have established him King of our souls; submit to him our souls, our hearts, our bodies, and may nothing within us move without his order, without his inspiration. Grant that united to him we may be borne to your bosom and consumed in the unity of your love.

O Jesus, unite us to you, in your all holy life, entirely consecrated to your Father and to souls. Be our justice, our holiness, our redemption, our all. Sanctify us in truth!

O Holy Spirit, love of the Father and the Son, dwell like a burning furnace of love in the center of our hearts. Bear our thoughts, affections and actions, like ardent flames, continually heavenwards into the bosom of the Father. May our whole life be a "Glory to the Father and to the Son and to the Holy Spirit."

O Mary, Mother of Christ, Mother of holy love, fashion us according to the Heart of your Son.

C. Marmion, *Consecration to the Blessed Trinity*, p.1

YEAR C

May our faith in you, one God in three Persons, be our pledge of salvation (RM, After Communion)

The cycle of the mysteries of Christ's life has been completed and today's Liturgy rises to the contemplation of the mystery of the Blessed Trinity. This mystery was unknown in the Old Testament; only in the light of the revelation of the New Testament can we discover some obscure allusions. One of the most significant of these is contained in the eulogy of wisdom, a divine attribute which is presented in the first reading as a person (Prov 8:22-31). There we read: "The Lord created me at the beginning of his work, the first of his acts of old . . . When there were no depths I was brought forth . . . when he established the heavens I was there . . . beside him like a master workman" (ib. 22,24,27,30); hence, as a person coexisting with God from all eternity, begotten by him, and collaborating with him in the work of creation. It is not difficult for a Christian to perceive in this personification of the attribute of wisdom a prophetic figure of uncreated Wisdom, the eternal Word, the second Person of the Trinity, of whom St. John wrote: "In the beginning was the Word, and the Word was with God, and the Word was God ... All things were made through him" (1:1,3). But the expressions that strike us most are those in which wisdom is said to rejoice in the creation of mankind and to set its delights within our reach. How can this not make us think of eternal Wisdom, the Word, who takes flesh and comes to dwell among us?

In the second reading (Rom 5:1-5) the revelation of the Trinity is made fully manifest. We behold the three divine Persons in their relations with us. God the Father justifies us and re-establishes us in his grace, the Son becomes man and dies on the cross to obtain this gift for us, the Holy Spirit comes to pour out into our hearts the love of the Trinity. In order to enter into relationship with the "Three", we must believe in our Savior, in the Father who sent him, in the Holy Spirit who breathes into our hearts love of the Father and of the Son. From this faith is born the hope of one day being able to enjoy "the glory of God" (ib. 2) in unveiled communion with the Blessed Trinity. The trials and tribulations of life cannot shake the hope of Christians; it is not vain because it is founded on the love of God, which, from the day of baptism, "has been poured into our hearts through the Holy Spirit who has been given to us" (ib. 5). Faith, hope, and love are the virtues which enable a Christian to begin on earth that communion with the Trinity which will become full and beatifying in eternal glory.

The Gospel of the day (Jn 16:12-15) throws new light on the work of the Holy Spirit and upon the whole mystery of the Trinity. When, in his discourse at the Last Supper, Jesus promised the Holy Spirit, he said: "When the Spirit of truth comes, he will guide you into all the truth" (ib. 13). Jesus also is truth (Jn 14:16) and has taught his disciples all the truth he has learned from the Father: "All that I have heard from my Father I have made known to you" (Jn 15:15)—; therefore the Holy Spirit will not teach things that are not already contained in Christ's message, but will rather make us penetrate their profound meaning and give us an exact understanding of them, thus preserving them from error. God is one; therefore truth is one; the Father possesses it totally and communicates it totally to the Son: Jesus will say: "All that the Father has is mine," adding that the Holy Spirit "will take what is mine and declare it to you" (Jn 16:15). Here Jesus is testifying to the unity of nature and to the distinction of the three divine Persons. Not only truth, but everything is common among them; they possess one single divine nature. However, the Father possesses it as source, the Son in that he is begotten by the Father, the Holy Spirit in that he proceeds from the Father and the Son. But the Father is not greater than the Son, nor is the Son greater than the Holy Spirit: in them there is perfect communion of life, of truth, of love. The Son of God came upon earth precisely to introduce man into this most sublime communion, making him capable through faith and love of living in the society of the Trinity dwelling within him.

> *You, O eternal Trinity, are my creator, and I am the work of your hands, and I know, through the new creation which you have given me in the blood of your Son, that you are enamoured of the beauty of your workmanship.*
>
> *O Abyss, O eternal Godhead, O Sea profound! What more could you give me than yourself? You are the fire which ever burns without being consumed; you consume in your heart all the soul's self-love; you are the fire which takes away all cold; you illuminate . . .*
>
> *By your light I know how to represent you to myself, O supreme and infinite good: good above all good, blessed, incomprehensible and inestimable good. Beauty above all beauty; wisdom above all wisdom; for you are wisdom itself. You, the good of the angels, have given yourself in a fire of love to men. You, the garment which covers all our nakedness, you feed the hungry with your sweetness. O Sweet without any bitter!*
>
> *O eternal Trinity, in your light which you have given me . . . I have known the path of supreme perfection, so that I may no longer serve you in darkness but with light, and may be the mirror of a good and holy life and arise from my miserable life, because of which I have hitherto served you in darkness . . . O eternal Trinity, you have dissipated the darkness with your light.*

> St. Catherine of Siena, *Dialogue* 167

298. CORPUS CHRISTI

Thursday or Sunday after Trinity Sunday

YEAR A

"Grant, O Lord, that we may share with faith in the holy mystery of your Body and Blood" (RM Collect)

The Church honors the Eucharist every day of the year, offering it to God in a sacrifice of praise, giving it as food to the faithful, and reserving it in tabernacles so that Christ's sacramental presence may be the center and the sustenance of their lives. Therefore, today's Solemnity is not so much the memorial of the institution of this Sacrament, as the celebration of a mystery that is always living and present. Let us consider today's Liturgy from this viewpoint. The first reading (Dt 8:2-3; 14-16) recalls an event which took place thousands of years ago, but which still retains its spiritual significance: the manna which fell from heaven and the living water which gushed from the rock to satisfy the hunger and thirst of Israel wandering in the desert. It was a theme to which Moses used to return insistently in order to keep alive the people's faith and gratitude. With all the more reason, the Church uses every means to keep the new people of God from forgetting an immensely greater gift—of which manna is only a weak image—a gift which is put daily within their reach, the Eucharist. This is not a physical food but a spiritual one, the very Body and Blood of Christ, offered for them as viaticum for their earthly journey. It is the "daily bread" which the faithful should ask for and eat every day, more hungry and eager for it than for earthly bread.

It is with just this in mind that today's Gospel (Jn 6:51-59) leads us to reflect upon the words of Jesus: "I am the living bread which came down from heaven; if any one eats of this bread, he will live for ever; and the bread which I shall give for the life of the world is my flesh" (ib. 51). The Eucharist is so life-giving a bread that it is the seed and the pledge of eternal life, because it is the Body of Him who is "life" (Jn 14:6). The Jews who ate manna in the desert are dead; but "he who eats this bread will live for ever" (Jn 6:58). The Eucharist is the memorial of the Lord's death and offers to the faithful the same body that Christ immolated for them upon the cross; it is also the memorial of his resurrection because it is "living bread" in which Christ is present and living just as he is in the glory of heaven. "Mystery of faith", the Church proclaims, each time she consecrates the Eucharist; "mystery of faith," we Christians should repeat every time we draw near to receive it. But it is likewise the mystery of love in which Jesus has carried the gift of himself to the highest degree: having given his life for us, he gives us himself as food, not once only but continually, daily, until his return. We must adore him, and love and thank him; we must draw near and eat. "He who eats my flesh and drinks my blood abides in me, and I in him . . . He who eats me will live because of me" (ib. 56-57). Sacramental Communion is the source of vital and permanent union with Christ, by which we truly live "through him", not only because we receive life from him, but because our whole existence is turned toward him.

The second reading (1 Cor 10:16-17) opens up another perspective: the Eucharist is also a source of union with our fellowmen: "Because there is one bread, we who are many are one body, for we all partake of the one bread" (ib. 17). Just as the eucharistic bread is but one—the Body of Christ—so also we who partake of it form in turn a single body, the Church, the Mystical Body of Christ. St. Paul has recalled elsewhere all the motives which pledge us to unity: "One Spirit . . . one hope . . . ; one Lord, one faith, one baptism, one God and Father of us all" (Eph 4:6). He is declaring that the strengthening food of this unity is the one eucharistic bread. "Precisely because we partake of one bread, we all become one body in Christ, one blood, and members of each other, having been made one body with Christ" (St. John Damascene, De fide orth. 4,13). Therefore we should draw from eucharistic Communion the fruit of a more intense communion with our brothers.

Praise to you, almighty Lord . . . You have come to free us from our sins. *We sing your praises, O wonderful Savior. You are the shepherd of the flock, sent by the Father . . .*

Grant that we may receive this Sacrament with reverence and be filled with your sweetness, O Christ. You have given us bread from heaven: we have eaten the bread of angels. Make us love one another, O God, because you are love. He who loves his brother is born of you and contemplates you; charity is made perfect in him.

cf *Prieres eucharistiques,* 47

Lord, you live in me by your grace, I delight in you above all things. I have to love you, thank you, and praise you; I cannot do less, because for me that is eternal life. You are my food and my drink: the more I eat the more I hunger; the more I drink the more I thirst; the more I possess you the more I desire you. You are sweeter than honey to me, far sweeter than any sweetness that can be tasted. There is always a hunger and desire for you within me, because I cannot exhaust your plenitude. Are you consuming me or am I consuming you? I do not know; because in the depths of my soul I feel both the one and the other. You want me to be one with you, I want to give up all my customary ways in order to surrender myself into your arms. I can only thank you, praise you, and honor you, because for me that is eternal life. I experience a certain impatience within me and do not know what it may be. If I could come to be but one with you, O God . . . then all my lamenting would come to an end. Lord, who know all my needs, do with me whatever you wish. I abandon myself completely to you and take refuge in you without fearing my suffering.

Ruysbroeck, *Oeuvres,* Vol 1

YEAR B

"I will lift up the cup of salvation and call on the name of the Lord"
(Ps 116:13)

According to the revised Liturgy, in today's solemnity the title of the "Blood" is added to that of the "Body" of Christ. This was always implicit—for where the Body is, there is also the Blood of the Lord and vice versa—but now it is explicitly proclaimed, thus drawing attention to the sacrificial aspect of the Eucharist. The biblical readings of the day converge on this theme. In the Book of Exodus (24:3-8; 1st reading) we read the text which gives the stipulations of the Covenant between God and Israel. Moses gathered the people together, built an altar, ordered young bulls to be offered in sacrifice, and then sprinkled their blood, half upon the altar and half upon the people while saying: "Behold the blood of the Covenant which the Lord has made with you in accordance with all these words" (ib. 8). "These words" were the words of God which had been previously read to the people, concerning the Ten Commandments which Israel had promised to observe, and the promises which God himself had pledged to accomplish. This bilateral pact would be formally established through the blood of the animals offered in sacrifice; this blood, sprinkled upon the altar and upon the people, signified the spiritual bond that united God and Israel.

The ancient covenant prefigured the new one which was ratified by Christ not by "the blood of goats and calves but [by] his own blood" (2nd reading: Heb 9:11-15). While in the Old Testament sacrifices were multiplied and had a purely external and symbolic value, in the New there is but one sacrifice, offered "once for all" (ib. 12) because its value is intrinsic, real, and infinite. In it there are neither slaughtered animals nor suffering human beings; victim and priest become identical in the Son of God made man, who "offered himself without blemish to God": his blood has the power to "purify our conscience from dead works to serve the living God" (ib. 14). It is no longer a question of an external purification, but of an interior one which transforms us from within, washing sins away, so that, "made alive" by grace and love, we may serve "the living God." The rebirth of the Christian takes place in the waters of baptism, which, however, derives its power from the blood of Christ, because "without the shedding of blood there is no forgiveness of sins" (ib. 22).

But before shedding his blood upon the cross, Jesus wished to anticipate this gift for his disciples with the institution of the Eucharist. Today's Gospel (Mark 14:12-16,22-26) speaks of this, using Mark's account, which, although more sparse in details than those of the other synoptics, does not omit an explicit reference to the blood of the old Covenant being definitively replaced by the blood of Christ. "And he took a cup, and when he had given thanks, he gave it to them, and they all drank of it. And he said to them: 'This is my blood of the covenant, which is poured out for many' " (ib. 23-24). From this time on the former sacrifices are ended and replaced by the new one, which is historically offered only once upon Calvary, but is sacramentally renewed every day in the Mass, so that its merits may be applied to the faithful of all times and enable all to approach and drink this Blood as the disciples drank it at the Last Supper. Thus the Church lives and grows through the Blood of Christ; the faithful are continuously purified from sin, watered with grace, strengthened by love, and brought together into one people. The Body and Blood of Christ are the heart and the support of the Christian life, but since they are immolated those who are thus nourished must accept sharing in Christ's immolation by embracing the cross with him, adhering with him to the will of the Father, even when it is crucifying, and offering themselves in a spirit of sacrifice and expiation to all the trials and hardships and sorrows of life. In such a way we live the mystery of the death of Christ through the Eucharist and are made ready to share in his eternal glory in a communion that will have no end.

O sacred banquet, wherein Christ is received, the memorial of his passion is celebrated, the mind is filled with grace, and a pledge of future glory is given to us. Oh how sweet, O Lord, is your spirit, who in order to show your sweetness to your children, feed them with the sweetest Bread from heaven, filling the hungry with good things.

St. Thomas Aquinas

O Lord, the soul's mouth ... lovingly tastes you; it savors the purity of the divine essence and of your humanity and attains to such a knowledge of your purity that that which used to seem virtue to it, now seems like a shortcoming both in itself and in others. Receiving the holy Sacraments which draw strength from your Blood and from your passion, we come by their means to taste the sweetness of the passion, and of the Blood that was shed therein. We savor this most fully when we receive the holy Sacrament of your Body and Blood, for there more than anywhere else this sweetness and grace are found hidden, when the Sacrament is really received with purity and honesty. Let whoever wishes to taste of your gentleness and sweetness approach this Blood and there he will find all rest and consolation. The soul will be washed in this Blood, adorned with this Blood, cleansed in this Blood, nourished by this Blood.

St. Mary Magdalen de' Pazzi, *Colloquies* 1, *Works* Vol 3

YEAR C

May I hunger for you, O "Bread of Life" (Jn 6:48)

In the Liturgy for today's Solemnity, the Body and Blood of Christ are presented in their relationship to the priesthood of Christ, whose supreme gift is the Eucharist: a Sacrifice offered to the Father, and a Banquet prepared for men.

The first reading (Gen 14:18-20) recalls the oldest figure of Christ the Priest: Melchizedek, king of Salem and priest "of God most high," who in thanksgiving to God for Abraham's victory offered a sacrifice of "bread and wine", a symbol of the Eucharist. The Bible gives us no information about this mysterious personage, either as to his origin or to his death. St. Paul wrote of him: "He is without father or mother or genealogy, and has neither beginning of days nor end of life, but resembling the Son of God he continues a priest for ever" (Heb 7:3). Melchizedek is called "a priest for ever" because we know neither about his birth nor his death. With much greater reason this title befits Christ whose priesthood is not of human, but of divine origin and is therefore eternal in the most absolute sense. The Church applies to him the words we repeat in the responsorial psalm: "You are a priest for ever in the line of Melchizedek." In the New Testament, since the levitical priesthood has come to an end, there is only the eternal priesthood of Christ, which is prolonged in time through the Catholic priesthood.

The second reading (1 Cor 11:23-26) shows us Christ the Priest in the act of instituting the Eucharist, the sacrifice of the New Testament. The account is what has been transmitted to the Apostle by tradition and what he himself has "received from the Lord" (ib. 23). Like Melchizedek Jesus offers "bread and wine", but his blessing brings about the great miracle: "This is my body which is for you . . . This cup is the new covenant in my blood" (ib. 24-25). It is no longer bread, but the true Body of Christ, no longer wine, but his true Blood. Jesus anticipates in the Eucharist the sacrifice that he will accomplish on Calvary in his tortured members, and in anticipating it leaves it as a testament to his followers, as a living memorial of his Passion: "Do this in remembrance of me" (ibid). Therefore, St. Paul concludes "as often as you eat this bread and drink this cup, you proclaim the Lord's death" (ib. 26). It is not a "memorial", limited to recalling a past event, nor an announcement in word only, because the Eucharist makes the Sacrifice of the cross and the banquet of the Last Supper actually present, although in sacramental form. This same reality will be offered to the faithful of all times so they can unite themselves to Christ's sacrifice and be nourished by his Body and Blood "in expectation of his coming" (RM).

The Gospel of the day treats of the Eucharist as Banquet under the transparent symbolism of the multiplication of the loaves (Lk 9:11-17). Here we have not only the ancient symbolism of the bread and wine offered by Melchizedek, but we see Jesus' action as an obvious prelude to the eucharistic Supper. Jesus takes the loaves of bread, raises his eyes to heaven, blesses them, breaks, and distributes them; these are all steps he will repeat in the Cenacle when he changes the bread into his body. Another detail attracts our attention: the loaves are multiplied in his hands, and pass from them into the hands of the disciples who distribute them to the crowd. Likewise it is always he who will accomplish the eucharistic miracle, though making use of his priests who will be its ministers and treasurers. Finally, "all ate and were satisfied" (ib. 17). The Eucharist is the banquet offered to all to satisfy their hunger for God and for eternal life. Today's Solemnity is an invitation to reanimate our faith and love for the Eucharist, so that we may hunger for it more ardently and approach it more fervently, and know how to arouse this saving hunger in our indifferent brothers and sisters.

Father, all-powerful and ever-living God, we do well always and everywhere to give you thanks through Jesus Christ our Lord. He is the true and eternal priest who established this unending sacrifice. He offered himself as a victim for our deliverance and taught us to make this offering in his memory. As we eat his body which he gave for us, we grow in strength. As we drink his blood which he poured out for us, we are washed clean.

Roman Missal, *Preface*

O new and ancient mystery! Ancient in its figure, new in the reality of the Sacrament in which the creature ever receives the greatest newness. We know well, and through faith we see with certainty, that, by divine power, that blessed bread and wine become substantially your Body and your Blood, O Christ, God and Man, with the words that you ordained and that the priest recites in this consecrated mystery ...

O God made man, you satisfy completely, you conquer, you superabound and fill your creatures with joy, above and beyond all things, without manner or measure ... O God that is not esteemed, nor appreciated, nor loved, yet found anew by those who yearn to have you fully, but cannot possess you totally! ... Let me come to you, O God, let me draw near so sublime a table with greatest reverence, much purity, great fear, and immense love. Grant that I may approach all joyful and adorned, because I am coming to you who are the goodness of all glory, who are perfect bliss and eternal life, all beauty, sweetness and sublimity, all love and sweetness of love.

Bl. Angela of Foligno, *The Book of Divine Consolation* II

299. THE SACRED HEART OF JESUS

Friday after the 2nd Sunday after Pentecost

YEAR A

"We know and believe in the love God has for us" (1 Jn 4:16)

The Solemnity of the Sacred Heart of Jesus celebrates God's love for men, which culminates in the gift of his Only-Begotten Son, who loved the world with a "human heart" (GS 22) which he took unto himself as an instrument of his infinite love. Let us follow these guidelines as we meditate upon the biblical texts of this day. The first reading (Dt 7:6-11) leads us to further consideration of God's love in the Old Testament, especially as revealed in his dealings with Israel. God chose this people, not because of any special merits on their part, but by the free choice of his love: "The Lord your God has chosen you ... not because you were more in number than any other people, ... for you were fewest of all peoples; but ... because the Lord loves you" (ib. 7-8). Israel's history has only one explanation: God's love. God chose Israel out of love, delivered her from Egypt, made a covenant with her, gave her possession of the promised land, and caused the Savior to be born of her race. The story of every man is modeled upon that of Israel: "I have loved you with an everlasting love; therefore I have continued my faithfulness to you" (Jer 31:3). God calls us into existence through love and through love he governs and directs the life of each one of us, desiring to make us sharers in his eternal bliss. Truly he "first loved us!" (1 Jn 4:19).

The second reading (ib. 7:16) pauses upon this truth; it is a truth that springs from another still greater truth: "God is love" (ib. 8:16). Since he is love, all his works are love; and the work that demonstrates this love in the highest degree is his having sent "his only Son into the world, so that we might live through him" (ib. 9). All that was needed to create man out of nothing was a simple act of God's will; to redeem us from evil, God pledged his own Son, willing him to assume a human body, and to sacrifice it "as the expiation of our sins" (ib. 10). Looking upon the Son of God who emptied himself, taking "the form of a servant" (Phil 2:7) in order to make himself our slave, and dying for us upon the cross, we can all repeat: "We know and believe the love God has for us" (1 Jn 4:16). Penetrating into this mystery we become capable of the fullness of love, first of all for God who first loved us, and then in him for our brothers, who are the objects like ourselves of his same love: "Beloved, if God so loved us, we also ought to love one another" (ib. 11).

The Gospel (Mt 11:25-30) brings God's love for us still closer by showing it to us in action in the behavior of Jesus, "gentle and lowly in heart" (ib. 29). He has immense pity for all the sufferings and miseries of mankind and says: "Come to me, all who labor and are heavy laden, and I will give you rest" (ib. 28). What weighs most heavily on man's heart is sin. To free him from this burden, Jesus will take it upon himself, he will carry it upon his cross and will destroy it by his death. Therefore he does not weary of going in search of sinners to be saved, of prodigal sons to be brought back to the Father's love, and of fallen women to be set again on the right path. The only condition he makes is that we go to him, believe in him, and, instead of the crushing burden of sin, accept the sweet burden of his law: "Take my yoke upon you . . . For my yoke is easy, and my burden is light" (ib. 29-30). Christ's law is a "yoke" because it requires control of our passions and denial of our love of self, but it is an "easy and light" yoke because it is a law of love. The more we know how to imitate the meekness and humility of the Heart of Christ, the more we will experience how sweet it is to follow him in obedience to the will of the Father, and how sweet to love as he loved, even when love exacts the greatest sacrifices. "Learn from me, for I am gentle and lowly in heart, and you will find rest for your souls" (ib. 29). The Heart of Christ is an inexhaustible source of comfort and of salvation, and at the same time an example of holiness.

O God, good Father, in the heart of your Son we celebrate the wonders of your love: from this inexhaustible source the abundance of your gifts is showered on us (Collect).

May the Sacrament of your love, O God, draw us to Christ, your Son, so that, animated by this same love, we shall know how to recognize his face in our brothers (After Communion).

Roman Missal

O Lord, gladden your servant's soul, because to you have I lifted up my soul. You are truly sweet and gentle ... You bear with our wretchedness, and in spite of everything, you wait for us to pray to you so that you can make us holy. And when we do pray to you, you give a happy welcome to our prayer and hear it ... Gladden the soul of your servant, for to you have I lifted it up. And how have I lifted it up? As best I could, according to the strength you gave me, and to the extent that I was able to catch hold of it as it was escaping ... O Lord! you are sweet and gentle! You are gentle in order to support me. Because of my infirmity I tend to dissipate my strength. Cure me and I shall be steadfast. Strengthen me and I shall be firm. But until I become all this, bear with me, because you are gentle and sweet, O Lord.

St. Augustine, *In Ps* 85,7

YEAR B

The thoughts of your Heart last through every generation to deliver us from death (Entrance Ant)

The purpose of today's Solemnity is to celebrate the wonders of God's love that are contained in the Heart of Christ which incarnates and expresses the divine goodness toward men. Therefore the Liturgy returns to the subject of God's eternal love which has never ceased to accompany man from the first day of creation. In the first reading (Hos 11:1,3-4,8-9) God himself reminds the people of Israel, in the words of Hosea, of how much he has done for them from the beginning of their history, leading them through the desert and loving and helping them as a father would a son: "I took them up in my arms ... I led them with the cords of compassion, with the bands of love, and I became to them as one who eases the yoke on their jaws, and I bent down to them and fed them" (ib. 3-4). Yet even this tender and solicitous love was not understood, and Israel abandoned its God. The Lord expressed his sorrow in very human terms: "My heart recoils within me, my compassion grows warm and tender" (ib. 8). But he is not like a man who lets anger overcome him; although he predicts punishment, he tempers it with "compassion." Israel will not be destroyed as it deserves, but will be punished in order that it may reform and return to its Lord. Such is the way that divine love acts in every age and for every individual: "The thoughts of his Heart last through every generation, ... (to) rescue them from death" (Entrance ant).

The Heart of God! In the New Testament this expression is no longer a metaphor; it is a reality because the Heart of Jesus, the Word made flesh, is both a true human heart and a true divine heart. The Heart of Jesus is a symbol not only of the human love that he possesses as a true man in its highest perfection, but also of the love of God which he possesses as true God because of being one Person with the Word. In Christ there is all the eternal and infinite love of the Father, of the Son, and of the Holy Spirit; he is the Sacrament which reveals it and distributes it to men. This is "the unsearchable riches of Christ" of which the second reading speaks (Eph 3:8-12,14-19). St. Paul's mission was to announce it to the world, revealing "the mystery hidden for ages in God" (ib. 9), that is, the eternal plan for universal salvation which is to be realized "in Christ Jesus our Lord" (ib. 11). Christ is the mediator between God and man; he brings God's love to men and in accordance with this love he saves them in order to bring them back to God; so that in him "we have . . . confidence of access to God" (ib. 12). Although through the meeting on the road to Damascus the Apostle was able to comprehend "the love of Christ, which surpasses knowledge" (ib. 19), he could not find words in which to express it, yet he wanted all to understand that "they might be filled with all the fullness of God" (ibid). In actual fact, such fullness comes to men through the mystery of Christ's love.

Today's Gospel (Jn 19:31-37) completes the picture of God's love for his creatures by showing us Christ's pierced Heart: "One of the soldiers pierced his heart with a spear and at once there came out blood and water" (ib. 34). How infinite and tremendous was the love of the Father who sacrificed his Son in order to save mankind; how infinite and tender the love of the Son who, to make reparation for sin, offered himself to the Father as a sacrificial oblation by which he purchased salvation for men. The blood and water shed by the Heart of Jesus attest to the full consummation of his sacrifice and are a most expressive symbol of the sacraments, in that they draw their efficacy from his blood; through their means all humanity is regenerated in Christ, and finds in him "confidence of access" to the Father. But just as Israel had once not understood God's love and had been unfaithful to him, so today men continue not to understand Christ's love, to reject him, and to insult him. For that reason devotion to the Heart of Jesus reminds us of our duty of reparation: to the Father insulted in his Son, to the Son whom men have crucified and continue to offend by sinning.

We give you thanks, always and everywhere, O Lord, heavenly Father, all-powerful and ever-living God, through Christ our Lord. Lifted high on the cross, he gave his life for us out of his limitless love; and from his wounded side there flowed blood and water, symbol of the sacraments of the Church, so that all men, drawn to the Heart of the Savior, may draw water with joy from the fountain of salvation.

Roman Missal, Preface

O my love, sweet Jesus, what made you come from heaven to earth? Love! What made you suffer such great and terrible torments even to death? Love! What made you leave yourself as food for the

The Sacred Heart of Jesus

soul? Love! What moved you ... to send the Holy Spirit to be our strength and our guide? Love! Many more things might be said of you. Only for love, you came into this world, in so vile and mean an outward seeming and did so humble yourself before the people that not only were you not acknowledged as God, you were hardly taken for a man. No servant, however faithful and loving, would bear as much for his master, even if he were promised Paradise, for without the inward love you give, no torment of soul or body can be borne patiently.

St. Catherine of Genoa, *Dialogue* p. 123

YEAR C

With joy we will draw water from the wells of salvation (Is 12:3)

Two images are interwoven in the Liturgy of this celebration: that of the Heart of Jesus in the proper of the Mass, and that of the Good Shepherd in the scriptural readings. They express one single reality: the infinite love of Christ who gave his life for his flock, and who let his heart be pierced that it might become the source of salvation for all.

There are many passages in the Old Testament that foretell the Messiah as shepherd. One of the most beautiful is without doubt the one which is read today in the first reading (Ezek 34:11-16). Following upon the banishment of the chosen people because of the negligence of their leaders, God personally declares his desire to assume their care. He will gather them around himself, will go in search of those who have been scattered and will bring them back to their country, to well watered and fruitful lands, like a good shepherd who gathers his beloved flock into the fold and leads them to fertile pastures. "I shall feed my sheep with good pasture; they shall lie down in good grazing lands" (ib. 14). To this loving solicitude for the entire people he will add a particular and even more tender concern for individuals. "I will seek the lost, and I will bring back the strayed, and I will bind up the crippled, and I will strengthen the weak, and the fat and the strong I will watch over; I will feed them in justice" (ib. 16). The messianic background of the prophecy is evident; it foreshadows and prepares the image of Jesus as the Shepherd, full of tenderness and love, who will come to rule his Father's flock with solicitude for even the least of its scattered and wounded sheep.

John's long discourse on the Good Shepherd (10:1-21) and Luke's account of the lost sheep in the Gospel of the day (Lk 15:3-7) are witness to this. Jesus does not limit himself to caring for his flock en masse, nor is he content that the majority are safe; rather, he leaves those sheep that are already in safety in order to seek the one sheep that is lost. It is no matter if the sheep's own action seems imprudent, or capricious, or stubborn, or even rebellious; it is a creature entrusted to him by his Father and it must not perish; therefore Jesus searches for it and pursues it until he succeeds in taking it on his shoulders and bringing it back to the fold. Then there is joy and celebration on earth and in heaven. We can each picture ourselves in such a situation. Resistance to grace, refusals, infidelities, the caprices of pride and selfishness—all are more or less serious evasions of the love of Christ; we must not be deaf to his calls but allow ourselves to be pursued and overtaken, to be taken up in his arms and carried back to the fold, and thus enter into a new deeper friendship with him. It is to this that the Sacred Heart of Jesus invites us.

Outside all allegory, St. Paul in the second reading (Rom 5:5-11) portrays Christ's love as the greatest proof of God's love for mankind. "God shows his love for us in that while we were yet sinners Christ died for us" (ib. 8). Indeed, divine love went beyond all measure when God gave his Only-begotten Son for the salvation of sinful man. And Christ himself, offering himself upon the cross gave the supreme proof of his love, beyond the measure he had already spoken of as being the greatest: "Greater love has no man than this, that a man lay down his life for his friends" (Jn 15:13). He alone had an even greater love, because he died for us "while we were still sinners" and were therefore "enemies" (Rom 5:8,10). From this fact St. Paul rises to immense hope and confidence: "Since, therefore, we are now justified by his blood, much more shall we be saved by him from the wrath of God. For if while we were enemies we were reconciled to God by the death of his Son, much more, now . . . shall we be saved by his life" (ib. 9-10). Since Christ's death, we can no longer doubt God's love and his mercy, nor be wanting in confidence for our own salvation, because the Heart of Christ is always there between ourselves and God to plead for us and "to make intercession for (us)" (Heb 7:25).

O God, who opened to us the treasures of infinite love in the heart of your Son, wounded for our sins, grant that we may correspond in generous reparation for the offering of your merciful love.
Roman Missal, Prayer

O good Jesus, how beautiful and joyous a thing it is to dwell in your heart! It is the rich treasure, the precious pearl which we have uncovered, hidden in the secret of your pierced body, as in a dug-out field . . .

O most gentle Jesus, I have found your heart . . . the heart of a king, the heart of a brother, the heart of a friend. Hidden within you, shall I not pray? Indeed I shall pray. Already your heart—I say it openly—is my heart also. If you are my Head, Jesus, how can what belongs to my head not be called mine? See, O Jesus, you and I have one and the same heart . . . Meanwhile, O most sweet Jesus, having again found this divine heart which is yours and mine, I will pray to you, my God. Receive my prayers into the sanctuary of your au-

dience chamber; even more, completely enrapture me in your heart. The tortuous crookedness of my sins would prohibit my entrance . . . But since an incomprehensible charity has opened and enlarged your heart, since you, who alone are, can make clean what was conceived unclean, O Jesus, my beautiful One, wash away my offenses, cleanse me of my sins. Then, purified by you, let me draw near to you who are all pure; let me enter and dwell in your heart all the days of my life, so that I may know and do whatever you desire of me.

St. Bonaventure, *The Mystical Vine* 3:3-4

300. SAINTS PETER AND PAUL

June 29

"The Lord will rescue me from every evil and save me for his heavenly kingdom" (2 Tim 4:18)

1. "These men, conquering all human frailty, shed their blood and helped the Church to grow. By sharing the cup of the Lord's suffering, they became the friends of God" (Ent. Ant.). The Liturgy unites in a single celebration Peter, the head of the Church, and Paul, the Apostle of the gentiles. Both are the living foundation of the Church, built up by their labors and their ceaseless preaching, and made fruitful in the end by their martyrdom. This is the first point brought out in today's readings. The first (Acts 12:1-11) records one of Peter's many imprisonments, which came about by the order of the political authorities who—as in Jesus' trial—wanted to do something "pleasing to the Jews" (ib. 3). Peter is thus involved in the same fate as Jesus. It could not be otherwise because "a disciple is not above his teacher" (Mt 10:24), and the Master had warned: "If they persecuted me, they will persecute you" (Jn 15:20). But the supreme hour had not yet arrived for Peter, and so, while "earnest prayer for him was made to God by the Church" (Acts 12:5), an angel of the Lord came to set him free.

Paul is also presented to us today in chains (2 Tim 4:6-8,17-18), but this is a final imprisonment which will end in his being condemned to death. Although the Apostle is aware of his situation, his words reveal no regret, but rather a serene happiness in the consciousness of having spent his life for the gospel: "The time of my departure has come. I have fought the good fight, I have finished the race, I have kept the faith. Henceforth there is laid up for me the crown of righteousness" (ib. 6-8).

The two Apostles in chains bear witness that only those who know how to face tribulations, persecutions, and even martyrdom for Christ are truly his disciples. At the same time their experiences show that Christ does not abandon his apostles when they are persecuted: he intervenes on their behalf to save them from danger—for instance, as Peter was freed from prison—or to sustain them in their vicissitudes, as Paul declares: "The Lord stood by me and gave me strength ... The Lord will rescue me from every evil and save me for his heavenly kingdom" (ib. 17,18). For a disciple who wishes, like Paul, to be united with Christ, martyrdom itself is a liberation; in fact, it is the definitive liberation, which leads through death into the glory of the Lord.

2. The Gospel (Mt 16:13-20) recalls the day at Caesarea when Simon Peter, urged on by the Master's questions, makes his great profession of faith: "You are the Christ, the Son of the living God" (ib. 16). Jesus answers, rejoicing with him for the divine light that made it possible for him to penetrate his mystery as Son of God and Savior of men; and, as if to reflect himself in the disciple who has recognized him, he makes Peter share in his characteristics and powers. Christ, the cornerstone of the Church (Acts 4:11), makes partnership with his Apostle as the foundation stone of his Church: "You are Peter, and on this rock I will build my Church" (Mt 16:18). He, who has received from his Father "all authority in heaven and on earth" (Mt 28:18), is transmitting it to Peter: "I will give you the keys of the kingdom of heaven," and confers upon him the supreme power to bind and to loose (Mt 16:19). Peter does not grasp immediately the full import of this investiture which binds him so closely to Christ; he will gradually come to understand it more and more fully through continual intimacy with the Master and the painful experience of his own weakness. When Jesus rebukes him for his protest when confronted with the announcement of the Passion, or when a glance makes him understand the cowardice of his denial, Peter will realize that the secret of his victory lies only in full union with Christ, animated by absolute confidence in him, and lived in conformity with his cross. Then he will be ready to hear him say: "Feed my lambs ... feed my sheep" (Jn 21:15-16).

When Peter is finally constituted shepherd of the Lord's flock, he will himself instruct the faithful on their relationship with Christ and their place in the Church: "Come to him, to that living stone ... and like living stones, be yourselves built into a spiritual house" (1 Pet 2:4-5). Just as the prerogatives of Peter continue to be those of the Pope, so also should the prerogatives of the early Christians be those of the faithful of all times. Close to Christ, the "living stone," and to his Vicar, the "foundation stone," so they themselves are "living stones" appointed to build up and support the Church. They do this through prayer, particularly prayer for the Pope—in imitation of the first Christian community which prayed for Peter in chains—through their offering of "spiritual sacrifices" made concrete in complete fidelity to the gospel, to the Church, and to the Vicar of Christ, in spite of difficulties and persecutions, trusting in him who said: "The powers of death shall not prevail against it" (Mt 16:18).

How can we thank you, O blessed Apostles, for all the hardships you endured for us? I remember you, O Peter, and stand amazed; I remember you, O Paul, and . . . I melt in tears. I do not know what to say, nor how to express myself when I contemplate your sufferings. How many prisons you made holy! How many chains you made honorable! How much suffering you bore! How many curses you endured! How far you carried Christ! What joy you brought to the Churches with your preaching! Your tongues are blessed instruments: your limbs have been covered with blood for the sake of the Church. You imitated Christ in everything! . . .

Rejoice, O Peter, to whom it was granted to savor the wood of Christ's cross. You wished to be crucified like your Master, not upright like Christ the Lord, but rather with your head towards the ground as if to set out for heaven from the earth. Blessed are the nails which pierced such holy limbs. You committed your soul with full trust into the hands of the Lord, you who assiduously served him and the Church, his bride; you, the most faithful of all the Apostles, who loved the Lord with all the ardor of your soul.

Rejoice also, O blessed Paul, whose head was cut off by the sword, and whose virtues cannot be explained with words. What sword could ever pierce your holy throat, that instrument of the Lord, so admired by heaven and revered on earth? . . . May this sword be like a crown for me, and Peter's nails like gems mounted in a diadem.

St. John Chrysostom, Sermon, (Metafraste)

O supreme and ineffable Godhead, I have sinned and am not worthy to pray to you, but you have the power to make me worthy; O my Lord, punish my sins and do not consider my frailties. I have a body which I surrender and offer to you: here is my flesh and here is my blood . . . If it is your will, crumble my bones and flesh together for your Vicar on earth, the only spouse of your bride, for whom I beg you to deign to hear me . . . Give him a new heart, continually growing in grace, a strong heart to raise the standard of the holy cross in order to make those without faith share like ourselves in the fruits of the passion and of the blood of your only-begotten Son, the spotless Lamb.

St. Catherine of Siena, Prayers

301. THE BLESSED VIRGIN MARY OF MOUNT CAMEL

JULY 16

Hail Mary, "the great glory of Israel, the great pride of our nation!"
(Judith 15:9)

1. Mary is truly "the glory and the honor of our race", honored as Queen and beauty of Carmel not only by Carmelites, but also by innumerable others of the faithful, scattered throughout the world. Devotion to her under this title can be traced back to the very beginning of the Carmelite Order, and tradition in its turn links it to the little white cloud that was seen from the summit of

Mount Carmel when the prophet Elijah was begging God to put an end to a long drought. This "little cloud like a man's hand" (1 Kgs 18:44) which rose from the sea and soon covered the sky with thick clouds heavy with rain, has been understood as a figure of the Virgin Mary who, by giving the Savior to the world, was the bearer of the life-giving water of grace. "Let the skies rain down the just one" chants the Church during Advent, repeating Isaiah's words (45:8). The mystical cloud that gives the Savior to the world is the Blessed Virgin, most holy and full of grace from the first moment of her immaculate conception.

Her children delight in applying to her, as does the Liturgy, the song of the prophet: "I will rejoice heartily in the Lord, my soul shall exult in my God; for he has clothed me with the robe of salvation, and covered me with the mantle of justice" (Is 61:10). These words, like a prelude to the Magnificat, are a beautiful expression of the Blessed Virgin's gratitude for the privileges with which God has adorned her in preparing her to be the mother of his divine Son. Indeed, from her as from a wonderful garden "he will cause righteousness . . . to spring forth" (ib. 11), that is, the blessed Jesus, "whom God made . . . our righteousness and sanctification and redemption" (1 Cor 1:30).

Mary does not jealously guard for herself the signal gifts with which she has been enriched, but shares them with everyone; she has given her Jesus to all, and desires to clothe every one in her "garments of salvation" and in her "mantle of justice," that is, with the grace and holiness merited by her Son. This is the significance of the scapular, the little "garment" of our Lady of Mount Carmel, an expressive symbol of her maternal concern for all those who are devoted to her and who choose her as their special patron.

2. The first hermits of Carmel built an oratory dedicated to our Lady in the midst of their cells and used to honor the Mother of God as the perfect model of their contemplative-apostolic life. From that time on, the Blessed Virgin of Mount Carmel was looked upon as the example and luminous sign of intimate union with God and of loving insight into the divine mysteries. This is in full harmony with the gospel which so often shows her in prayer. At the annunciation of the angel, during her visit to Elizabeth, at the birth of Jesus, in the temple when she presented her Son and again when she found him there among the doctors of the law, at the wedding in Cana, as at the foot of the cross or in the Cenacle, Mary always appears praying. She is listening to the word of God, or singing his praises, meditating and "pondering in her heart" (Lk 2:19) upon all that she has seen and heard about Jesus; or perhaps discreetly pointing out some one else's needs to him, or again, entreating the Holy Spirit on behalf of the young Church. Her prayerful attitude is the living representation of Carmel's ideal which, following her footsteps, places prayer at the center of one's life as the essential means for union with God and for a fruit-

ful apostolate. For this reason Carmel is wholly filled with Mary and constantly turns to her as to its Mother, its model and guide in its life of prayer.

But the particular aspect of Our Lady's prayer which is most esteemed and loved in Carmel is the one she took upon herself at the foot of the cross when Jesus in his agony proclaimed her Mother of men, saying to John and through him to all of us: "Behold your Mother" (Jn 19:27). At that moment Mary's prayer reached the high point of sacrificial offering: she offered her beloved Son to the Father for the salvation of the new children who were being entrusted to her maternal love, so that in her Son's offering her own is included, intimately associated with his passion. To copy her prayer means that we place sacrifice in the foreground of our prayer, so that our own prayer is transformed into an offering of self that is united with that of the Blessed Mother and of her divine Son. It is this prayer which, like Mary's, draws down the Holy Spirit upon the Church and obtains grace and salvation for all mankind and gives glory to God.

> O Mother, what a friend of the Lord you are! How close, indeed how intimate with him you deserved to become! What grace you have found in his sight! He dwells in you and you in him; you clothe him and are clothed by him. You clothed him with the substance of your flesh and he clothes you with the glory of his majesty. You clothe the sun with a cloud and are yourself clothed with the sun.
>
> Now, O Mother of mercy, humbly prostrate at your feet and trusting in your most tender, pure love, we call upon you with devout entreaty as our mediatrix with Christ, the Sun of justice. In your light may we contemplate the Light, and through your intercession deserve to receive the grace of Him who loved you above all other creatures, and clothed you with the mantle of glory, crowning you with a diadem of beauty. You are full of grace, full of celestial dew, leaning upon your Beloved, overflowing with delights. O Lady, feed your poor ones today! Like the little dogs beneath the table let us also have a few crumbs to eat, . . . and draw water from your brimming jar.
>
> St. Bernard, *De duodecim praerogativis B.V.M.* 6,15

> O Mary, you are the model of interior souls: those whom God has called to live within themselves in the depths of the bottomless abyss. In what peace and recollection you lived and acted! You sanctified the most trivial actions, for through them all you remained the constant adorer of the gift of God. Yet this did not prevent you from spending yourself for others when charity required it (1 Retreat).
>
> O Mary, Queen of Virgins, you are Queen of Martyrs too, but it was within your heart that the sword transpierced you, for with you everything took place within your soul. How beautiful you are when I contemplate you during your long martyrdom, enveloped in a majesty both strong and sweet, for you learned from the Word himself how they should suffer who are chosen as victims by the Father: those whom he has elected as associates in the great work of

redemption, "those whom he foreknew and predestinated to be made conformable to his Son", crucified by love.

You are there at the foot of the cross, standing in your strength and courage, and my Master says to me: "Behold your Mother." He gives you to me for my Mother! And now that he has returned to the Father and put me in his place on the cross, so that "in my flesh I (may) complete what is lacking in his afflictions for the sake of his Body, that is, the Church", you are still there, to teach me to suffer as he did, to tell me, to make me hear, those last outpourings of his soul which only you could catch (2 Retreat).

Elizabeth of the Trinity

302. ASSUMPTION OF THE BLESSED VIRGIN

August 15

All generations will call you blessed for he who is mighty has done great things for you (Lk 1:48:49)

1. "A great sign appeared in heaven: a woman clothed with the sun, with the moon under her feet and a crown with twelve stars on her head" (Ent ant). Thus the Liturgy honors Mary, assumed into heaven, applying to her the words of the Apocalypse (12:1) which also occur in today's first reading. In John's prophetic vision this extraordinary woman is seen in expectation of a son, engaged in a struggle with the "dragon", the eternal enemy of God and of men. Such a picture of light and darkness, of glory and battle, brings to mind the fulfillment of the messianic promise contained in the words spoken by God to the deceitful serpent in the garden of Eden: "I will put enmity between you and the woman, and between your seed and her seed: he shall bruise your head" (Gen 3:15). All of this comes to be through Mary, the Mother of the Savior, against whom Satan hurled himself, but by whom he was definitively overcome. Christ, the Son of Mary, is the victor; yet, for mankind to enjoy to the full the victory he has won for it, mankind, like himself, must keep up the struggle. In this stubborn combat we are sustained by our faith in Christ and by the power of his grace; we are also upheld by Mary's motherly protection, for amid the glory of heaven she does not cease interceding for all who follow her divine Son. These will conquer by virtue of the blood of the Lamb (Rev 12:11), the blood that was given to him by his Virgin Mother. Mary gave the world its Savior; therefore, by her means, "salvation and the power and the kingdom of our God and the authority of his Christ have come" (ib. 10). All this has happened because it was "the will of Him who decreed that we should receive *everything* through Mary" (St. Bernard, De aquaed. 7).

When the apocalyptic vision shows us the son of the woman "caught up to God and to his throne," which is an allusion to the ascension of Christ into heaven, it also shows us the woman herself fleeing towards "a place prepared by God" (Rev 12:5-4), which is symbolic of the assumption of Mary into eternal glory. Mary is the first to share fully in the destiny of her divine Son; she is bound to him as mother and as "an associate of unique nobility" who "in an utterly singular way . . . cooperated . . . in the Savior's work" (LG 61), and, assumed body and soul into heaven, shares in his glory.

2. The concept expressed in the first reading is completed in the second (1 Cor 15:20-26). Speaking of Christ, the first fruits of those who are risen, St. Paul concludes that one day all the faithful will have a share in his glorification. Yet there is a gradation of merit: "First Christ, the first fruit, then . . . those who belong to Christ" (ib. 23). Among "those who belong to Christ", the first place undoubtedly belongs to Our Lady who was always his because she was never touched by any sin. She is the one created being in whom the brightness of God's image was never dimmed; she is the "immaculate conception", the untouched work of the Trinity, in which the Father, the Son, and the Holy Spirit have always been well pleased, always receiving from her a total response to their love.

There are echoes of Mary's response to God's love throughout today's Gospel (Lk 1:39-59), whether in the words of Elizabeth exalting the great faith which led Mary to adhere without hesitation to the divine will, or in the words of the Virgin herself as she sings her hymn of praise to the Almighty for the great things he has accomplished in her. Mary never casts a glance at herself except to acknowledge her littleness, and from this lowly point rises up to God to extol his condescension and his mercy, his great works and power on behalf of the little ones, of the lowly and the poor, to whom she joins herself with extreme simplicity. Her reply to the immense love of God who chose her from all women as the mother of his divine Son is invariably the one which she gave to the Angel: "Behold the handmaid of the Lord." (ib. 38). For Mary, to be a handmaid means to be totally open to God and to be at his disposal: he may do what he wishes with her. And after God has associated her with the passion of his Son, he will one day exalt her by fulfilling in her the words of her canticle: "He has put down the mighty from their thrones, and exalted those of low degree" (ib. 52). The humble handmaid was truly "taken up body and soul into heavenly glory . . . that she might be the more thoroughly conformed to her Son, the Lord of lords" (LG 59). In Mary, taken up into heaven, all Christendom has a powerful advocate as well as a magnificent example. We can each learn from her how to acknowledge humbly our own littleness, how to offer ourselves to God in complete submission to his will, and how to believe in his merciful and all-powerful love with unshakeable faith.

O love of Mary, O ardent love of the Virgin, you are too ardent, too immense . . . a mortal body cannot contain you; . . . too burning is its fire to be concealed under this poor ember! Go ... shine out in eternity, go, blaze and burn before the throne of God, ... be extinguished and multiplied in the bosom of this God who alone is able to contain you.

J.B. Bossuet, Assumption of the Virgin

O immaculate Virgin, Mother of God and Mother of men! With all the fervor of our faith we believe in the triumphal assumption of your body and soul into heaven, where you are acclaimed Queen by all the choirs of angels and by all the ranks of saints; we unite with them in praising and blessing the Lord who has exalted you above all other creatures, and we offer you all the yearning desire of our devotion and love.

We know that your glance, which so lovingly caressed the humble, suffering humanity of Jesus on earth, is now completely satisfied in heaven with the sight of the glorious humanity of uncreated Wisdom, and that the happiness of your soul in contemplating the adorable Trinity face to face makes your heart beat fast with blissful tenderness; and we, poor sinners that we are, whose bodies weigh down the flight of our souls, beg you to purify our senses that, beginning here on earth, we may learn to enjoy God, and God alone, in the charm of his creatures.

We are confident that his merciful eyes will look kindly upon our sufferings, on our struggles, and on our weaknesses; and that your lips will smile upon our joys and our victories, and that you will hear the voice of Jesus, saying to you about each of us, what he said of his beloved disciple: "Behold your son"; so that we who call you our Mother may take you, as John did, as guide, the strength and the consolation of our mortal life.

From this earth, where we journey along as pilgrims, fortified by faith in our future resurrection, we look to you, our life, our sweetness and our hope; draw us by the gentle sweetness of your voice, so that after our exile you may one day show us Jesus, the blessed fruit of your womb, O clement, O loving, O sweet Virgin Mary.

Pius XII, Prayers

303. MARY OUR QUEEN
August 22

He who is mighty has done great things for you, and holy is his name (Lk 1:49)

1. Today's feast continues and completes the theme upon which we meditated on the Solemnity of the Assumption. Having in fact been "taken up body and soul into heavenly glory," Mary was "exalted by the Lord as Queen of all in order that she might be more thoroughly conformed to her Son, the Lord of lords and the conqueror of sin and death" (LG 59). Mary who was so closely

associated with Christ during her earthly life and who was conformed to him even to having her soul pierced by his passion as she offered him, dying, to the Father, had also to be united with him in glory. The Liturgy therefore acknowledges her title as Queen and honors her as Queen enthroned beside her Son, the King: "The Queen stands at your right hand" (Ps 45:10; Resp. Ps of the Assumption). Mary is resplendent through her immaculate conception, by the fullness of grace that adorns her, by her privilege as Mother of God, by the painful martyrdom she suffered in union with her Son, her boundless faith, her perfect virginity, her profound humility, and her measureless love. These are the prerogatives that constitute Mary Queen of the apostles and of the martyrs, of confessors and of virgins, of all the saints and even of the angels. Her royal status has no earthly origin; it is exclusively derived from that of her Son. Isaiah had spoken of him in prophecy as the one who will have "the government upon his shoulder, and his name will be called . . . everlasting Father, Prince of peace" (9:6). The angel Gabriel also clearly declared him: "Son of the Most High" to whom "the Lord God will give the throne of his father David; he will reign . . . for ever; and of his kingdom there will be no end" (Lk 1:32-33). By becoming Mary's son, Jesus received human nature from her and made her share in his divine royalty. The Church applies the touching words of the psalmist to the Virgin who is so humble and so exalted: "Hear, O daughter, consider, and incline your ear; forget your people and your father's house; and the king will desire your beauty" (Ps 45:10-11). No creature has ever been so loved by God as Mary was, and no creature has ever loved him in return as Mary did, who gave herself to Christ, her King and her Son, forgetting for his sake every privilege of her own.

2. The first to proclaim Mary's greatness was the Angel who greeted her: "Hail, full of grace, the Lord is with you!" (Lk 1:28); he was with her in such a way as to become her Son. For a mere creature, could there be dignity greater than this? Next was Elizabeth who "exclaimed with a loud cry: 'Blessed are you among women, and blessed is the fruit of your womb . . Blessed is she who believed that there would be a fulfillment of what was spoken to her from the Lord'" (ib. 42,45). God's greatest blessing descended upon Mary, making her fruitful in virginal and divine motherhood. Mary is proclaimed blessed because she is the Mother of the Lord and blessed because she believed his word. Many years later, another woman will praise her by making the admiration directed toward her Son redound upon her: "Blessed is the womb that bore you and the breasts that you sucked!" Mary was conscious of the great things worked in her and so transparently humble that she could sing without being disturbed: "All generations will call me blessed, for he who is mighty has done great things for me" (Lk 1:48-49). She prophesied most humbly of her own glory without holding on to the least particle of it for

herself; her glory must serve only to glorify him who was able to make the Mother of God out of a mere creature.

Mary's royal status is entirely pervaded by this sweet humility, which makes her much more Mother than Queen. Still, she is a royal mother, with a kindly and most gentle queenship of which she makes use to bring men to the salvation which her Son has merited for them. Her motherly queenship makes her powerful over his heart for obtaining the graces of conversion and of pardon; it makes her powerful in reclaiming sinners, in upholding the weak, in infusing courage into the fearful and fortitude into the persecuted, and in attracting those who are far off and scattered. The Church invokes her with confidence and invites its children to implore of her that "exalted as she is in heaven above all the saints and angels ... she may intercede with her Son, ... until all the peoples of the human family ... are happily gathered together ... into the one People of God, for the glory of the most holy and undivided Trinity " (LG 69).

> *Where your glory is concerned, O Mary, neither is devotion content to remain silent, nor is the arid mind capable of formulating something worthy of you ... The very inhabitants of heaven, surprised at what is happening, ask themselves in amazement: "Who is she coming up from the wilderness, overflowing with delights?" ... Who is she rising up here from beneath the sun, where all is toil and sorrow and affliction of spirit, superabounding in spiritual delights? ... O Queen of the world, when you ascend from the desert, ... you are enchanting in your beauty and delightful in your sweetness.*
>
> *So to you, O spring of life, our thirsting soul draws near, and to you, O treasure of mercy, our misery has recourse with all haste. O Blessed Virgin, let your compassion reveal to the world the favor you have found with God: by your holy prayers you obtain forgiveness for the guilty, healing for the sick, strength for the weak, comfort for the afflicted, help and deliverance for those in danger. On this day of peace and happiness, lavish the abundance of your favors upon us your poor servants who call upon your sweet name as we praise him who is your Son, Jesus Christ our Lord, God blessed above all things for ever and ever. May he do all this through your intercession, O merciful Virgin.*
>
> St. Bernard, *In Assumptione B.V.Mariae* 4:1,9

> *Hail Mary, delight of the Father, through you the knowledge of God has spread to the farthest ends of the earth. Hail, dwelling of the Son from which he came out clothed in the flesh. Hail, ineffable sanctuary of the Holy Spirit. Hail, holier than the Cherubim; more glorious than the Seraphim; greater than the heavens ... Hail Mary, whose name the apostles made heard throughout the whole world; splendid witness of the martyrs; acclaimed in every eulogy of the patriarchs; highest ornament of the saints; conciliating queen of peace; immaculate splendor of mothers. Hail, mediatrix of all that is*

*under heaven, refuge of all the world; hail full of grace, the Lord is
with you; he who is before you is born of you in order to live with us.*
St. Tarasio, Patriarch of Constantinople

[End of Vol. III]

INDEXES OF ABBREVIATIONS

SACRED SCRIPTURE

The abbreviations used for the various books of the Bible are
those given at the beginning of the RSV version. Unless otherwise
noted, all scriptural quotations are taken from the RSV Common
Bible.

THE DOCUMENTS OF VATICAN COUNCIL II

AA	Laity	LG	Dogmatic Constitution on the Church
AG	Missions	NAE	Non-Christians
CD	Bishops	QE	Eastern Churches
DH	Religious Freedom	OT	Priestly Formation
DV	Revelation	PC	Religious Life
GE	Christian Education	PO	Priests
GS	Church in the Modern World	SC	Liturgy
IM	Social Communication	UR	Ecumenism

The text used is "The Documents of Vatican II" edited by Walter
M. Abbott, S.J.

AUTHORS AND WORKS FREQUENTLY CITED

T.J.	ST. TERESA OF JESUS *Works*	J.C.	ST. JOHN OF THE CROSS *Works*
F	Foundations	Asc	Ascent of Mt. Carmel
IC	Interior Castle	Cs	Counsels to a religious
Life	Life	Ct	Cautions
Med	Meditation on the Song of Songs	DkN	Dark Night
Sol	Soliloquies (Exclamations)	Let	Letters
Sp	Spiritual Testimonies	Say	Sayings of Light and Love
Test	(Relations)		
Way	Way of Perfection	Sp C	Spiritual Canticle
		Fl	Living Flame
		Note:	Fl and SpC are generally cited from redaction B; where A is used, it is in-

		dicated by SpC-A and Fl-A.
T.C.J. ST. THERESE OF THE CHILD JESUS	E.T.	SR. ELIZABETH OF THE TRINITY
Writings		*Writings*
Auto Autobiography, Autobiographical Mss.	1 R	First Retreat
NV Last Conversations (Novissima Verba	2 R	Second Retreat
	Let	Letters (French Edition)

For the works of St. Teresa of Jesus (except for the Foundations, not yet published), St. John of the Cross and St. Therese of the Child Jesus, the ICS texts have been used throughout, except in rare cases which are noted in their proper places. An English version of the works of Elizabeth of the Trinity is in preparation.

MISCELLANEOUS

RB	Roman Breviary	cf	compare
RM	Roman Missal	Let	Letter
RRo	Roman Ritual—old	p.	page
Lect	Lectionary	v.	volume

BIBLIOGRAPHY

ALACOQUE, Margaret M., St.
—La vita della Ven. Margherita Maria, G. Languet, A. Poletti, Venezia, 1740

ANGELA of Foligno, Bl.
—The Book of the Divine Consolation of Bd. Angela of Foligno, Trans. M.G. Stegman, N.Y. 1909

ANSELM, St.
—Proslogion, Wisdom of Catholicism, ed. by A. Pegis, New York, Random House, Inc., 1949

AUGUSTINE, St.
—The Soliloquies of, New York Cosmopolitan Science & Art Service Co. 1943
—The Confessions of, New York, Sheed & Ward, 1943
—On the Psalms, Vol. 1, Ancient Christian Writers, Vol. 29, Westminster, Md., Newman Press, 1960
—The Trinity, The Fathers of the Church, Vol. 45, Wash., D.C., Catholic University of America Press

BERNARD, St.
—Sermons on the Canticle of Canticles, Vol. 1 Dublin, Browne & Nolan, 1920
—On the Love of God, New York, Spiritual Book Associates, 1937

BLOIS, Louis (of)
—The Works of Louis of Blois, B.A. Wilberforce & D.R. Hudleston, London 1925-26

BONAVENTURE, St.
—The Mystical Vine, Fleur de Lys 5, London 1955

BOSSUET, J.B.
—Meditazioni sul Vangelo, Vol. 1, (1930); Vol. 11 (1931), V. Gatti, Brescia
—Elevazioni a Dio sui misteri, SEI, Torino, 1933

CANOVAI, G.,
—Suscipe Domine, Madrone, La Civilta Cattolica, Rome, 1949

CATHERINE of Genoa, St.
—The Treatise on Purgatory and the Dialogue, New York, Sheed & Ward, 1946

CATHERINE of Siena, St.
—The Dialogue of, New York, Benziger Bros. 1925
—Preghiere ed Elavazioni, I. Taurisano, Ferrari, Roma, 1939
—Epistolario, 6 Vol., Misciatelli, Giuntini-Bentivoglio, Siena

CARMELA dello Spirito Santo, Sr.
—da Suor Carmela dello Spirito Santo, O.C.D. Monastero S. Giuseppe, Roma, 1954

CHAUTARD, Dom J.B.
—The Soul of the Apostolate, Abbey of Gethsemani, Trappist, Ky., 1941

CHEVRIER, A.
  —Il vero discepolo di Christi, Vita e Pensiero, Milano, 1950
  —da L'esprit et les virtus du venerable A. Chevrier, Vitte, Paris, 1926
CLEMENT of Rome, St.
  —Epistle to the Corinthians, Ancient Christian Writers, Vol. 1, Westminster, Md., Newman Press, 1946
CYPRIAN, St.
  —Letters Complete, The Fathers of the Church, Vol. 51, Wash., D.C., Catholic University of America Press
EARLY CHRISTIAN PRAYERS
  —A. Hamman, Chicago, Regnery, 1961
ELIZABETH of the Trinity, Sr.
  —J'ai Trouve Dieu, Oeuvres Completes, Tome Ib, II Paris, Les Editions du Cerf, 1979, 1980
de FOUCAULD, Charles
  —Meditations of a Hermit, Burns & Oates, London Orbis Books, New York, 1981
  —Ecrits Spirituels, J. Gigord, Paris, 12 ed., 1951
FRANCIS of Assissi, St.
  —The Writings of St. Francis, trans., P. Robinson London, 1906
FRANCIS de Sales, St.
  —A Treatise on the Love of God, trans. by John K. Ryan, Doubleday, Image Books, New York
  —Spiritual Conferences, Westminster, Md., Newman Press, 1962
GAY, Msgr. Charles
  —The Christian Life and Virtues, Vols. I, II, III Burns & Oates, London, 1879
GERTRUDE, St.
  —The Exercises of, Westminster, Md., Newman Press, 1956
GREGORY the Great
  —Moralia, 2 Vol., Ed. Paoline, Roma, 1965
GUERRA, E. Bl.
  —Il fuocho che Gesu porto sulla terra, E. Nucci, Pescia, 1900
HILARY of Poitiers, St.
  —The Trinity, The Fathers of the Church, Vol. 25, Wash., D.C., Catholic University of America Press
IGNATIUS of Antioch, St.
  —Epistle to the Romans, Ancient Christian Writers, Vol. I, Westminster, Md., Newman Press 1946
JOHN XXIII, Pope
  —Prayers and Devotions, New York, Doubleday Image Books, 1969
JOURDAN, R.
  —Contemplatione sull'amore divino, L.E. Fiorentina, Firenze, 1954
a KEMPIS, Thomas
  —Following of Christ, Catholic Publications Press, New York, 1924

LEBRETON, G.,
—Il Padre L. de Grandmaison, Morcelliana, Brescia, 1936
LYONNET, P.,
—Scritti spirituali, Borla, Torino, 1963
MARMION, O.S.B., Abbot
—The Trinity in our Spiritual Life, Westminster, Md., Newman Press, 1953
NEWMAN, J.H.
—Meditations and Devotions, Longman's Green & Co., New York, 1907
PAUL VI, Pope
—Teachings of Paul VI, Office of Publishing Services, U.S. Catholic Conference, Wash., D.C.
de' PAZZI, St. Mary Magdalen
—The Complete Works of, Carmelite Fathers, Aylesford, Westmont, Illinois, 1974
PHILIPON, O.P., M.M.
—The Spiritual Doctrine of Sr. Elizabeth of the Trinity, Westminster, Md., Newman Press, 1962
PIUS XII, Pope
—Prayers of Pope Pius XII, Westminster, Md., Newman Press, 1957
PLUS, Raoul
—Christ in His Brethren, London, Burns, Oates and Washbourne, Ltd., 1925
de PONTE, Louis
—Meditations on the Mysteries of our Holy Faith, Trans. by John Heigham and Thomas Richardson, 1852
REDI, Teresa Maragaret, St.
—Gabriel of St. Mary Magdalen, La Spiritualita di S. Teresa di Gesu, E.L. Fiorentina, Firenze, 1950 Margherita del Cuore
RUYSBROECK,
—Oeuvres de Ruysbroeck l'Admirable, 3 Vol. Vromant, Bruxelles, 1922
SEZZE, St. Charles of
—Autobiography, trans. by L. Perotti, Chicago, 1963
SUSO, Bl. Henry
—The Exemplar—Life and Writings of Bl. Henry Suso, 2 Vols. trans. by Sr. M. Ann Edward, O.P., Dubuque, Iowa Priory Press, 1962
de SOUBIRAN, Bl. M. Teresa
—La Beata M. Teresa de Soubiran, Instituto Maria Ausiliatrice, Roma, 1946
THOMAS AQUINAS
—Preghiere, Firenze, 1963
Refer to a patristic collection for the texts of the Fathers and early ecclesiastical writers.